SENATORS ON THE CAMPAIGN TRAIL

THE JULIAN J. ROTHBAUM DISTINGUISHED LECTURE SERIES

SENATORS ON THE CAMPAIGN TRAIL

The Politics
of Representation

By
RICHARD F. FENNO, JR.

UNIVERSITY OF OKLAHOMA PRESS : NORMAN AND LONDON

ALSO BY RICHARD F. FENNO, JR.

Home Style: House Members in Their Districts (New York, 1978)
The Making of a Senator: Dan Quayle (Washington, D.C., 1988)
The Presidential Odyssey of John Glenn (Washington, D.C., 1990)
Watching Politicians: Essays on Participate Observation
  (Berkeley, 1990)
*The Emergence of a Senate Leader: Pete Domenici and the Reagan
  Budget* (Washington, D.C., 1991)
Learning to Legislate: The Senate Education of Arlen Specter
  (Washington, D.C., 1991)
When Incumbency Fails: The Senate Career of Mark Andrews
  (Washington, D.C., 1992)

Library of Congress Cataloging-in-Publication Data

Fenno, Richard F., 1926–
    Senators on the campaign trail : the politics of representation /
by Richard F. Fenno, Jr.
        p.   cm. — (The Julian J. Rothbaum distinguished lecture
series ; v. 6)
    Includes bibliographical references (p.   ) and index.
    ISBN 0–8061–2827–5 (alk. paper)
    1. Electioneering—United States—Case studies. 2. Legislators—
United States—Case studies. 3. United States. Congress. Senate—
Elections—Case studies. 4. Representative government and
representation—United States—Case studies. I. Title.
II. Series.
JK2281.F46   1996
324.7'0973—dc20   95–42282
                                                                              CIP

Series design by Bill Cason.

Senators on the Campaign Trail: The Politics of Representation is Volume 6
  in the Julian J. Rothbaum Distinguished Lecture Series.

1   2   3   4   5   6   7   8   9   10

CONTENTS

LIST OF FIGURES AND TABLES

FOREWORD

AMONG THE MANY GOOD THINGS that have happened to me in my life, there is none in which I take more pride than the establishment of the Carl Albert Congressional Research and Studies Center at the University of Oklahoma, and none in which I take more satisfaction than the Center's presentation of the Julian J. Rothbaum Distinguished Lecture Series. The series is a perpetually endowed program of the University of Oklahoma, created in honor of Julian J. Rothbaum by his wife, Irene, and son, Joel Jankowsky.

Julian J. Rothbaum, my close friend since our childhood days in southeastern Oklahoma, has long been a leader in Oklahoma civic affairs. He has served as a Regent of the University of

Oklahoma for two terms and as a State Regent for Higher
Education. In 1974 he was awarded the University's highest
honor, the Distinguished Service Citation, and in 1986 he was
inducted into the Oklahoma Hall of Fame.

The Rothbaum Lecture Series is devoted to the themes of
representative government, democracy and education, and
citizen participation in public affairs, values to which Julian
J. Rothbaum has been committed throughout his life. His lifelong dedication to the University of Oklahoma, the state, and his
country is a tribute to the ideals to which the Rothbaum Lecture
Series is dedicated. The books in the series make an enduring
contribution to an understanding of American democracy.

CARL B. ALBERT

Forty-sixth Speaker
of the
United States House of Representatives

ACKNOWLEDGMENTS

THIS BOOK COULD NOT HAVE BEEN WRITTEN without the help of many people who went out of their way to facilitate my work. First and foremost, I wish to express my appreciation to Julian J. Rothbaum and his family for making possible the Rothbaum Lecture Series, under whose auspices this book first took shape. The Rothbaum Lectures were delivered at the University of Oklahoma in October 1993. For their good advice and warm hospitality on that occasion, I wish to thank Joel Jankowsky, Ron Peters, Gary Copeland, Alan Hertzke, and LaDonna Sullivan.

My greatest debt and my deepest thanks go to the senators who were willing to take me along and talk with me about what they were doing and why—Dick Clark, William Cohen, John Culver, Wyche Fowler, John Glenn, Tom Harkin, Paul Tsongas, Claiborne Pell, David Pryor, and Dan Quayle—and to senatorial hopeful Richard Leone.

I have had the opportunity elsewhere to publicly thank the staffs of Senators Glenn and Quayle. Here, I should like to acknowledge the invaluable assistance of other Senate staffers who helped me on the trail: in Arkansas, Don Harrell, Carmie Henry, Ann Pride, Kelly Robbins, James (Skip) Rutherford, and Raymond Scott; in Georgia, C. J. Jackson, Bill Johnstone, Chris Schepis, and Fran Weis; in Iowa, John Frew, James Larew, Andrew Loewi, Mike Naylor, and Jack Wertzberger; in

Maine, Thomas Daffron, Dale Gerry, Ted O'Meara, and Robert Tyrer; in Massachusetts, Richard Arenberg, Christine Briand-Naylor, Dennis Kanin, and Toby Dilworth; in Rhode Island, Jack Cummings, Fred Hashway, Thomas Hughes, and Leo Skenyon. Other friends to whom I owe thanks for their aid in a variety of ways are Merle Black, Charles Bullock, Diane Blair, Ernest Dumas, Patrick Fett, John Geer, Jay Goodliffe, Julian Kanter, Douglas Madsen, Samuel Patterson, Lynda Powell, Catherine Rudder, Stephen Salmore, Byron Shafer, Wendy Schiller, Randall Strahan, Darrell West, and Gerald Wright.

For their major contributions, I am especially indebted to two colleagues, Gary Copeland and Roger Davidson. They read and commented on the entire manuscript. I cannot thank them enough for their guidance.

The manuscript was prepared by Rosemary Bergin. I thank her for her expertise, her enthusiasm, and her good humor. At the University of Oklahoma Press, I have been fortunate to have worked with an expert, Kimberly Wiar, and to have had the intelligent editorial assistance of Sheila Berg.

To Nancy, whose strong sense of partnership made my guilt level manageable while I was on the trail, I owe the very most—as always.

SENATORS ON THE CAMPAIGN TRAIL

Introduction

THE CAMPAIGN TRAIL

THE VANTAGE POINT

POLITICAL SCIENTISTS KNOW A LOT about America's politicians. But there is a lot we do not know. This book reports on one effort to learn more. The effort is worth reporting because its observational approach has not been widely employed by political scientists. And because it might help. I believe we can learn something about our politicians by watching, listening, and talking to them as they go about their business, by staying close to them, and by looking over their shoulders to see the world as they see it. I believe also that what we learn by personal observations of this sort can reinforce, highlight, and augment what we already know. The book should be read as a report, from an inveterate politician watcher to his fellow students of American politics.

It is a report that comes from a special vantage point—from the campaign trail.[1] Off and on for the past eighteen years, I have been observing—up close, but not too personal—some aspiring and some sitting U.S. senators. Between 1976 and 1994, I traveled in sixteen states with twenty senatorial candidates. I first met and talked with each of them and their staffs in the midst of an election campaign. I conducted a follow-up interview after most campaigns. I observed the winners as they worked in the Senate. So I got to know all of them as campaigners before I got to know them as senators. I met most of them in 1978 and 1980. And, in the case of the 1978 and 1980 winners, I continued to follow them at least through their subsequent election campaigns, six years later.

All told, I visited thirty-one election campaigns, twenty-two successful ones and nine unsuccessful ones. I averaged about three and a half days per trip; and the time spent with each campaign ranged from one day with two senators to thirty days with one senator. This book is about ten of them. The who and the when of these exploits are detailed in Table 1, following this introduction.

SOME GLIMPSES

One might reasonably ask, what is it like, this drop in/drop out, tag along/hang around kind of research? And what can we learn from it? Some introductory glimpses from the campaign season of 1980 will convey the flavor of the enterprise.

In September and October of that year, the eight candidates with whom I traveled included Senators John Culver of Iowa and John Glenn of Ohio, both first-term Democrats running for reelection. Also included were Arlen Specter, a Pennsylvania Republican, and Jim Folsom, an Alabama Democrat, each running to fill an open Senate seat. I watched both Culver and Glenn speak to groups of their organized labor supporters. And I watched Specter and Folsom as each confronted the importance of "the issues" for his political persona. These paired comparisons may illuminate some of the possibilities of a research method I once summarized as "soaking and poking."[2]

In September 1980, Senator Culver spoke to the United Auto Workers at their union hall in Des Moines, Iowa. He received an introduction that emphasized his "100 percent voting record for labor" and his "100 percent voting record for senior citizens." It was interrupted twice by standing ovations. When he got up to speak, the audience rose and rocked the hall for two or three minutes chanting, "Cul-ver, Cul-ver Cul-ver." He responded with a sweaty, rip-roaring, podium-pounding speech blasting the conservative record of his opponent and warning of the dominance of "the oil lobbyists," "the chemical companies," and the "radical New Right" if his opponent were elected. It was punctuated by frequent cheers and more standing ovations. As we drove away, he exclaimed, "Wasn't that enthusiasm something, that spirit. You could feel it, couldn't you?.... Did I make it too hot? Huh? It was there, wasn't it? They wanted red meat, didn't they? Huh?" The next day, he commented again on the chemistry of his relationship with his supporters. "That group last night—I could have said 'Off with your heads' and they would have done it."

A month later, Senator Glenn spoke, following a reception, to the members of Boilermakers Lodge 85 at their union hall outside Toledo, Ohio. After the introduction by the union president—"He was an astronaut and all. The world is proud of this man and his achievement"—the woman sitting beside me added, "He was a Republican at the start, but now he is more with labor." Glenn delivered a short, standard pep talk about the need to get out the vote, to fight complacency, and to discount his own big lead in the polls. It drew little audible reaction from his audience of plumbers and pipe fitters. He received a routine round of applause, jumped down from the stage, and was halfway out of the hall when the president returned to the microphone, thanked him for coming, and remarked that Glenn was once a plumber, too.

When Glenn heard that, he stopped and shouted, "That's right, I was a plumber, too." He turned and ran back toward the stage. The president said to him, "You didn't have to come back." But Glenn grabbed the microphone and said, "My dad was a plumber in New Concord. I spent my summer digging holes for septic tanks and I hated every minute of it." The union members responded with laughter. "I was the pipe threader and reamer and cutter; and I cut, threaded, and reamed miles of pipe. And that was before you had machines. That was hard going."

The union members responded with cheers. Glenn waved, jumped down off the stage, and left in a changed mood of good feeling. In the car afterward the driver said, "These people were our enemies in 1974 [in the primary].... Now they are great supporters." But no one mentioned that the campaigning politician approaching an obvious opportunity to identify with these newfound supporters had not known instinctively how to do it.

Culver and Glenn both assumed they were meeting with reliable union supporters. Yet there were substantial differences in the intensity of each candidate's union support and in the ability of each candidate to cultivate that support. Firsthand observation of this sort might help us to think about varying patterns of presentation and constituent support.

During the same 1980 campaign season, in Pennsylvania, I watched aspiring Republican candidate Arlen Specter campaign with the help of a 108-page, inch-thick package of "position papers" addressing twenty-four separate issues of public policy. He used them to buttress his policy discussions, to generate a stream of press releases, and to differentiate himself from his opponent. Specter carried a package to every media source we touched. When he brought one to his endorsement interview at the *Harrisburg Patriot and Evening News* in September, the editor quipped, "I thought you were campaigning, Arlen, not going into the publishing business."

During the interview, Specter told his questioners, "The most important difference [between me and my opponent] is the intensity of my campaign and the evidence it gives of my willingness to work hard." As evidence, he added, "I've produced a sheaf of position papers three inches thick and my opponent has none." As we rode along afterward, he returned to this issue advantage over his opponent. "He is vague on the issues. When you research him, there's nothing there. He has no position papers. He meanders during the campaign, always changing priorities. Whatever position I take during a debate, he takes in the next debate." To my question, "What has been the most enjoyable part of the campaign?" he answered, "The debates."

A month later, during my first day in Alabama with the Senate campaign of aspiring Democrat Jim Folsom, the phone rang in his Montgomery headquarters. I listened as two campaign staffers wrestled with the call. "This guy wants to know Jim's position on the Davis Bacon Act," said the man at the phone. As the other staffer walked over to the counter where Folsom's campaign materials lay, he said, "We aren't supposed to know anything about that, are we?" "You're supposed to be our issues director," replied the man holding the phone. "The guy says it has something to do with labor." "Tell him we'll have to call him back later," said the "issues director" as he inspected the campaign materials. Later I went over to the counter to have a look. Folsom's issue material consisted of one single page. It was entitled "The Issues." It devoted a total of 21 lines to eight policy subjects.

Two days after I first saw "The Issues" page, the following conversation took place between candidate Folsom and his campaign manager—at the same counter.

> FOLSOM: When is our new statement on the issues coming out?
> MANAGER: This is it right here [pointing to "The Issues"]. I didn't know we had a second one.
> FOLSOM: I heard we did. The people in [the] Birmingham [headquarters] are complaining. They say people are coming in asking them what the issues are.
> MANAGER: You mean they want things to talk about.
> FOLSOM: Yes.
> MANAGER: Well, "Jim is for the balanced budget." We could write that one up.

A couple of days later they released a new version of "The Issues" page by simply adding two new lines to the original twenty one. One of the new lines read: "Believes that the federal budget must be balanced."

Both Folsom and Specter were in the business of presenting themselves to their prospective constituents. But a vast difference was observable in their orientation toward policy issues and in the weight each gave to the issue component in his presentation of self to constituents. Again, firsthand observation of this sort might help us to think about varying patterns of candidate presentation and of constituent support.

SOME VIRTUES

These glimpses from the campaign trail may, of course, suggest to some readers only the limitations of this kind of research. They may trigger only negative reactions: too subjective, too episodic, not enough cases, too few angles of vision, unsystematic collection of evidence, insufficiently susceptible to testing. The list of problems is amply sufficient to induce modesty, but not quite sufficient to kill the notion that close personal observation of some politicians in action might have some benefits. Or to kill the notion that it might be especially beneficial for people who know our politicians mostly in the aggregate or at a distance. To people who do not engage in personal observation, this book suggests that the approach has some modest virtues to recommend it.

First and foremost, the quick glimpses above remind us that it is, after all, flesh and blood individuals, real *people* we are talking about when we generalize about our politicians. And we are reminded, too, that it is a set of very specific activities that we are talking about when we generalize about the behavior of politicians. For analytical purposes, we political scientists typically fold candidates like these into all-encompassing categories such as incumbent and challenger and into subcategories such as quality challenger and nonquality challenger. Similarly, we calibrate their behavior by using all-encompassing measures such as voting scores, expenditure of money, visits home, and media attention. Our categories and our measures permit the statistical presentation of evidence. And they serve our explanatory purposes well.

But the argument for observation is that there is something to be gained by occasionally unpacking our analytical categories and our measures to take a firsthand look at the real live human beings subsumed within. And we can look, too, at what they actually do. Political scientists rely routinely on detailed and nuanced tracings of the politicians who occupy the presidency, but close attention to individual politicians in Congress is deemed forbidding or unprofitable. As our four early glimpses indicate, however, there may be substantial differences among individuals within categories and substantial magnitudes of difference in some standard behavior patterns. There should be some value in reminding ourselves, occasionally and concretely, what kind of people populate our categories and what behavior we are measuring.

The constituency-related behaviors we just glimpsed are among the building blocks of our generalizations about political activity. Indeed, after watching politicians in action, it is hard to imagine that we can achieve the depth and the solidity of understanding of them we seek without some minimal ground-level exposure to them—or to firsthand reports of their adventures.

Secondly, observation of politicians on the campaign trail is helpful because it takes us to the *place* where our representative form of government begins and ends—to the home constituency. At bottom, our scholarly interest in Congress is stimulated and sustained by our broader interest in representative government. And representative government is built out of many separate and distinct legislator–constituent relationships—relationships that get forged in the constituency, one campaign, one election, one politician at a time. Representative government has local roots and a bottom-up logic. And that is precisely the perspective of the observational research that is conducted on the campaign trail.

Representation involves the relationship between elected politicians and private citizens, one in which the politicians act in the place of, on behalf of, and in the interest of the citizens. In a representative democracy such as ours, these politicians are freely and competitively elected by—and are kept electorally accountable to—the citizens for whom they are presumed to act. A system of accountability presumes a system of representation.

Elected representatives organize themselves as a legislature for the purpose of taking collective action on public matters. Our national legislature is the most representative of all our national political institutions. It is better at reflecting and recording citizen attitudes, values, and preferences than either the President or the Supreme Court. As such, Congress is the bedrock of our representative system of government. Moreover, its representational strengths are its greatest strengths as an institution. That is to say, the content of its decisions is less important than its representational contribution to decision making.

Its representational strengths, however, are only as strong as the underlying political processes by which individual politicians win the right to represent certain citizens and the processes by which they work out a representational relationship with those citizens. For it is this underlying "politics of representation" that renders the collective action of the legislative institution acceptable and legitimate in the eyes of the citizenry. The politics of representation originates in individual activity—activity that is considerably less publicly scrutinized than the collective activities of the legislature. Such activities, of the sort we glimpsed earlier, can usefully be found, described, and assessed in the place where they most often occur—in the constituency. There are, of course, local media accounts of individual political activity. And I shall rely on them for verification throughout.

A third virtue of the observational method is contained in its useful reminders about *time*. By watching and talking to the same individual over time, we become sensitized to the passage of time, to its effects, and to the importance, in general, of a longitudinal perspective for understanding politics. For the individual politician, the time-oriented question, When shall I act? is as critical as the substantive question, What action shall I take? And in the broader sense, representation is not a static condition but a *process* that develops over time. Representing is an activity that politicians may or may not learn over time. It will be helpful, therefore, in conceptualizing representation as a process if our research has a longitudinal, over-time perspective built into it from the outset.

That proposition becomes even clearer when we identify the several underlying representational processes of greatest interest to us, that is, the processes by which a politician decides to become a representative, becomes a representative, and works at being a representative. More specifically, I shall focus on politicians as they pursue a career, campaign for election, and build a constituency. All three activities are developmental in character. They depend on continuous, over-time negotiation between politicians and citizens. All three are better captured by longitudinal analysis than by cross-sectional analysis.

Because of my interest in these relationships, this work will be more concerned with the process of representation than with the outcome of representation. In particular, it will focus much more on election campaigns than on election results. I shall endeavor to tell the reader what elective politicians are like and how they can influence election outcomes without, at the same time, purporting to explain election outcomes. Explaining outcomes tends to put the focus on the voters, whereas my intention is to place the focus on the politicians. The narrative treatment given to them and to their developmental activities buttresses that intention.

The three virtues of observational research I have suggested pertain to *people*, *place*, and *time*. They should be seen as adding qualitative dimensions to a dominantly quantitative corpus of research on politicians. My hope is that they will reinforce by illustration, and thus strengthen our confidence in, what we already know and that they will, in turn, enrich and encourage ongoing research. More ambitiously, they might convince us to rethink the importance of, some of what we already know. And there is also the possibility that a firsthand look might uncover some underappreciated patterns of perception or behavior and thus suggest some promising new avenues of research.

POLITICIANS AND CRITICS

Even as we put forward qualitative suggestions, the world around us resounds with other qualitative assessments of our elected politicians and of the Congress. Most of them are highly critical. Their tone ranges from cynicism to contempt. And the sins of the few are quickly accepted as the norm of the many. People who could not name ten members of Congress fearlessly assert that they are all bums, crooks, or worse. People who have not the slightest idea how much time members of Congress spend at home or what they do there state unequivocally that they are all out of touch with their constituents.

The summary headline of a 1989 national opinion survey captures the prevailing public attitude. It reads, "They're All Crooks—Whatever Their Names Are; Americans Don't Know Much About Congress, Except That They Can't Be Trusted."[3] One of the enduring strengths of a representative democracy is, of course, its capacity for self-criticism. And where Congress is concerned, this capacity has never been underutilized. Even so, this book is being written amid a good deal of citizen ignorance and an unusual outpouring of citizen criticism.

It is difficult to say whether contemporary public criticism focuses first on the institution and then trickles down to discredit the individual members or whether public criticism begins with the individual members and bubbles up to discredit the institution. Complaints about congressional inaction suggest the trickle-down sequence; but complaints about the behavior of individual legislators—the Keating Five, or the Anita Hill–Clarence Thomas interrogators—suggest a bubble-up sequence. Most likely, both types of criticism have combined to bathe the contemporary Congress in citizen distrust and anger.

It is not my purpose to join the chorus or add to the popular distemper. It would be the easy course. Criticizing the Congress is like shooting fish in a barrel; and the institution is surrounded by trigger-happy critics firing assault weapons. Indeed, much of what citizens know about our congressional politicians comes

directly from a drumbeat of disparaging commentary about
them—from journalists and talk show hosts, cartoonists and
comedians. What is lacking is breadth of understanding. And
under the best of circumstances, Congress is, among all our
national political institutions, the most difficult to understand.
My view is that understanding ought to accompany, if not
precede, criticism and that there remains room to improve our
understanding.

Research conducted through personal observation, however,
carries a built-in obstacle. The activities of politicians that I
report will be to a very great extent what the politician says they
are. And since my analysis depends so heavily on the expressed
words of the politicians, its auspices will be suspect. There needs
to be a willingness to set aside our ingrained distrust of these
words and accept—conditionally at least—that what politicians
tell the researcher is pretty much what they think, believe, and
act on.

Admittedly, this willingness comes a lot easier for the author,
who is dependent on the cooperation of politicians and who
spends a lot of time with them, than it does for the reader, who
is bombarded on all sides with the cynical view that nothing
a politician says can be believed or accepted at face value. The
author's low gullibility quotient provides some protection for
the reader; but still, the author accepts as data much of what
he is told. And my suggestion to the reluctant reader is to
do likewise—subject to whatever discount seems appropriate
upon careful inspection of the data.

Assuming some such generosity of disbelief on their part,
the critics, too, might benefit from exposure to the qualitative
reminders I have outlined. If congressional critics explored these
qualitative dimensions, they might be induced to take a more
selective look at the politicians they so roundly condemn as a
collectivity.

Critics, too, operate with their own all-encompassing catego-
rizations of our legislators—as "careerists" or members of "the
political class" or simply as "politicians," whose only goal in

life is to stay in office. Their relentless pursuit of this goal, say the critics, outweighs, detracts from, and militates against any good they might do by way of representing their constituents. And these undiscriminating premises quickly lead to undiscriminating reform proposals—such as a single arbitrary and legally imposed limit to the longevity of all legislators. One formula—term limits—fits all.

We Americans seem to have an infinite capacity for disillusionment when it comes to our politicians. Yet surprisingly, we know that when citizens do take a fairly careful, qualitative look at individual politicians—that is, at their own member of Congress—they tend to like what they see. While any wholesale effort to rehabilitate the rest of the congressional politicians would surely be doomed, it is not beyond hope that a retailstyle, one by one by one, close-up look at a few representatives might cause some critics to question the wisdom of their blunderbuss condemnation of all of them. Lumping them together is a device that facilitates criticism. It is also a device that makes lowest common denominator-type denunciations practically inevitable. However, accountability is a one-on-one relationship between a single politician and his or her constituents. And a few one-on-one critical assessments might inject discriminating judgments into the prevailing culture of condemnation.

SENATORS

In the pages that follow, the politicians under scrutiny are aspiring or sitting U. S. senators. If any set of politicians can be described as especially appropriate subjects of a one-by-one, individual-level qualitative scrutiny, surely it is the members of the U. S. Senate. For the Senate is routinely and invariably described as a highly individualistic institution.

Students of the contemporary institution—Barbara Sinclair, Ross Baker, Steven Smith, Roger Davidson, Lawrence Evans— agree that "individualism" is the Senate's basic contemporary characteristic.[4] The Senate is an institution, they tell us, in which each individual member has access, resources, and rules that combine to give him or her enormous independent influence in decision making. Life inside the institution is described as an entrepreneur's dreamworld, as "everyone for himself or herself." Senate politicians are notably unconstrained in their choice of behavior patterns.

To separate out these politicians for individual scrutiny does little violence, therefore, to their lives as independent, individualistic, and powerful members of the Senate. Nor does it lead to a distorted view of the Senate. To the contrary, as we focus our learning on senators as individuals, we can hardly help learning something useful about the Senate as an institution. Moreover, when our perspective comes from the campaign trail, we will be learning something important. Donald Matthews, in his groundbreaking study of the institution, wrote, "It is difficult, really, to understand the senators, how they act and why, without considering what happens to them when they are running for office."[5] In that spirit, I shall assume that the individualistic, candidate-centered campaigns I study are relevant for the understanding of an individualistic, senator-centered institution.

There is nothing especially noteworthy about the group of politicians discussed in this book. They were not chosen with this particular book in mind, only with the intent of studying senatorial activity in general. They were chosen to represent something of the variety among senators in terms of constituency, party, ideology, and career experience. Most are Democrats, but only because I have written more extensively about Republicans in previous studies on the Senate.[6] Otherwise, they are, I think, fairly typical of the elective politicians who try to make our system work, as good a group as any with which to explore the politics of representation. To be sure, there is more information here about some individuals than most readers will ever want to know. For that, I apologize. But the events, anecdotes, conversations, newspaper accounts, and personal recollections that generate such bulk are the essential evidence on which the narratives depend.

The plan is to explore, in rough order, some careers, some campaigns, and some constituency connections. My main focus will be on campaigns, where research affords maximum leverage. But individual campaigns, I argue, cannot be understood apart from the careers and the constituency connections of the politicians involved. Nor can the politics of representation be understood without all three focal points.

The first two chapters are devoted primarily to careers, the next four to campaigns, and the last two to connections. In representational terms, "careers" focus on the seeking of representation, "campaigns" on the testing of representation, and "connections" on the achievement of representation.

Table 1. Campaigns Visited, 1976–1992

	Winners		Losers	
	Challengers		*Challengers*	
Non-incumbents	William Cohen (R/Maine)	1978	Philip Hayes (D/Ind.)	1976[1]
	Paul Tsongas (D/Mass.)	1978[1]	Richard Leone (D/N.J.)	1978[1]
	Dan Quayle (R/Ind.)	1980	Jim Folsom (D/Ala.)	1980[2]
	Tom Harkin (D/Iowa)	1984		
	Open Seats			
	David Pryor (D/Ark.)	1978[2]		
	Mark Andrews (R/N. Dak.)	1980		
	Arlen Specter (R/Penn.)	1980		
	[1]Won primary (visited) and election.		[1]Lost in primary.	
	[2]Won primary and election (visited).		[2]Won primary; lost in election; election visited.	
Incumbents	Pete Domenici (R/New Mex.) ('72)[1]	1978, 1984, 1990	Dick Clark (D/Iowa) ('72)[1]	1978
	Claiborne Pell (D/R.I.) ('60, '72)[1]	1978, 1984, 1990	John Culver (D/Iowa) ('74)[1]	1980
	John Glenn (D/Ohio) ('74)[1]	1980, 1986	Robert Morgan (D/N.C.) ('74)[1]	1980
	Orrin Hatch (R/Ut.)	1982	Donald Stewart (D/Ala.) ('78)[1]	1980[2]
	Pat Moynihan (D/N.Y.)	1982	Mark Andrews (R/N. Dak.) ('80)	1986[3]
	William Cohen (R/Maine)	1984, 1990	Wyche Fowler (D/Ga.) ('86)[1]	1992[4]
	David Pryor (D/Ark.)	1984		
	Dan Quayle (R/Ind.)	1986		
	Arlen Specter (R/Penn.)	1986		
	[1]Previous Senate elections; not visited.		[1]Previous Senate elections; not visited.	
			[2]Lost in primary runoff.	
			[3]Visited both elections.	
			[4]Lost in election runoff.	

10 nonincumbent campaigns

21 incumbent campaigns

Totals:	12 winning candidates	9 losing candidates
	22 winning campaigns	9 losing campaigns

Other data: 20 campaigners; 16 states; 8 election years.
14 had previous election-year electoral experience; 6 had none.
Length of visits: 1 day (Moynihan, Harkin); 14 days (Cohen), 30 days (Fowler)
4 primary elections; 27 general elections; 1 primary runoff (Stewart)
1 election runoff (Fowler).

CHAPTER 1

PREPOLITICAL CAREERS

CAREERS AND AMBITION

ON THE CAMPAIGN TRAIL, an outsider's overwhelming first impression is one of indecipherable motion and flux. Having stepped into a moving stream and perception of events, there is an immediate need to catch up and get one's bearings. The following are givens: Every Senate candidate is seeking the right to represent a statewide constituency; they all want to win, and they are working at it. An ongoing campaign features David Mayhew's "single-minded seekers of reelection" (or of election) in its purest form.[1] And his generalization helps us to begin by focusing, first of all, on the candidate's progress toward the clear-cut electoral goal.

However, there is much more to be learned on the campaign trail. And much of what an observer learns is gleaned from the kind of informal, disjointed, meandering, event-stimulated conversations I shall call "travel talk." It is a form of conversation more open-ended, more expansive, and more unpredictable than the structured, inhibited interviews conducted in the cocoon of Capitol Hill. A lot of travel talk is about careers.

The earliest effect of campaign travel talk is to make you acutely aware that the campaign you are watching is but a small slice of the candidate's ongoing political life. It becomes clear that much of what the campaigning candidate is thinking and doing depends on what he or she has thought and done before you got there—sometimes long before. It becomes equally clear that your understanding of the politician you are following may depend on your understanding of where each one has been before you got there and where each one might want to go after you have left. In sum, the short-term campaign you have stepped into is embedded in a long-term *career*.

Not that you hadn't thought of careers before. And not that you could possibly have neglected the idea during your travels. At every campaign stop, several times each day, the candidate is introduced with the same chronological recitation of his or her personal milestones to date—experiences, accomplishments, honors, offices—usually read from a résumé carefully calibrated by the campaign staff. Candidates are recognized, remembered, and evaluated by their career milestones—by the path and the content of their careers. Candidates could not shed this badge of identification even if they wanted to. Which they don't, since they offer their career milestones to the voters as criteria for recognition and for choice.

As an observer on the campaign trail, therefore, the idea of a career is constantly put before you. And it soon becomes both a central way of identifying politicians and a major organizing idea for your research. The task I have set, of differentiating among individual politicians, can usefully begin with the differences in their careers. Much like the injunction given to investigative journalists to "follow the money," the guiding injunction of this chapter is "follow the career."

The engine that powers political careers is ambition. All politicians, we say, are ambitious; and it is ambition that most often links the milestones of a political career to one another. Legislative careers begin with the ambition for elective office. While many observers treat political ambition as dangerous and political careers as an enticement to corruption, most political scientists treat the two phenomena as neutral objects of study. Career studies by Joseph Schlesinger, David Rohde, Linda Fowler, and others have focused interest on those politicians who move (or who deliberately decline to move) from the elective office they hold to a more desirable elective office.[2] Those who want to move and try to do so are said to display "progressive ambition."

Their career decisions, it is said, can be explained by the interplay of ambition, opportunity, and calculation. The idea is that their ambition will be constrained by a historically established, hierarchical structure of elective offices that governs the opportunities for advancement. The ambitious occupant of any given office will, that is, typically contemplate moving upward to another office along the most well-traveled career paths. Thus local officeholders can reasonably contemplate a move to the U.S. House of Representatives, a House member to the Senate, a senator to the presidency or vice presidency. The decision of whether to climb this ladder will depend on a set of individual calculations involving the probability of winning, the willingness to take a risk, and the assessment of the opportunity.

All the senators I have observed have been driven by progressive ambition. This idea will be helpful in analyzing their careers. But observation on the campaign trail suggests that it is necessary to expand the scope of career analysis, too. For there is more to ambition than striving for elective office, there is more to opportunity than a structure of elective offices, and there is a lot more to a career than the move from one elective office to another.

As the idea of progressive ambition suggests, we should think of a career as a developmental phenomenon. The milestones of a career—the experience, the accomplishments, the offices listed in the résumé—accumulate over time. And careers get shaped by the learning, the growth, the adaptation to changing circumstances by individuals over time. A career is also an incremental phenomenon, since development is usually a step-by-step process. Some career steps are large and visible, for example, a climb from the House to the Senate. But other career steps are small and harder to see, for example, a shift in positions or policy interests inside the Senate. All of them are traceable. And so, too, are the constraining—or liberating—effects of any one career step on subsequent ones.

A career is a contextual phenomenon, too, in the sense that every step—every politician's career calculation—is affected by the context in which it is made. The two large contexts affecting senatorial careers are the constituency at home and the legislature in Washington, D.C. And there are subcontexts in each location. Entries in the campaign résumé come from both contexts. Encouragement and sustenance for the politician's career can be found in both contexts.

The work of Gary Jacobson and Samuel Kernell has led the way in examining the outside context in which "strategic politicians" make career calculations.[3] And John Hibbing's research has pioneered the study of careers inside the Congress—opening up the inside career, the institutional career, to analyses similar to those developed for careers in the home constituency.[4] Accordingly, the elective, legislative politicians in this study are seen as pursuing two careers—a career at home powered by *elective office ambition* and a career in the Senate powered by *institutional ambition*. And I will discuss also the relationship between them.

Thinking about careers leads an observer to think in developmental, incremental, and contextual terms. On the campaign trail, it is the developmental aspects of a career that present themselves most forcefully. How far back, one asks oneself, do I have to go in this person's career to understand what I'm seeing and listening to now? The answer would seem to be, at least to the immediate pre-Senate career and as far back beyond that as there are direct, substantial, and palpable links to the present career. In some cases, this means going back to the *prepolitical career*—to the career before a person's first run for elective office. This is not an invitation to plumb the childhood or psychological makeup of the candidate. It is only a recognition that the proximate prepolitical experience can have an important effect on the political career that follows and may, therefore, have to be incorporated into our thinking about politicians.

JOHN GLENN, OHIO, 1980–1986

Prepolitical Career

For me, the definitive case for the relevance of the prepolitical career was that of Democrat John Glenn. I first met him on the campaign trail in Ohio in 1980, when he was running for his second term in the Senate. The career milestones of his résumé outlined a truly spectacular prepolitical career. Most of it, twenty-six years, was spent in the U.S. Marine Corps. As a wartime fighter pilot, he had been awarded five Distinguished Flying Crosses and the Air Medal with eighteen clusters. Then, in 1962, as the first American astronaut to orbit the earth, he had become this nation's greatest space age hero.

Everywhere we went, he was besieged by autograph seekers. At every meeting, he was introduced as "a great American" and "a national hero," with comments such as "The world is proud of this man and his achievements." At the end of my two-day visit, I wrote in my notes, "He has had such a rich life that I despair of catching up." To which I added a ray of hope: "One thing I could ask him point blank is to talk about the relationship between his past and present. How has it affected his view of politics?" It was the right question. But it took six years of occasional conversation and campaign visits to construct an answer.

John Glenn's prepolitical career turns out to be the major influence on his elective office career. Most obviously, it endowed him with the spotless, all-American reputation for courage, character, and charm that made his political career possible. As a hero and a political amateur, however, he would have to learn to be a politician. From this angle, and less obviously, his prepolitical career was not so helpful. For it left

Glenn with a view of and attitude toward politics that made political learning difficult for him. In the end, I argue, his prepolitical career kept the hero from having as successful an elective office career as he wanted.[5]

Glenn sees politics as public service. For him, the decision to enter politics was a natural extension of what he had been doing all of his adult life—serving his country. Running for the Senate was the political equivalent of signing up for one more hitch in the marines. And he approached it with the same gung ho, "let's set goals and go for it," optimism and enthusiasm he displayed as a fighter pilot and astronaut. For him, public service is the highest calling, requiring the highest degree of personal integrity and the purest of motives. He believed that his prepolitical career exemplified those qualities. He further believed that his exemplary performance had earned him the right to run for the Senate and that the voters would easily recognize his qualifications for that job. His prepolitical behavior patterns had gotten him into politics and, he believed, would ensure his success.

His self-confidence was grounded in a core belief that having already received the unbounded acclaim and adulation of his fellow citizens, he would be a different—and better—kind of politician than most. Having no need for glory or self-gratification, he would be better motivated than others and would have an edge over others in discerning the public interest. The distinction between public service politics and ego trip politics became fundamental to his thinking about his political career. Shortly after reaching the Senate, in 1975, he expressed his view of the job this way: "You can help work out problems and plan for our future and, by God, that's exciting. But do I enjoy being a politician? Good Lord, no. I've had all the ego trips I could handle in seventeen lifetimes."[6] Voters who appreciated this difference, he believed, would recognize the merits of his case and support him as "the best man" for the Senate.

In keeping with these views, Glenn believed that he could succeed in politics without engaging in as much of the grubby, ground-level, constituency-building, party-stroking activity as the typical politician. In this respect, it is important to note that while the prepolitical careers of some military men, Dwight D. Eisenhower, for example, required an ability to win support from others through coalition-building efforts, Glenn's prepolitical career required only solo performances, in the cockpit and in the capsule. He neither knew nor enjoyed the workaday business of politics. So John Glenn came to politics directly from a prepolitical career that left him with a somewhat negative, somewhat disparaging attitude toward working politicians, toward the everyday political arts, and toward the political profession.

This set of views was, of course, most strongly expressed in the early stages of his political career. Nonetheless, it continued to dominate his career for the six years, the two Senate campaigns, and the presidential campaign during which I watched and listened to him. When we talked, for example, in 1984, after he had abandoned his quest for the presidential nomination, he commented,

> I didn't get in the race for the glory. I got in it because I believed in principles I felt were for the greater good of the country. [Walter] Mondale got in it so early that it seems to me crass or cynical or all of the above. He got in it for reasons of personal advancement. He didn't wait to see what would happen in the country. He said, "I'm going to run no matter what." I know this sounds self-serving, but I wanted what was best for the country. I got in for principle.

His core distinction between well-motivated public service politics and less well motivated ego trip politics was alive and well. And he still believed that his public service orientation made him the best man for the job.

Hero, Constituency, and Reputation

On the campaign trail in Ohio in 1980, he came across as a natural hero but an unnatural politician. In unstructured, one-on-one personal encounters—picking out a pumpkin for his wife at a farm market, buying corn dogs for some high school leafletters at a county fair—he was spontaneous, warm, and appealing. In situations structured as political—a get-out-the-vote rally in a union hall, a Democratic dinner party to roast a local politician—he was awkward, aloof, and, at the dinner, admittedly uncomfortable. In my notes I wrote, "He asked that I sit beside him as he drove to the fair so we could talk. And he tried hard to answer my questions. Some worked, some didn't, because he is essentially nonpolitical."

Among the questions that did not work were those that invited him to give some definition to his various supportive constituencies—especially the distinction between his very strongest, thick-and-thin supporters and his less reliable, fair-weather supporters. Try as I might, I could not coax him into any delineation except that he enjoyed "across the board" support from "the people."

I operated from a concentric circle formulation that made a major distinction between a candidate's primary (or strongest) constituency and his or her reelection (or weaker) constituency.[7] Glenn operated from what he called his "theory of three concentric circles"; but his three circles were Ohio, the nation, and the world. And Ohio, he said over and over, was "a microcosm of the United States." I began with the statewide constituency and worked inward. He began with the statewide constituency and worked outward. It was a mental construction that eliminated any need to delineate intrastate constituencies.

Within Ohio, I concluded, he recognized only the broadest, most general, national constituency—that is, the hero's constituency, the one he had brought with him ready-made from his prepolitical career. If he could not conceptualize a hard-core Ohio constituency or a solid Ohio political base, then he had little chance of connecting with them or activating them. Nor was he likely to develop any distinctions to help him think strategically about representation.

In none of the three election contests I watched did I ever encounter a cadre of enthusiastic, dedicated volunteer campaign workers ready to fight, bleed, and die for John Glenn or ready to state any strong reason for doing so. Nor did I ever find the morning, noon, and night devotion among his campaigners that was common elsewhere. His Ohio campaign staff kept banker's hours. His presidential campaign staff was top heavy with self-seeking mercenaries. The absence of a primary constituency, or any developed strategic sense for building one, remained a permanent characteristic of the hero's incomplete adaptation to politics.

But Glenn had obviously learned enough about constituency cultivation to win a Senate seat. He had learned from an unexpected Democratic primary defeat in 1970 that a pure, nonparty hero's campaign was not enough. As a reporter put it, "John's platform was essentially, 'I'm a hero, elect me.' "[8] He had learned, from a bitter primary victory in 1974, that he had to identify himself with the party rank and file in order to win a primary.

But that lesson was counterbalanced by another one. From that same primary experience he had also learned the overwhelming importance of his personal integrity. When we talked, his most vivid recollection of that 1974 primary victory was his emotional and intensely personal defense of his prepolitical marine-astronaut patriotism against the charge of his opponent, Howard Metzenbaum, that he had "never held a job." In the opinion of his press secretary, Glenn's ringing defense of his patriotism was the decisive moment of the campaign. "It wasn't my checkbook, it was my life that was on the line," he replied to his opponent. "Go with me and tell a Gold Star mother her son didn't hold a job."[9]

When I asked his campaign manager to describe Glenn's support in that crucial primary, he said, "I hate to say it, but it's the truth—the people." Once elected, Glenn became a major Democratic party asset, and he never had to face another primary. So long as he ran only in general elections, he could rely heavily on his "across the board" hero's constituency, "the people." And he would not have to pay for his inattention to primary constituency building. By 1975, he was probably in a position to be a senator from Ohio as long as he wanted.

But that was not all he wanted. He had progressive ambition. In David Canon's important distinction, John Glenn was an ambitious amateur.[10] And from the day he was elected to the Senate, the national political elites—the media and the politicos—encouraged him. Two years into his Senate career, he became one of five finalists for the vice presidential nomination. But a bromidic convention speech that failed utterly to connect with the party faithful cost him that chance. While deeply disappointed, he was not discouraged. He interpreted his overwhelming reelection victory in 1980 as legitimating a run for the presidential nomination in 1984. That, too, ended in disappointment.

Traveling with him in the presidential campaign, I observed the same lack of strategic sense about supportive constituencies as I had worried about in Ohio. His 1983–84 problem nationally was the same as his 1970 primary problem had been in his home state—to locate and assemble a nominating constituency from among his fellow Democrats. But he could not do it.

I observed firsthand his failure to communicate either by message or by personal persuasion with several types of potential primary supporters—with black leaders at their 1983 NAACP meeting in Mississippi, with Democratic state chairs from Delaware, Missouri, North Carolina, and Tennessee at Philadelphia's 1982 mini convention; with Arkansas Governor Bill Clinton at the 1982 Jefferson Jackson Day dinner in Little Rock; with Mayor Jane Byrne at a 1981 Democratic party dinner in Chicago; and with core Democratic caucus-going constituencies in Iowa in 1983. He could not speak to any of these Democrats in terms of shared attachments, sensitivities, or intensities. All of them recognized him as a remarkable astronaut, but they could not yet be drawn to him as a winning politician.

Only twice in seven days on the campaign trail did presidential candidate Glenn look and act as if he was in total command of an event and completely comfortable. That occurred at two full dress anniversary dinner-dance celebrations of his own U.S. Marine Corps—the only two nonpolitical events out of twenty-one campaign stops. And he acknowledged—"I guess you could tell that"—the accuracy of my observation.

John Glenn campaigned for the presidency by pursuing the same "across the board" hero's constituency he had emphasized from the beginning of his political career. His campaign-planning document called for "a broad-based and all-inclusive coalition of Democratic elements." His campaign consultants later conceptualized it for him by stating that his nomination strategy should activate "the constituency of the whole." Glenn "swallowed that argument hook, line, and sinker," said a disappointed longtime aide, "because he could be the hero and avoid the dirty political work." And when it was over, another veteran staffer explained, "He's an amateur—not because of ability, but because of arrogance. He thought that all he had to do was to enter the race—John Glenn, the big hero—and everyone else would be blown away." They, too, were talking about the incomplete transition from hero to politician.

As I traveled with him during his presidential campaign and later during his 1986 reelection campaign in Ohio, I concluded that it was as much Glenn's ambivalence as his inability that accounted for his political difficulties and disappointments. And his ambivalence was the product of his career. For he came to politics with not one but two ambitions—to achieve higher elective office *and* to preserve his prepolitical reputation. He wanted to protect his hero's reputation, I argue, almost as much as he wanted to further his ambitions to achieve elective office.

He was quick to perceive and take offense at the slightest slur on his personal integrity or his public service. During our travel talks, the one political subject that invariably commanded Glenn's attention was not outreach but outrage—at the personal, negative campaign tactics of his adversaries of the moment. He not only construed political attacks in personal terms, he invariably pictured himself as the injured party in every confrontation.

During his campaign for the presidential nomination, he talked about his early confrontations with Mondale.

> I had always hoped that we could conduct the campaign on the issues and not get into personal attacks on one another. But it didn't work out that way. And I was the aggrieved party.... [When] Mondale lit out after me on a number of things, I had to defend myself. So I hit back, but I said I hoped that would be the last of it.... Then he printed that three-page attack on me.... Each time I said I hoped that would be the end of it. And each time they started it again—the worst kind of flat-out demagoguery I have ever heard. It makes me mad and I don't know what to do about it. I may have to take him head on and all out.... I can't let them get away with that garbage.

When presidential opponents Fritz Hollings and Jesse Jackson made jokes about Glenn's astronaut past, he reacted,

> I never brought it up first. Two of them brought it up in a very deprecating way, and I'm very proud of those days. When people deprecate that, they deprecate me, they deprecate my family, they deprecate something that this country thought was important.... To have someone cast disparaging remarks at the kind of dedication we had ... that does hurt.[11]

On the trail in Ohio in 1986, he complained about Republican Tom Kindness.

> My opponent is conducting a completely negative campaign.... This guy is saying things about me that are absolutely outrageous. I'd love to stomp him 95 to 5 or 90 to 10. I'd love to get a vote of 75 to 80 percent so that I could say that we won't have that sort of thing ever again in Ohio.... This is the first time I've ever had an opponent whose principal effort has been to tear me down.... He's attacking my integrity—with absolute untruths.

These reactions were cut from the same cloth as his winning counterattack against Howard Metzenbaum in 1974.

Glenn's hair-trigger defense of his hero's reputation was partly to protect his own greatest political resource, but it was also, I believe, to preserve a national resource. No politician I have ever met felt more sincerely or more passionately than

John Glenn about love of country. He was immensely proud
of what he had done for his country. And he did not want his
accomplishment or the national memory of it to be sullied by
conventional politics.

The desire to protect his reputation—for both personal and
national reasons—is the main explanation for his incomplete
transition from hero to politician. His pursuit of his reputational
goal severely constrained the range of political behavior
available to him in pursuing his office-seeking goal. He would
not submerge the recognizable astronaut persona sufficiently to
take on a more recognizable political persona. In the end, it was
too high a price to pay for America's greatest peacetime hero.
And so he remained, for too many of his fellow citizens, more
astronaut than political leader.

The dilemma is understandable. Indeed, it is hard to imagine
any final resolution. John Glenn's prepolitical career made
his political career possible, but at the same time, it was
the overwhelming influence of the former that inhibited his
political learning and impeded the development of the latter.
The successes, the disappointments, the unresolvable tensions,
the genuine ambivalence of his political life were built into it, I
concluded, by the prepolitical career path that had brought him
to that life.

Conclusion

What tentative notions about political careers might be drawn
from the case of John Glenn's elective office career? First and
most important, the proximate prepolitical career may be highly
relevant for understanding the political career. And its relevance
may be long-lasting as well. Since some proportion of legislative
candidates will always be "ambitious amateurs," it will be
important to devote continuing scholarly attention to the impact
of their prepolitical careers. If the proponents of term limits are
able to recruit the amateurish "citizen legislators" they desire,
then the need to understand prepolitical careers will become
even greater.

Second, the development of Glenn's career suggests that a representative's career might usefully be viewed as a sequence of learning experiences as new career steps bring new challenges and opportunities. In Glenn's case, the important lessons involved the identification and cultivation of supportive constituency relationships. At some points, he learned enough to succeed; at other points, he did not. When he had time to learn, he did; when he came fresh to a new context, as in 1970 and 1984, he did not. In a representative system of government, a supportive constituency may not tell us all we need to know about just who it is that a politician represents. As a major component, however, it does provide a good starting point.

Third, the Glenn case suggests the importance of personal *reputation* for the study of careers. As we have seen, a politician's reputation can facilitate, shape, and constrain his elective office career—and, perhaps, his institutional career as well. A career is a summary of a person's experiences and actions. A reputation is a summary of other people's knowledge and interpretation of those experiences and actions. Career and reputation are related to one another, and they affect one another. As a politician's career proceeds, and is scrutinized by others, a reputation develops, changes, or crystallizes. At each stage, it affects the politician's relationship with others.

If salient and favorable, a reputation is one of a politician's most treasured resources. The more salient and favorable, the more strenuously—as in Glenn's case—will the politician work to protect it. If otherwise, it is a major hurdle to overcome. Either way, reputation is harder to understand and more qualitative in its impact than other familiar career-building resources such as money or organization or office experience. Reputation is a resource that can be explored by close, personal observation. The interplay between John Glenn's reputation, his protection of it, and his career illustrates how that can be done and why it should be done.

DAN QUAYLE, INDIANA, 1980–1986

Prepolitical Career

In all probability, the Glenn case belongs at the high end of any scale that measures the eventfulness of prepolitical careers. Among the senators with whom I traveled, the case of Dan Quayle belongs near the uneventful end of such a scale.

I began my travels with Dan Quayle in Indiana in the fall of 1980, at the same time I began traveling with John Glenn in Ohio.[12] Moving from one campaign to the other produced a stark career comparison. Quayle was a thirty-three-year-old, two-term congressman reaching for the Senate. He had been only two years out of law school, working on a family-owned newspaper, when he ran successfully for Congress in 1976. Until a nearby newspaper editor suggested it to him that year, he said, "I had never thought about running for Congress." Indiana's governor commented that "most voters didn't know whether they were sending him to Congress or to camp."

Travel talk on the campaign trail with Quayle and his campaign staffers produced almost no conversation about his prepolitical career. I got only the skimpiest clues as to what prepolitical experiences, intellectual or practical, might have affected Quayle's political career. He occasionally mentioned his grandfather, an influential, conservative newspaper publisher who probably sensitized him to politics and, perhaps, to ideology as well. And he said it was a patronage job in the governor's office—which he described only as "fun"—that started him thinking about running for the state legislature.

To be sure, he had not had a long prepolitical life. Still, none of our travel talks between 1980 and 1986 contained the slightest indication that college or law school or work on the newspaper had influenced his political life. Neither he nor any staffer ever mentioned any prepolitical accomplishments, and none was contained in his very short résumé. When his closest political friends wondered what prepolitical experiences they could exploit in his campaign advertising, they joked that the only alternatives were "Dan Quayle, student," "Dan Quayle, lawyer," and "Dan Quayle, father." And one of them summed up, "We'll just say you never did anything else." As far as I could tell, they were right.

So Quayle entered politics with no name recognition, no accomplishments, no reputation, and, the pundits said, no chance to win. But he had nothing to lose—no career investments or commitments. While he got no positive thrust from his prepolitical career, he was not constrained by it either. He had no career-long record to defend. He had an abundance of self-confidence; it was free-floating and not born of accomplishment. And his goal was to build a reputation, not protect one. Quayle was as unconstrained by his prepolitical career as Glenn was constrained by his. For Glenn, entering politics was the continuation of a serious lifetime commitment. Quayle, however, was free to take a plunge, to treat politics as a youthful adventure— to see how he liked it and how well he might succeed.

When I caught up with him, he was trying to parlay the momentum from his two House victories into a Senate seat. But except for the victories themselves, he remained a blank slate. He was introduced everywhere as the architect of a stunning upset win in 1976 and little more. He had no recognizable House record. His campaign literature called him "a rising star"—all future, no past. He was trying to turn his youthfulness into an asset by campaigning for "a new generation of leadership." His message was standard, boiler plate, Republican conservatism, enlivened only by an especially strident anti-Washington, anti-incumbent theme.

As a bread-and-butter campaigner, Quayle possessed the talents and the instincts that Glenn lacked. He threw himself into the daily fray with youthful enthusiasm. When asked to rank the twelve events of our three-day trip in terms of how comfortable he felt, he gave first place to ninety minutes of shaking hands with blue-collar workers during a shift change at an Alcoa plant gate. "Some Republicans aren't comfortable at factory gates. I am. I like it." He ranked that campaign stop even higher than

his talks to realtors and to dentists—"our natural constituency."
His presentational skills helped me to understand his political
success. But they did not help me to understand why he was
doing it. On that subject, too, his prepolitical career offered no
assistance.

Ambition and Accomplishment

There could be no doubt of Quayle's ambition. "He is," said a
longtime friend, "the kind of person who is always climbing
a mountain, and always looking ahead to the next one." In
1980, he made the same set of calculations he had made in 1976.
Once again, he was taking a risky political plunge against heavy
odds. Once again, he was confronting a strong and popular
incumbent—this time a three-term, eighteen-year incumbent
senator. Once again, he had started out far behind—by at
least thirty points—in the polls. Once again, he exuded self-
confidence. But why was he doing it?

He was doing it primarily, I believe, because the Senate was
there, just above the House in the hierarchical structure of
opportunity. "Ever since I was elected," he said, "I had thought
about the Senate if anything came up." What had "come up"
was a challenger vacuum—into which he moved before anyone
else. "Right after my reelection in 1978 I started to go around
talking to people." And he had never stopped campaigning. "I
spent my first term running for reelection to the House and my
second term running for the Senate."

Dan Quayle had the purest kind of progressive ambition.
He conformed to every generalization in Rohde's authoritative
formal analysis of that phenomenon.[13] Quayle would reach for
any office that presented an opportunity to him. His personal
calculations were relentlessly optimistic about the opportunity
before him and about the probabilities of winning. He was
unconcerned about the costs of losing; and he was perfectly
willing to accept the risk involved. The absence of a prepolitical
career had, I believe, reduced the stakes attendant on a political
career. He had plunged in; he liked it; he was good at it; so he

would just keep going. If he lost, even if he lost his secure House seat, his attitude was "No big investment, no big problem."

On the trail in 1980, he expressed the belief that he could accomplish more in the Senate than in the House. "It's an awful job—especially being a Republican in the House," he said. "You can't get anything done. I couldn't be satisfied just taking care of my district and getting reelected. If I had not run for the Senate, I would have run for one more term in the House and then I would have looked around for something else. I might have gotten out of politics." Later he added, "In the Senate, you can work with the guys—the top twenty guys—to get something done. I'll like that about the Senate." But he never identified with any specificity or passion just what it was he wanted to get done.

When he made his first important career decision inside the Senate—his committee assignments—he demonstrated the same pattern of ambition without focus. As he described it,

> I wanted [the] Governmental Affairs [Committee]. But I sat there watching and I saw that I could be third ranking on [the] Labor and Human Resources [Committee]. . . . I didn't have any interest in it to tell you the truth. I hadn't even thought of it. But if I were third ranking and Bob Stafford retired next year, I could be second—assuming Orrin Hatch is reelected. So I said to myself right there, "Why not take it?"

It was an on-the-spot choice that eventually led to his most important Senate accomplishment. Moving up to a better office had been his electoral office ambition; and moving up to a better position inside the Senate was his institutional ambition. It was moving up that mattered.

When we talked at the end of his first year about his career aspirations inside the Senate, he answered in terms of reputation: "I want to be known as an effective senator." And he added, "But it isn't clear yet what issues I'll be working on. . . . It's hard to tell whether I'll be known as someone who initiates legislation or someone who takes issues that come to him and moves them through the Senate."

And he added, "I got the most satisfaction out of getting involved in the issues, taking some initiatives, doing the work, and getting things accomplished." When I asked him for a highlight he answered, "There was no one highlight. The highlight was getting involved in a whole lot of things." As for his reputation, "It's too early to tell. I haven't developed any themes yet." As a legislative politician who had, as yet, no legislative accomplishment, I assumed that his institutional ambition was "to accomplish something." The substance was not important to him. The accomplishment was.

In my notes after the 1980 trip, I speculated on Dan Quayle's future career: "He's just a kid—or so he seems to me. I wonder what gives a kid of thirty-three the confidence to go around his state calling for a new generation of leadership for the 1980s and the twenty-first century.... All this raises an interesting challenge for DQ. Can he grow? If he makes it, will he grow?" As it turned out, I had the opportunity to watch him and to record his efforts as he took hold of his most important leadership opportunity in the Senate, engineering the passage of the Joint Training Partnership Act (JTPA) through the Senate and into law in 1982.[14] It had given a temporary focus to his desire to get things done. As chairman of the relevant subcommittee and the unquestioned leader of an important and complex legislative effort, Quayle displayed a breadth of view, a sense of responsibility, a coalition-building talent, and an independence of judgment sufficient to answer my question concerning his growth. Yes, he had grown—a lot.

In 1980, the majority leader, Howard Baker, asked him to take on a sensitive institutional task, chairing a committee to revise the Senate's committee system—which he did.[15] By 1986, the beltway media were describing Quayle as "one of the most active and successful members of the Republican class of 1980," whose "legislative record is among the most productive of the 1980 class," who "has built a reputation as a pragmatic, thoughtful senator," and one of the three "potential Senate leaders" in the class of 1980.[16] He was becoming the effective senator he had wanted to be. What John Glenn had done outside the Senate, Dan Quayle was doing inside the Senate—learning what he had to, to further his political career.

By the time I began to follow his reelection campaign in 1985–86, it became clear that Quayle's substantial JTPA accomplishment had underwritten the continuance of his political career. It had driven all serious Democratic opponents from the field. It had given his Indiana constituents both a substantive policy reason and a personal leadership reason for supporting him. He had finally made a mark by which he could be judged.

On the campaign trail, he was invariably introduced, with lavish praise, as the author of the JTPA—"one of the best legislative success stories in America ... a great legislative achievement and a sign of the great ability he brings to public life," as the lieutenant governor put it to a group of party leaders. His campaign manager summed up the political potency of his legislative achievement: "JTPA is the whole campaign. It's everything. It's the first thing he talks about everywhere he goes.... It sews everything together. He brings home the bacon; he is a national leader; and the program embodies his philosophy of public/private partnership.... JTPA is his suit of armor." He won a very easy, very large reelection victory. It was a convincing example of the mutuality of institutional ambition and elective office ambition.

Between campaign stops, however, our travel talk did *not* center on JTPA but on his political future. He expressed little sense of any enduring commitment to the policy area he had so largely affected. Politics, not policy, remained his primary interest. Taking his reelection for granted, he worried out loud about his victory margin: "I have to get 55 percent. I'm counting on that. If I didn't get 55 percent, I don't know what I'd do. Anything between 55 percent and 60 percent is adequate. I couldn't complain. Anything over 60 percent would be great. That would bring a lot of national attention." He was planning to hire a speech writer, he added, to help him "take part more on the floor, write op-ed pieces for the paper and magazines, and give more in-depth speeches on the subjects that interest me." His second-term goal was to build on his legislative reputation to achieve some national recognition. He was as ambitious as ever to move up—whatever that might mean substantively.

The constant factor in Quayle's personal calculations about opportunity and risk in 1976 and 1980 had been his self-confidence. And that remained undiminished during our conversations on the trail in 1986. "I have complete confidence that whatever I want to do, I can do," he said. "I haven't had many failures. So I just keep going on the theory that when you're hot, you're hot.... It's a matter of self-confidence. In my first race and in my Senate race—I surprised everyone but myself. I've risen very fast—first office Congress, then two terms, and then the Senate. I never earned my spurs, as they say. And I guess I'm still flying high." When I left him that October, he remained the youthful, self-propelling risk-taker I had met six years before—still embarked on a "let's go for it and see what happens" political career, still "flying high" and still contemplating an upward trajectory. I believed at the time that the inside political skills he had displayed on JTPA had put him on the road to Republican party leadership inside the Senate.

Conclusion

The Quayle case, added to the Glenn case, illustrates the considerable variation we might expect in the impact of prepolitical careers on political careers. It tells us that ambitious individuals come to politics at very different stages in their lives. And it alerts us to take note of the stage at which we have entered the career of each politician. It tells us that there will be cases in which the impact of a prepolitical career is almost nonexistent and leaves no positive mark on the political career. But the Quayle case also suggests that even under these circumstances, the prepolitical career is worth thinking about, if only to conclude that its very absence may still have consequences for the political career.

My suggestion here is that Dan Quayle's career ambitions—to move up somewhere and to accomplish something—may be understood if we recognize the marked lack of any guiding or shaping experiences in his prepolitical life. He began his political career in the House without any well-formed concept of politics or any well-rooted agenda. And he acquired neither while he was there. So he came to the Senate still young and unformed, but still confident and eager to tackle whatever came up. The first Washington journalist to interview him extensively in 1979 entitled her profile "The Charmed Life of Indiana's Golden Boy: Dan Quayle's Smooth Passage to the Senate."[17] His career remained an adventure for the young and restless. Unencumbered in his political career by any prepolitical career experience, or any prepolitical reputation to protect, he was able to improvise as he went along. And he did.

PATTERNS

My personal observation of any one politician never encompassed the entire career. All observation-based discussions of a certain career therefore involved career segments.[18] After I had completed my observation of one segment, however, I wondered about its connection with later ones.

It has been eight years since I completed my intensive research on John Glenn and Dan Quayle. And the question arises, What has happened to them since? Have their careers followed the paths and taken the shapes I expected during the six-year period I was watching them? Did the differing patterns of ambitions, motivations, and reputations inside and outside the Senate have any durability? Did my six years of observation have any diagnostic value for understanding their subsequent political careers? While necessarily speculative, the answer is, to a large extent, yes. A longitudinal look-in has promoted the discovery and the elaboration of some long-lasting career patterns.

When I left John Glenn in 1986, I believed that all opportunity for another elective office had ended. But it hadn't. He had to endure one more disappointment, for the familiar reasons reaching back to his prepolitical career. In 1988, he was one of the two finalists as Michael Dukakis's choice for vice president. He wanted it. As he had commented after his presidential bid, "You keep climbing."[19] But he lost out to his colleague, Lloyd Bentsen. According to the newspaper accounts, it was the memory of Glenn's disastrous 1984 campaign for the presidency that did him in.[20]

So for the third time his hero's reputation made him a serious contestant for national office; and for the third time his incomplete persona as a political leader kept him from winning. In 1992, however, he won reelection to the Senate. And that victory—also for the third time—followed a familiar pattern. It was the third of his winning Senate campaigns (1974, 1986, 1992) to be dominated by his fierce rebuttals to the perceived attacks on his personal character and integrity. "It's smear tactics, a character assassination, and I resent it," he said of Michael Dewine's campaign.[21] And his victory comments were carbon copies of 1986. "Tonight," he said, "I hope Ohio has signaled the beginning of the end of the politics of sleaze and smear."[22] The hero's reputation and the politician's career had proved terminally incompatible nationally, but again they had remained perfectly compatible in Ohio. For anyone who began an analysis with John Glenn's prepolitical career, these persisting patterns offered no surprises.

It cannot be said of Dan Quayle's post-1986 career that it contained no surprises. When George Bush chose Quayle to be his vice-presidential running mate in 1988, the decision was a surprise. But the surprise pertained, of course, to Bush's choice. It was not a surprise to witness Dan Quayle's ambition for the office—not, at least, for anyone who understood his all-purpose progressive ambition to "move up" and "accomplish something." From Quayle's point of view, the vice presidency was simply the logical next step up the career ladder. It came as no surprise at all, then, to learn from later reporting that Quayle had coveted the job, had engaged in "subtle, even stealthy planning," and had "worked for six months to be picked by Bush."[23] For the third straight occasion, therefore, he had surprised everyone except himself. And his career took its third consecutive move up the elective office ladder. It was the straightforward continuance of his established career pattern.

But in the aftermath of his selection, one of the established features of his career took on a new importance. The very freedom from a highly constraining prepolitical career—the freedom that had encouraged his progressive ambition and facilitated his meteoric political career—turned out to contain some career-threatening liabilities.

In the vastly larger national political context, under the scrutiny of the vastly more adversarial national media, Quayle was hit with an avalanche of negative publicity. And almost all of it was based on the years of his life before Congress— the part that I had found to be neither textured nor relevant to his political career. The political reporters were not a bit interested in the accomplishments or the overall development of his praiseworthy and promising Senate career.[24] Instead, they focused their formidable investigative resources on his skimpy prepolitical career to construct a profile of a rich boy, a weak student, and a draft avoider—all in all, a privileged, unqualified, unaccomplished lightweight. Within a few weeks, that national reputation had been promulgated; and it had quickly hardened. It plagued him throughout his vice presidency. And with the reelection defeat in 1992, it promised to thwart further movement up the career ladder.

With a longer, more accomplished, and better-known pre-political career or a favorable pre-Senate reputation of some sort, Quayle might have been able to withstand the national onslaught or deflect it away from his private life and toward his public career. In the end, the absence of a prepolitical career may have kept him from trying to extend his public career as far as his progressive ambition would otherwise have driven him. With respect to their loftiest career ambitions, it seems John Glenn had too influential a prepolitical career and Dan Quayle had one that was too uninfluential.

CHAPTER 2

POLITICAL CAREERS

AMBITION AND CAREERS

THE CAREER PATHS of John Glenn and Dan Quayle amply illustrate the driving force of ambition in seeking elective office. Indeed, without ambition, there are no careers in politics. So, granted that ambition is the engine that powers political careers, what is the fuel that fires the engine? What is it that stimulates and sustains political ambition? Judging by the Glenn and Quayle cases, the motivations that lie behind elective office ambition and the satisfactions that flow from its achievement are a good deal more variable than the presence of ambition itself.

If we want to relate the ambitions of politicians to their behavior, it will help us to explore the variability of motivations, attractions, and satisfactions. It is particularly important to consider that variability if we want to relate ambition to long-term career patterns. The idea of progressive ambition applies to a politician's career inside the legislature as well as outside—to the *institutional career* as well as the *elective office career*. Knowledge concerning the differing incentives that shape one aspect of the career will help us to understand the other. And we would expect some short-term convergence of the two elements of the career and some long-term patterning of the two elements over the length of the career.[1]

I will pursue this further exploration with three candidates I first joined on the campaign trail in 1978—Paul Tsongas, Democrat of Massachusetts, William Cohen, Republican of Maine, and David Pryor, Democrat of Arkansas. Their elective office ambition—their progressive ambition—was amply documented by the ladder of offices each had already climbed when I met him. Tsongas had already been a city councilman and a county commissioner and had served two terms in Congress. Cohen had already been a city councilman and a mayor and had served three terms in Congress. Pryor had already served in the Arkansas House of Representatives, in the U.S. Congress, and as governor of Arkansas.

From their campaign travel talk and from our conversations later, as I followed them in the Senate, it became clear that their political careers had been stimulated and sustained by quite different sorts of motivations, attractions, and satisfactions. In each case there was complexity, but in each case one motivation was sufficiently well articulated to provide a long head start toward the explanation of that person's behavior. For Tsongas, it was the desire to exercise policy leadership. For Cohen, it was the desire for a job that would keep him totally engaged. For Pryor, it was the desire to be a politician. I suggest that an understanding of these differences is not only important to understanding their elective office ambition but their institutional ambition as well.

In my discussion of the latter, I shall pay special attention to choice of committee assignments. A long time ago, Lewis Anthony Dexter told us that the most important question every senator faces is, "What kind of a senator do I want to be?"[2] It still is. It is, in fact, the institutional ambition question. The answer to it will emerge only over time, but expressions of committee assignment preferences contain early clues. For no matter how individualistic and freewheeling the Senate may be and no matter how many noncommittee opportunities for goal achievement are available, for most senators most of the time, life inside the institution still revolves around their committees.

A senator's reputation inside the Senate takes shape first within his or her committees, that is, with those people (colleagues and staff) with whom he or she has the closest and most regular working relationship. Senators, as compared to House members, are less constrained in their work by their committee boundaries. Nonetheless, a senator's governing accomplishments—initiatives taken, provisions inserted, bills passed, money allocated, coalitions created, explanations devised—will be disproportionately committee-centered.[3] In any case, the division of institutional responsibility for policy making is authoritatively established when senators are assigned to their various committee jurisdictions. Their committee assignments are essential building blocks of their careers; and committee assignment choices are milestone career choices. I shall treat them as having diagnostic value for the examination of institutional ambition.

PAUL TSONGAS, MASSACHUSETTS, 1978–1984

Paul Tsongas's prepolitical career, like that of John Glenn, had a major impact on his political career. But unlike Glenn's case, Tsongas's prepolitical career facilitated the development of his political career. It gave him a motivation and a direction that propelled him into public life and up the elective office ladder without ambivalence or setbacks.

Tsongas joined the Peace Corps after law school and spent two years as a teacher in Ethiopia. There he developed a taste for getting involved in public policy and changing the world. In the process, he changed himself. When we first met in 1978, he said, "The major formative influence of my life was the Peace Corps and all the Peace Corps stands for. That's where I'm coming from." And he added, "I went there a conservative Republican and I came back a liberal Democrat." More to the point, he returned as a policy activist; and his elective office ambition was fueled by a passion for solving public policy problems.

When we met on the campaign trail in 1978, he had already propelled himself up the elective office ladder as he reached for ever bigger and better forums in which to frame the policies that interested him. He catalogs his first House campaign in 1974, for example, simply as "the first time I got involved in national issues." He was, he said, "carried into Congress on the wave of Watergate." As a member of the class of 1974 in the House, he helped engineer the largest reform package in half a century.

He made it clear that he was in the business because of the issues. His reason for leaving the House was as follows: "I could look ahead for 8, 10, 12 years before I could get to be chairman of the only subcommittee that interested me. There were seven or eight guys ahead of me." He was reaching for the Senate, he said, "because it's the best place to be if you're issue-oriented." He first thought seriously about reaching for the Senate when he became angry "at the way [the incumbent] was handling the Panama Canal issue—first up the hill, then down the hill." Everything about his pre-Senate career showed him to be a policy activist.

Tsongas and Quayle came to the House together in 1974 and left together in 1978. Both men ran first against an incumbent House member and then against an incumbent senator to get where they were; and both men began their two races as challengers behind in the polls. Both men declared in 1978 that they would not have stayed in the House more than one more term. Both men were skilled in diagnosing the presence of opportunity.

If we were to view their political careers only from the standpoint of their shared progressive ambition, the similarities are most striking. They were a pair of prototypical, progressively ambitious politicians. But in terms of what underlay their ambition and what sustained their careers, they could not have been more different. To know only about their progressive ambition is not enough to uncover their motivations or explain their behavior.

Tsongas's ambition was fueled by a passion about public

policy problems that predated his political career and imparted a purposeful direction to it. In sharp contrast to Quayle, he had well-rooted and very specific policy interests. His Senate television campaign featured tangible legislative accomplishments in the House (as Quayle's campaign could not): the establishment of the first urban national park in his hometown of Lowell, and a $6 million grant to hasten the commercialization of solar energy through the development of photovoltaic cells. Our 1978 travel talk was heavily oriented toward policy, stimulated by these accomplishments and spilling into the broader areas of which they were a part. When we talked shortly before he was sworn in, he declared, "Cities is our number one issue, then energy, then third world, and then environment. I can be good on these four issues because I'm interested in them. I'd be just as interested in them if I stayed in private life."

Accordingly, the three committees he asked for were Energy, Foreign Relations, and Banking. He knew Banking would be easy; but in the two months before he was sworn in, he went to Washington "four or five times" to lobby for the first two. "Eventually," he said, "I'll be on Foreign Relations and Energy. The only thing that makes sense is to stay with the issues you came here with. Anything else is a damned waste of time." All this was in the sharpest contrast to Dan Quayle's uncertainty and impulsiveness in making committee assignment decisions.

Tsongas talked constantly about "my four issues." And he generalized about them. For example, when I asked him before he was sworn in whether his issues differed from that of his Massachusetts colleague, Ted Kennedy, he said, "Yes, the issues that I'm into reflect another generation. He tends to be into human resources issues, Great Society issues. Mine are more technological, more future-oriented—energy, environment, Africa, the restoration of cities. Those are different kinds of issues than health care, the criminal justice system, or welfare would be." He quickly established five citizen advisory groups in different issue areas, and he described his meetings with them as "the most enjoyable things I do."[4] He was, and would remain, the most issue-oriented, issue-driven senator of all those with whom I traveled.

Combining his elective office ambition and his institutional ambition, the goal of his political career was to achieve policy leadership. Neither he nor any of his staffers ever showed the slightest interest in party leadership positions. He had propelled himself up the elective office ladder by searching for ever bigger and better forums in which to frame and promote the policies that interested him. He had come to the Senate, he said, "because it's the best place to be if you're issue-oriented." His desire was, in his words, to get "out front"—first intellectually and then politically—on his issues.

The intellectual part of his leadership was crucial; if he did not feel he was out front intellectually on a particular issue, he would lose interest. "There's no point in my getting involved in issues where I basically play a support role or am second string," he explained.[5] Typically, getting out front involved a major intellectual effort and the preparation of a fat report or position paper— his Lowell Plan for urban revitalization, his Massachusetts Plan on energy, his compromise plan for bailing out the Chrysler Corporation, his foreign policy for southern Africa, his book proposing a neoliberal agenda for the Democratic party. His passion was "to plant the flag and say 'follow me.' "

Within six months of taking office, Tsongas was hard at work on his four issues. Listen to him: "I'm clearly the most out-front senator on the African issue." "We see a lot of people who are thinking seriously about energy, because we are out front on the issue." "I probably spend more time on urban revitalization than anyone in the Senate." When asked in June what he wanted to accomplish in six years, he said, "I would hope that on the issues we worked on—energy, the cities, Africa—we will be seen to have been credible."

His immediate institutional ambition was to achieve credibility on his issues, out of which would grow policy leadership. Within two years, he had worked, within his committee assignments, to craft two crucial compromises—on the Chrysler bailout from the Banking Committee and on the Alaska lands bill from the Energy Committee. In both cases, he worked across party lines to work out his solution. He received reputational credit—from the media and from his colleagues—for these achievements.[6]

In early 1981, he talked about them in terms of their effect on his reputation.

I felt we hit our stride when we got the Chrysler bill through. It showed we could accomplish something. It was the first time I went against my natural constituency. I have to show a willingness to rethink the issues if people are going to take me seriously. I have done that—starting with the Chrysler vote.

I feel very comfortable in the Senate, and it's not social. I think people respect me. The Alaska lands issue had a lot to do with that—with Republicans as well as Democrats. I understand there are little cliques that get together. Not only do I not do that, I don't know who they are or where they meet. But I think people know that my word is good. I also think people know I will give them a good hard fight and that I don't fight just for the sake of fighting.

As far as I could tell, he was well on the way toward the reputation he wanted for credibility and leadership on the issues.

In 1980, Tsongas told a constituent with a large export business,

We're not newcomers to this area. I'm on the International Trade Subcommittee [of the Banking Committee] and someday I want to be chairman of that subcommittee—however long it takes. So I'm going to be dealing with export problems for a long time. I want to build a reputation in the field that will stand me in good stead way down the line. We've already started. We've passed every one of our export amendments in committee.

Four months later, when a vacancy opened up on Foreign Relations, he went to the chairman of the Banking Committee to ask for the chairmanship of the International Trade Subcommittee. And he canvassed the more senior committee members to see if he could pull it off. When he found his path to the subcommittee chairmanship blocked, he left Banking for Foreign Relations. A veteran staffer explained, "His interest is in the issues. He will go to any committee that will enable him to take a bite out of the issues he's interested in. He doesn't mind giving up seniority. The trappings of power don't interest him."

Not surprisingly, after four years in the Senate, his issues had changed. When I asked him what happened to the four issues he had brought with him to the Senate, Tsongas said, "Psychologically and philosophically, I am still interested in those issues. But times change. Issues come and go. If you stayed with one set of issues, you'd be standing in the backwater. I have backed away from the energy area. The problem is you can't get anything passed. So you walk away from it. You go on to other things." Somewhat later, he said, "Africa was the classic example. I was the most learned person on Africa ever to sit in the Senate. It never amounted to a damn. Events didn't require it."

Four years into his term, one of his longtime aides described Tsongas's ceaseless drive for policy leadership. "There was his El Salvador–Central America phase; then there was the Japanese challenge phase; there was the nuclear freeze; then he came back to the Japanese issue; then there was the ERA [Equal Rights Amendment] phase; and now there is the Lebanon issue." He added, "He keeps saying [to the staff], 'Bring me some issues!' He wants to be out front on everything." The staffer summed up:

It's like the endless summer. He keeps looking for the perfect wave. He's a great political surfer. He's got fantastic instincts for finding the wave just as it's beginning to form and getting out ahead of everyone else on the crest of the wave. That's how he gets his satisfaction. You can take the one hundred senators and ask each one what gives him the greatest satisfaction. For a lot of them, satisfaction comes from the power and prestige of just being a senator. It is enough to push the buttons and pull the levers. For Paul, that is not satisfying. He likes to get out front on an issue, analyze it, work out a position on it, and then dig in to explain it to others.

The closest Tsongas came to the perfect wave during his six years was a policy effort that reached beyond committee-based leadership to Democratic party leadership. He got "out front" in July 1980, with a speech to the traditional liberals of Americans for Democratic Action (ADA) in which he called for a revision of liberalism that would be less reflexively anti-business and pro-labor, that would emphasize economic growth and prepare the country for survival in a newly competitive, high-tech world.[7] Two weeks later, he said, "My speech to the ADA got the most attention of anything I've done. There has been an incredible reaction." And he said later, "It developed a momentum. Two weeks before the election, Walter Mondale's office asked for a copy; Exxon covered it in their annual report."

The timing of the ADA speech—*before* the election of Ronald Reagan—put Tsongas on the crest of the Democratic post-election soul searching. He said in March,

> It was obvious to me that this was an opportunity, that what I had been saying was going to be heard. A friend came up to me and said, "Paul, you went from heretic to prophet in 24 hours." The ADA speech had given me credibility. It was important that I had said it before the election. I started to write a book in December. I began to be interviewed constantly. Reporters said to people, "If you are writing about the Democrats and where they are going, the first person to talk to is Tsongas." There was the sense that people should touch base with me.

He was not the only person talking revisionism or new liberalism—Gary Hart and Bill Bradley were two compatriots—but he was out front. "Mine will be the first book out," he said. "I'll be the first to give [the Democrats] something to read."

It was, he recognized, the Senate that had given him the forum in which he could be heard. "If I had been exactly this same person, written exactly the same book, said exactly the same things, as a House member, no one would have been interested. As a senator, the publishers are competing with each other for my book." He added, "This is the best job there is."

Paul Tsongas left the Senate in 1984 at the end of his first term, after he was diagnosed as suffering from cancer. When we talked after that decision, he described the ADA speech as "the most important thing I've ever done and the thing I'm proudest of." And, without prompting, he spoke of catching the wave. "The Democrats," he said, "are getting bombarded by the baby boomers this year, because they haven't caught the wave. If the wave is coming and you see it, you can get out ahead of it and have a lot of impact. If you see it, you won't be the only one who sees it. Others will see it too, which means there is something there. And you get the chance to lead." "Now," he said, "my issues are high tech, education, Central America, and arms control." He smiled. "So much for 'my four issues.'" He was excited about his upcoming trip to El Salvador, having been accepted by both sides as an honest broker in their civil conflict. Other seasons, other waves, but he was still surfing.

When I left him that day in August 1984, his final comment was about ambition and opportunity. "Another thing about the Senate," he said, "you are always thinking up. In the House, it's the Senate. When you get to the Senate, half the people around you are running for president. You see them and you think you are just as good as they are. It's almost like a dare. So you start to think about running yourself or having someone pick you for vice president." However he meant it, I took it as a valedictory comment on what might have been. For several years, I had believed that of all "my" senators, he was the one most likely to become president.

WILLIAM COHEN, MAINE, 1978–1984

Bill Cohen saw his career as the product of a series of unplanned and incremental steps. "I never planned to make politics my career," he said. "Things just happened that way." He often said of himself, "I never know what I'm going to do next." Unlike Tsongas, his career had not been driven by policy concerns. His career decisions are made as he responds to a personal challenge he finds himself confronted with. Step-by-step, these challenges and responses have driven and shaped his political career.

Listen to his travel talk concerning his career calculations.

First, his move to law school: "I majored in the classics, studied Latin, and wanted to be a Latin professor. I had no interest in politics, took no political science courses. Then in my senior year, I got bored with it and decided to go to law school. But I had no burning desire to be a lawyer."

Second, his move to Congress: "When I ran for Congress, I had no idea what a congressman did. I didn't know what the pay was or what the job entailed. I ran because I was bored to death with my law practice

Third, his move to the Senate: "I had three alternatives this year [1978]. I could have run for governor, which I didn't want, I could have run for the Senate, or I could have retired from politics. It was a very iffy proposition between the last two. Staying in the House was not an alternative. I couldn't stand another term in the House. . . . I considered very seriously getting out and trying something else. But I thought that if ever I was going to make a try for the Senate, this was the time."

In each of these cases, he had become bored and was ready for a new challenge; he then identified and accepted a challenge; and his decision had altered his career. On the trail in 1978, he described his motivation this way: "What is that line Fleetwood Mac sings: It's not the outcome, it's the action. It's the chase I care about. And I care less about the prize. I don't want to be anything but thoroughly engaged in whatever I do." He added, "I can do a lot of things other than politics in that big ocean out there."

Indeed he can, and he does—filling up the time when he is not fully engaged politically by writing poetry, nonfiction and novels. During his first year or so, he kept (then published) a detailed diary of Senate life. "I can't justify what I'm doing with my life when all we do around here is wait. So I keep writing." His passion is to stay completely occupied. So long as his political career is fulfilling this purpose, fine. But there is always the subtext that he could find satisfaction elsewhere. "I almost decided not to run again," he exclaimed when I rejoined his reelection campaign in 1984. "I had the novel I wanted to finish and I said, What am I doing wasting time in the Senate? On the other hand, I said, I'm a senator. Why am I wasting my time worrying about this novel?"

Others sense this career ambivalence. In that same year, a top aide to Senate Republican leader Howard Baker said to me, "Bill Cohen is a great person, the kind who should run for president of the United States. He's thoughtful. He's got a mind of his own. He gets the job done. He can become one of the great senators. My only worry is that he'll look at all the nonsense that goes on around here and say the hell with it, I'm going home to write poetry." Cohen often asks out loud, "Why am I doing this?" Or in one of his favorite ruminations, "I keep thinking of that Peggy Lee song, 'Is That All There Is.'"

His answer seems to be to throw himself into situations that promise "more," probably for the sheer challenge. "I've just published a book of poems," he told me as we campaigned in 1978. "It may have been a foolish thing and fatal to my career." "Why did you do it?" I asked. "Because I felt like it." Two years later, we had the same conversation about the publication of his Senate diary. "If there's hostility to it around here, I'm finished." "Why did you risk it?" "Because I wanted to."[8]

Cohen's travel talk turns up less intellectual examples of challenges accepted amid potential disasters. Many of them allow this serious person to have a hearty laugh at his own expense. There is a tryout with the Boston Celtics in a team uniform several sizes too large, when his slipping shorts produce more pratfalls than points. There is his participation in a local automobile race—helmeted, strapped in, and "terrified" in a 200-mile-per-hour race car. There is his after-speech effort at dancing during which the constituent couples he jostles outnumber the constituent couples he pleases. Characteristically, he throws himself into these unlikely adventures for the sheer challenge of it.

Cohen's introspection should not be taken to mean that the outcome of a challenge does not matter to him. Quite the opposite. Engagement energizes all his faculties; and he becomes fiercely competitive. He is a former star athlete who is not accustomed to losing. He hates to lose. He speaks admiringly of his father, a baker, who at the age of eighty-six still works eighteen-hour days, "trying to bake the perfect roll." And he tells the story of his father watching him play basketball. One day, "I scored 43 points. I came off the court grinning from ear to ear. I asked him, How did I do? He said, 'If you hadn't missed those two foul shots, you'd have scored 45.' His desire for perfection has been a great example to me." While Cohen may now describe his first campaign for the House diffidently, as the result of happenstance and boredom, once he committed to that contest, he walked six hundred miles across his huge district to win it. "I wore out several pairs of shoes," he recalled. "I had to go to the hospital three times with blisters, they were so bad."

Six days after candidate Cohen had become Senator Cohen, I talked with his top adviser about what lay ahead. It was reassuring to hear him talking, in Washington, about the same person I had met in Maine. "Bill has a very low threshold of boredom," he said.

> He was bored in the House and he used to say, "I'm going to quit this job." I told him it would be better in the Senate, and it will be. . . . It's a big challenge. Whenever he's been faced with a challenge, he's always concentrated on the job and done it well. He knows he's on trial and he knows he doesn't want to fall on his face. Frankly, I hope things get started pretty soon, because he's already sitting around being bored.

In this general pattern—boredom, challenge, engagement, competitiveness—there are clues to his political behavior and his political career.

When I met him in 1978, the biggest and most important challenge of Cohen's political career most probably lay behind him. Four years earlier, he had been a member of the House Judiciary Committee during the impeachment proceedings against President Richard Nixon. For six months, it had engaged him fully. The publicity attendant on the hearings had turned a talented but obscure young Maine congressman into a national celebrity—first, because he was both telegenic and articulate as he discussed the dilemmas involved, and second, because he had ultimately voted to impeach a president of his own party. He emerged from that experience with a reputation as a thoughtful, moderate, and independent politician with a sky's-the-limit career ahead of him. He emerged, too, with an enthusiastic bipartisan supporting coalition at home on which to float such a career.

The impact of Watergate was constantly with us on the campaign trail in 1978. It permeated Cohen's travel talk. He spoke of the agonizing and exhausting process, of the national publicity he had received, and of the enmity he had provoked among many Republicans. At the time, he said, "I felt certain I would lose [the next election]. I was resigned to being defeated." He spoke, too, of how, in the end, he had benefited from "a combination of the wide exposure and the good feeling about the process and the outcome." It was in the aftermath of Watergate, he said, that he first thought seriously about the Senate: "somewhere toward the middle of 1975, when I was at the height of my popularity."

But he had waited until 1978. And now that he was running, Watergate still loomed large in his strategy. "I need to find a way to touch on that moment in 1974. In Democratic areas, where I expect to do well, that's the one reason they will vote for me, because of what I did on impeachment—that I voted my conscience and not the party." Six years later, the incidence of Watergate travel talk had declined precipitously. Even so, every master of ceremonies still included a favorable mention of it; and every handshaking tour turned up at least one person who said, "I'm a hard-line Democrat, but I've always voted for you. Do you know why? Watergate!" Cohen's Democratic support remained, in 1984, the very baseline of his reelection campaign strategy.

Like John Glenn's prepolitical past, Bill Cohen's cast a long shadow over his subsequent career. In Cohen's case, however, the shadow fell not across his elective office career but across his career inside the Senate. Cohen came to the Senate with the kind of media-generated public reputation that could impede the development of his institutional career. "I came over here carrying a lot of baggage," he said early on, "and not all of it favorable. I had gotten a lot of publicity. People thought I was cocky, arrogant, a guy who throws rocks in the water, anti-Nixon, anti-Republican." He was anxious to subdue his pre-Senate reputation and start anew. His Watergate experience had left him supersensitive to the media's capacity for making and breaking reputations.

Cohen's sensitivity to the media was our constant companion on the campaign trail. "They enjoy watching you rise to prominence," he said. "Then when they have you puffed up, they enjoy taking a pin, pricking you, and watching you collapse." He believed the press was waiting to knock him off his Watergate perch. "If I took the lead [on a policy matter]," he told one news reporter, "you guys would pull me down as fast as you could. You'd say, 'That guy Cohen is still suffering from withdrawal after Watergate.'"

He carried that wariness with him into the Senate. And the media followed. On the day before he was sworn in, the *Washington Star* gave him a three-page, three-photo spread billing him as "almost too good to be true. The perfect image of the modern politician, easily packaged and merchandised."[9] It was no help. There was some early talk, too, about his presidential or vice presidential possibilities. That did not help either. The challenge he faced in the Senate was to produce an inside reputation that was not Watergate-and-media controlled, but Cohen-and-Senate controlled.

After three months on the job, Cohen described his institutional ambition: "I've been working very hard to get a reputation as a substantive senator. I have been studying hard, doing homework, showing up on time. During the campaign, I had to confront the 'show horse/work horse' argument. I've been trying to be a work horse. People make judgments about you very quickly. And it was especially important in my case to start quickly." A couple of months later, he said, "I have stayed away from the press—deliberately. I've done very few interviews— almost all of them off the record. I'm asked to do them all the time, but I've been refusing. I'm keeping a low profile, avoiding publicity. I've turned down *Issues and Answers* and a lot of the magazines." "Some people," he added, "are asking, 'Where are you?' I tell them I'm doing my work in the Armed Services Committee." That was the place, he believed, where he could become the kind of senator he wanted to be.

The other legislative career path—in the Republican party leadership—was not realistically open to him, as it surely was, for example, to Dan Quayle. Cohen's Watergate behavior stamped him as both independent and moderate in a party increasingly dominated by ideological conservatives. During one period of party leadership changes, I asked him if he had thought about it. "People ask me why aren't you running for something?" He answered, "I say, because I don't want to lose what I've got. I can vote the way I please."[10] There remained a lot of the independent Judiciary Committee member in the senator.

Even if his colleagues had wanted a moderate leader, Bill Cohen would not have been chosen. In terms of both temperament and intellect, he was a loner.[11] I had observed this basic characteristic of style from my earliest moments on the campaign trail in 1978. For the first three days, we campaigned by walking eight miles along the Maine coast. On the first day, after two miles spent walking with a small group of local candidates and supporters, Cohen started running, and disappeared from view, went the next six miles alone, leaving the rest of us to walk by ourselves for the rest of the afternoon. That evening he apologized to me. So why had he done that? Out of boredom? Surely, that was a part of it. But there was something else, his preference for his own company rather than that of a group.

As a senator, he remained something of a solitary jogger. "I'm afraid I'm getting trapped by the image I have of always reading," he said in 1981. "I'm not sure I like it. But I'm not sure I can do anything about it.... I should mingle more and backslap more.... [But] I have to think and read or else I don't feel I've done anything with my day." His decision to write *Roll Call* did nothing to move him along the path toward senatorial camaraderie. It was certainly natural for colleagues to keep a distance from someone who might write about them. As a veteran staffer of his put it, "He's never going to be elected president of the class."

So the initial challenge of Bill Cohen's legislative career—to achieve a substantive reputation based on subject matter expertise—centered on the Armed Services Committee. But this inside institutional challenge came about in the same unplanned and reactive way that his outside career-shaping challenges had. He pursued his institutional goal in a less purposeful way than Tsongas. "I had no intention of getting on the [Armed Services] committee," he said. "I didn't do anything. I was very cavalier about it.... I honestly didn't know what I wanted to do." He continued, "I took Governmental Affairs first. Then a vacancy opened up on Armed Services on the second round, so I said why not. It was just happenstance. It's consistent with everything else that's happened to me in my life.... The opportunities just opened up." The challenge had been defined and presented to him, and he responded with another career-shaping decision.

His first description of his work, in 1979, reflects the early pursuit of committee-based expertise.

> Ninety percent of my time has been taken up so far with Armed Services. I'm learning all the acronyms—studying a great deal. I enjoy it.... I knew almost nothing; and I have tried to start right in learning. Staff people on the committee know who is interested and who is not. If you take an interest, they will pile material on you. They have been briefing me and giving me tons of things to read. You make a reputation with the staff, and that's very important. They want to work with someone who has a substantive interest. If you have an interest, they will feed

you information. The more information you have, the more your reputation grows.

Two years later (in 1981), as a new subcommittee chairman, he was following the same prescription.

Ninety-five percent of my time is spent with my subcommittee on sea power. We've been holding hearings for three weeks. I can't keep up with all the material I'm supposed to read. The military people are crawling all over me with information. And I'm enjoying every minute of it. I'm supposed to be an expert on all these things, not because I really am, but because I'm chairman of a subcommittee.

A year later (in 1982), just four years into his Senate career, he was slightly more willing to admit his expertise.

I know more about defense than most senators; and to that extent, I'm an expert. But there is so much to know. I understand something about sea power; I know something about manpower problems; and I know a smattering about strategic systems from having gone through SALT [Strategic Arms Limitation Treaty]. I do think people feel that I know something about defense and that they think of me as an expert. That has two effects. First, it makes you want to be more of an expert, to learn more. So it has a reinforcing effect. Second, it gives you more weight in defense matters than most other senators. . . . By being on this committee, you are surrounded by experts. You have more expertise than you can use. Expertise is all relative.

Maine observers had begun to think of Cohen as "one of the youngest defense specialists [whose] peers look to him for advice."[12]

Later that same year, I asked him the general question, "Do you think you are getting the substantive reputation you want?" He answered in terms of his work on the Armed Services Committee.

When the defense bill was being debated on the floor, an awful lot of people came up to me and said, "Bill, we know you are moderate and thoughtful on defense matters. What do you think?" Not the older ones, but all the guys in my class and the younger ones came up. Even the hard-liners asked, "What do you think? We know you aren't a 'knee-jerk' in this field." That was the test for me. It showed that people do think I'm thoughtful on defense matters. It was the same reputation I had in the House— that I'm moderate and thoughtful and have good judgment. So I'd say, yes, I do have that substantive reputation.

He continued, "I'm enjoying the job. I'm not climbing anymore. That gives me a good feeling." "So, will you run for reelection?" I asked. "I'm inclined to run. But if I could find something else that allowed me as much of a challenge, as much stimulation, I might take it. I just can't think of a job as good as this one." It was still pure Cohen!

He achieved his most notable substantive success in 1984, when he and Democratic expert Sam Nunn sold their build-down proposal to the Reagan administration as a basis for arms negotiations with the Soviets.

Joe Biden and I went to Russia to explain the idea to them. It took me five years before I got to that point. It was a five-year process of building up my self-confidence. When I began I didn't know squat about defense systems. I spent the first year just learning the names. Then I went to the Indian Ocean to watch the carriers; I flew in fighter planes; I went to the Middle East and visited Mubarak; I went to Central America; I lectured in Europe; I talked with NATO officials. I was instrumental in working on the dense pack idea with the Scowcroft Commission. [One group of senators] asked me to carry their position on dense pack to the administration. I did. It failed. I was active in the military caucus and at the Center for Strategic Affairs at Georgetown. But it all culminated in the build-down proposal. There was a vacuum in the administration and we moved in. So my most important accomplishment came in my sixth year. It gave me a lot of satisfaction to have had a little bit of influence.

By his own calculations and those of Washington's insiders, he had met his original senatorial challenge.[13]

On the campaign trail, in that sixth year, his public presentations on defense policy and negotiating strategy were as impressive as any I had ever heard—in or out of a university. He

had gone a long way toward fulfilling his institutional ambition
to be a substantive senator.

DAVID PRYOR, ARKANSAS, 1978–1984

Senator David Pryor of Arkansas got into politics early in life.
And he has stayed in politics ever since, for one reason: he loves
it. "I don't know why I wanted to be a senator—to serve people,
to pass legislation, or to fulfill an ambition," he said in 1979. "But
my attitude toward politics was portrayed in the movie *Patton*.
There is this battlefield scene. Patton rides in and stands there
in his Jeep taking it all in. And then he says, 'I love it, I love it.'
That's just the way I feel about politics." He cannot remember
a time when he lacked elective office ambition. He came by it
honestly. "My mother was the first woman in Arkansas to run
for county clerk," he relates. "My father and grandfather served
as sheriff. I had politics in my blood, and I loved politics. I would
hand out cards at the rallies and the feeds."

Surely, Pryor never experienced a prepolitical career, relevant
or irrelevant. He was born political. "I've been running for
something all my life," he says.

> I remember when four of us ran for president of the third
> grade of Cleveland Elementary School in Camden. Miss Mary
> Bragg Wheeler told the four candidates to leave the class. We
> all went into the hall. I prayed. I prayed that if I just got elected
> president of the third grade, I would never aspire to another
> office in my life. Miss Wheeler came out into the hall. She said,
> "David, congratulations. You've been elected president of the
> third grade." Before I got to my seat, I was trying to figure out
> how I could get to be president of the fourth grade.

He dubbed his campaign for reelection to the Senate in 1984,
his "toughest race since the third grade." Almost since the third
grade, he has been running for the U.S. Senate. When he was
sixteen, Pryor spent a summer as a House page and visited the
Senate.[14] And from that day on, the office he wanted was that
of U.S. Senator.

His progressive ambition is written all over his political career—elected to the Arkansas House at age 26, to the U.S. House at age 32, to the governorship of Arkansas at age 40, and to the Senate at age 44. It was a sequence much like that of Tsongas and Cohen. Except that unlike them, Pryor had one setback: as a two-term House member, he challenged incumbent U.S. Senator John McClellan in the 1972 Democratic primary and lost. His loss forced him to take a detour. Two years after his defeat, he won the first of two terms as governor. And when McClellan died, Pryor seized the opportunity and captured the open Senate seat in 1978. When I met him that fall, he had already won a tough primary and runoff. And he was coasting to the finish line.

Mostly, he was performing his ceremonial duties as governor and, as he said, "doing nothing to call attention to the campaign." What I have called his love of politics was conveyed during that visit by his obvious gregariousness and by his stream of good-humored, self-effacing observations and stories about the small-scale, human aspects of his business. His travel talk was not nearly as introspective as Cohen's, or as policy-centered as Tsongas's. And he was far more gregarious than they. His was a people-oriented view, one that he summed up in such comments as: "Politics is people," "If you like people, you'll like politics," "If you can't laugh at yourself and poke fun at yourself, you won't like politics."

When we next met, one week after his swearing-in, his absorption in politics was beginning to manifest itself in an absorption with the Senate. In his office, he greeted me, arms extended. "Well, here I am. Is this what I've wanted for so long? I don't know." But the rest of our conversation left little doubt. "We won one victory already," he continued. "We got an office here in the Russell Building [the oldest of the three]. It's much more, what would you say—senatorial. Who do you suppose has sat in this office? Henry Cabot Lodge, Arthur Vandenberg, Jack Kennedy. I'm going to find out. There's a history to this place and I want to know it."

He said he had found the orientation sessions helpful in meeting other new senators. And he wanted to keep up those personal contacts. "I'm trying to put together a meeting of all the new Democrats to extend the orientation program. On issues, we don't agree, but on the nuts and bolts of the Senate, we could share information." It was the kind of collegial initiative that would never have occurred to Paul Tsongas or Bill Cohen—or interested them. That same day, I asked Paul Tsongas, "How many new people have you met?" "None," he answered. "I didn't go to the introductory sessions." And when, later in our conversation, veteran Virginia Senator Harry Byrd, Jr., dropped by Tsongas's office to "welcome" him to the Senate, Tsongas turned to me afterward and said, "What the hell was that all about?" It was a question David Pryor would never have to ask.

Tsongas's and Cohen's institutional goals were less all-consuming than Pryor's. Tsongas wanted to use the institution as a policy amplifier. Cohen wanted to use it to test a variety of talents. The sum of David Pryor's career ambition was to become an integral part of the institution—nothing more, but nothing less.

Five months after my first Senate visit, he was clearly just where he had always wanted to be. "When I was here as a page," he said, "there was, to me, a distinct smell to the Capitol. It was part smoke, part granite, part leather, and something else, I don't know what. The other day I got a whiff of that smell I remembered as a boy." He has a strong sense of place; and the Senate was, for him, a distinct place. "The other day, I took a constituent on a twenty-minute tour of the Capitol," he said several months later.

> We went to the Senate gallery and then to the House gallery. It was the first time I had been back to see the House in action since I left it. Looking down on it, it gives you the impression of a metropolitan area. The buses are going every which way; the horns are honking. It's disorderly and confusing. When you look down on the Senate, you see a small New England town, with shade trees, no noise on the streets, and everything in its place.

He saw the Senate as the kind of community an individual could fit into and participate in.

When he wasn't experiencing the Senate, he was learning about it. "I spend a great deal of time on the floor—more than most freshman senators. I preside as often as anyone. . . . I want to learn the rules, and I know that the longer you're here, the less time you have to learn them. Every day, I try to learn something about the Senate," he said. And he passed along things he had learned in the chamber.

For example, "Each person is a little island and every other member of the Senate respects the integrity of that little island. That's the strength of the institution, the beauty of it. That's what makes it a club. Each member will protect the right of every other member to be heard." Or, "In the Senate, honesty counts and intelligence counts, but the thing that counts the most is whether you are prepared when you get up to speak." He admitted, too, that he was not yet as much at home on the Senate floor as he hoped to be. "The House is a large hall, and you must shout to be heard. The Senate is a small room. The best speakers are those who speak as if they were in a living room, in a conversational tone. They are comfortable in their surroundings. I do not feel comfortable in that room yet and do not have a conversational tone." For a senator who had put himself under pressure to fit in, his own sense of "confidence" and "comfort" would be important measures of his success.

"Two weeks ago," he added, "I dusted off *Profiles in Congress*. I hadn't read it in four years. It's a pretty good history of the institution. It's a fascinating institution." Judging by his fund of anecdotes, his fascination covered everything from the seating arrangements in the public and private Senate dining rooms to instances in which an individual's rights were protected at considerable cost to institutional efficiency to the substantive prowess of Sam Nunn and the procedural prowess of Majority Leader Robert Byrd. Speaking of Byrd, he chuckled, "A month or so ago, he sent the Democrats a note thanking them for the good job they had done. We all took out our letters and compared them. Did he say 'good,' 'nice,' 'very good'? We laughed over our report cards." Pryor's own six-month summary was satisfaction. "I like the Senate as an institution. I like the people. I like the staff who run it. I like it a lot."

For all his love of the institution and his desire to fit into its internal life, his pre-Senate career indicated that he was less likely to succeed by way of specialized substantive expertise than either Tsongas or Cohen. Pryor was, at heart, a reformer and an investigator, someone who was energized by a cause and tended to lose interest when the investigative chase was over.

Thinking ahead about his choice of committees, Pryor commented, "Frankly, I'm not worried about my committee assignments. I once said that if I got elected, I wouldn't ask for any committees. I'd rather be a free spirit, a rover, a hummingbird sipping nectar from many different flowers. I'm undisciplined. I don't like to sit there for hours on one subject."

Of course, he made choices—purposeful choices that proved important to his career.[15] "During the campaign, I said I wanted to get on [the] Agriculture [Committee]. I regard that as a commitment ... [but] the Finance Committee is the one I really want." Agriculture was no problem. When he found out that Finance—the most powerful and prized of all Senate committees—was impossible, he opted for the Governmental Affairs Committee because, he said, "they handle a broad range of issues across the government." "It suited me," he said later. "I'm a generalist."

Certainly, the Governmental Affairs Committee fit his investigative enthusiasms. And his work as chairman of its Post Office and Civil Service subcommittees produced his earliest senatorial reputation for his investigation of abuses in the hiring of government consultants.[16] Two years into his term, Pryor looked back on that investigation quite self-consciously as a way to get adjusted.

It helped a lot to give me credibility with my colleagues and with the people who run the Senate—with the Capitol Hill community. It was a case of stalking, searching out, and capturing an issue. You become identified with something; and that is especially helpful for a senator in his first couple of years. My only problem was not to make too much of it. I did not want to become a one-issue senator.

He has, however, returned to the issue, off and on and in one form or another, ever since.

Pryor's gadfly predisposition should not be taken to mean that when he wanted a position of influence inside the institution, he could not get it. And that is what he wanted. Two-thirds of the way through his first term, he renewed his lobbying for the powerful Finance Committee; and he defeated Michigan's Don Riegle in the Steering Committee by more than two-to-one for the single vacancy there.

In November 1980, the Democrats lost control of the U.S. Senate for the first time in thirty-six years. The shock threw each Democratic senator, accustomed to being in the majority, into a private, soul-searching tizzy. What shall I do now? What kind of a senator do I want to be now? The three Democrats I had been following made very different midcareer choices. John Glenn decided to run for president. Paul Tsongas decided to write a book about the plight of the Democratic party. David Pryor decided, in his words, "to be a constituency senator." Glenn and Tsongas, in pursuit of progressive ambition, reached for wider constituencies. Only Pryor decided to improve his communication with the constituency he already had. His choice was every bit as political as theirs, but its focus was very different. The three choices were diagnostic for their own different political ambitions.

"We're trying to adjust to being minority senators," Pryor said in February 1981.

I don't think there is any major across-the-board legislation a minority senator can introduce or be associated with.... So we are gearing up, for the next six months anyway, to emphasize constituency service—more newsletters, more radio, more personal telephone calls instead of letters, more visits in the state. We are going to target certain counties in the state where there are scars left from … [previous] campaigns. I'm going to be a constituency senator. We are going to have staff meetings each week to give the staff a stronger sense of constituency service, constituency relations. I'm excited about it. I was down for a while after the election, but now I'm really excited about all the things we can do to communicate with constituents.

His decision reflected his essential contentedness as a member of the Senate. He was where he had always wanted to be. And he wanted most of all to be able to pursue his career just where he was.

During Pryor's years in the minority, he worked out a way to reconcile his strong desire to be part of the institution with his reformer instincts. That is, he would work to reform the institution; but he would do it by emphasizing the *collective* benefits of his reforms—efficiency, morale, and public reputation. In that way, he could become the kind of senator he wanted to be—an institutional reformer and, at the same time, a senator's senator.

In the summer of 1982, our conversation centered on his reformist effort.

I'm just about as frustrated now as I was when I left the House to make that crazy race for the Senate.… For the last month, we have done nothing in the Senate but hang wallpaper. The Senate is not working well. I'm in the process of getting together a group of eight senators, all of whom came to the Senate in 1979, to come out to my house to talk about how we could reform the Senate. We'll cook some steaks and sit around and talk about what can be done about things like the budget process, the filibuster rule, the germaneness rule.

A month later, he reported,

A few of us got together at my house the other night. We had a good discussion about the germaneness rule and the filibuster. One senator tied up the whole Senate last Friday night by threatening a filibuster. Everybody had to change plans, cancel plane reservations. I'm going to talk to [the former parliamentarian] next week. I'm going to pick his brain. I had an intern study the amount of time spent in quorum calls. She found that we spent exactly one-third of the session in quorum calls. There is something wrong with the system when one person can hold up everything and we spend one-third of our time in quorum calls.

In 1985, after watching Pryor for six years, his institutional efforts had led to his selection by the Democratic party leadership to chair the ad hoc Quality of Life Committee to think about reforms that would enhance the workaday life of the Senate.[17] It placed him at the center of the Senate's institutional life and invited him to become an institution builder.

For someone who wants to become an institution protector and builder, the early signs of success are associated with a growing sense of being confident and comfortable as a member of the institution. Back in Arkansas, on the reelection trail in 1984, he summed up, with evident satisfaction, his first six years inside the institution. "I'm very comfortable in the Senate," he said.

> I'm comfortable with the procedures and the people. I've felt that way for three or four years. When I first went there, and I got up to make a speech, I was scared stiff. It was peer pressure, pure peer pressure. I was afraid I would make a fool of myself in front of my peers. I still don't do a lot of speaking in the Senate. But when I do, I am very comfortable. I feel like I have made it in the Senate. I know I have a long way to go before I am completely accepted. But I am comfortable with my peers. I know … that I am respected and that when I say something, I get attention. … You can't say how you've made it in the Senate. It comes little by little. People talk to you about other colleagues. People come over and visit with you and joke with you. It's a sense you have, a feel.

It was, again, a highly people-oriented view of the political institution of which he had wanted to become an integral part. With his elective office ambition having been met, he seemed well on his way toward the fulfillment of his institutional ambition.

PATTERNS

It has been ten years since I carried on any continuous monitoring of these three political careers. Again, as with Glenn and Quayle, early patterns have persisted and have diagnostic value for their careers.

After I left Paul Tsongas, he retired to battle his illness. And a different Greek from Massachusetts climbed to the topmost rung of the Democratic party ladder. But when Tsongas recovered, he took up where he left off in the very last moments of our very last conversation—that is, by "thinking up." As issue-driven as ever, he decided to reach for America's biggest and best forum in which to amplify his policy views and seek policy leadership.

In familiar fashion, he worked to get himself out front, on the crest of the policy wave—and once again with a fat position paper, "An Economic Call to Arms." And for a while in the 1992 presidential campaign he was, indeed, out front. He was the first candidate in the race and the first to call for citizen sacrifices to ensure economic growth. The motivational and career pattern I identified in the Senate candidate of 1978 and in the senator of 1979–84 was almost perfectly preserved in the presidential candidate of 1991 and 1992. No surprises there.

After I left Bill Cohen in 1984, his importance as a player in national security matters steadily grew. He became vice chairman of the Senate Intelligence Committee; and he was selected as a member of the Joint Committee to Investigate the Iran-Contra affair. Not surprisingly, he wrote a book about it—with his Maine colleague, George Mitchell. In Washington, he had a reputation as "a clear-minded authority on defense and intelligence" and was "widely respected as an artful legislator conversant [in] ... the complexities of defense and foreign policy."[18] As a moderate, he was called "a barometer of middle-of-the-road congressional opinion" on these matters. "As Cohen goes, so goes Congress," wrote one D.C. observer.[19]

In Maine, his reputation was similar—as "one of Congress' leading experts on defense issues, who holds a position of real power as a swing vote."[20] In both places, his early reputation for "fair-minded independence remained central to his persona."[21] Looking forward to 1990, his campaign manager was making familiar calculations. "With people over forty who remember Watergate, Bill is rock solid—and he gets 56 percent of the Democrats, too. Our job is to reach the younger people, some of whom were just being born at the time of Watergate."

When I rejoined Cohen on the campaign trail in 1990, he declared, "I look forward to running this time. I was actually eager to run." No sooner had I joined him than he was called to the White House to meet with the president on the Persian Gulf crisis. And for the rest of my visit he was hounded by the national news media for his comments on that crisis.[22] He seemed to be totally engaged. Indeed, working from his Watergate and Iran-Contra experience, he had become a forceful defender of legislative prerogatives in relations with the executive branch.[23] He was easily reelected.

A month later, however, I received a call from one of his long-time associates. Could I come down to Washington and have dinner to talk about the senator's career. "Of course," I said. "What's up?" "He's getting bored again," he said. No surprises there.

Shortly after I left David Pryor in 1984, he was reelected by a sufficient margin (57 percent) to underpin his growing self-confidence as a senator. In 1986, he ran for and defeated Pat Leahy to win the third-ranking position in his party—as the secretary of the Democratic Conference. "Running for a job in the U.S. Senate," he said afterward, "whether you win, lose, or draw, is one of the great educations of mankind. I have not met a more intensified personal, one-on-one campaign for anything since I ran for the president of my third grade class."[24]

In 1990, he wanted to move up the ladder to the party's number two position, as whip; but the senator just ahead on the ladder laid claim to the job first, and, after scouting out his chances, Pryor desisted.[25] He was, of course, the one person among the senators I have discussed whose career aspirations had from the beginning led in the direction of inside institutional power.

Eighteen years after I had watched him enter the Senate, he was still telling listeners, "I love the Senate. I have a job I love coming to every day."[26] "I've always been infatuated with the Senate. I've always been fascinated with its makeup and how it operates. It suits my personality, I think."[27] As a top party leader from 1992 to 1994 and as the "best friend" of the president (throughout), Pryor has gone regularly to the White House where he has sat at the table a few places away from his Arkansas friend, Bill Clinton.[28] And he has served as a point man for the president inside the Senate. When party leader George Mitchell retired in 1994, Pryor decided not to run for that job; and he relinquished his party position. This *was* a mild surprise.[29] Still, he has been in a position of greater influence than any of "my" other senators—that is to say, exactly where he always wanted to be. No big surprise there.

CONCLUSION

The view from the campaign trail teaches us something about our politicians' similarities and something more about their differences. It suggests that we can usefully differentiate among our politicians in terms of their careers. And it further suggests some of the attributes of careers that might help us make that differentiation.

The crucial commonality among members of Congress is their political ambition. It is ambition—elective office ambition and institutional ambition—that has driven all the senatorial careers I have followed. Ambition creates the résumé by which senatorial candidates are known on and off the campaign trail. Ambition lies behind the willingness of most candidates to present themselves to their fellow citizens for judgment, for the furtherance of competition, and for accountability.

For critics of Congress, the ambition–career connection is not so neutral. For them, "ambitious politician" is an all-purpose epithet, and long-running careers are a danger to the republic. The case of John Glenn case may suggest to them, however, that even the most exemplary of our public service oriented citizen-politicians will be driven by career-level ambition. And the other cases discussed above do not confirm the belief that ambition is an enemy of talent or that careers are an ally of corruption. There would seem to be no prima facie reason to heap public disparagement on all senators who chose the job, like the job, have learned to do it well, and want to keep it. It is difficult to see how a democratic system of government could survive unless it consistently attracts a large number of ambitious and talented people, willing to make serious career-level commitments to ensuring that representative government works.

Ambition, however, is only the beginning of a study of politics. Beyond the commonality of political ambition lie large differences in the stimuli and in the subsequent patterning of political careers. My approach has been to study a few careers by observing them over time. The accompanying notion about careers is that they are not fixed but provisional and subject to change over time. One career event, like the margin of an election victory, or the choice of a committee assignment, or a switch in chamber majorities, can change subsequent career possibilities in ways that are unpredictable beforehand. Career limitations develop over time, and yet some open-endedness remains in almost every career. Because that is so, it is best to examine each politician's career at several points in time. The argument here is that drop-in/drop-out observation—however episodic and brief—can provide some diagnostic tracings of political careers and some suggestions about their distinguishing characteristics.

Among the distinguishing characteristics, I have emphasized the importance of the prepolitical career, wherever applicable. And I have also emphasized, for five senators, the varying motivations or the goals—electoral and institutional—that have both stimulated and sustained their political ambition. There were differences in motivation among them in the degree to which they emphasized their desire for public service, general accomplishment, policy leadership, personal challenges, and political involvement. And there were satisfactions with the job that placed distinctive emphasis on protecting a reputation for integrity, moving up the ladder, getting out front on policy, gaining a reputation, and becoming a senator's senator. There is no "best" motivation or satisfaction, nor is there a "best person" for the job. All five were effective senators.

Neither the critics nor the students of Congress are at a loss in dealing with the commonalities discussed here. The scholars are likely to be more tolerant of ambition than the critics. But both groups find it convenient and useful to throw a descriptive or prescriptive blanket over the members of Congress and to proceed with their analysis on the basis of broad categories. A final message from the campaign trail is simply that neither critics nor students should consider their tasks completed unless they take time out occasionally to take a look at the individual differences in ambitions and careers to be found within their operative assumptions and categories.

CHAPTER 3

PRIMARY CHALLENGER CAMPAIGNS

CAMPAIGNS

POLITICIANS' CAREERS ARE INSEPARABLE from their campaigns. In a representative democracy, the essential requirement of every political career is the ability to get elected and stay elected. And that ability is tested in an election campaign, in which careers are launched, extended, or terminated. Successful campaigns become career milestones in every politician's résumé. In combination, careers and campaigns are foundation elements in the infrastructure of representative democracy. The career question, Why do I want to be a representative? is tightly bound to the campaign question, How do I get to be a representative? If you want to be a representative, you must campaign for it. And for as long as you want to remain a representative, you must keep on campaigning.

Campaigns help to establish, maintain, and test the connections between politicians and citizens—connections that constitute the very core of a representational relationship. It is through a campaign that a candidate is introduced to the electorate. It is through a campaign that a candidate locates and builds a constituency. It is through the interpretation of a campaign that the winning candidate derives some of the impulses, interests, and instructions that shape his or her subsequent behavior as a legislator. It is through a campaign that a legislator explains his or her legislative activity to the citizenry. And it is through a campaign that a legislator's contract is renewed or rejected.

In all these ways, campaigns connect politicians and citizens and make possible the accountability of politicians to citizens that representative government requires. In short, no campaigns, no connections; no connections, no accountability; no accountability, no representative government.

Not surprisingly, when people worry about the health of our representative system, they criticize those features of our campaigns that tend to impede or to distort candidate-citizen connections. For example, negative campaign advertising can distort the explanatory connection that runs from the candidate to the citizen. The distribution of campaign money can distort the influence connection that runs from the citizen to the candidate. And the unfair treatment of campaigning candidates by the media can distort the connection as it runs in both directions.

These kinds of distortions contribute to citizens' sense—now quite widespread—of being *disconnected* from their elected representatives. Several research groups in the 1990s, among them the Kettering Foundation and the Harvard Press-Politics Institute, have highlighted a voter feeling of "disconnectedness" from elected politicians. Reporters covering the political beat have voiced a similar disenchantment.[1] In everyday parlance, life "inside the beltway" is said to be unconnected to life "beyond the beltway."

To the degree that a feeling of disconnectedness does exist among the populace, it increases the negative stereotyping of our politicians, it attenuates the lines of accountability of politicians to citizens, and it threatens the legitimacy of collective legislative action. Citizen criticisms of campaigns provide additional evidence of the relevance of campaigns for effective representative government. As such, they may act as a stimulus to reform or, in this book, as a spur to further examination.

Political scientists have devoted more time and energy to the study of elections than to any other subject. Since most political scientists live in representative democracies, this is not surprising. What is surprising to someone who follows the exploits of campaigning politicians is how little of our huge elections research effort has gone into the study of campaigns. An election is, after all, a two-sided business. Campaigning candidates are trying to influence the behavior of voters. But for most political scientists most of the time, the study of elections has meant only the study of voters and their voting behavior.

Thinking only of the Senate, for example, a comprehensive 1990 article entitled "Voting in Senate Elections: A Review and Future Research Agenda" draws on 93 relevant references—only one of which has the word "campaign" in its title.[2] For that same year, a pathbreaking research proposal, "The Systematic Study of Senate Elections, 1990–1993," lists 133 relevant references, only five of which have the word "campaign" in their titles.[3] Judging strictly from bibliographical evidence, it seems apparent that the study of Senate elections has meant the study of voters, not the study of campaigns.

The scholarly neglect of campaigns—at all levels of politics—can be traced to the eagerness of researchers to explain election outcomes and to their belief that campaigns have only a minimal impact on election outcomes.[4] Recently, there has been some drift away from this belief, as evidence from both aggregate and case study analysis suggests that it is not accurate. Senate campaign studies by Mark Westlye, Charles Franklin, Gary Jacobson and Raymond Wolfinger, Edie Goldenberg and Michael Traugott, and Samuel Patterson and Thomas Kephart support, in an aggressively positive manner, the proposition that campaigns do matter for election outcomes.[5] Each of these studies depends on a fairly detailed analysis of voting behavior to make the argument. And all but the last suggest, in varying degrees, that it is the effect of the mass media, as an information source, that provides the best supporting evidence. As a group, these studies have created a receptive climate for the study of Senate campaigns.

The vantage point and the interests of this study, however, are quite different. Here, the primary focus is not on the behavior of voters or on the outcomes of elections, but on campaigning politicians—what candidates do when they campaign, how their performance affects their campaigns, and what their campaigns tell us about their political careers and their representational relationships. In focus and in angle of vision, this study most closely resembles the work of Barbara Salmore, and Stephen Salmore, except that their observations draw most heavily on the views of campaign consultants rather than the candidates themselves.[6]

We shall, of course, have quite a bit to say about voters and election results. But, in these areas, we will operate with some large simplifying notions. In terms of voters, we will operate with the voter-oriented, but campaign-friendly, theorizing of Samuel Popkin. Voters, he says, pick up useful information during campaigns and combine that information with everyday experience to form reasoned candidate choices. A great deal of this useful information, he says, comes from the performance of the candidate during the campaign. "People learn to read the political and personal strengths and weaknesses of individual candidates."[7] Popkin's theory is about voters, but it buttresses our observations by telling us that campaigns and candidate behavior in campaigns matter. And there is comfort in his conclusion that "the better we understand voters and how they reason, the more sense campaigns make and the more we see how campaigns matter in a democracy."[8]

In terms of election outcomes, there is comfort in the scholarly consensus that contemporary political campaigns are "candidate-centered."[9] With political parties having lost their commanding control over nominations and elections, ambitious individuals now declare their own candidacies, recruit their own staffs, find their own supporters, raise their own money, fix their own strategies, and conduct their own independent campaigns for elective office. Since candidates make their own campaigns, election outcomes are more than ever heavily influenced by what candidates do. Linda Fowler explains this family of propositions in her analytical overview.[10] Alan Abramowitz and Jeffrey Segal test them in their broad-based study of Senate elections. They conclude that "candidate characteristics clearly emerge as the strongest influence in individual contests."[11]

These two arguments—that voters are influenced by campaigns and that campaigns are heavily influenced by candidates—constitute an invitation to take a look at some campaigns and some candidates. That is what I do in the next four chapters.

A campaign is a representational activity. It is also something of a negotiating activity. Candidates and citizens both have something the other wants and something to offer in exchange. Candidates want support, and they offer responsiveness; citizens want responsiveness, and they offer support. Both have advantages. Candidates have the initiative, but citizens have the choice. Neither party can dictate the terms of a settlement. Both must make adjustments.

The adjustments and the settlements can be viewed in the short run and in the long run. In the short run, a campaign is part of the effort to negotiate the terms of a one-shot, election day settlement. In the long run, a campaign is part of an effort over multiple campaigns to negotiate the terms of a continuing career. In either case, the negotiations can be viewed developmentally. They take place over time and are very nearly continuous. Every settlement is contingent and will be subject to renegotiation. To the degree that we can think of campaigns as a negotiation between politicians and citizens, it will be that much easier for us to conceptualize representation itself as a process.

As with careers, life on the campaign trail impresses this developmental outlook on the drop-in/drop-out observer. My first question to each candidate or staffer is always "How's it going?" It is the quintessential catch-up question. Short-term answers involve the progress of the campaign against the opponent—its course to date, its current condition, and its future prospects. Long-term answers often place the campaign in the perspective of the six-year interval since the last election. A generation of events may have taken place during that interval and may have settled such matters as the vulnerability of an incumbent or the availability of a challenger.

Janet Box Steffensmeier and Charles Franklin differentiate, similarly, between "the short campaign" and "the long campaign." And they suggest that some citizen perceptions of a candidate are influenced more by the latter than the former. Their work lends credence to a developmental perspective and underscores the catch-up problem facing an observer.[12]

In all campaigns, the question "How's it going?" yields an early acquaintance with basic elements of a candidate's negotiation—context, resources, and strategy.[13] Context involves such matters as the makeup of the constituency, the nature of the opponent, and the prevailing issue climate, both national and local. Resources refers to such matters as money, organization, experience, reputation, workers, and supporters. Strategy concerns decisions such as where to look for votes, how to allocate funds, and what theme to adopt. Sometimes a campaign will have a model—a notion of how these negotiating elements ought (or ought not) to relate to one another—often based on some knowledge about or participation in a previous campaign.

The presence of a model does not mean, however, that a campaign negotiation will run according to plan. There are always unforeseen circumstances that arise out of the changing context or out of the confrontational dynamics of the campaign itself. Because campaign negotiations develop over time, candidate and campaigners often update their assessments with meteorological metaphors: "The wind is at my back," "The tide has turned in our favor," "The skies are darkening," "The barometer is holding steady," "The campaign is heating up." Perhaps the nightly weather report reminds campaigners of the hazards of prediction and their limited control over the elements with which they must cope. If the observer heeds the meteorology of the campaign, some appreciation of matters such as uncertainty and control and timing may follow.

In generalizing about campaigning politicians, political scientists utilize broad categories such as "candidate characteristics," "quality candidates" and "weak candidates," or "hard-fought campaigns" and "low-key campaigns," or "effective campaigns" and "ineffective campaigns." It is, of course, necessary that we do so in order to make general statements about campaigns. This study, however, reminds us that many details of the activities of real flesh and blood individuals get subsumed within these categories, that these activities are the building blocks of our generalizations, and that we ought to unpack them occasionally to see what's there. If there are some underappreciated candidate perspectives, calculations, and activities that lie within our working categories, some qualitative explorations may bring them to light.

PRIMARY CHALLENGERS

In 1978, I traveled with two candidates in Democratic Senate primaries. In both cases, the candidates I watched were out-party challengers, running in a multicandidate field for the right to oppose a veteran Republican incumbent. Richard Leone was one of three candidates seeking to challenge four-term Senator Clifford Case in New Jersey. Paul Tsongas was one of five candidates seeking to challenge two-term Senator Edward Brooke in Massachusetts. Leone's primary campaign failed; Tsongas's succeeded. There were enough similarities in the two campaigns to fortify our understanding of would-be challengers and their campaigns. And there were enough differences to stimulate further thinking about candidates and campaigns in general. I will call the two candidates "primary challengers."

Among students of congressional elections, an early explosion of interest in the advantages of incumbency has been followed by another burst of interest in the disadvantages of challengers. Those disadvantages, we now know, have to do with poor candidate quality, lack of name recognition, inadequate finances, and insufficient media attention.[14] We would not expect observational research on challenger campaigns to call into question the essential importance of these four variables. But a close-up, over-time look might shed light on them and on interactions among them. As neither of the campaigns was a direct challenger-incumbent campaign, they are not strictly comparable to a partisan contest. However primary challenger campaigns do give special visibility to the very earliest stages of campaign development.

RICHARD LEONE, NEW JERSEY, 1978

Candidate Quality

Observation from the campaign trail places heavy emphasis on the personal aspects of campaigning. Among the variables used to explain challenger difficulties, therefore, the one most likely to come under scrutiny is challenger quality. Paul Tsongas was, by every measure political scientists have developed, a "quality challenger." But Dick Leone was not. Most measures of Senate candidate quality require previous elective office or, perhaps, a previous run for elective office; Leone had neither. [15] Political scientists would have to classify him as a poor-quality candidate and would emphasize that factor in explaining the failure of his campaign.

In examining Leone's precampaign career and listening to him, however, I came to the judgment that he was, in fact, what reasonable people would consider a high-quality candidate. And with this judgment came resistance to the idea that his losing campaign could be explained on the basis of his quality as a candidate. This resistance, in turn, suggests that we need to keep thinking about how we measure candidate quality, what we mean by it, and what weight we should give it in explaining election outcomes.

Dick Leone's career résumé included such milestones as the first Ph.D. graduate of the Woodrow Wilson School at Princeton University, executive director of the White House Task Force on the Cities, campaign manager of New Jersey Governor Brendan Byrne's first successful campaign, three years as the appointed New Jersey state treasurer, lecturer in public finance at Princeton and top campaign adviser to Governor Byrne's successful reelection campaign. In their election eve editorial, the *New York Times* said of him,

> [He] has been active in New Jersey reform politics for almost 15 years. As Governor Byrne's State Treasurer, Mr. Leone was the architect of the state income tax, of the fiscal arrangements that led to the construction of the Meadowlands sports complex and of an innovative bond program that rescued hard-pressed cities. . . . If experience and outstanding service matters, as they should, Mr. Leone . . . would seem to deserve the edge.[16]

Though he had never run for elective office, he was steeped in the campaign politics and public policies of New Jersey.

"What I like best," Leone told me, "is meeting with small groups and talking issues. Answering questions—that is what I like best of all." He was every bit as knowledgeable, as articulate, and as excited about public policy issues— national and local—as Paul Tsongas. To the degree that candidate quality is intended to measure previous public political accomplishment, Leone was a high-quality candidate. And to the degree that candidate quality is intended to measure campaign experience, he was at least a medium high-quality candidate.

In both respects, Leone was certainly a higher-quality candidate than his primary opponent. Indeed, he said of his opponent, "His candidacy offended me, because I did not think he was qualified to be a senator." His opponent's career résumé consisted of two milestones, both of them prepolitical. He had been a Rhodes Scholar at Princeton; and he had been a highly publicized basketball star with the national champion New York

Knicks—a focus of athletic interest in the New York/New Jersey media market. His prepolitical career did not fit, either, with conventional ideas of candidate quality, as Canon's studies of ambitious amateurs have taught us.[17]

Nonetheless, his prepolitical career alone had made Bill Bradley an attractive and visible candidate. To the degree, therefore, that candidate quality is intended to measure favorable, personal recognition of whatever sort, Bradley was a higher-quality candidate than Leone. And it was Leone's misfortune to be matched against an opponent who had such recognition—what Leone called "the celebrity advantage."[18] But that does not make Leone a low-quality candidate. He will be treated throughout as a high-quality candidate who lost. And the campaign will be treated as one in which our conventional ideas about candidate quality were useless.

In the first stage of his campaign, Leone's one campaign leaflet spoke only of his own record. Its headline read, "For over a decade, he's been in the forefront of every important fight for reform in New Jersey." When I arrived in New Jersey two weeks before election day, his second leaflet had appeared with a headline that jabbed at his opponent: "The next time a candidate tells you what he's going to do for New Jersey when he gets to Washington, ask him what he did for New Jersey while he was in New Jersey." As he campaigned, he would ask, "Where was Bradley when I was in all the fights in this state?" "You have to remember," he would say, "that I've been involved in every reform fight in this state for ten years. What I've done matters more than what his name is."[19]

But he was wrong. His description of Bradley as an unqualified "celebrity" who was "just passing through" New Jersey and "playing games" with the voters to satisfy his personal ambition never took hold. It simply did not matter how Leone compared their qualifications. In mid-May, Leone's name recognition among prospective Democratic primary voters stood at 33 percent; Bill Bradley's stood at 60 percent.[20] A horse race poll showed Bradley at 34 percent and Leone at 9 percent.[21]

Qualification is important to a quality candidacy. But recognition is a candidate attribute that must come first, it seems, in the campaign context.

From a developmental perspective, the campaign of a primary challenger against other primary challengers places the observer as close to the postrecruitment phase of a campaign as it is possible to get. The observer is in a position to contemplate the earliest sequences in the life of the campaigning politician. Leone's campaign had two distinct stages—a highly successful takeoff period of about four months and a highly problematical growth period of about two months. Indeed, from December 1977 (when he suddenly decided to run) until April 1978, the Leone campaign was a model for a winning campaign by a primary challenger.

The earliest goal of every campaign is to achieve credibility, to be taken seriously. For Dick Leone, the first task was to establish himself as the most credible liberal candidate among the three clearly recognizable liberal aspirants—Congressman Andrew Maguire, State Senator Alex Menza, and himself. This he did; and it was the triumph of his campaign. First, he located his hard-core primary supporters—"liberal intellectuals, mostly Jewish, people I have been involved with in the state for a long time, including those who urged me to run" and "ethnic support among Italians that wells up spontaneously wherever I go." Second, he raised $150,000 in three months.[22] And his planned budget of $300,000 was more than had ever been raised before for a Senate primary race in New Jersey. Among his one-thousand contributors, he said, "there are two bulges, the $500 to $1,000 contributions mostly from Jewish liberal activists and the smaller contributions mostly from party people." His support base was clearly the product of his prior political experience.

Third, he had hired one of the nation's premier political consultants, David Garth, a man he had worked with before when he ran the Byrne campaign.[23] Fourth, he used his fund-raising prowess to persuade Congressman Maguire (who subsequently endorsed him) to abandon his fledgling Senate campaign—for lack of money—in February.[24] Fifth, he spent $60,000 on a television blitz in March to place a convincing distance between himself and Menza, who was the only conventional "quality candidate" in the race. "My early TV has made all the difference between me and Menza," he explained. "We started with the same name recognition, the same libreal background, and we've gotten the same news coverage. My recognition went from 14 percent to 33 percent after two weeks of TV. That's as big a jump as you can make in two weeks."

By the beginning of April, Leone had secured a primary constituency, launched a credible campaign, and trimmed his competition. He had developed first-stage momentum. Until April, he said, "I had the best time I ever had in my life." And this success could be attributed very largely to his political experience—to the fact that he was, despite most political science measures, a quality candidate.

Candidate Control

During the early, takeoff stage of the Leone campaign, Leone and his staff did what was needed, in the proper order. That early stage can be characterized as a campaign under control. What I saw in mid-May—during the second stage—was a campaign out of control. By that time, the campaign seemed to be at the mercy of everyone but the campaigners themselves. The candidate described the situation: "The campaign has been blown off-course by events over which I had no control." He added, "In the beginning, I had to establish my credibility as a candidate. I talked about the issues. Now all we talk about is the campaign. The campaign has taken on a life of its own."

The turning point came in April, when their money dried up. "We raised only $3,000 or $4,000 in the first two weeks of April," he said. "Our campaign was on the verge of collapse. We were thinking that we might have to drop out of the race. It was a disaster." The underlying cause was Leone's inability to expand his electoral support beyond the hard core and the consequent loss of the financial potential of a broadened group of supporters. The group he wanted and needed to complete his electoral coalition was the Democratic party organization—its leadership and its voters in such traditional urban bastions as Jersey City, Newark, and Camden.

As a practical matter, that meant the support of Governor Brendan Byrne and his allies in the old-line party organization. It was to be an odd coalition—"Never the twain shall meet," Leone quipped—of liberal intellectuals and machine politicians, of outsiders and insiders. He believed that his public service involvement had earned him the partisan loyalty of the Democratic organization just as much as it had earned him the policy and reformist loyalty of the liberals. The second stage of his campaign was to be dominated by the endorsement and the fund-raising support of the party. It did not happen. And that became the defining circumstance of the campaign's last two months.

Hudson County was the largest of the state's local Democratic organizations—and the prize of the primary. Leone's expectation was that Governor Byrne would give him a strong pledge of support and would persuade other organization leaders, like Tommy Smith, mayor of Jersey City, to do likewise. Byrne gave Leone a minimal public endorsement: "All things being equal, I have to support Leone."[25] But that was all. There was very little persuasion and even less money. The campaign never achieved second-stage momentum. "By all the rules of politics," said the *New York Times*, "it should have been over when Governor Byrne endorsed Mr. Leone. . . . However, the endorsement failed to sew up the nomination for Mr. Leone."[26]

As we drove to Democratic gatherings in Jersey City and Bayonne, Leone described his plight.

> If the governor had gotten Tommy Smith in line, as soon as Smith indicated he was wavering, I would have locked up the nomination right then. But he did nothing, and the genie got out of the bottle. We had to make the best of a bad situation and it took two weeks to put things back together with some sort

of compromise. That took a lot of my time—time spent away from my natural constituency, the liberals. I have to deny Bradley Hudson County if I am to have any chance.... I should come back here four or five times between now and election day—once a day even.

The "compromise" was a minimal public endorsement by Tommy Smith—"I'm for Brendan Byrne . . . and if he's for Leone, I'm for Leone"—plus his prediction of a normal 30,000-vote plurality for Leone.[27] But he denied Leone the more substantial prize of the "organization line" on the ballot, opting, instead, for an unusual open primary free from official party endorsement.[28]

Smith, it turns out, had been sitting on the New York Knicks bench with Bradley and shooting baskets with the team. And the demographic group that Leone felt least able to connect with was "blue-collar males"—a group quite likely to have heard of Bradley's athletic exploits. In Leone's calculations, a primary victory would have to include a 20,000-vote plurality in Hudson County. On election day, his plurality was 1,600 votes. Other Democratic organizational bastions proved even less friendly.

When I was with him, Leone's short-term answer to "How's it going?" was, "We are behind." But with the undecided vote at 60 percent, he clung to the possibility that if he could become better known, he could fashion a narrow plurality at the polls. "Among people who know both of us," he told his audiences, "I'm considered much better qualified, but more people know him." And he told his staff, "My theory is that between now and election day, the undecided voters will get one or two pops on the election and that will swing it. How many automobile ads are there in the paper every day—hundreds. But you don't notice them till you're interested in buying a car, do you? It's the same with elections."

But he would need money to deliver those "one or two pops." And he was broke.

I'll tell you, we have only $8,000 left for TV. We'll have to go off the air for the next five or six days and then—if we can raise $20,000—we'll go back on for the last week. We have no money;

and this is the most expensive state to run a [TV] campaign in.
You have to buy the whole market [in New York]; but you use
only a quarter of it.

His problem was no secret. Nor was Bradley's kitty of
$500,000. The comparison convinced the media that Leone
was behind in the horse race. "We're in trouble," he said,
"partly because the press keeps saying we're in trouble."[29]
His hopes were reduced to whimsy. "If the media will start
playing up our campaign in the last week, maybe I'll be a
celebrity, too, by election day." For the two days I was with
him, the campaign ran out of control, because it was caught in
a downward media-money spiral. In order to raise money, he
had to project a credible campaign. In order to project a credible
campaign, he needed media attention. In order to get media
attention, he needed to look like a winner. In order to look like
a winner, he needed money. His dilemma reminds us of the
continuous interaction of money with other variables such as
media attention. And to understand campaigns, we must study
the interactions as well as the variables themselves.

In Leone's case, he could break this downward spiral only
with a timely infusion of money from committed loyalists or
with a timely burst of attention from an interested media. The
candidate's constant dilemma was how to spend his time—
on the phone raising money or going places to attract media
attention. Whatever Leone decided to do with his time, his
choice usually brought disappointment. What I witnessed was
a losing effort to attract media attention.

The first afternoon he scheduled a tour of a Newark senior
citizens housing project that, as state treasurer, he had helped
to finance. But nobody from the media was there. "It was a
waste of time," he said as we left. "We did it hoping the media
people would come. It would have been a great media event.
But it's a crapshoot. I should have spent the time on the phone
[raising money] as it turned out." That evening, we went to a
rally for the uncommitted Essex County (Newark) Democratic

leader. "He's liable to blurt out an endorsement that will hurt us," he said. "But I'll take that risk because I'm behind.... If good things happen there and I get a good story, it will mean votes." Nothing good happened. When we got there, we found that Bradley had come and gone. So, too, had the television crews and half the two-thousand Democrats. "I wonder what I'll do if I lose," he reflected on the way home. "Maybe I should begin to think about that."

The next morning, as we were riding in the car, he flipped through several papers looking for coverage of the six events of the previous day. "Remarkably little press," he mused. "Nothing in the *Daily News*, nothing in the *New York Times*. Well the rain falls on everyone evenly." The media was, however, devoting most of its attention to the (losing) primary campaign of Republican Senator Clifford Case. And Democrat Leone was devoting all his attention to Democrat Bradley. He did not have to—and hardly did—mention Case. We were driving, at the time, to a chemical plant site where Leone was to be endorsed by a Princeton student who had built an atomic bomb—a pure media event. An NBC television crew appeared, but the reporter complained because no people came to supply a background. And he produced no story.

Later that day, we got stuck in a traffic jam as we headed for another tour of a Leone-financed senior citizens housing project in Elizabeth. "I should be on the phone instead of going to these things. They would be fine if we had a station wagon full of press people traveling with us.... I should be making phone calls to the three most important papers in the state and here we are sitting in traffic. My life blood is dripping away." A photographer from the *Elizabeth Journal* did take his picture there. But the delay caused us to miss his next scheduled meeting with the Elizabeth Democratic leaders.

This high proportion of missed opportunities during two days on the trail was doubtless partly attributable to an inefficient, if not amateurish, campaign organization. "The biggest difference," said Leone, "between this campaign and the ones I ran is that when I told people to do something then, they did it." At day's end, he likened his situation to a wartime siege. "It's like the last days in the bunker when you are moving paper battalions from place to place and no one does anything." And then to meteorology. "We're waiting for the clouds to break and the airdrop to come."

The clouds never broke and the airdrop never came. Ten days later, Bill Bradley got 61 percent of the vote. Dick Leone got 27 percent.

Postmortem

In our postmortem conversation, he was generous in his praise of Bradley's strengths as a candidate. "He had a terrific reputation. He was not just a jock. If he had been just a basketball player, we might have done something about it." This judgment recalled the very first campaign comment he had made to me when we met—that the Princeton Ph.D. had, in effect, been neutralized by the Rhodes Scholar. "This is the first time in my political life," he had said, "when I'm not considered to be the intellectual. And that hurts." No matter what strategy he had followed, he said afterward, "it would have been tough against Bradley." Publicly he acknowledged that "we were not in a position to overtake Bradley's celebrity status and recognition."[30]

Still, he speculated about what might have been. And these speculations revealed a highly personal ingredient in his campaign. As a candidate, he said, he had made—all by himself—two large miscalculations. One involved the intensity of some supporters, the other the intensity of his ambition.

His support problem arose from the unwillingness of the governor and two of the governor's major Democratic fund raisers to help him. Leone simply assumed they would. The governor, he believed, let him down from the very beginning. "If Byrne had acted differently and had moved in January and February to put things together, he could have forced Bradley out of the race. . . . I hoped he would. I was optimistic about him when I should have known better. You misjudge a lot of people in life—you have, I have. But this was a judgment that meant more to my life than any other one, and I was wrong."

In the second stage of his campaign, when he needed money to sustain his momentum, said Leone, Byrne's posture of minimal support had been adopted by two other top party leaders whose appointed positions Leone had helped to secure. "They could have raised the money for me, and they didn't. If ever there were three people who, according to conventional wisdom, were obligated to me politically, it was the three of them. . . . Never have I misjudged any people in politics as I did these people." And he added, "If I had known that I would have to run without the resources, I might have behaved differently. I'd never run again without the resources in hand." "I should have known," he concluded, "that they would not help, but I cannot believe that about human nature."

I do not know enough about New Jersey politics to assess Leone's overall postmortem. But, from a larger perspective, it seems likely that what was involved was less personal perfidy than a changing political context in which organizational loyalties and capacities were breaking down. In which case, voters were becoming attracted to political outsiders like Bill Bradley.[31] And old-line machines were becoming loathe to challenge them. Bradley's television advertising proclaimed, "We've had enough politicians cut out of the same mold,"[32] and his campaign brochure touted him as "a citizen politician," "cast in a different mold."[33] CBS-TV endorsed him as "a fresh face."

If basketball brings far more recognition than public service does, then the quality candidate or quality challenger concept cannot be measured by political experience alone. In a television age, we shall have to think of all possible bases for visibility. And we shall have to think of "quality" as a comparison among actual sets of candidates, in ever-changing contexts. Better still, when we want to determine a candidate's "quality," we should look at the campaign.

Dick Leone's second personal miscalculation, he said, involved the lack of intensity and focus in the pursuit of his ambitions. It was a matter of the fuel that fired his political ambition. When I asked him why he ran, he answered, variously, "I thought Case was vulnerable," "A lot of people encouraged me to do it," "I was bored at the time," "It solved a lot of my personal problems as to what to do—that's a major reason. I wasn't doing anything at the time." It was a tepid expression of ellective office ambition. In a strategic sense, his uncertain ambition created a problem of timing. He waited too long to decide. And the lateness of his decision to run severely constrained his strategic possibilities.

"My biggest mistake of all," he said afterward,

> was not deciding early enough that I wanted it. If I had decided right after the election in 1973—when I could do no wrong—that there was a Senate seat up in 1978 and that I wanted it more than anything else, there are a thousand things I would have done differently; and I would have been in a much different position than I was in December of 1977. Anybody in politics thinks about the Senate now and then. But I didn't think seriously about it. When my name came up, I told people I was not interested. In August of 1977, I told Bill Bradley and Andy Maguire that I wasn't going to run. They asked me. I talked to Dave Garth about it in September, and we decided not to do it. In December, I decided to do it.

By contrast, he noted, "Bradley had been running for the Senate since 1974. I knew that. He told me. I didn't think he was qualified to be a senator; but I didn't think much about it. I told him he ought to get into state government and work up. He campaigned for four years. There was never a place I went during the campaign, but what Bradley hadn't already been there. Now he wants to be president." And he concluded, "If there's one thing I've learned that is true for all of politics, the person who single-mindedly wants a particular office has a big advantage over everyone else. He can bend everything he does in that direction. Once in a while an accident may come along to make it possible, but it's the people who plan way ahead who get it."

It was House Speaker Tip O'Neill who said, "Everything in politics is timing."[34] And Dick Leone would doubtless agree. As his case suggests, ambition influences timing. The reason may be that ambition sensitizes politicians to the existence of opportunity; and an opportunity seized is likely to yield effective timing. By the same token, to bank the fires of ambition may mean an opportunity lost.

To the degree that the term "quality candidate" is intended to apply only to those who have previously put their careers on the line, Dick Leone's personal reflections may, indeed, portray him as something less than a high-quality candidate. Had he run before, he might well have understood better than he did the minimal value of personal endorsements and the very great importance of determined ambition.

What, then, might students of elections and campaigns learn from this observation-based, qualitative discussion of the Leone campaign? First, the idea of candidate quality may be more complex and its relevance more dependent on specific candidate comparisons in context than current measures allow. Second, intensity of commitment matters a lot in politics, and a candidate's misestimate of intensity can be crucial. In this case, the candidate overestimated the relevance of his public accomplishment and his endorsements, while underestimating the relevance of his own desire for the job. Third, the interaction over time of campaign variables—such as money and media—may need to be stipulated very clearly when the two are included in an explanation of campaign success. And the degree of control over their interaction requires investigation.

PAUL TSONGAS, MASSACHUSETTS, 1978

The Candidate: Recognition and Qualification

Congressman Paul Tsongas got to the Senate in 1978 by winning a five-person Democratic primary and then by defeating two-term Republican incumbent Edward Brooke. My main interest here is in the primary campaign, during which Tsongas accomplished what Leone could not. The Leone campaign had a successful takeoff and then stalled out, whereas the Tsongas campaign followed a steady, upward trajectory to the end. Its crucial decisions were made in its earliest stage and it was never "blown off-course" in any succeeding stage. As a top aide traced it, "Our campaign ran in a straight line from May 17 to November 7"—that is, from announcement to victory. And as Tsongas said of his primary campaign, "It was perfect. We didn't make a single mistake.... It was incredible." His success story provides us with some more, perhaps some sturdier, suggestions concerning such qualitative notions as strong candidates and effective campaigns. In so doing, it may help us to better understand what primary challenger campaigns are all about.

When I first met Paul Tsongas, he was greeting the early morning shift at several mill gates in Fall River in late July. Two hours and several hundred handshakes later, I asked him, "Did any of those people recognize you?" "No," he answered. "Why should they?" He was eight weeks into his primary campaign with eight weeks to go. But his candidacy was still in its earliest stage.

As a sitting congressman, he had strong support in his own Fifth Congressional District, which contained his home city of Lowell and a ring of Boston suburbs whose liberals Tsongas considered his "natural constituency." From this strong and secure base, he had been raising money and recruiting volunteers, resources with which he hoped to expand into the other eleven districts statewide.

His early samplings had revealed that only 12 percent of the Massachusetts electorate had heard of him. And his June poll put him in second place, twenty-four points behind the equally young, equally liberal secretary of state, Paul Guzzi—with three other candidates strung out behind. The state's major newspaper, the *Boston Globe*, later described the situation as I found it: "Paul Guzzi, the only candidate with a state-wide constituency, became the instant favorite when he announced his candidacy June 22, with his level of support at least three times that of any other candidate."[35]

At breakfast that first day in Fall River, Tsongas told a small group of potential contributors, "My problem is recognition. People don't know who I am or what my record is. Our polls tell us that among people who know all candidates, I'm favored. But I'm way behind Paul Guzzi in name recognition . . . . I have so little recognition, I have campaign paranoia." Indeed, he did not give his campaign workers the actual poll figures, because, he said, "it would have scared the hell out of them." Later that week, the *Boston Globe*'s chief political columnist weighed in with his confirming opinion: "Tsongas hopes to break through with his Washington experience ... but the candidate best known, Mr. Guzzi, will be the one to beat the early line shows."[36]

Like Dick Leone, Tsongas was the underdog. But he had three advantages Leone did not have. First, he had a driving and focused political ambition—always, in his own words, "thinking up." Second, he was an experienced candidate. Referring to his first race for Congress, against an incumbent, he commented, "I've been in the underdog position before. In June, I was 22 points behind in the polls. In November, I beat him by 21 points, a switch of 43 points in six months. . . . So it doesn't bother me. I know what movement is all about." Third, he had a legislative record, one more easily linked than Leone's public record to the legislative job he sought. And he was, as we know, a person with a very strong policy orientation. "Our whole campaign," he said, "is based on what I have done as a congressman."[37] These ingredients placed Tsongas perfectly within the conventional idea of a quality candidate and a quality challenger.

When we talked about the origins of the campaign, he disavowed any long-term ambition for the Senate.

> The first time I ever thought of the Senate was this spring. I got mad at Brooke for the way he was handling the Panama

Canal issue. One day I called Dennis [Kanin, his administrative assistant and campaign manager] and Rich [Arenberg, his legislative assistant and pollster] into my office and said, "What would you think about a Senate race?" Before that, whenever anyone ever mentioned the Senate, I always said, "I'm in the wrong state. You've got Kennedy and you've got Brooke."

Whatever he said, however, Democrat Tsongas had in fact been eyeing Republican incumbent Brooke for a long time. Ever since May 1975, five months after he became a congressman, he had been placing items about Brooke in his own Fifth Congressional District polls. Twice in 1975, four times in 1976, once in 1977, and once in 1978, for example, he had probed Brooke's favorability/unfavorability ratings. And the distinct weakening of these ratings between September 1977 and April 1978—from 67–24 to 54–34–was instrumental in persuading Tsongas to pursue his elective office ambition.[38]

The years spent assessing Brooke's vulnerabilities gave candidate Tsongas a resource Leone never had, never developed, and never showed—a well-crafted challenger argument, a reason to vote against the incumbent. Tsongas's pollster thought of his Fifth District as a "bellwether" for the state, especially for "the crucial group of independent, issue-oriented, Route 128 ring-around-Boston segment that votes Democratic but crosses over to vote for Brooke." What he found among the voters in the Fifth District was "a hardening of attitudes toward Ed Brooke, a vague sense that he hasn't done very much, no real accomplishment. Ask about Ed Brooke and you draw a blank. And then there's the whole thing about his being absent from the state." "Brooke's strength is a surface strength," Tsongas told his July listeners. "Scratch it and there's nothing there. He hasn't done his homework and that's why I'm running."

Tsongas had his anti-incumbent argument fully prepared by July. "Ed Brooke has to answer two questions: What has he done? And when was the last time you saw him? His problems are performance and accessibility." Throughout the primary, Tsongas was armed with an explanation for why he was challenging Brooke and why he, in terms of performance and accessibility, was the most viable alternative. From July to November, his argument never changed.

Pursuing his own ambition and relying on his own polls, Tsongas became the first Democrat to enter the Senate primary, which gave him the organizational advantage Leone felt he had lost. But the timing of Tsongas's decision gave him yet another advantage. Eleven days after his May 14 announcement, the *Boston Globe* broke a story about discrepancies in Senator Brooke's personal finances—discrepancies that had surfaced during his already messy divorce proceedings. The story produced media attention at home and an Ethics Committee probe in Washington that seriously weakened the incumbent. Only *after* the story broke did the other four Democrats decide to run—a sequence that left Tsongas holding the high ground as the only sincerely motivated, nonopportunistic challenger.[39] At the Fall River breakfast, he was quizzed in detail about this matter of timing. He commented, "That sequence has not been lost on the voters."

Most probably, Senator Brooke's personal troubles were the largest single factor in his eventual defeat. That is the conclusion of the scholarly postelection analysis by Gilbert Scharfenberger.

> The most important variable in the vote choice for the election were candidate images. The image perceptions of Tsongas as a good leader and Brooke as a bad person were the two most important predictors in voting for Tsongas.... It appears that the unraveling of Brooke's personal life, coupled with concerns of integrity, became the salient forces of image judgment. In contrast, Tsongas was portrayed as a counterpoint to Brooke along these concerns.[40]

Tsongas's own postelection poll produced evidence that his "performance and accessibility" argument against Brooke did take hold—evidence, therefore, that Tsongas proved to be a strong opponent. A summary of its findings noted, "Of those who voted for Tsongas, the top three issues were effectiveness, accessibility and personal qualities."[41] Most probably, however,

Brooke would have been vulnerable to other Democrats as well. "I'd like to think they voted for me," said Tsongas when it was all over, "but when you run against a 12-year incumbent ... I guess it's a sort of referendum."[42] All of which returns us to the primary campaign as *the* crucial Democratic contest.

Every primary campaign can be thought of as an effort by a candidate to locate a constituency and to begin to negotiate a representational relationship between candidate and constituency. The words "locate" and "begin to negotiate" are used to indicate that the primary occurs early in the overall electoral sequence and thus is particularly helpful in revealing the rock-bottom ingredients of the candidate–constituency relationship. In Dick Leone's case, we saw that to get off the ground, a candidate must establish early credibility. The Tsongas case, because it was successful, helps to elaborate what is meant by credibility—especially early credibility—for the campaigning candidate.

If we think of credibility as the threshold requirement of every primary campaign, it presents two personal thresholds for the candidate. The first is that he or she be *recognized*, at least by name.[43] The second is that he or she be thought to be *qualified*, at least by some body of strong supporters and by elite opinion. Recognition and qualification are the minimal connections of any representational relationship. They are, therefore, the earliest goals of most challenger campaigns. When a candidate has crossed both thresholds, he or she is deemed to be credible, that is, thought to be worthy of serious attention and thought to be plausibly electable. That legitimating judgment will be heavily influenced, of course, by the conduct of the campaign itself, but important, too, by the running evaluation of the campaign by elite political opinion, especially by the media.

The Campaign: Teamwork and Television

The second time I dropped in on candidate Tsongas, in August, he had completed a two-week television blitz and had taken another poll. His name recognition had jumped from 12 to

40 percent, and instead of trailing 34 to 19, with 21 percent undecided, he was now behind by only 21 to 19, with 40 percent undecided. He had broadened his support beyond his own district and gained the kind of second-stage momentum Leone could not achieve. And he was talking like Leone had talked about his first stage. "This is the most enjoyable campaign I've ever run."

His travel talk was all about the movement of polls and money. "When we were in Fall River," he recalled, "no one at the factory gates knew who I was. Now, after the TV ad has run for two weeks, the difference is phenomenal. Our poll shows I'm taking support from Guzzi, my support is the most solid of any of the candidates, [and] more are moving into the undecideds. Guzzi's coming backwards, we're going forward, and we aren't far behind. The momentum is ours, and it's ours because we spent $200,000." "The knock on me," he added, "has always been 'good congressman would make a good senator, can't be elected, can't raise money, can't organize.' That's buried. These poll results are the last nail in the coffin."

For fund-raising purposes, he had located the Greek business community—both in and out of Massachusetts. "This was the first time," he said later, "that the Greek community has been important to me, and did they come through! Whenever I wanted anything, there were two groups I could go to—liberals and Greeks. And they were ideologically inconsistent. I spent a lot of time with my roots." In the end, he collected 40 percent of his money from the Fifth Congressional District and an additional 30 percent from inside the state and 20 percent from outside.[44]

We all know—as Dick Leone's case surely reminds us—that money for television is a necessary resource of every contemporary campaign. How and why that resource gets used, however, is something we know less about. And it is something we need to know about to understand campaigns and their success. The Tsongas case tells us that to learn about television usage, it is important to know who, and what kind of group, makes the strategic decisions about usage.

Tsongas's decisions were made by a campaign team that had worked together in his congressional office and in his two previous campaigns. Only one of three media people was new to the top group of seven—and he was a television producer who answered an ad asking for volunteers. The Tsongas team was homegrown and devoted. They knew their candidate intimately; they had worked regularly with one another; and they had no other commitments.

"There's an integration in our campaign," said one, "that's hard to understand if you operate a hierarchy of consulting groups that work by memo. Our great strength is informal contact." Paul Guzzi, by contrast, had hired the biggest polling firm and the biggest ad agency in Boston. Another Tsongas aide said, "The amazing thing about our campaign was the organic quality of the effort—the batting back and forth, the constant interaction among us. That was the secret." Tsongas himself put the importance of his team this way: "If we had not had the experience of four years in Congress and the experience of running for Congress, we could never have hoped to put it together." It was to Tsongas's personal credit that he had put together and kept such an ideologically, politically, and personally committed staff.

As a general proposition, students of elected politicians will want to learn what they can about the people around the politician—the staff on Capitol Hill, the circle of campaigners on the trail. When political scientists plug "experience" into statistical analyses as a surrogate for "challenger quality" in explaining outcomes, a big part of its explanatory power may come from a smart, seasoned, integrated, and devoted campaign team. Quality campaigns require quality teams; and quality teams help to make quality candidates.

In a strategic sense, the object of every campaign is to manipulate the agenda confronting the voters. Each side works to define the issues in such a way that the answer will be favorable to its candidate. Each struggles to frame the contest so that the voters will face the question each side wants them to face. If you can control the agenda and the question, you have the best chance of controlling the dialogue, the answer, and the result. For the Tsongas team, that meant first getting him known and then framing the choice in terms of his superior qualifications for the job.

To capture control of the contest, the Tsongas campaign team made two early decisions, decisions that face every Senate candidate: the timing and the content of the television campaign. Both decisions were crucial and problematical; both were crowned with success; and neither depended on any preconceived campaign model. "We were flying blind," said one strategist. "We knew of no other campaign like it."

Recall that his June poll results showed Tsongas far behind and with very little name recognition. His longtime pollster and legislative assistant commented, "It was important to read that poll right, because we were so far behind them. The obvious instinct was to attack. But our interpretation was that there was no need to attack. We believed that Guzzi's support was soft [i.e., based entirely on name recognition] and would melt away if we could increase Paul's visibility."

It was the Tsongas campaign's strategic premise that if they could connect with the voters by crossing the recognition threshold, they would then surely connect with voters by crossing the qualification threshold. They believed their candidate had a more substantive policy-oriented outlook and record than Guzzi. "My opinion has always been," Tsongas said in August, "that if I could get known and get my record across, I would win, but that you can't penetrate people with a record if they don't know who you are." Their question was, how to "penetrate"? And their answer was, by going on television before anyone else and spending all their money.

"Our most important strategic decision," said the pollster,

was the decision to go for visibility and to get on before Guzzi. . . . It is axiomatic that if you don't save enough money for the end of the campaign, you don't win. So everybody saves something to use for TV at the end. We put all our chips on two weeks of early television and gambled that the increase in visibility would produce enough momentum so that we could raise more money for the last couple of weeks.

"It was a gamble," said another team member. "Sometimes you blow your whole wad and nothing happens." Conventional wisdom might have dictated both attacking and husbanding, but the campaign team chose a different course on both counts. Tsongas's team recognized the possibility of the kind of downward spiral that trapped Leone. The Tsongas gamble, however, paid off in more recognition, more money—$250,000 more from mid-August to primary day—and a come-from-behind upward spiral.

The team's second key decision was to keep their television content positive and pro-Paul Tsongas. Negative advertising was never considered. "The idea of a campaign," said one media aide, "is to get out of the way and let your candidate communicate with the public. In order to do that, you have to know your candidate well." Another one said, "There's a big difference between a commercial and a campaign." A campaign, that is, must present—and must be consistent with—the real person. A third media aide agreed. "We wanted people to get to know Paul Tsongas as he is. He's quiet, he mumbles and stumbles, doesn't look energetic, doesn't smile a lot. But he cares. And he has more integrity than other politicians. People like him and trust him. And he gets things done."

Their first recognition commercial was a perfect fit with their wry, self-deprecating candidate. It was a catchy ad in which several people struggled but mispronounced his name, after which a bright-eyed kid finally came up with the pronunciation "Tickets!" The candidate smiled, mentioned several of his congressional accomplishments, and said he wanted "to tell you what I've done as a congressman." And a voice intoned, "The closer you look, the more Paul Tsongas is doing for Massachusetts." In three other ads that ran during the two-week blitz (and later), he elaborated what he had done: a $40 million bill establishing "America's first urban park" in Lowell, development money for solar energy, his idea for home equity conversion for the elderly. These policy accomplishments and interests would, they believed, carry him over the qualification threshold.

"It was," one aide said of their television blitz, "a characterization—qualified. The point is, here is a guy who is really qualified, who can talk to you, who has depth.... It was important that he was 'Congressman Tsongas.' But that alone wasn't enough. If it weren't for the fact that he was substantive, the cutting edge with Guzzi wouldn't have worked."

When the blitz was over, Tsongas had turned the corner. "Our August poll showed that everything we had projected was happening," said his pollster. "We wanted to see what impact our media had. We wanted to know whether the visibility ("Tickets") ad was working, and we saw that it was. That was the time I stopped worrying about the race. I thought it was right on track."

The Tsongas–Guzzi comparison worked, as the Leone–Bradley comparison did not. Tsongas raised enough money to advertise his public policy record, to gather second-stage momentum, and, eventually, to win credibility with the media.

A few days before the election, the *Boston Globe*'s chief editorial writer provided the kind of elite certification so necessary to a challenger's qualification when he acknowledged, grudgingly, that the evaluation of Tsongas as "the heavyweight" and Guzzi as "the lightweight" had become "the centerpiece of the race."[45] The judgment brought the free media into line with Tsongas's paid media advertising in presenting himself to the voters. It meant that the free media were finally framing the issue in terms of candidate qualification—exactly as the Tsongas team wanted.

In their eyes, *Boston Globe* certification did, indeed, come "eventually," "grudgingly," and "finally." The paper's reluctance to grant them credibility was a major campaign irritant.

As Tsongas said afterward, "The *Globe* didn't take me seriously. In terms of their coverage, they were fair. But in terms of their editorials and what their editorial writers were saying, they assumed Guzzi would win. We really spent May, June, July, and most of August wandering in the wilderness. The *Globe* wasn't alone. It was the prevailing wisdom."

For the final two weeks of the primary campaign, the media team prepared their concluding ad called "Son of Tickets," in which the adults from the first ad pronounced Tsongas's name right, but the kid still pronounced it 'Tickets.' Whereupon the candidate commented, "Well, three out of four isn't bad." And then, he talked about his accomplishments—opening and closing his discussion with the phrase, "What I've done in Congress."

"I felt," said a media adviser, "that the [five-person] primary would be decided in the end by people electing someone who would not be known all that well. The best thing was to tie Paul back to that kid without any issues or cutting edge. Here's a nice guy who can laugh at himself." And another added, "At the polls [on election day], whenever the kids would come by, they would pronounce Paul's name or else they would say, 'Tickets.' " "Everything we did," said his campaign manager, "was designed to raise Paul's recognition."

In September, Tsongas got 35 percent of the vote to Guzzi's 31 percent. (He carried his Fifth District base by 67 percent.) The next day when we talked, he said, "This is a time for great savoring. We took on Paul Guzzi, the two biggest political consulting firms in the state, and the *Boston Globe*. If we win in November, that will be nice. But it will never replace this one." "We'll have to be conciliatory to the *Globe*," he added, "even though they pushed for Guzzi." At the press conference that followed, he gave first mention to "the media campaign that was put together for me." And he quipped, "If my name were Smith, I probably would have lost."

His underdog primary campaign made for an easy transition to a general election campaign. "The image of David beating Goliath," he said, "and the catapult effect of that, put me in a good position for the general election."[46] That campaign, against the wounded incumbent, was a straightforward extension of his primary campaign—no change in argument, no change in strategy. "The basic thrust in terms of the image we were trying to project was the same," explained his campaign manager.

> We emphasized what Paul had done [and] we continued to raise Paul's recognition.... The major thing we had going for us was Paul's low recognition in some areas. We figured we could hit a lot of people we hadn't hit in the primary ... raise their consciousness. That basically dictated our strategy. And it worked beyond anything we expected. In the places where we had done poorly in the primary, we did very well in the general.

An effective primary campaign and the recognition-qualification strategies of the primary campaign had put Paul Tsongas in the U.S. Senate.

Paul Tsongas's success story tells us that campaigns cannot be neglected in explaining election outcomes. At the same time, it suggests some ingredients of an effective campaign that deserve the fullest exploration in campaign studies. They are the previous accomplishments of a candidate's career, the working relationship of the campaign team, the strategic decisions regarding the timing and the content of television, the consistency between television ads and the candidate's strengths, and the legitimating evaluation of the free media. These ingredients, when incorporated into our thinking about campaigns, will get incorporated into our thinking about representational relationships.

CONCLUSION

The primary challenger campaigns of Dick Leone and Paul Tsongas illuminate the beginnings of a politician–constituency negotiation. Primary campaigns can be divided into two stages. In the early stage, the central activity is identifying and organizing a support base—a primary constituency of workers, donors, and people associated with them. In the later stage, the central activity is to broaden favorable judgments by means of paid media and free media. The object of both stages is to achieve credibility as a candidate. The essential ingredients throughout are recognition and qualification. And at the center of the effort is the candidate.

While it may be true that a few candidates will be recognized *because of* their qualifications, these cases suggest that for most challengers, recognition—or "visibility"—will have to come first. After a sufficient level of recognition has been reached, qualification can become a determining factor. Tsongas achieved that level; Leone did not. And it may be that the only way to find that "sufficient level" is to wait for the evidence that qualification has, in fact, kicked in. An important piece of evidence is elite certification, as reflected in media commentary. Once achieved, candidate credibility brings constituent connections and a personal reputation at home that will underpin a future political career.

On a final developmental note, the two campaigns suggest that there may be important campaign and candidate characteristics that are difficult to pick up in aggregate cross-sectional analysis and are more readily available to observers on the campaign trail. One is the degree of control exercised by the candidate and the campaign team over the course of the campaign. The other is the timing of candidate and campaign decisions. In both these respects, the rhythm and the flow of the Tsongas campaign was exemplary, while the Leone campaign suffered. Control and timing are likely to be matters of consequence to all candidates, their campaigners, and their campaigns. More generally, because this developmental perspective comes so naturally to the drop-in/drop-out researcher, the perspective may be a special contribution that the observational approach can make to the study of campaigns.

CHAPTER 4

A SEQUENCE OF CAMPAIGNS

TWO INCUMBENTS AND A CHALLENGER

Every campaign is part of an ongoing career and an ongoing representational negotiation. A campaign observer is always an intruder. In chapter 3, I described my intrusion into two primary campaigns, to watch a pair of challengers attempt to negotiate their earliest statewide constituency connections and, perhaps, launch a statewide career. To explore the full complexity of senatorial careers and connections, I observed the ongoing campaigns of some incumbents—at varying stages of their tenure.

Twenty-one of my thirty-one campaign intrusions involved incumbent U.S. senators. They were at a very different stage in their careers than the two challengers had been. The campaigning incumbents were renewing, reinforcing, refining, or reshaping—in a word, renegotiating—constituency connections that they had established in previous years.

A majority of those incumbent campaigns—fifteen of the twenty-one—involved *first-term incumbents*. For them, we would expect that the threshold connections of name recognition and qualification had been crossed six years earlier. As

Charles Franklin has shown, "senators enjoy most of their visibility advantage from the very start of their careers ... [and] the first campaign seals their visibility advantage."[1] The first reelection campaign can thus be seen as a test of the minimal connections of the first campaign and, further, as a test of six years of activities undertaken to negotiate a renewal of the relationship with a constituency.

In 1978, as I was watching the campaigns of Dick Leone and Paul Tsongas, I was also watching the campaign of first-term incumbent Democratic Senator Dick Clark of Iowa. He was widely expected to win reelection, but he did not. His losing campaign, however, was altogether a more uncertain and more complicated matter than Dick Leone's losing campaign had been.

After Clark's defeat, my curiosity turned to the upcoming campaign of Iowa's other first-term Democratic senator, John Culver. Culver and Clark were pre-Senate friends, working associates, and ideological soulmates. In 1980, Culver would be facing the same reelection test Clark had faced—and in the same constituency. Would he do any better, or any differently? And if he did, why? Would he learn anything from the Clark campaign? And if he did, would it matter? These questions sent me back to Iowa in 1979 and 1980 to observe the Culver reelection campaign. He, too, lost; but his campaign generated some instructive comparisons with the Clark campaign.

These Clark–Culver comparisons whetted my appetite for still one more adventure with the Iowa Democrats. When, therefore, the Republican who had defeated Dick Clark came up for reelection in 1984, I went back to have a look at the campaign of his Democratic challenger, Congressman Tom Harkin. He won. Comparisons among these three Democratic candidates added to my data. And the sequence of campaigns, in a single state, added another set of questions concerning the personal and developmental influences on campaigns and hence on representation.

The sequential perspective draws on the idea of "observational learning," as developed in the campaign studies of Marjorie Hershey. It is important to study campaigns, Hershey says, because campaigning politicians learn from previous campaigns and apply the lessons learned to their subsequent campaigns.[2] Politicians might learn something about negotiating, either from their own previous campaigns or from the previous campaign of another, similarly situated candidate. Tsongas would be an example of the first. But I am interested, here, in the second possibility. Hershey argues that to our notion that campaigns are important to careers we should add the notion that campaigns are important to other campaigns.

The three campaigns in Iowa provided a test of her proposition.[3] Because the three candidates shared their Democratic party affiliation, their liberal ideology, and their geographic constituency, it seems reasonable to assume they would pay attention to one another's efforts to negotiate connections with various elements in that constituency and to learn from them. Contextual differences would, of course, call for some discounting of such lessons. But the constancy of party, ideology, and constituency would make the matter of sequence more salient and make candidate learning more traceable than if these three key variables differed across the candidates. Holding these three conditions constant should also make it easier to discern the impact of candidate factors that both stimulate and constrain the learning process.

In the Clark-Culver-Harkin sequence, the Clark campaign offers a baseline. The two candidates who followed him could take his experience as an informational starting point and derive object lessons from it. John Culver's losing campaign is the pivotal campaign in the sequence. It could have been influenced by the campaign that went before, and, in turn, it could have influenced the campaign that came after. Tom Harkin's winning campaign, last in the sequence, could reflect lessons learned from both predecessors. While it may not be possible to demonstrate that the earlier campaigns "influenced" the later ones, it is possible to demonstrate, in every case, that the later candidates did think about, talk about, and compare themselves to the earlier candidates. And that provides sufficient incentive to explore the three campaigns—individually and in sequence.

DICK CLARK, IOWA, 1978

The Campaign

Senator Dick Clark was a former college professor whose pre-Senate political career had been entirely organizational and administrative.[4] He was a nuts-and-bolts architect of Democratic party resurgence in Iowa in the 1960s. He was an organizer of Congressman Culver's 1964 victory there. And he became Culver's administrative assistant in Washington. When Culver unexpectedly decided not to run against Iowa's two-term Republican incumbent in 1972, Clark hurriedly decided that he would.[5]

As a challenger, he had faced far bigger threshold problems than Paul Tsongas—albeit in a smaller territory. "I was totally unknown when I first ran," he said when we met in Iowa. "I can tell you honestly that I never thought of running for the Senate until seven days before I filed—never in my life." He began with 20 percent name recognition and very little money.[6] He was devoid of progressive ambition, and he was not, by accepted standards, a quality challenger. He was far behind in the polls; and he was given very little, if any, chance by the pundits.[7] But he conducted an eye-catching campaign, and he scored a major upset victory.

As a challenger, Clark successfully negotiated the recognition threshold, but not through television. He did it by walking 1,312 miles across the state of Iowa.[8] It was, he recalled, a desperation strategy.

> I had to do something. State Representative _____ told me one day that I should do it. I thought it was crazy, and I dismissed it out of hand. Several weeks later, he asked me what progress I was making in the campaign. I said, "Not much." I had no money and wasn't known. He said I ought to consider the walk. I realized that I had to do something, so I thought it over and

decided I might just as well. After the first day, I knew I had done the right thing. It got people interested in politics who had never been interested before. I walked 1,300 to 1,400 miles. That was *the* campaign. The results were amazing.

As he explained in 1972, "People respond to a candidate who meets and talks with them in their own surroundings. I have heard dozens of Republicans and independents say they will vote for me because of my personal effort."[9]

It was a spectacularly successful campaign. And it was based largely on his highly accessible personal approach to the voters.

In the Senate, Clark was a strongly committed liberal, with a serious, unassuming personal style. He served on the highly relevant Agriculture Committee. But he was best known for his leadership in reforming the procedures of the Senate and in keeping the United States out of the civil war in Angola.

When I dropped in on him in mid-October 1978, Clark was running on the basis of 89 percent name recognition and an "excellent job rating" (63%–25%)—as revealed in his earlier 1977 baseline poll. Clearly, he had crossed the recognition-qualification threshold that he had faced as a challenger. And, we might assume, he had negotiated an increasingly complex relationship with his constituents during his tenure in office. That relationship would be tested in November. To a greater extent than in 1972, Clark would be judged on his record—whatever that might mean. And, of course, both he and his opponent would have something to say on that score.

Incumbent Clark's early October poll showed him with a thirty-point lead—57 to 27 percent—over his opponent. I found him running an extremely low-key campaign, against former Lieutenant Governor Roger Jepsen. For two days, we drove across the state in a two-car caravan—senator and staff in the car up front, reporters and political scientist in the van behind. We were summoned, one at a time, to the lead car. He was seeking media attention from speeches and from media interviews in seven communities from Marshalltown to Mason City.

He had opened his campaign with a brief reprise of "the walk"—enough to justify a television commercial—but he had quickly discontinued it. "[Walking] was a lot more productive than this type of campaign and a lot more fun," he said as we rode along. "Here we are spending all our time in the car. We ride for hours to talk to eighty people who have made up their minds long ago. Maybe three or four of them are changeable. But it's a media thing now. That's why television is so important. Everybody watches it." What I saw was described this way by a leading Democrat. "The Clark campaign was by and large media oriented in its entirety. I mean, the campaign operation was basically [to] raise money and spend it on TV and radio."[10]

Clark had recently begun to rotate six forty-second television commercials. Four of them featured his work in the Senate—one on Angola, one on Senate ethics, one on sunset legislation to cut budgets, and one on a set of three additional Senate battles. The other two commercials featured his attentiveness to Iowans—one about the value of the walk, one about his frequent trips home. All six ads were totally positive, pro-Clark commercials. They contained no hint of his opponent, nothing negative. Their net effect was to portray Dick Clark as an active and effective legislator. He had no plans to add to them.

His six speeches on our trip were sober, bland discussions of political reform issues involving political action committees (PACS), ethics, and sunset regulations together with equally earnest expressions of his interest and accomplishments in agriculture. His ten interviews produced highly intelligent, analytical, and probing discussions of policy alternatives and decision-making dilemmas.

There was no sense whatever that Dick Clark was, or could be, in trouble. I heard only one cautionary note: "Whatever the farmers thought of me in 1972, it had to do with the walk; that I came to their towns, stopped in the stores, the grain elevators. That isn't there this time, and so the farmers have a different picture of me than they did. I don't expect to do as well in the rural areas."

His recent poll had turned up one issued-based vulnerability, his controversial pro-choice position on abortion. But the poll also showed that the strongest anti-abortionists "break 51 to 25 *for* Clark" and that "two-thirds of the voters currently cannot say what Dick Clark's position on the issue is." His offsetting strategy was, as he said later, "to try to duck it" and, as his pollster advised, "to present a large enough number of issues to obscure the issue context somewhat and make the emphasis lie on caring."[11]

When queried about this single-issue vulnerability, Clark would invariably reply, "Not many people are going to vote on the basis of one issue." And he believed it. As a top staffer put it, "That's what we thought. That's what all the national columnists were telling us. That's what all the Iowa writers were telling us. That's what the polls were telling us." By way of bolstering this conventional wisdom, Clark answered my question about his area of strongest support by asserting, "I do well among Catholics." As it turned out, he was wrong about both rural voters and Catholic voters.

If there was a theme that tied Clark's own reelection thoughts together, it was the importance of the constituency connection. Both his 1977 and his 1978 polls had told Clark that his solid reputation for "caring, communicating and working for the people is your greatest electoral strength."[12] This was the extra ingredient that the six-year incumbent had added to his less-complicated challenger's credentials. He assumed—as his polls suggested—that he would win because he had worked so hard to build a stronger connection than that with which he had begun.

"The great problem in the society is alienation," he reflected as we rode along,

the feeling that you elect people and they go off somewhere and forget about you. They want you to be around, to listen, to talk with them, to hold open office hours. People will forgive you almost everything if you stay in touch. That gives you latitude when you vote in the Senate. For me it is the only way I could survive. When I went to Washington, I decided I was not going to "throw" votes ... to please people. So I have to come back here all the time. I spend all my spare time here—all my vacation time. If I didn't get back here a lot and talk about agriculture and know a lot about it, people would never forgive my interest in Africa. Again, that gives me latitude. Coming back here, being accessible, listening, that's my strength.

The *Des Moines Register*'s lengthy profile of Clark—which he distributed as a campaign document—began with his comment "Home holds no fear for me," followed by his criticism of certain colleagues who "are terrified of being sent home."[13]

He was laying claim, now, to a record of representation—in this case, strong *personal* representation. In our conversation, he made much of the average of eighty-eight days a year he spent in Iowa. And his campaign commercial reminding people about the walk told viewers that he had spent five-hundred days in the state. At the same time, there he was, campaigning in a caravan—the farthest possible cry from his solitary, grass-roots walk of six years before. Furthermore, his television campaign was placing a distinctly secondary emphasis on his accessibility and virtually no emphasis on his interest in Iowa agriculture. As we got out of the car, he repeated, "That's my strength, no doubt about it—'He's responsive, he's accessible, he's around a lot.' " All in all, however, he did not seem to be conducting a close-to-the-citizen campaign.

Postmortems

Three weeks later, Clark was defeated 52 to 48 percent. It was called a "shock" and a "stunning upset."[14] When we talked afterward, I asked him, "What happened after I left you at the Mason City airport?" His answer was, "Nothing much happened. With respect to any obvious difficulties, we didn't think anything *had* happened—until the returns came in." A top campaign adviser described their total surprise.

"We were so goddamned confident." Election day was beautiful, the nicest November day you could have in Iowa. When we saw that, we knew we were going to win. That settled it. It was in the bag. The first bad news we heard was in the early afternoon when the *Des Moines Register* poll of people as they came out of the voting booth showed Jepsen, 56; Clark, 44. We didn't put any stock in it, figuring it was a bad sample. We just didn't believe it. Then, around nine o'clock, just before the polls closed, we learned the *Register* had scrapped the poll because they felt the sample was all screwed up. "Well, that clinches it," we said. And we were happy as could be. Twenty-five minutes later, ABC declared Jepsen the winner.

The meteorology of the campaign—from sunshine to storm—could not have been that sudden. But the unexpected shock that came afterward does help to highlight the serene confidence that reigned beforehand.

Something had changed the campaign dynamic in those last three weeks. And the campaigners had missed it, or underestimated it, very badly. That "something" turned out to be the launching of a heavy negative campaign against Clark by single-issue groups spearheaded by Iowa's anti-abortion, Pro-Life Action Council, but supported by the National Rifle Association, the National Right to Work Coalition, and an anti–Panama Canal Treaty group. The negative campaign stimulated a negative vote. "The voters voted against me—on abortion, Panama, gun control," Clark said. "Nobody said Jepsen would make a good senator."

The anti-Clark attack was funded independently and conducted out of plain sight via direct mail, mailgrams, and leafletting. As a postelection survey put it, "Jepsen owned the last three weeks of the campaign." To which Clark merely responded, "Some things were happening, but we didn't think they would have an overwhelming impact." "The one thing I feared," he said, "was a candidate who would pour so much money into the tube ... that he would buy the election from us. But he had no TV the last three weeks. ... We assumed he was out of money. Suddenly we got this spurt in every other form."

From Jepsen's point of view, the timing of the "spurt"

was exquisite, an anti-Clark barrage that surfaced too late to allow for a counterattack. The anti-abortionists, for example, distributed 300,000 leaflets to churchgoers just three days before the election.[15] "Our polls showed that people didn't know my position on abortion," Clark said. "What happened was that a lot of them got informed the last Sunday. The anti-abortionists did a great job, no doubt about it. They were out in force and they plastered every church." Surely, their campaign helped to produce Clark's career-ending surprise.

In the wake of the electoral surprise, explanations flourished. The pro-life group claimed credit for the outcome—a claim that energized the group but has not been supported by subsequent analysis.[16] Democratic party people, who had tied Clark's hopes to a big turnout, emphasized the low turnout—10 percent lower than assumed by the Iowa Poll.[17] When we talked, Dick Clark acknowledged the relevance of both these factors but expressed overall bafflement. "I don't have any solid conclusion about it at all. What is there you can say, scientifically, about this business?"

He placed heavier emphasis on two other factors—one developmental and one personal. There was, he said, a six-year public mood swing that made for a changed electoral climate. There was also his own staunch liberalism.

> When I went in, in 1972, the Vietnam War was still on. The fellow I ran against was closely associated with that effort; and that was of interest to people. There was not building that avalanche of antigovernment feeling, in the sense that government could not solve problems. The lack of faith that government can be useful has grown enormously in six years—the Goldwater spirit that government never has done anything right and never will—so the mood had changed in six years. The impact was very great, I think. People said, "Dick Clark is not a bad guy. He works hard at it. He's honest. He comes back. But he's just too liberal. He hasn't kept up with this change and is holding out for old ideas. There's nothing wrong with him, but his views."

One 1979 study found Clark to be the only liberal senator whose (near-perfect) rating by the ADA did not decline as his

1978 reelection approached.[18] And a close adviser volunteered that "his voting record would never change no matter what he heard at home. I noticed that his conservative coalition score came out after the election and it was just the same as it had been every other year." Clark's best overall guess, then, was that the combination of a changed context and his own committed liberalism was most responsible for the outcome.

My analysis is not designed to explain the election outcome, but rather to assess the Clark campaign as it may have contributed to that outcome and as it may have been an object lesson for succeeding Senate campaigns in Iowa. My assessment is that the campaign was ineffective and that its ineffectiveness was an important factor in accounting for Clark's defeat. It may also be the case that the pundits in predicting his victory erred because the "minimal effects" perspective on campaigns led them to discount the possiblity that the campaign could have a detectable influence.

If, as Clark's pollster told him later, "Jepsen owned the last three weeks of the campaign,"[19] we are led to wonder what information the Clark people had available to them at the time the campaign dynamic was changing. Mostly, it turns out, they were relying on the information gathered from their own poll of October 4–6. And this was a large problem. So confident were they of his thirty-point lead that the rest of the month they took no other polls. So they detected no slippage. They seemed not to credit the Iowa Poll, which showed him with a smaller though steady 10-point lead.[20] And they never altered the positive, unemotional, low-visibility campaign I observed during my October 14–16 visit.

"Had we assumed we were in more trouble, we would have come back at him," Clark said in the aftermath.

And we could have done it, because he was not a good guy. He was vulnerable. But with the poll showing a thirty-point lead, we thought the last thing we needed was to create more interest in the campaign. We had a great reluctance to make the campaign any more visible than necessary. With our poll being so lopsided,

God, you don't take chances. It's like a football game in which
you have three minutes to play and are three touchdowns ahead.
You don't pass.

When I asked his top campaign aide, "Would you have done
anything differently?" he answered, "Nothing. It was out of
our hands. Working with the information we had at the time,
there was nothing else we could have done. Why would you
do anything differently when the polls tell you you are thirty
points ahead?"

One obvious answer is, keep polling. If as was suggested
in chapter 3, all campaigns have short-run dynamics, then
the closing month of any campaign is no time to navigate
without updated information. Clark's pollster, Peter Hart,
acknowledged the error. "I did not serve Clark well," he
admitted when it was over.[21] And in his apologetic postelection
survey report showing that "Jepsen easily won the last month,"
Hart acknowledged "our failure to conduct later polling which
might have detected the shifts, and our inability to fashion
a strategy for preventing voter defections."[22] Hart concluded,
"We set our strategy in concrete too early."

The danger, not uncommon in campaigns, is to miscalculate
by assuming that a poll snapshot tells you what you need to
know about the dynamics of a campaign. It doesn't. "Early
leads," Hart wrote afterward, "are just the tip of the iceberg. It
is necessary to understand what the dynamics of the election
are." And he added, "The old approach of not mentioning
one's opponent will not do anymore. A candidate should go
aggressively after an opponent ... [and] develop an offensive
strategy." It is hard to believe that this experienced pollster
could not have provided this very same advice *during* the
campaign. Thinking about the continuous, undivided attention
to Paul Tsongas's campaign by his pollster suggests that Hart—
who was serving twenty-nine other politician-clients in 1978—
may have simply been too busy to keep a close weather-eye on
Iowa.[23]

However, while Hart's polls were overly optimistic, they still contained plenty of information, both cautionary and advisory, that could have been put to good use by the rest of the campaign team, especially by Clark's television advisers, Michael Kaye Associates. But it wasn't. For example, the early October poll showed that room for substantial voter shift remained. Sixteen percent of the voters were still undecided. An additional 21 percent described themselves as weak Clark supporters; and only half of them "expressed positive feelings toward the senator."[24] Furthermore, with respect to a battery of issues, Hart reported that "on none of the issues tested do more than 49 percent see him as in step with their thinking—a far cry from the 64 to 74 percent who see him as responsive." Even on the responsiveness measure, Hart noted that 44 percent of the respondents "agree with the statement that Dick Clark is not as close to Iowa as he used to be."

"Our overall judgment," Hart summarized, "is that his reputation for caring is the strongest thing Dick Clark has going for him—especially among crucial segments of the electorate." And he urged Clark to exploit that reputation. On the theory that "the only way for Jepsen to win is to get people to vote negatively against Dick Clark," Hart advised that "the Clark campaign step up a negative campaign against Jepsen.... The message should be that Dick Clark cares and Roger Jepsen doesn't.... We advise making as vivid a contrast as possible between the man who really cares and the one who does not." In short, Hart was cautioning the Clark team against overconfidence and he was advising them to make changes in their campaign strategy.

An observer of the Clark campaign might wonder why, with what a top team member said was "plenty of money to do anything we wanted to do," the October poll summary did not produce a fresh television ad—one featuring the Clark–Jepsen contrast on Clark's own terms. But it didn't. One part of the answer may lie in the unrecognized power of hardball negative campaigning, only then coming into its own. Today, candidates grab instinctively for the attack ad. But in 1978, the technique—full-blown, down and dirty—was in its infancy, at least for incumbents. The Jepsen campaign—late breaking and negative—may well have been a first for Iowa. Another part of pollster Hart's problem may have been a lack of experience with the phenomenon.

Clark's problem, however, stemmed in large part from the general inadequacies of his own campaign. All the advice in Peter Hart's 1977 and 1978 polls emphasized, as Clark himself did, that his representational strength lay in his personal responsiveness to the citizenry, in their feeling that he was in touch with them and cared about them. In the 1977 memo that helped lay the campaign groundwork, Hart wrote, therefore, that "more than any other single goal, the Clark campaign must establish responsiveness as *the main issue* of the campaign."[25] He elaborated, "He must *show* how he has stayed in close touch with Iowa and how he has represented Iowa's thinking in Washington." With explicit reference to television, he emphasized that "[Clark] should be depicted in a more aggressive posture, fighting to represent the views of Iowans in Washington; he should also be pictured in Iowa, seeking out the views of his constituents." More pointedly, Hart suggested that "the kind of responsiveness he should be emphasizing should be, perhaps, a little more along the lines of caring about and understanding the ordinary person." The television campaign that resulted was badly mismatched with this advice.

The six commercials composing Clark's television campaign were only marginally related to the candidate's political strengths. They did show Clark "fighting" "tough battles" in Washington, but three were devoted to battles over Senate ethics, over Angola, and over the budget. Agriculture, Iowa's dominant interest, was relegated to one of three fights (against corrupt grain interests) incorporated in a fourth, Washington-centered ad. But in this ad, two boxing puppets did the fighting and Clark himself never appeared. Indeed, Clark spoke in only one of his six commercials. As a cluster, therefore, the net effect of these four ads was to emphasize the candidate's greatest electoral weakness—his liberalism in Washington—and to downplay his greatest electoral strength—his responsiveness at home.

Two of the six ads were devoted to the responsiveness theme. The "walking" ad pictured him cooling his feet in a tub of water and talking into the camera—not talking to citizens. His "commuting" ad pictured him standing by an airline baggage claim waiting for his bag, smiling and nodding at people who remained off camera. Neither was shot against an Iowa background. And neither of them focused sharply, as Hart advised, on "how he has stayed in close touch with Iowans" or "seeking out the views of his constituents" or showed him "caring about and understanding the ordinary person." The two ads were not forceful portrayals of his home connection. Clark's television campaign was neither a dominating nor a sharply focused nor a persuasive presentation of his putative campaign message of responsiveness. As a packaged effort to carry out Hart's advice and to communicate Clark's brand of personal representation, they badly misfired.

Afterward, one of his television consultants acknowledged the failure: "The idea of 'keeping in touch' was put forward, but in my estimation, *not* with sufficient strength. . . . We might have made a mistake in not using our media more effectively to convey that story. . . . We should have had our media emphasize the fact that Senator Clark has kept in touch with Iowa and this is the evidence. We should have shown him in What Cheer, meeting with constituents." If Clark was correct about the strength of his accessibility, then it was certainly not highlighted or reinforced by the story his television commercials told.

Again, the contrast with the Tsongas campaign is striking. Tsongas's television message was markedly consistent with his presumed personal strengths. Clark's was not. Michael Kaye Associates was as distinguished in the political advertising field as Peter Hart was in the field of political polling. But the two did not operate on the same wavelength. Dick Clark did not have the kind of steeped-in-the-context, close-to-the-candidate quality campaign team that Tsongas had. All in all, Clark's television campaign seems to have been markedly inappropriate and ineffective.

If his TV campaign failed to hit hard on the accessibility-responsiveness theme, then the burden of carrying that theme rested heavily on the campaigning candidate. But the candidate was deliberately conducting a low-key campaign and relying on the free media to convey his I'm-in-touch message to the electorate. Beyond that, in keeping with his background as a get-out-the-vote organizer, he was relying heavily on the Democratic party's voter identification program and its election day organization to produce voters at the polls. The only memorable campaign speech I heard Clark give was his detailed and technically oriented reminiscences about his early successes in election day organization—to a small group of hard-core Blackhawk County Democrats. Apparently, that did not work. And many Democrats blamed the depressed 1978 turnout directly on the low-key campaign of their Senate candidate.[26]

When I asked a close adviser afterward, "If you knew then what you know now, would you have done anything differently?" he answered, "I would attack Jepsen. I would face up to the pro-lifers directly as radicals who are persecuting Dick Clark. Overall, I would raise the emotional level of the campaign and give our supporters a reason to go out and vote. It was our supporters who didn't turn out. They thought everything was going so well, they didn't have to. After all, the press told them it was all over." "Could you have persuaded your candidate to run such a campaign?" I asked. "That would have been hard," he said. "We ran an unemotional, positive kind of campaign because that's the kind of guy Dick Clark is." For Clark, campaigning simply did not involve a high emotional content. In addition to context, campaign team, and campaign dynamics, there is always the influence of the *candidate*—in this case, a steadfast liberal with a preference for a low-key strategy.[27]

We might wonder, moreover, if Clark was as well connected at home as he believed. If he was, how could he have remained so unaware of the marked Iowa mood swing he emphasized afterward? Why was he content to let his television campaign so underplay his accessibility at home? Why did he conduct the punchless, good government campaign I saw and others described? Why did he predict more constituent disaffection in Iowa's rural areas, where his support held up, than in its Catholic areas, where it did not? Finally, does it help us to answer these questions about the accuracy of Clark's perceptions to note that, despite his campaign put-down of politicians who did not like to go home, Clark himself did not go home again? He has lived in Washington—not Iowa—ever since his defeat.[28] Did the Iowa voters sense this lack of a strong attachment to home?

Comparing challenger and incumbent campaigns, we are led to speculate whether former challengers like Clark might not have to adopt a changed campaign outlook once they become incumbents. Challengers like Dick Leone and Paul Tsongas, it was said, need to negotiate a threshold constituency fit in terms of name recognition and qualification. But another kind or another quality of connection might be called for when the incumbent first runs for reelection. Put differently, it is possible that a challenger's victory, despite the "visibility advantage" it bestows, provides only the most tenuous of citizen connections. And it may be tempting for the incumbent to overestimate the durability of those connections.

I will have more to say about this intercampaign dynamic later. For now, the moral is clear: No matter how well you did in your first campaign, run hard and run scared in your second campaign. Senate incumbent Dick Clark did not.

JOHN CULVER, IOWA, 1979

Two Styles, Two Constituencies

With first-term Senator John Culver facing reelection two years

later, I wondered how, if at all, his campaign might be affected by
the Clark campaign. Would one candidate learn anything from
having observed the failure of another candidate? Constant
factors like statewide constituency, party, and ideology would
create conditions favorable to such observational learning. Yet
variable factors, like electoral context and personal style, would
create conditions that constrained learning. So how much and
what kind of intercampaign learning would take place? How
would John Culver interpret the defeat of his former aide and
friend, Dick Clark? And how, if at all, would Culver's campaign
be affected by that interpretation?

When I met Culver in the fall of 1979, I did not have to wait
long to satisfy my initial curiosity. Yes, indeed, the Clark defeat
had affected candidate Culver. The senator's lengthy answer
to my very first question, "How's it going?" made that much
amply clear. "When Dick Clark was defeated, the party was in
shock," he said.

> There was even disbelief. The party was demoralized. There were
> a lot of guilt feelings; people felt they hadn't done enough. And
> there was a lot of pessimism about the future. Clark and Culver
> were Tweedledee and Tweedledum. Now that Clark has gotten it,
> Culver's next. Culver is vulnerable. The media people crowded
> around asking me if I was going to run. Frankly, if Dick Clark had
> won, I would not necessarily have run again. But with Clark's
> defeat, I felt I had to run. As I began to think about it, it seemed
> that my job was to get out in the state and change the psychology
> of the thing.... And I thought that my personality, my style, my
> chemistry was right for the job. I could energize the party people.
> I could do the exhortation that was necessary to ... rechannel
> the thinking of the party, the media, the opposition and change
> the dialogue. One of the things the Clark campaign lacked was
> intensity, a depth of commitment. People like Dick Clark. But his
> support was a mile wide and an inch deep. In January, we started
> going around the state, hitting hard on the theme that we could
> win and rallying the elements of the old liberal coalition, making
> the party activists optimistic and getting them committed.

His lengthy answer suggested several effects. The Clark

defeat had, for the time being at least, foreclosed Culver's career choices. More than likely, it also reminded Culver of the need to run scared. Almost certainly, the defeat had given a thrust and a rationale to Culver's early campaign activity. And, surely, it had provided him with an example to learn from—as indicated by his brief references to the absence of intensity and commitment in the Clark campaign.

One stimulus Culver did *not* get from the Clark defeat was the "personality," "style," and "chemistry" of which he spoke. In Culver's speech to the United Auto Workers mentioned in the introduction, we caught a glimpse of what those attributes might be—energy, aggressiveness, and passion. Culver's high-intensity campaign style was very different from Clark's. It was genuinely his and was in no sense adopted in response to Clark's defeat.

Because of Culver's campaign style, it is impossible to determine how much his campaign behavior was influenced by the Clark defeat and how much it was simply a matter of doing what came naturally to him. He certainly criticized the Clark campaign and he certainly behaved differently, but it is difficult to untangle the causal relationship. The Clark defeat may only have reinforced Culver's stylistic preferences. In which case, the Clark campaign— and Culver's interpretive assessment of it—probably encouraged Culver to turn his stylistic preferences into strategic behavior as well.

Culver's operative critique of the Clark campaign became clearer as I watched him talk to Democratic-leaning groups of Iowans during our first day together. For he sought "commitment" with "intensity." It was not commitment to the party he sought, but commitment to his candidacy based on a shared interest in public policy. Culver presented himself as a person of strong policy views seeking policy-based support. In that respect, he closely resembled Paul Tsongas. So it is not surprising that Tsongas spontaneously named John Culver and Jacob Javits (R/N.Y.) as the two senators he most admired.

In the morning, Culver exhorted a group of teachers.

I remember when teachers were second-class citizens. I know how far you've come. And I've supported you all the way. No one has a better record on education in the United States Congress than I do—100 percent. But I'm not going to be around in a couple of years unless people like you get off their tails, stop sitting around saying "Isn't it terrible," and get to work. The people who disagree with you will work against me because they know my record.... They say they'll take care of you. Oh, you bet they'll take care of you! They're just dying to take care of you!.... If you don't see your own self-interest, then you're hopeless. Frankly, the teachers have been a disappointment thus far. I need your help. I don't want your money.... I want your time and your commitment. You know what my record is.... You should organize your block, talk to your friends, and work.

"It was shock therapy," he said as we left.

I tried to give them a pronounced sense of urgency. We should be all right with the teachers. But they need energizing. I was trying to weld some personal bond—even with a little black coffee that made me rough, raw, aggressive, and acerbic. If we can pick up a few workers from that group, it will have been worth it.... What discourages me is the laid-back attitude.... It's time for them to show some appreciation for what I've already done and go to work.

After lunch, he solicited the same kind of policy-based "appreciation" from a student environmental group. "I am the subcommittee chairman and the author of the reauthorization of the Endangered Species Act," he told them.

I've been the leader on the Tellico Dam dispute—the snail darter. I'm the one who thinks it's important to keep this legislation on the books; and I have resisted attempts to do without it. Those people who are opposed to me know what my position is. The environmental movement needs to be informed and get its act together. You are not well organized. I've led the fight three times, but if people who agree with me sit back and think great thoughts while I get my head bloodied, I won't be back for a fourth time. If you are interested and agree with me, you should say "Thank you."[29]

In both cases, his goal was to consolidate and to exploit the special allegiance of people who shared his policy views.

In the evening, he continued on this mission by cementing relations with yet another liberal policy ally. He was guest of honor at a huge union-sponsored "appreciation dinner" celebrating his success in securing a large grant for the troubled Rath meat-packing plant. On our way in, the Clark campaign again came to mind.

> Dick Clark did a lot of things for people. But Dick Clark did not exploit the things he did. You've got to rub peoples' noses in it—not offensively—and tell them that you're the one who did it.... To do all the work and then not come to an appreciation dinner is to miss out on capping your role.... A cross section of the community will be here. I'm here to collect my chips.

On our way out he exclaimed, "That was a great political hit." And he returned to his favorite idea of "appreciation" as a constituent connection, one that created bonds of loyalty and obligation. "Rath needs the grant; you need Rath. It's as American as apple pie."

"The phase we're in now," he said, "has no master plan. It isn't as if a brain trust sat around a table and planned tactics and strategy. It's just a matter of doing what you feel comfortable doing." But these three events displayed a clear strategic pattern. He was reaching out to consolidate his natural support base, a base he could count on for extra help at election time because of what he had done for them in policy matters, both national and parochial. And he was doing it according to a strategic pattern of early-stage campaigning: "With the teachers and the students, we were trying to energize people to work in this campaign. We're doing a lot of that now, stirring up the liberal elements you have to have to win. Later, we will begin to pick targets of opportunity, target other groups, and move out to broaden the appeal."

Whether challenger or incumbent, the first campaign requirement is committed supporters. Some of these supply money.

Others supply work. Culver was prospecting for campaign workers, laying the groundwork for what he called "the long season."

At day's end, Culver formulated a proposition about campaigning that shaped his interpretation of the Clark campaign. "There's a big difference," he said, "between the people who are for you and the people who are excitedly for you; between those who will vote if they feel like it and those who say 'The only election is Culver's election.' You need as many of that group as you can get."

That is the group Culver spent most of his day negotiating with. And as he saw it, that is exactly the kind of intense, committed support Dick Clark, with "inch-deep support," did not have. Culver was articulating a crucial distinction between a strongly supportive *primary constituency* and a weakly supportive *reelection constituency*. It was the distinction John Glenn never made. It was a fundamental qualitative distinction; and Culver's concern, at this early stage, was for the *quality* of his connections to a primary constituency.

Another of the day's events—an afternoon tennis game with some well-known university coaches—prompted Culver to articulate a second proposition about the quality of his constituent connections. And it, too, prompted a comparison with the Clark campaign. After noting that he had heard reports of his upcoming tennis game throughout the day, he generalized about Iowa campaigns. "Iowa is a word-of-mouth state," he said.

> One of the ingredients I felt was missing from the Clark campaign—in addition to the intensity factor—was the one-on-one aspect.... They felt that all they had to do was come into a community, hit the media, and get out. After all, if you were on NBC News in Council Bluffs, you got the largest audience in the state. But they didn't make personal contact wherever they went. So they missed the rich relationships that help people get to know you. I don't think people get to know you on that damned tube.

Culver believed, as I suggested earlier, that Dick Clark did indeed underestimate the strength of his constituency connections. Clark certainly was "around a lot," but, in Culver's view, he mistook quantity for quality in designing his campaign strategy.

By contrasting his campaign to Clark's campaign, Culver was formulating a different view of the essential representational relationship—one that emphasized the quality of the legislator/constituent connection, not the quantity thereof. And quality meant both intensity of policy commitment and the intimacy of personal contact. He believed the Clark campaign suffered from too little commitment on the constituency side and too little personal contact on the candidate side. For Culver, it was less important that he be around a lot than it was to apply the right connective chemistry when he was around. From Culver's qualitative viewpoint, Clark's lopsided reliance on his media campaign was a strategic mistake, since media campaigns are directed at a candidate's weakest supporters and can, therefore, only create low-quality connections.

Two Contexts, Two Careers

Throughout my 1979 visit, Culver campaigned with confidence as a policy leader in the Senate. That was his self-image, and it set the tone for all his public appearances. He wanted to use his Senate accomplishments to connect with his hard-core supporters. And his travel talk was full of his private reflections on the Washington–home relationship. He expressed the hope that the overall electoral context would be more favorable for his Washington strengths than it had been six years earlier. "In 1974, I never mentioned the fact that I had served five terms in the House," he said. "The mood was not favorable to experience. Now maybe it will be. Maybe my kind of leadership and effectiveness in Washington will be back in style by 1980."

There was ample evidence at hand that Culver enjoyed a very favorable reputation in Washington. *Washingtonian* magazine had rated him one of the eight most respected Democratic senators.[30] The veteran Washington journalist Elizabeth Drew had written a lengthy, admiring series about him in the *New Yorker*. It became a book entitled, simply, *Senator*, in which his standards and his performance in the Senate were held up as a model for U.S. senators.[31] He was hoping to turn this favorable Senate reputation into a favorable Iowa reputation.

But he worried about it. For one thing, voters might not make the connection. "I'd like to see someone ask every member of the Senate to rank each senator in terms of his effectiveness and his respect among his fellow senators," he said,

> and then I'd like to have that ranking correlated with each senator's popularity rating among the people of his state. I'll bet that there is no correlation between the two. It's easy today for members to look good at home ... to thumb their noses at everything in Washington and pile up huge popularity margins at home. Yet in the Senate, they are useless.... What discourages me is that most people do not care about your leadership in the Senate. And it's so hard to communicate that to your constituents.

For another thing, people who are in a position to communicate that linkage to constituents will not do so. "The media doesn't help," he continued. "They only focus on the things that make news. Leadership doesn't make news. The media does nothing to increase respect for members of Congress. If there's one ember of confidence left, they consider it their duty to stamp it out." His was another reminder that the media does act, or can act, as the guardian of a candidate's reputation at home and, in that way, affect his or her constituency connection.

All candidates complain about the media. But the burden of each complaint has to be considered in the context of the campaign in question. Culver's complaint—that the media did not communicate his Washington reputation for leadership— reflected his felt need for electoral help beyond his hard-core supporters. The party activists, the unions, the teachers— his primary constituency—knew enough about him. It was the people in the much larger, less supportive reelection constituency that needed more information. A campaign consultant put the problem this way: "There are four groups of voters: strong incumbent supporters, weak incumbent supporters, strong challenger supporters, undecideds. The challenger will get 85 to 100 percent of the undecideds. That's a law of politics, like the law of gravity. The strong supporters will stay strong. The battleground is the *weak incumbent supporters*" (emphasis added). Culver's concern for the quality of his constituent ties had not been duplicated in a concern for their quantity.

With his weak supporters and the undecideds, John Culver was in trouble. In his March 1977 survey for Clark, Hart had found Culver ranking well below Clark in recognition (-12%), job performance (-20%), and attractiveness (-19%). Culver, Hart wrote, "is barely known to a large number of Iowa voters" and "has much work to do if he is to be a strong candidate for reelection in 1980."[32] The first Iowa Poll in April 1979 gave him a horse race lead of only 35 to 31 percent over a possible (and eventual) challenger, Congressman Charles Grassley.[33] Apparently, Culver had not made a lot of progress in the two years between 1977 and 1979 in strengthening his overall constituency ties. If, as was suggested earlier, the media is the most effective vehicle for widening constituency support, then Culver's dismay at the media's reluctance to communicate his Washington reputation to the home folks is understandable.

Now that he had returned to campaign for reelection, Culver had become quite aware of his problem. Several times during our 1979 visit, he mentioned it. "One thing I have not done since I have been in the Senate is to become well known in Iowa. I have not defined myself in the state. Perhaps it has been a misuse of my incumbency. I have a very diffuse image in the state." Or, "In five years, I haven't become enough of an established personality in the state. There isn't much warmth of identification with me." He ended his discussion of "one-on-one contact" with the comment, "I know I have a long way to go in this state. I have no illusions about that."

Culver quoted with approval a veteran party leader's

comment that "Dick Clark's support was a mile wide and an inch deep; and John Culver's support is an inch wide and a mile deep." And not surprisingly, when Clark's defeated campaigners contemplated Culver's early prospects as of 1979, they used some of the same words. One said, "Culver is the opposite of Dick. He never goes back to Iowa. He's never in the papers. He doesn't give a damn. He ran five times for the House and he's tired of going back to the district all the time. He stays in Washington.... His support is deeper than Dick's in some places.... But his support isn't as wide.... Fewer people like him than like Dick. But he can generate more emotional support than Dick."

We might wonder why a politician of this description had been able to win election to the House five times. One answer might lie in the greater constraints of the two-year term and the difference, therefore, in time horizons. When the constituency delivers a report card every two years, the legislator is encouraged to stay regularly attentive to home and to be content to develop Washington influence at a slow pace over several elections. A six-year term, by contrast, allows for lapses in attentiveness to home and encourages legislators to believe they can achieve Washington influence within a single term. In the House, senators say, you're on a much shorter leash.

But the larger point is this: In career terms, Senator Culver had made a choice in balancing a Washington career and a constituency career. He had chosen to pursue his institutional ambition—to become a respected policy player inside the Senate—at some cost to his elective office ambition. How great a cost, and how irretrievable a cost, was the question in 1979. He was hoping to catch up during his campaign. But there was little doubt that he had created a classic "out of touch" problem for himself at home, that he had not kept his constituency career in an optimal balance with his Washington career. This large vulnerability, incidentally, had gone unrecognized in Elizabeth Drew's admiring, but lopsidedly Washington-oriented, study.

My own sensitivity to his problem was stimulated by small

incidents on the trail. It struck me as odd, for example, that he would let himself be taken to the National Cattle Congress parade in my car with its New York license plates. As we left the Waterloo fairgrounds, having parked prominently near the entrance gate and having said good-bye to the parade organizers, he parodied their likely reaction. " 'He's not from Iowa,' they say. Where'd they ever get that idea? 'He's arrogant, insensitive, out of touch.' What makes them think that? Huh? 'He votes more with the East than the Midwest.' Where'd that idea come from? Huh? All I'm doing is riding around with New York plates on my car!" He was sensitive to his weakness but was not treating it seriously.

Later that day, after a game of tennis, sitting in a high school locker room swapping stories with a couple of college coaches, it struck me that former athlete Culver was much more on the fringes of the conversation than he would have been had he "been around more" and kept in touch. The coaches' stories revolved around the current prospects of various Iowa athletes; and Culver's information seemed to end at the point where he went away to college. "I think I played against him in high school," he said. Or, "Is he as good now as he was in high school?" Or, "Where did he go to college?" Culver's own stories were about freshman basketball at Harvard and his tattered hand-me-down sneakers given to him by his former Harvard roommate, Ted Kennedy. They were both enjoyable stories, but they stamped him as Harvard, not Iowa.

While the senator's locker room conversation did not seem encouraging, his attitude toward the tennis game itself gave cause for hope. He had limped into the locker room with a bloody knee and elbow from a tumble on the asphalt surface. "I'm mortally wounded," he said. "But I made the shot! Just as I was going to fall, I reached out and, wham, I hit the ball right past Jim for a winner. I figured if I was going to do down, I would go in glory." The attitude was authentic Culver. But whether, in 1980, he would "make the shot" or "go down in glory" remained to be seen.

JOHN CULVER, IOWA, 1980

Campaign Plan

For incumbent senators, "campaigning" can go on throughout the six-year interelection period. But "the campaign," or "the short campaign," typically gets acknowledged when the challenger becomes known. When I traveled with Culver in September 1979, he not only did not know who his opponent might be, he openly speculated that his eventual challenger, Congressman Charles Grassley, might decide not to run. He was campaigning without a plan, doing whatever "felt comfortable." When I returned to Iowa in September 1980, Culver was fully engaged in an electoral battle with Grassley, who had won the Republican nomination in a June primary. And he spoke more purposefully about the stage he was in. "For the last sixty days, we've been campaigning hard, night and day," he said. "Really, we've been campaigning hard for twenty-two months. But it wasn't till after the Republican primary when we knew who our opponent was going to be that we could know what we had to do and focus on a plan."

Culver's campaign plan was the exact opposite of Dick Clark's. Almost everything Culver did was calculated to raise the intensity, sharpen the differences, increase the visibility, and magnify the stakes of the campaign. As much as Clark's low-key, personal style helped to shape his strategic preference, John Culver's high-octane, high-decibel personal style helped shape his strategy. As much as the Clark campaign had been low profile and media centered, the Culver campaign would be high profile and candidate centered. In presentational style, it was the difference between a rumpled, pipe-smoking former professor and a sweaty, pile-driving former fullback and marine. Culver in action displayed passion and competitiveness. In Washington, his admirers described him as "principled" and "courageous." His opponents called him "pugnacious" and "combative."[34] It was a forceful personal style that was better tailored to attract quality than quantity of support.

On the trail in 1980, his public presentations blended three themes. His central campaign message was a policy message.[35] He described the contest as "a classic race" between a conservative and "a liberal who won't back down from his views." "Nowhere in the country is there a clearer choice.... I invite you to compare our records." He regularly cited his differences with Grassley on a whole range of domestic policy issues—fuel for the elderly poor, windfall profits for big oil companies, food stamps, fair housing, toxic substances, soil conservation, wildlife protection. Culver explained,

> We had researched his record and we knew that, if we were going to win, we would have to take the fight to him on the issues— that we would have to make his record the main issue of the campaign. So we prepared a set of detailed papers on several of the key issues ... comparing my position and Grassley's, about a half-dozen in all. Two weeks after the Republican primary, we started around the state, meeting with the media people and explaining the material in the issue papers.

Basically, Culver was staking his election on his policy record. Second, as support for his policy message and his policy record, Culver sought to distinguish himself from Grassley in terms of legislative competence and potential for leadership in Washington. Culver's argument was that Grassley could not match his legislative accomplishments or the respect of his colleagues. But he made it implicitly, not directly. "It's not just how you vote. It's the ability to do the work in Washington. What is your demonstrated ability to convince others." "There are a lot of bumps on a log down there. The question is, Who can persuade fifty other senators to do what he wants them to do?" He did not have a high opinion of his opponent's legislative accomplishments. And he was putting into operation his belief—or hope—that leadership in the Senate ought to count for something at home.

Third, Culver waged a frontal assault on the New Right, conservative groups, which had targeted him for defeat.[36] He described such groups as the National Conservative Political

Action Committee (NCPAC) and Christian Voice as "radicals working outside the system," as "outside hate groups" that are "poisoning the political atmosphere." And he told his audiences that "this is one target who is going to shoot back." Culver knew that he would face the same strong anti-abortion opponents that damaged Dick Clark. And his strategy was the one Clark's campaigners said they would have adopted if they had it to do over again. He sought to attack and isolate the leaders as radicals, then appeal to the moderate instincts of rank-and-file anti-abortion sympathizers to support him on the basis of his overall policy record.

"By taking on the New Right," he explained, "we are shaking up the apathetic majority they feed on. And by shaking up the majority, sharpening the issues, increasing the intensity of the campaign, we have gotten people thinking about the campaign." By energizing the general electorate, he believed he would at least help to avoid the low turnout problem that many party people had blamed for Clark's defeat. But he hoped it would also help him reach the broad electorate, to bring to his side many "decent, fair-minded, tolerant, and moderate" Iowans "who had never voted for extremes."

Whereas Clark thought of his constituency strengths in terms of *personal representation*, Culver thought of his constituency strengths in terms of *policy representation*. He saw himself as a person of strong convictions about what was best for the country and for Iowa, as a person who fought for his views and was willing to live or die by them. When Dick Clark lost, Culver recalled, "The media began to ask if I was going to change. I told them, hell no, I'm not going to change! I've been in Congress for fifteen years. I'm proud of my record and I'm going to run on that record. If I lose doing it that way, then I'll be comfortable with that. But I'm not going to change."

On the trail, his travel talk was loaded with similar sentiments. After he had been interviewed by one national reporter, he exploded.

Since when have the media become so cynical that they no longer believe people go into public service because of the ideas and values they believe in—that they work hard to enact policies embodying those ideas and values, that they win some and lose some. I don't mean to be self-serving, but whatever became of the notion that people go into public life because they believe in certain things and fight for them?

Later that day he picked up the thread.

I don't mean to sound noble in any silly-assed way, but I'd a hell of a lot rather fight for my beliefs than whore around. I'm not so naive as to believe that most politicians feel this way. But shouldn't that be the standard? I'm a lot more concerned about what my grandchildren and great-grandchildren will think about what I did. I want them to be able to say, "There was a son of a bitch who stood for something and fought for something—in good times and bad."

This was John Culver's self-image—policy-oriented, consistent in his policy beliefs, and seeking reelection largely on that basis. This persona accounted for his great strength within his activist primary constituency. It raised anew, however, the question of his ability to negotiate enough additional support in the wider electorate.

Campaign Dynamic

When I arrived in September, answers to "How's it going?" were upbeat. The week before, Culver had pulled even with Grassley in the Iowa Poll, after a summer in which he had trailed by as much as seventeen points.[37] The first event of my trip was the initial Culver–Grassley debate. Culver used all three of his themes to such good effect that the first edition of the *Des Moines Register* carried the headline, "Culver Puts Grassley on Defensive in Debate." Recalling his summertime travels peddling his issue papers, Culver exclaimed, "We had all that substantive stuff marinating in the state. We are now in a position to control the dialogue, to set the terms of the debate, to talk about our issues and not be on the defensive.... More than any other campaign I've ever been in, we have had a thematic, rational strategy."

The campaign weather report was favorable. "I know it's up for grabs," said Culver, "but it's nice to be sailing with the wind instead of bucking a head wind." And his campaign manager echoed, "The tide that had been running against us has turned and is going our way.... It's a lot easier swimming with the current."

His optimism was strengthened by the existence, now, of "a dedicated, committed campaign organization," "the best I've ever had or ever seen." The recruitment effort I had observed in 1979 was now paying off. And the qualitative comparison with the Clark campaign surfaced again. "We've been so lucky with our campaign staff," he said.

> It's like a family. Dick Clark didn't have that relationship with his staff. He was aloof. He was almost too professional, too academic.... With the unions, the auto workers, the party, the teachers, and the other elements you need, we have a much more constant and close communication than Dick Clark had. His staff didn't have the close relationship our staff has with them. People had a lot of respect for Dick Clark, but less depth of commitment than they feel for us. Dick thought that you already had the Democrats, so he reached out to others. But that was a mistake because he lost the intensity of commitment among the true believers.... He lost his foot soldiers. You can't do it with media alone, not in this state.

As he talked about the commitment of his own foot soldiers, he added to his critique of Dick Clark's campaign an idea that had not developed (or was not articulated) the year before. The idea was that every candidate needed a hard-core constituency that would battle through thick and thin *because* when trouble came to a campaign, as it inevitably would, these were the supporters you would need to weather the storm. And these were the very kind of supporters Clark did not have. "That was the trouble with Dick Clark's campaign," he told a fund-raising group. "It lacked intensity, passion. So when the negative stuff came, it blew him away."

As we left a small-town picnic of his strong supporters, Culver again noted that "Dick Clark did none of this in 1978." And he developed his broadest interpretation of the Clark campaign.

In some ways, the Clark campaign failed because it was so exquisitely rational. It was laid out as scientifically as you can do it with the use of polls, the analysis of the issues, and the knowledge of the media markets. Dick's idea was to hit all the media markets in the state, to get into town and out again as fast as he could, just so long as he got on the media.... So there was no people-to-people contact, no word-of-mouth politics.... In fairness to Dick, he thought he was ahead. And maybe he thought you didn't need anything except media. Which was ironic, because he won in 1972 because of the walk. He got media from the walk because it was people-to-people politics.... I think you can be too rational about politics.... There is an important place for passion, for personality, for personal chemistry between the candidate and his supporters. Dick Clark didn't have that intense communion with people. And that's why, when he came under attack, there were no people to fight back on his behalf.

Culver never made it clear just what it was that Clark's supporters might have done to fight back. But he did express an inordinate degree of confidence in the capabilities of his organization. And he believed that a quality campaign organization could prepare and defend him against the kind of attack that blindsided Clark.

"In my opinion, the greatest strength we have in this campaign is our organization," he said.

Pretty soon this whole thing is going to grab hold, and when it does, our people will be ready. You've got to have a plan, but you've also got to have the people in the trenches to carry out the plan.... You need a plan so that when things go bad, you have something to fall back on.... You know you will make mistakes.... [But] campaigns are won by people who make the least mistakes and who can repair them once they are made. That's where a good campaign organization comes in. If we win, our organization will have been very important, if not decisive.

By all the qualitative measures of support, John Culver believed he was running a more effective campaign than Dick Clark. In keeping with his emphasis on the quality of his relations with his strongest supporters, his was an organizationally intensive campaign.

Reelection Constituency

Culver's electoral problem, as he acknowledged from the outset, was to reach beyond those people "for whom the only election is Culver's election" to a broad reelection constituency made up of weak supporters and undecided voters. Quality alone was not enough; he needed quantity. Stanley Kelley has suggested that "all campaigns can fruitfully be viewed as a *set* of campaigns." And he distinguishes between campaigns aimed at "the mass public" and those aimed at "more limited constituencies."[38] In that vein, I distinguish between the primary constituency campaigns and the reelection constituency campaigns of incumbent candidates. John Culver's problem centered on the latter.

Within his reelection constituency, the target of opportunity Culver most often talked about during my visit was the 35 percent of the Republicans who had supported the more moderate candidate, Tom Stoner, in their primary. That was the group he hoped to attract by associating Grassley with the New Right. "The group to watch are the moderate Republicans," he said. "They don't like extremism. A lot of them are going to say that they can't vote for Culver the liberal, but they may vote for me if they see me as a decent, reasonable person—as an alternative to the New Right. I think the Stoner vote may come over to us in time. I see signs of it, in the poll, in what people say. It could be a key development."

Early in the first debate, Culver reached for their support by describing his "record of achievement and accomplishment that's very much in the mainstream of the progressive tradition of our state." "I submit that it is Congressman Grassley who is really out of step and, frankly, it's because he identifies with a very ultraconservative, radical wing of the Republican party."

After the debate, he specifically mentioned pro-choice Republican women. "Two nights ago, we had a real good meeting sponsored by twenty-one women's groups. A lot of Republicans came. The people there were mostly Republicans. I was relaxed. My talk went well. Then there were five-hundred women at their conference the next morning." He was optimistic about winning their reelection support.

At the same time, his travel talk revealed his difficulties within larger segments of his prospective reelection constituency. "The Iowa Poll did a break-out on our strengths and weaknesses," he reported, "and we did pretty well in all groups. The only place where we were weak was among the farmers." Despite good prices, he continued, farmers "are still complaining." And he told a story. "Don't quote me on this, but one old farmer asked me the other day, 'Do you know how you can tell whether a baby is going to be a farmer? He's the one who cries before you hit him.' That's just about it. But if you quote me on that, I'm dead." Unlike Dick Clark, Culver did not sit on the Agriculture Committee. And he admitted, "One group I've never felt quite comfortable talking to are the farmers." This sense of distance had to be a not inconsiderable problem in a major farm state.

The farm and rural vote that Culver understood the least was in the western part of the state, the part most distant from his old congressional base in eastern Iowa. "Western Iowa is different from eastern Iowa," he explained as we rode west one day.

Farming is different—more cattle, less cash grain crops. There is no major university in western Iowa and no large medical facility. Western Iowa feels a little like a stepchild. The hold of the *Des Moines Register* there is tenuous. Council Bluffs is more oriented

toward Omaha and the conservative *World Herald*. Sioux City
... is more oriented toward South Dakota and Sioux Falls. So
western Iowa has taken some learning for me.

Whatever normal problems Culver might have had connecting
with the farmers of his state would surely be exacerbated in a
region where people had feelings of inferiority.

Chuck Grassley, in contrast, was a farmer. Not surprisingly,
he understood Culver's lack of strong, close identification
with large numbers of Iowans. And his opening salvo in their
debate produced the sharpest contrast to Culver's emphasis
on his Washington accomplishments. Grassley emphasized his
understanding of the problems of Iowans, because, he said, "I
have been on the job with them." He continued,

> John has none of this [understanding] for, other than being an
> attorney for a short time, John has not worked in Iowa in his adult
> life. There's an old Indian saying, "To really understand a person,
> you must walk in his moccasins." As a farmer, I've overcome the
> perils of hail, drought, embargoes, and inflation. As an assembly
> line worker for ten years, I worked to supplement my farm
> income, attending union meetings, being on strike, being laid off,
> and standing in unemployment lines because of factory closings.
> I taught school at half pay because there was not enough money
> for full pay. I have been there, as many Iowans have. Because
> of our background differences, John and I differ dramatically on
> how we vote.... The record shows that I voted on the side of the
> majority of Iowans and John is on the side of New York City and
> the Washington bureaucrats.

It was a classic "I am one of you" appeal for broad support. It
gave him an underpinning for his policy record: "I voted as you
would have voted." It was a presentation of self Culver could
not match.

Grassley pushed his advantage in his television campaign.
In a quiz show, push-the-right-button format, he asked the
questions: which candidate had been a farmer, a teacher, a
factory worker, had never missed a vote, had never gone
on a junket. The quiz show format was used to further

underline Grassley's "I'm in touch, he's out of touch" theme
by challenging specific Culver votes—for the congressional
pay raise, for the New York City bailout, and against ending
the grain embargo. By posing mismatches between Culver
statements and votes, the challenger exploited Culver's weak
identification. It begins with the satirical "Fighting John Culver
is at it again." And it ends, "In Iowa, he says he's for it;
in Washington, he votes against it. Where does John Culver
stand?"

In his pro-farmer commercial, Grassley stands first in front
of a house with a sign reading Member, Farm Bureau, Charles
Grassley and then in a field with a farmer's cap on while a
list of five agricultural accomplishments scrolls up the screen.
In sharp contrast, Culver's pro-farmer ad consisted of a series
of boilerplate testimonials by farmers describing the senator
as a "fighter," but without mentioning specific pro-farmer
accomplishments and without Culver on the scene.[39]

Just before I left the campaign trail, Culver talked about his
own television strategy.

> The challenge now is what to do in the next sixty days. What
> should we do with our media campaign? Now that the wind is
> at our back, should we let out all the sails or should we tack?
> Should we be positive in our media [campaign] or negative?
> Should we stay on the attack now that we are even in the polls?
> When you're ten points down, you have to attack. But maybe we
> should be more positive now. I've always believed in the positive.
> But I'm afraid that people are so cynical now and so used to
> negative campaigns that their tolerance for negative campaigns
> has become very high.

He could not decide what to do. But the decision was important
to his campaign for a reelection constituency. If, that is, he saw
television as the only way he could reach weak supporters and
undecided voters.

Culver's television campaign was a conventional mixture of
pro-incumbent testimonials (including one on Elizabeth Drew's
book) and attacks on the voting record of his opponent. He used

Grassley votes for tax breaks for oil and gas and against home heating assistance to paint his opponent as a special interest, anti-elderly politician. And, later, he adopted Grassley's quiz show format to attack these and other votes—with the message that Grassley was more interested in helping the well-off than the less well-off. His tag line was, "A fighter for Iowa and for you" or "A senator who fights for Iowans."

It is not possible to say anything definitive about the impact of his ads. But, on viewing the two full sets of commercials, two professional observers agreed unreservedly that Grassley's ads were "more aggressive," "stronger," "more vigorous," "faster-paced," and altogether "superior" to Culver's.[40] Culver's negative ads were not strongly negative. They were comparison ads, not attack ads. And his positive ads did not emphasize his accomplishments. They did nothing to convey or to complement the forceful, leadership aspects of Culver's political persona.

Near the end, Culver chose not to launch a more strongly negative, attack-style campaign against his opponent. On October 12, Culver pulled ahead in the Iowa Poll.[41] "And that," said one aide, "was when Culver made the decision: no negative ads." Another top campaigner elaborated. "Two weeks before election day, Culver said that there would be no negative ads. Grassley spent $200,000 on negative ads the last two weeks, calling John a liberal spender. They hurt John. Grassley's pollster said that we were ahead until those last two weeks. And he said they were ahead by the weekend before the election."

The ad in question was a jigsaw puzzle, the pieces of which gradually formed Culver's face, as a series of charges were leveled against him: twenty-two votes to raise the debt limit, a vote for the largest tax increase in history, votes against foreign aid cuts, and six years of support of all spending bills. When the puzzle was complete, Culver was called "the biggest spender in Washington—of your money." "I'm sure the image of big spender was a factor," Culver said afterward. "When Grassley got behind in the polls, he put on a series of very effective negative spots. And we went down a little in the polls."

Still, he continued, "the polls continued to be good until the last weekend when the [Iowa Poll] dipped and had us four points down.... Even with that news, I thought we would win. I knew we had the organization to get out our vote." "We never used any negative ads," said his campaign manager, "because our polls showed the positive stuff was working so well." His final commercials were informal interviews with Culver, alone or with his wife. To the end, the incumbent's television campaign was more pro-Culver than anti-Grassley. But from a distance, at least, it seemed uninspired, and uninspiring and unlikely to attract adherents he did not already have.

Post Mortems

John Culver lost his reelection bid by 54 to 46 percent. Again, it is not my intention to explain an election outcome. But the Culver campaign was not like the Clark campaign. Candidate campaigns, we might speculate, establish the framework for accountability. Dick Clark's low-key campaign, when coupled with his opponents' late-breaking, low-visibility campaign depressed his accountability to the voters. The two campaigns combined to deprive the citizenry of the opportunity to hear and to choose between two strong and positive candidate appeals. John Culver was defeated, too; but his campaign and that of his opponent combined to enhance his accountability. Each candidate argued his best case vigorously and fully; and, in open combat, they clarified their differences. More than in the Clark case, Iowa's voters would know who and what they were voting for. Neither Culver nor any of his campaigners nor the media blamed his campaign for his defeat. The consensus was that he ran a strong campaign, that he made himself fully accountable to his constituents.

Culver's view of the outcome was that his collapse at the end was heavily influenced by President Jimmy Carter's simultaneous collapse at the head of the Democratic ticket. "From the time you left," he told me afterward, "the campaign continued upward so that I thought we were going to win. The polls continued to be good until the last weekend ... when the *Register* had us four points down.... Even with that dip, I thought we would win. I knew we had the organization to get out our vote.... What can you say? We didn't make any mistakes. He seemed to be stumbling around. The last minute suction—the hostages, the Reagan thing—turned it all around. That's about it."

A team member agreed. "The main thing was that people wanted a change. I don't think there is any way we could have won it. After all, the difference was 100,000 votes and eight percentage points." These electoral context explanations are buttressed by the large contingent of liberal Democratic senators that went down to defeat in the same election.

Some Senate liberals did survive the Reagan tide, however. And from the perspective of sequential campaigns, the outcome was dependent on candidate as well as context. That is, some of Culver's own shortcomings limited the effectiveness of his campaign and could, therefore, be studied with profit by later campaigners.

The reluctance to go negative may be one. This was the only campaign decision that got second-guessed afterward. "I was one of those," said another top aide, "who said we should have hit back hard with negative media. [But] we stayed with soft, positive stuff because we were ahead. Grassley kept hitting us, hitting us hard."

Grassley's negative ads appear more negative, more assertive, and altogether more persuasive than anything Culver had in his repertoire. If Culver learned by watching the Clark campaign that candidates need a strongly supportive constituency, the lesson he did not learn was the power of last-minute negative campaigning to attract a weakly supportive and indecisive constituency. To the degree that Grassley did overtake Culver at the end, Culver may have suffered the very fate he thought he could avoid by campaigning differently from Clark—that is, the lack of residual constituency support when the opposition turned up the heat. He was not blindsided like Clark was. He simply chose to rely on the strength of his qualitatively stronger support base and his organization. And they couldn't save him.

Culver's five-year failure to lay the groundwork for a campaign among his reelection constituency is another of his shortcomings. "Most people believe we lost it in the last week of the campaign," said one top aide, "but [our pollster] Peter Hart disagrees. He says we lost it in the first three and a half years—that Culver failed to make any impression. The Iowa Polls on job performance consistently said 40 percent good job, 12 percent poor job, 48 percent no opinion. They never changed."[42] In this view, the campaign registered the negotiating failures of his constituency career.

There is evidence of candidate weakness in the election results. Recalling his lack of familiarity with western Iowa, we can note, for example, that he failed to carry a single county in the western one-third of the state. And he did not do as well as Clark in this respect. (See figs. 4.1, 4.2.) Recalling Culver's insecurity in dealing with farmers, we should note that the final Iowa Poll showed him trailing 68 to 31 among farmers.[43] And a Democratic postelection analysis of support among a number of broad voter groups indicated that the greatest slippage between Clark's and Culver's support levels (from Clark's 43% to Culver's 34%) came among farmers.[44]

The final Iowa Poll also showed Culver trailing Grassley 61 to 36 in small towns.[45] And a postelection county-by-county analysis showed that Culver suffered his second greatest loss of support, from his own 1974 totals, in Iowa's "most rural counties."[46] Again, Clark had done marginally better in both these categories.[47] Culver understood all this well. "As near as I can tell," he said in our postmortem conversation, "it was the sons of bitchin' rural vote that turned out in force; and that is poison to me. You just look at all those little towns—1,000 votes, 2,000 votes, 3,000 votes. They killed me."

Compared either with Culver's 1974 performance or with

Dick Clark's 1978 performance, Culver's support among Catholic voters registered the same slippage as the farm-rural vote.[48] It indicated the failure of his effort to attract support among pro-life sympathizers. And, in this respect, Culver's own postmortem reflections pointed up the limitations of his strongly supportive hard core. In bellwether Catholic areas, he had effective organization. But it was not enough.

> In Dubuque, we had the mayor, who is a nun, and other Catholic leaders taking out newspaper ads that urged people to take my entire record into account—not just abortion. And I went in there—it was my old district—and campaigned on that theme. Dick Clark stayed away from Dubuque and never had that kind of support. I did better than he did, but in no way commensurate with the difference in our campaigns. In Carroll County, three of the top leaders in the community, the Democratic leaders worked for me from the first day of the campaign. They never turned a finger for Dick Clark. For me they swallowed hard and took the whole package.... Dick Clark never got that kind of community help. Yet he carried the county and I lost it. How do you explain it?

Mile-deep support helped Culver, and milewide support helped Clark. Neither was sufficient.

In sum, Culver failed to make a strong enough connection with those constituents who were positioned beyond his strongest supporters. Indeed, with rural-farm and Catholic voters in the reelection constituency, Clark did better than Culver. And it was more a six-year failure than a campaign failure.

To make matters worse, Culver's weakness was his opponent's strength. As a farmer-congressman, Grassley enjoyed an ease of identification with his prospective reelection constituency. "The root of Grassley's political strength," says one observer, "is that Iowans view him as one of them, which he is."[49] And an Iowa Democratic leader recalled that Grassley had succeeded in framing the contest in exactly those terms—terms least favorable to Culver. Grassley, she said, "hammered to death the idea that John was not an Iowan and didn't care about folks there. He hit a nerve, because some people thought there was a grain of truth to it."[50] For the broad Iowa reelection constituency, it was Grassley, not Culver, who controlled the campaign dialogue. An intriguing indicator that Culver and Clark may have shared a debilitating constituency weakness is the fact that Culver, like Clark, never returned home from Washington to live in Iowa.

In the final analysis, Culver's institutional ambition may have been stronger than his electoral ambition. For four or five years, it seems, his personal goal was to become a respected policy player in the Senate. He achieved that goal. But the price he paid was neglect of his reelection goal. He knew he had to catch up if he was to achieve that goal. And he hoped that his Washington achievement would contribute substantially to his achievement in Iowa. It didn't.

Ironically, it may even have hurt. Trying to explain what happened at the end, Culver said,

> When people got into the booth, the desire to protest took over. If you want to vote against the leadership of the country, if you want to kick them all out, then vote against the president and the senator. By the time they get to the congressmen, the feeling is, "There's old Joe, he's not to blame!" So the congressmen all survive. If I had been a congressman, I would have survived, no doubt about it. But if you're a senator, you are up there in the leadership with your ass sticking up in the air, waiting for lightning to strike.

If, indeed, people voted against him because they saw him as part of the leadership, he had been campaigning in double jeopardy. Not only did he not get any credit for his Washington reputation but he got punished for it as well. He remarked afterward, as he had earlier on, how unhelpful the local media had been in their conception of Congress. "Nothing," he said, "was more frustrating than to deal with the press people at home, to get through that ignorance, to filter through their ignorance to get to the people."

Institutional accomplishment—at least with the broad reelection constituency—looks like a very unlikely substitute for carefully cultivated home connections. An over-the-shoulder look at the Clark and Culver campaigns indicates that constituency connections need to be both more than an inch deep and an inch wide. And representational relationships probably need to have both personal and policy dimensions. Furthermore, these balances will have to be negotiated during both the six-year term and the actual campaign.

TOM HARKIN, IOWA, 1984

Four years after Culver's defeat, five-term Iowa Congressman Tom Harkin—a protypical quality challenger—decided to run against the man who had defeated Dick Clark. And just as Culver had critiqued the Clark campaign, I assumed Harkin would take a similar interpretive interest in the Clark and Culver campaigns.

No sooner had I arrived in Iowa than Harkin's campaign manager said, "The first thing Tom did after he announced his candidacy was to go see Dick Clark and John Culver and have long talks with them. What did you do? What didn't you do that you should have done? What can I expect? He went to school with Clark and Culver." If we are going to think of Harkin as a quality challenger, we must include, among his resources, the accumulation of information he received from his two defeated Democratic predecessors.

As we might expect, Harkin's working assessment of the two preceding campaigns reflected his assessment of his own situation. From Clark's failure, he learned the need to counteract negative campaigning. From Culver's failure, he learned the need for more encompassing constituent support. And he believed that he brought distinctive resources of background and support that would make his campaign different from the two preceding ones.

As a challenger, he was particularly interested in the confrontational dynamics of the Clark campaign, about which he had strong opinions. "There is absolutely no way Dick Clark should have lost that campaign," exclaimed Harkin. "He ran a poor campaign, a complacent campaign. He could have clobbered Roger Jepsen if he had hit at him and hit at him. But he didn't. And so he lost."

When I arrived in Iowa in 1984, Harkin and his opponent were trading negative commercials in now-familiar rapid-fire, point-counterpoint fashion. The exchange was described by journalistic observers as "a nasty fight, bitter and personal," and as "uncommonly negative for clean politics Iowa."[51] "We didn't know about negative campaigning when Dick Clark ran," said Harkin. "We had not had any experience with it at that time. Dick Clark didn't expect negative campaigning and didn't know how to handle it. I can take it and I can give it back." Which he did, to the very last week, with a very negative "Isn't it time to close the book on Roger Jepsen?" ad. Looking back to 1980, one Harkin aide recalled, "Grassley turned up the heat and made Culver the issue [at the end]. And that's what we did. We made Jepsen the issue."

Moreover, Harkin believed that his Catholic background put him in a much stronger position than either of the others on the question of abortion—an issue that had hurt the two strongly pro-choice candidates, Clark and Culver. Though Harkin's position was no different from theirs, he said,

> I think I know how to talk about it, because I know how Catholics think about it and what worries them. They did not think Dick Clark or John Culver cared one bit about the issue.... With me, they'll say, "that kid went through parochial schools, we know what he's been taught, we know how he thinks—he can't be in favor of abortion." The reason I'm going to carry [the Catholic city of] Dubuque, which neither Clark nor Culver could carry, is because they will say "he is one of us" and give me the benefit of the doubt.

Harkin seemed to agree with Culver's assessment that he had a quality campaign team and Clark did not. "I have a stronger

organization than Dick Clark ever had," said Harkin. "Not better than Culver. He had a good organization. But better than
Clark." His critique of the Culver campaign focused, instead,
on matters of strategy and personal style. And it reinforced the
idea that candidate Culver had, indeed, been a factor in his own
defeat.

> Traditionally, the Democrats have campaigned statewide by
> establishing a base in the east and then coming out to western
> Iowa. And western Iowa has been the Achilles heel of the
> Democrats. John Culver's base ... was concentrated in eastern
> Iowa.... He got 40 percent of the vote in my district. I got 60
> percent. My base is western Iowa—in the most conservative,
> most Republican district in the state. I thought that if I could
> establish my base of support in the west and then move east
> into the traditional Democratic strongholds, I could win. It's a
> strategy that has seldom been tried.

He continued.

> Traditionally, Democrats had concentrated their campaigns in
> the cities. They did not pay as much attention to the rural areas
> as they should.... I thought I had the time to campaign in the
> rural areas and that I knew how to campaign in the rural areas.
> I spent all of last year and most of this year campaigning ... in
> every Timbuktu town in Iowa. We would go into a town, go to
> the cafe for a couple of hours and talk, visit with the banker,
> have our pictures taken with him, and then go around to the
> newspaper.... Dick Clark knew how to campaign in a rural area,
> but John Culver did not. It takes time and he didn't take the time.
> He campaigned in the cities. We spent a year and a half staying
> away from the cities.

During my late October visit, Harkin's campaign manager
added, "We have given special emphasis to agricultural
policy—against the background of a rural strategy.... Right
now [in the polls] we are tied [with Jepsen] among the farmers.
Can you imagine being that close? If we break even with the
farmers, we'll win."

What Harkin learned from the Culver campaign was the
need for a different strategy. What he did not learn, but had

available to him, was the ability to implement the strategy. With his attention to farmers and small towns, Harkin was building into his campaign the very kind of reach to a broad reelection constituency that Culver lacked. Explaining his "rural strategy" to reporters, Harkin commented, "We all farm in Iowa. One way or another, we all farm. We either farm directly or we farm the farmer."[52]

A campaigner who served on both Culver's and Harkin's teams combined strategy and personality in comparing the two candidates.

> We began by going to every small town in Iowa so people could see Tom Harkin as a man, not as a politician. We wanted them to get to know him, to feel that he is one of us. His district is rural, and Tom is comfortable in the rural areas. John Culver was not. . . . Tom can go into a cafe and sit for two hours just talking with people. It wasn't that Culver didn't like these people; he would just get tired of small talk. He'd want to talk to them about the Trilateral Commission. . . . Tom never tires of small talk; one-on-one he just melts people. Culver consolidated his base in the cities and then moved into the rural areas. But it was too late. By the time he got around to the small towns, people saw him as a politician and they weren't interested.

Harkin's was a broad-based "I'm one of you," strategy, like Grassley's.

On election day, Harkin defeated Dick Clark's conqueror with 55 percent of the vote. The burden of my postmortem conversation with his campaign manager was that Harkin's one-of-us presentational strategy—as focused heavily on the rural/farmer/western constituency (see fig. 4.3)—had worked. "We carried twenty-five counties and we didn't lose a congressional district. We did better in the cities than the Democrats usually do; so in a normal year that might have been just enough to pull us in. But we won it out in the rural areas. . . . We split even with him there. Traditionally, Democrats don't come anywhere near even in rural Iowa. The rural vote came through. It was worth all that time." "We talked to Clark and Culver on election night," he added. "They were beaming all over." After three tries, the Iowa Democrats were victorious.

CONCLUSION

We can draw some conclusions from these campaign stories. One is simply that candidates and campaigns do make a difference in the election outcomes. Students of election outcomes cannot leave campaigns out of their calculations. And students of campaigns should recognize the ways in which candidates can shape their own campaigns and the limitations to their influence. For the Clark and Culver campaigns suggest that quality candidates can lose and good campaigns can be unsuccessful. A related conclusion is that campaigns are an integral part of the continuous negotiating process by which elected officials forge and test, reforge and retest, their connections with their constituents. Further, the nature of the campaign affects the accountability of the candidate to the citizenry. By the time they went to the polls, the voters had better information by which to judge John Culver than they had by which to judge Dick Clark.

The Clark-to-Culver-to-Harkin learning sequence suggests, too, how inexact a science the negotiation of a constituency fit is, how much a matter of trial and error the representational process is. Taken together, the three campaigns suggest that this trial-and-error negotiating process develops across campaigns as well as within campaigns. Election campaigns are evaluated after the fact by interested political people; and these evaluations are incorporated into guidelines for future candidates in succeeding campaigns. Campaign sequences serve to update a candidate's information about his or her own constituency fit. They also serve to update the stock of information available to other campaigners within the same political community. Candidates can combine ideas from their own prior campaigns with ideas from the more recent campaigns of others.

The Clark and Culver cases suggest that negotiating durable constituency connections—especially for first-term incumbents—is no easy task. Whereas a challenger campaign can be won by meeting the threshold requirements of recognition and qualification, something more will be needed the second time around. A second success cannot be expected on the same basis as the first one. Constituency connections will be more complicated for incumbents than for challengers and, perhaps, a lot more fragile than the highly touted incumbency advantage might suggest.

Students of campaigns and representation need to keep in mind the two quite different types of constituencies with which politicians must connect. They are the strongly supportive, fight-bleed-and-die activists of the primary constituency and the weakly supportive, undecided or fairweather citizens of the reelection constituency. First-term incumbents need to find a balance between the Clark milewide and inch-deep support pattern and the Culver inchwide and mile-deep support pattern to avoid their support problems. There is a hint here, too, that personal campaigning may be most appropriate in locating and securing a solid primary constituency, while media campaigning may be most appropriate in locating and securing a less fragile reelection constituency.

It is important as well to distinguish between personal connections and policy connections, as the first was expressed in the Clark campaign and the second was expressed in the Culver campaign. It will be useful to carry forward these types of connections as two—perhaps *the* two—bases of the representational relationship between elective politicians and their constituents. And it would be helpful if we could probe the ways in which politicians use different types of connections with different types of constituencies as they negotiate their representational relationships.[53]

We may draw from the Culver and Clark reelection campaign stories the final suggestion that lasting connections may require a certain degree of candidate consistency. For example, Dick Clark could have shown a greater consistency of personal touch between his first and second campaigns. And the paid media of his second campaign could have been more consistent with his presumed constituency strengths. John Culver might have worked out a greater consistency between his Washington career and his constituency career. Problems of candidate consistency may be found both within and across campaigns.

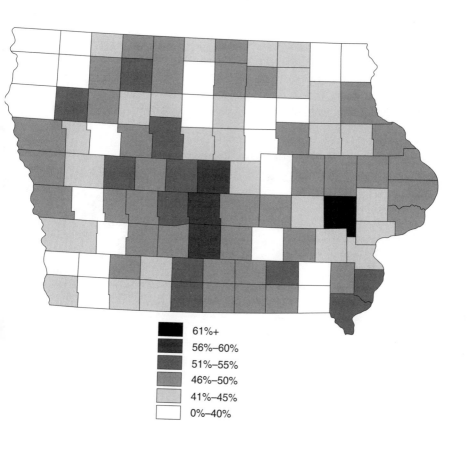

Figure 4.1. 1978 Iowa Election Results, Dick Clark

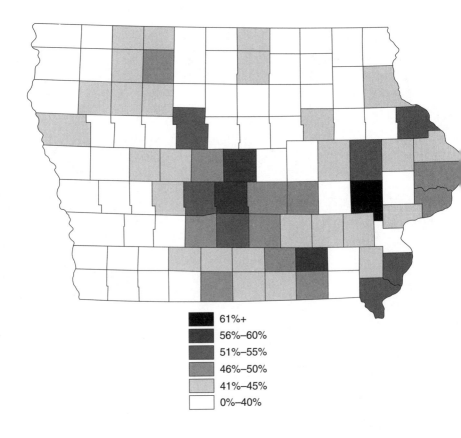

Figure 4.2. 1980 Iowa Election Results, John Culver

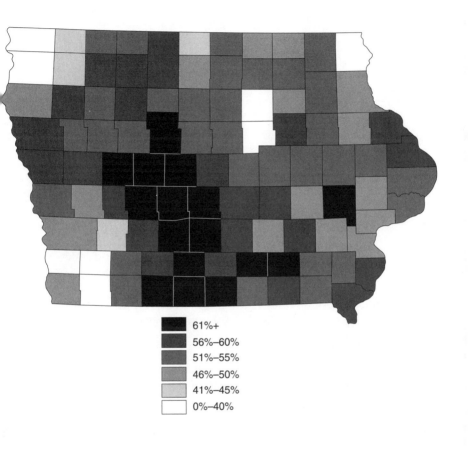

Figure 4.3. 1984 Iowa Election Results, Tom Harkin

CHAPTER 5

A CANDIDATE AND A CAMPAIGN I

WYCHE FOWLER, GEORGIA, 1991–1992

IN AUGUST 1991, fifteen months before national election day, I journeyed to Georgia to begin following the reelection campaign of the freshman Democratic senator, Wyche Fowler. At regular intervals thereafter, I returned to the campaign trail in Georgia—six times in all, for a total of twenty-one days, ending in mid-November 1992. It was my most intensive and extensive acquaintance with a single campaign. It proved to be a campaign that really mattered, and one that the political scientists' favorite prognosticators did not understand.[1]

The bare outline of the campaign story is this: Wyche Fowler served five terms as a congressman from Atlanta before his election to the Senate in 1986. In that year, he won a Democratic primary and then defeated the incumbent Republican senator—in each case with less than 51 percent of the vote. In 1992, in the race I watched, he was defeated for reelection by Republican Paul Coverdell in a November 24 runoff election—again, by less than 51 percent of the vote. On national election day, November 3, Fowler had won a 49.3 percent plurality of the vote. In any of the other forty-nine states, he would have been reelected. But in Georgia, Senate candidates need a majority vote; and Fowler fell 0.6 of a percent, or 17,000 votes, short.

The result illustrates the small margin that can separate winning from losing and also how important winning can be. Indeed, this campaign may some day qualify as a relevant data point in the realignment of southern politics. For now, my concern is to point out that although we should beware of overinterpreting the results, even partial explanations are important.

From the perspective of the Fowler campaigners, the November 3 result—his victory without victory—was the election they should have won and the election that most needs explanation. Accordingly, it will be the focus of attention here. Like first-term incumbents Clark and Culver, Fowler's experiences raise the general question, What sorts of connections do incumbents require after six years in office to secure the support of their constituents?

If candidate-centered campaigns are the contemporary norm, political scientists will want to learn all we can about the relationship between a candidate and his or her campaign. That is the intention of the next two chapters. They present an in-depth exploration of a single candidate and his campaign. They are predicated on the notion that campaigns do affect election outcomes; and they emphasize the candidate's own contribution to his campaign. They attempt to enrich our understanding of the candidate–campaign–outcome relationship by emphasizing the continuing effects of a career and a set of constituency connections on the campaigning politician. And in so doing, they encourage the further study of campaigns, not just to help us explain election outcomes, but to help us explain representational relationships as well.

Interpretation: The Challenger's Campaign of 1986

Campaigns are sequential activities. In the previous chapter, campaigning candidates observed, interpreted, and learned from the campaigns of preceding candidates. In this chapter, campaigns are also treated as sequential—but in the life of a single candidate, who observes, interprets, and learns from *his own* previous campaign.

Wyche Fowler's previous campaign was his unexpected, come-from-behind upset victory in 1986. When we first met in Washington to discuss my research plan, he commented,

> No one thought I could win. I was the only one. I wasn't about to give up ten years of seniority in the House and membership on the Ways and Means Committee unless I thought I could win. It was a very interesting campaign, slogging all over the state. We were twenty-five points down with four weeks to go. We peaked at 2:00 A.M. the night before the election.

The mid-October prediction of *Congressional Quarterly*—that challenger Fowler would *not* win—can be taken as an initial indicator that the campaign *did* indeed strongly affect the election outcome.[2]

By the time I arrived on the scene, Fowler's 1986 challenger's campaign had become a local legend. The legend had it that a five-term white congressman who represented a 65 percent black district in Atlanta had done the impossible, by successfully negotiating the Scylla and Charybdis of Georgia politics, race, and region.

First in a primary against Democrat Hamilton Jordan and then in the general election against incumbent Republican Senator Mack Mattingly, he had surprised elite opinion. "Too liberal for Georgia," had been the refrain of both his opponents.[3] Neither they nor the pundits believed that an urban liberal, with a voting record to match, could win the support of rural white conservatives in a state with "a larger number of rural Democratic voters than any state except Texas."[4] In the history of Georgia, no Atlanta-based candidate for governor or senator had done it. But Fowler had.

And he had done it, according to the legend, by means of a model campaign. His campaign manager was given the Campaign Manager of the Year award by the trade magazine

Campaigns and Elections. His campaign team—manager, pollster, and media consultant—gave numerous seminars when it was over. The campaign was detailed in Stephen Salmore and Barbara Salmore's fine political science textbook as a campaign that had unquestionably shaped the election results.[5]

From my perspective, the important feature of Fowler's 1986 campaign was its sequential effect on his 1992 campaign. And the linking mechanism was the *interpretation* that Fowler, his campaigners, and other observers placed on the previous campaign. My earlier research on senatorial careers, completed before I began tagging along with Fowler, had convinced me of the following proposition: The interpretation placed by successful candidates on their successful campaigns will have important effects on their subsequent political behavior.

In five lengthy studies, I found that candidate interpretations of their own successful campaigns helped to shape such subsequent senatorial activity as a run for the presidency, independence in Senate voting, renewed devotion to old political habits, and newfound dedication to public relations.[6] In her studies of interest groups and the media, under the rubric "constructed explanations," Marjorie Hershey has documented similar effects of post hoc interpretations of campaign events and outcomes.[7] Campaigns may help us explain outcomes. But it is the interpretation of those campaigns by the politicians involved that helps us to explain their future actions. And it is those actions that are of primary interest here.

The reigning interpretation of Fowler's 1986 campaign held that it was a personal triumph for the candidate. The centerpiece of all the retrospectives I heard or read about was the personal presentational skill of Wyche Fowler. According to everyone's interpretation, it was not just a candidate-centered campaign. It was a candidate-dominated campaign—about as candidate-dominated as a candidate-centered campaign could be.

We had "a great candidate ... unsurpassed as a campaigner," said Fowler's broadly experienced pollster. Georgia's Democratic state chair called him "the best personal hands-on, look-'em-in-the-eye, out-in-the-street campaigner I have ever known." People who had opposed him in the Democratic primary described him as "smart, capable, charming, and well organized," "a smart and able campaigner."[8] The nonpartisan "Political Report" said of his victory that "the candidate—in personality and style—may have made more of a difference than anyone ever anticipated."[9] The Salmores called him "charismatic."[10] *Politics in America* called him "a master campaigner" who triumphed by "sheer political skill."[11] The *Almanac of American Politics* called him "one of the most skillful political practitioners around," with "a knack for politics."[12]

The Georgia political commentator Rick Allen summarized the 1986 victory: "Here you had a guy who had been representing the Fifth District in Atlanta go down to South Georgia and get white votes, white Georgians to vote for him. It was a fascinating thing, very unusual. How did he do it? He did it, I think, on charm, on charisma. It was personality that got him in in 1986." It was a consensus opinion.

In that 1986 campaign, Fowler had turned away from ideology—his great weakness in a conservative state—to a theme of personal connectedness. He stressed his identification with, and his representation of, the average Georgian, based on the sharing of Georgia values and a concern for local problems. He campaigned—in the primary against Jordan and in the general election against Senator Mattingly—as he put it, by "slogging," "the old-fashioned way" through all of Georgia's 159 counties. He identified himself with voters as a "seventh-generation Georgian," as "born and raised in rural Georgia," as "a bass fisherman, a baseball fan, and a country guitar picker."[13] In face-to-face meetings, he used his down-home storytelling gifts to evoke populist values. He emphasized his accessibility and his interest in diverse local issues. By contrast, he "called into question Mack Mattingly's inclination to even appear locally and press the flesh, much less address local issue concerns."[14] "The more Fowler campaigned," wrote one analyst, "the more he dispelled any images that he was too liberal for the state."[15]

Fowler's personal presentation to voters was perfectly reinforced by his presentation on television. As one team member put it, "We circled him with a moat of Georgia values." According to his singing television biography, "He was born and raised in Georgia and his values make him strong. He knows her small towns and her family farms, and he knows what's right and wrong." His other commercials told his prospective constituents in South Georgia that he "will represent the values we learned growing up here, hard work, discipline, love of family, and certainly our religious faith," that he will be "a proven, effective partner that you can get to and talk to and trust."

These promises were completely consistent with his reputation as a congressman. "In 1985," said his pollster, "he was a blank canvas for most voters. [But] voters in his Fifth District were favorably disposed. His positives were: he's sensitive, he delivers, he puts the Fifth District first. He had very few negatives. Our task was to build on their favorable impressions." His campaign brochure featured an *Atlanta Magazine* reader's poll that found him the "most trusted" public official, plus an *Atlanta Journal-Constitution* endorsement of him as "the most effective congressman in Atlanta history ... [whose] foremost asset is his ability to get things done at home." As one of Fowler's television spots put it, "He has done it for Atlanta, now for all Georgia."

Fowler was blessed with a tightly knit and very disciplined campaign team. It was headed by campaign manager Bill Johnstone, who was also Fowler's top senatorial aide. Their pivotal strategic decision was an unorthodox one, to husband their limited financial resources—even though they were being pounded by the incumbent—until they could put their television commercials on the air and stay on the air with a continuous, high-octane purchase. This meant waiting until three weeks before election day. And it meant enduring months of opposition attacks on Fowler's spotty attendance record and his liberalism. "The low point in the campaign," said a friend, came when Mattingly poured $3 million into his 'Fowler, Absent for Georgia' television campaign. All Wyche's friends were spooked. 'We've got to get on TV.' Wyche stayed steady in the boat, while everyone else was spooked. It was like Kipling said, 'Keep your head, while all about you are losing theirs.' He just went on campaigning with great availability everywhere, while Mattingly played tennis in Georgetown.

A team member described the strategic considerations.

The conventional wisdom is that you don't want to leave a negative unanswered, that a negative unanswered is a negative confirmed. I give credit to Bill Johnstone for our endgame. He had a game plan; and he was absolutely unflappable. We had to play rope-a-dope like Ali did against Foreman in Zaire. Ali laid on the ropes, Foreman punched him out, and Ali came off the ropes and destroyed him. It was excruciating. But we knew that if we were going to win, we would do it in the last three weeks.

In Fowler's first horse race poll, in October 1985, he trailed Mattingly 30 to 55; one year later, on October 16, at the beginning of his television campaign, he still trailed 31 to 55. The campaign dynamics of the last three weeks produced a 26-point swing to 51 to 49. Two other essential elements in this television-dominated endgame swing were Fowler's performance in the only televised debate (watched by an estimated 60 percent of the potential audience) and the strongly supportive televised endorsement by conservative Georgia icon, Senator Sam Nunn.[16]

I have gone into Fowler's 1986 campaign at length because I think the interpretation of it is, from a developmental perspective, the most important contextual element in the 1992 campaign. Since the consensus interpretation was that Fowler won in 1986 on the basis of his individual campaign performance, campaigners and observers alike believed he could and would repeat that success in 1992. So, too, I believe, did Fowler. To be sure, there are other elements of context that would be important if we were explaining election results.[17] But they are not important in explaining the campaign.

Career

To intrude on a campaign, I have said, is to discover immediately that the campaign is embedded in a career. We cannot
understand Senator Fowler's interpretation of his 1986 campaign success, I believe, until we step back and take a look at
his pre-Senate career. It was a career marked by progressive ambition, fueled by enthusiasm for public service, and sustained
by entrepreneurial skill. From a developmental perspective, his
highly personal campaign success in 1986 must be seen as but
one more in a career-long string of personal successes in which
he was able to put his political abilities to work in the service of
his electoral and institutional goals. His career—from congressional aide to Atlanta alderman to president of the Atlanta City
Council to House member to the House Ways and Means Committee to the Senate and, finally, to assistant floor leader in the
Senate—reveals an unusual degree of personal resourcefulness
in recognizing and creating opportunities to further his political
ambitions.

A classmate and fraternity brother at Davidson College, who
says that he and Wyche "would talk for hours and hours about
our lives and what we wanted to do and so forth," asserts that
"Wyche always wanted to be a United States senator." True
or not, Fowler obviously spent a lot of time, in Paul Tsongas's
words, "thinking up." And because his 1992 campaign must be
understood in the context of his career, I will trace it in some
detail.

As a young soldier stationed at the Pentagon, Fowler
volunteered to work after hours in the office of Atlanta's
freshman congressman, Charles Weltner, who became his
closest friend. "He was my first intern," said Weltner. "He came
in after work and we put him to work on the robotyper." Shortly
after his discharge, he joined the office staff full time. He soon
became the congressman's administrative assistant. And, said
Weltner, "He ran my office during my second term." Weltner
decided not to run for a third term. Fowler returned home to

enter Emory Law School.

During his freshman year, Fowler observed that Atlanta's City Hall was closed in the evening. He suggested to Mayor Ivan Allen that an office be kept open at night to provide ombudsman services to working people who had no time to contact City Hall during the day. As Fowler tells the story,

> The mayor said to me, "What fool would want to take a job like that?" I sold myself—as a former nighttime duty officer at Fort Benning. He thought it was a great idea to have a duty officer at night, to unstop the sewer and collect the garbage. Of course, as soon as the press came down they said, "What are you doing here, Fowler?" I said, "I'm the night mayor." Allen picked up the paper the next morning and saw the headline, "Night Mayor at City Hall." He didn't speak to me for a month!

Weltner laughed as he recalled the advantageous payoff for Fowler's political creativity. "Why any mayor would agree to let some college kid become night mayor with all that publicity, I don't know. But when Wyche ran his first race for alderman, he ran with the slogan, 'Night Mayor Runs for Alderman.' In that race, he took the seat from a man who had been in office for 30 years. . . . It was a most improbable victory for a young man who was still in law school."

"When we were on the Atlanta City Council," a colleague recalls, "Wyche used to go way out to Buckhead after meetings to shake hands with people in the movie lines. He had figured out how to campaign in movie lines—start at the box office and work back. I said to him one day, 'Why do you go way out there to shake hands?' And he said to me, 'You never can tell.' "

Within a couple of years, Fowler was running for president of the City Council.[18] He recalled that contest: "You had the candidate of the white establishment—they called him the picture book candidate—running against a well-known leader of the black community from the Martin Luther King era. While they battled each other, no one paid any attention to me. I was just out there shaking hands and winning votes." A friend added, "He won the race with shoe leather, going door-to-door. He had no money for advertising. But he had innovative ideas like three-cornered signs to put on the tops of cars parked in shopping centers." They said, Fowler for President. As president of the City Council, he reached beyond his current constituency. "I lived in Northeast Georgia at the time," said a third friend, "and he would come up from Atlanta to Rotary Club meetings and Kiwanis meetings in Gainesville and Commerce and Toccoa—all preparatory to someday running for the Senate." He was "thinking up."

Fowler lost his first race for Congress—against Andrew Young. But when Young joined the Carter administration, Fowler was elected to the seat he would hold for five terms, defeating, among others, the current congressman, John Lewis, and the man who would oust him in 1992, Paul Coverdell.

After one term in the House, Fowler sought membership on its most powerful committee, Ways and Means. "I knew tax law," he said, "and there were five Democratic vacancies on the committee." He told another story of his entrepreneurship in producing a most unlikely result.

I went to talk to [Committee Chairman] Danny Rostenkowski first.... He told me that the slate had already been chosen and that was the way it was going to be. So I read the rules. And the rules said that the Steering Committee proposed a slate to be ratified by the caucus; but they also said that anyone not on the slate could present himself to the caucus for a vote. So I went to [Speaker] Tip O'Neill.... He told me that I had a right to run under the rules and that he would not stop me. He also told me that I would make people mad and that I would not win.... [Majority Leader] Jim Wright called me and said, "Fowler, what makes you think you're so smart that you can substitute your judgment for the wisdom and experience of the leadership?" I sat down by the telephone for fifteen hours straight and called every Democrat in the House to ask them to vote for me. I tracked them down wherever they were. My argument was that I was trying to beat the system and that the system was too rigid.... I was the only one who called them to ask for a vote. What I didn't realize until the day of the vote was that in order to be elected, I had to beat the entire slate! I beat the slate by fifteen votes.... without the help of a single lobbyist, a single special interest group, or a single campaign contribution.

It was an unprecedented reversal of the leadership. And it proved that he was as resourceful in pursuing his institutional ambition as he was his elective office ambition.

Fowler's success in achieving both goals in the House was repeated in the Senate. First of all, there was his unexpectedly successful 1986 election campaign. Then there was his immediate elevation onto the Senate's leadership ladder. Again, it is a story of opportunity recognized, created, and exploited—this time in the context of a tight three-way contest among the Democrats for majority leader.

When George Mitchell came to me to ask for my support, I told him that I was going to support him, that I would do so publicly from that moment on, and that I would do whatever I could to help him get elected. I told him that I would like to help him on the policy side of things, that I would like to be included in the internal work of the party, that I thought I could help on the inside.... I think I was his first southern connection.... On the night before the vote, Mitchell called me and asked if I would second his nomination. Each candidate can have two people speak for him; he asked John Glenn to speak first and me second. That was only the second conversation I had had with Mitchell.... He had gone all over the country making speeches for other Democratic candidates.... But he had never come to Georgia. Like everybody else, he thought I didn't have a chance.... After he won, he called me and said he was going to create a new position, assistant floor leader, and he was appointing me. It meant that when there are leadership meetings, I'm involved, or when the Democratic leaders go to the White House, I go.

Two days later, he beat out three fellow southerners for a coveted assignment to the powerful Senate Appropriations Committee.[19]

In 1992, Majority Leader Mitchell did come to Georgia to campaign for Fowler. "I chose him [as assistant floor leader]," said Mitchell, "for his uncanny ability to work with senators on both sides of the Senate. His wit, his intelligence, and his grasp of issues enable him to build consensus. As majority leader, I listen to the voice of the Dixie Limited. And the voice I hear most often is that of Wyche Fowler." [20] Had Fowler remained in the Senate, there is little doubt he would have been in the 1994 succession race that followed Mitchell's retirement.

The candidate I met on the trail was a person of commanding abilities and superior presentational skills. He was broadly interested, widely read, and engagingly funny. I could easily see why he could be thought of as the perfect candidate running a perfect campaign. He was unusually self-confident, self-sufficient, and free-spirited.

When we first met in his Senate office to discuss the possibility of my following his campaign, he pointed to his longtime administrative assistant, Bill Johnstone, and said,

> Our real campaign staff is right here—the two of us. We run a very informal campaign, more informal than any other Senate campaign. We don't have a big organization with lots of experts and lots of high strategy meetings. I hope you won't find this a big disappointment. I don't mean to say we do it by the seat of our pants. . . . We do not have a big, well-organized staff operation with lots of meetings.

With some pride, Fowler described himself as a "low-tech" campaigner who had won in 1986 without a car phone or a fax machine. It was my first clue to the self-described "independent cuss" I would follow. A veteran staffer summed him up by saying simply, "He's his own man." He was a person who wanted to operate free from any and all encumbrances. A large campaign staff was apparently one such encumbrance. And I would find others as I went along.

Fowler's progressive ambition was fueled by his strong attraction to public service. That is the way he talked in public and in private. On election night, he told his supporters, "Shed no tears for me. Whether I am Senator Wyche Fowler or citizen Wyche Fowler, I will find other ways of public service."[21] For me, the most convincing measure of this basic desire was his steadfast devotion to the public institutions in which he served. In dozens of public appearances and in hours of private conversation, I never heard him bash the Congress—as so many of his colleagues eagerly and regularly do.

He was electorally and institutionally ambitious to reach ever more influential institutions and to become an influential player in each of them, from congressional office to city council to House and to Senate. His parting comment to nearly every politically interested group he met on the trail was, "Thank you for your public service." And that is the judgment the defeated candidate would wish to receive from them.

Miscalculation

Politicians, we know, are calculating individuals. And sometimes, of course, they miscalculate. I believe that Fowler's self-confidence, drawn from his remarkable career-long string of personal political successes—strongly reinforced by everybody else's interpretation of his challenger's success in 1986—led him to miscalculate in 1992.

My central purpose is to explain candidate behavior, *not* to explain the election outcome. But Fowler's miscalculations were probably sufficient to have cost him his seat in the Senate. Indeed, the judgment of local observers is so uniformly strong on this point that to argue otherwise would be to assume an almost impossible burden of proof. My view is that Fowler's self-confidence caused him to underestimate certain things he needed to do in the campaign to win: to settle on a campaign theme, to take his opponent seriously, to win back disaffected supporters, to use television effectively, to cultivate the media.

His bottom-line miscalculation was expressed when we talked afterward. "Not until one hour before 11:00 o'clock [on runoff election night]," he said, "did I ever think—not for one minute had I ever thought—that I might lose." Many candidates say this before the election; many fewer say it afterward. But I was not surprised to hear it from him. During our first meeting, long before he had a challenger, he described the upcoming race as close. "My margins are always small," he said, "51 percent, 52 percent, not much higher." To the very end, he never predicted more for himself than 53 percent. But neither did he ever, at any time, predict less than 51 percent.

With the election still a year away, he had prophesied, "[any opponent] will have to bring me down a few points negative *and* gain six points or so [positive] from a big Bush win. They can't beat me with either one standing alone." With the election two weeks away, he had offered, "Let me predict it for you—sixteen points. Well maybe twelve points—53 percent–41 percent–6 percent [for the third party Libertarian candidate]." In the midst of the runoff, he predicted, "It will be close, 51 to 49. But we'll win and I'll be known for the rest of my life as landslide Fowler." These were not egregious miscalculations. On November 3, he almost won. But as expectations, they were not helpful.

When a challenger defeats an incumbent, as Fowler did in 1986, two broad interpretations of the campaign and its outcome are available to the winner: it was the incumbent's failure and it was the challenger's success.[22] For the first-term incumbent facing reelection, the "incumbent failure" interpretation is the conservative, albeit the less flattering, one—that the previous campaign was a referendum on the former incumbent and revealed little if anything of what it would take for last time's winner to win reelection. The second interpretation may be more tempting to the new senator, but it is more risky. It assumes that the previous winning campaign established or at least pre-figured constituency connections that will provide substantial carryover strengths in a reelection campaign.

For a candidate like Fowler, whose prowess as a challenger had become legendary, the temptations of the winner-centered interpretation would be especially strong. And the risk is that it would lead to a misestimation of what Fowler, the successful challenger, would need to do to succeed as an incumbent. Because the reigning interpretation of his past success held that his superior campaigning abilities had carried the day, it was hard to resist the expectation that he could do it again and to calculate accordingly.

Early in the summer, Fowler's campaigners worried about his transition from challenger to incumbent. As one consultant put it,

> For every incumbent, the first reelection is the most vulnerable time. Wyche is a first-termer; and he beat an incumbent. When an incumbent is beaten, it means the incumbent was fired. The challenger didn't win; the incumbent was fired. Challengers hate to admit it. They like to think that there were two equally shiny apples on the shelf, and the voters picked one. In reality, their first reelection will be the first substantive introduction of the challenger to most of the electorate.

And a second campaigner echoed, "I don't think 1986 will have any carryover for Wyche.... We don't know whether he'll do as well now that he is the incumbent. He may have been at his best attacking an incumbent." They did not believe that the history of 1986 would automatically repeat itself.

With these worries framing their thinking, Fowler's campaign consultants confronted a distressing but fundamental fact. However self-confident Fowler might be, he was, according to the polls, an incumbent without much "substance" to work with. A summary of his January poll described Fowler as "a very vulnerable incumbent going into 1992" and explained, "Most of the problem is that Georgia voters don't have any idea of what the hell Wyche Fowler is doing for them in Washington." In June, another consultant commented, "The only thing people know about him is his name. They don't know anything about him. He has a lot of educating to do."

In a summer focus group—dubbed by the staff "the focus group from hell"—ten people were asked to name Fowler's "issue priorities." Their answers were as follows. First person: "I do not know." Second person: "I think he serves on the Agriculture Committee." Third: "I don't know." Fourth: "I haven't a clue." Fifth: "What does he do?" Sixth: "He goes to a lot of baseball games with Ted [Turner]." (Laughter) Seventh:

"He answered a letter I wrote him. I got a letter." Fourth person again: "That's one out of two." (Laughter) Eighth, ninth, and tenth persons: head-shaking silence.

However well he had negotiated a personal recognition threshold as a challenger, he did not seem to have negotiated much understanding of his performance since then. In a challenger's campaign, where recognition and qualification are the main goals, constituent connections can simply be asserted. In a reelection campaign, however, some demonstrable connections will need to be added.

Later, when it was all over, a top adviser said, "Our basic problem was that nobody knew who he was. He had no record. We crawled through his record looking for things to write about.... There were strands of a record, but nothing you could weave into whole cloth, nothing people would recognize. This showed up in all our focus groups. People simply did not know who he was or what he had done." All three top campaign advisers used the same phrase to describe their incumbent senator: "a blank slate."

Candidate Fowler was certainly aware of the problem. "People like me," he said when we first met, "but they don't have any idea of what I've done or what my views are. One of the things I'm working on now is to take the twelve things I could talk about and reduce them to three things I will talk about. We will have to repeat, repeat, repeat those things." He was articulating the need for a campaign theme. But the interpretation of his 1986 victory and the lessons of his career led him to overestimate his carry-over strength from his challenger's campaign; and this combination led him to underestimate the severity of that need. Certainly, he behaved as if this were the case.

Themes

In the absence of a high-profile legislative record, candidate Fowler had two generic campaign themes available to him—two choices of the sorts of things he could "repeat, repeat,

repeat." One theme, in a manner similar to John Culver, would emphasize his policy connections to his constituents. The other theme, in a manner similar to Dick Clark, would emphasize his personal connections to his constituents. They are not incompatible. But they produce different thematic arguments. All campaigns can be thought of as efforts to negotiate policy and/or personal connections with constituents. These are the two main bases of representation. And, explicitly or implicitly, positively or negatively, all campaigns are about representation.

What, then, was Fowler's reaction to this choice? His choice was not to choose. "In 1991," explained a top adviser, "we tested two themes and wrote a stump speech for each one. One was that Wyche Fowler was accessible and he got things done for Georgia.... The other was that Wyche was an agent of change in fields like health care and education. We were unable to agree on either one—or on any other message.... Neither stump speech nor message was ever approved by Wyche or used by him." "We could never get him to adopt a thematic focus," echoed another adviser. In all of my visits, I never witnessed any effort to articulate a campaign theme. I never saw a basic campaign brochure; I never heard a campaign slogan. And I never heard Fowler mention his thematic choices one way or another.

In an April interview, he had this exchange with Atlanta's television political reporter, Bill Nigut.

NIGUT: And what are you gonna stand for? What's your message gonna be to the voters this year?
FOWLER: Well, a couple of things. I haven't, I mean I've got a lot of governing to do before we get to the fall and the heart of the campaign. But I think accountability is a big issue—not only accountability for the Congress but the executive branch. I want to make sure that we're forced to live under the laws that we put all of the majority and all of Americans under. I mean that's been a proposal of mine for three or four years. I'm about to get support and get it passed. But also I want to make the case for the fact that we can now invest in our country. Now we don't have to defend Germany and Japan—about $100 billion a year that

we've been spending to defend these countries that are perfectly capable of defending themselves—to do what we should have been doing in our schools and health care system and housing and provide jobs for people. I'll have specific proposals on how to do that, and they've all been put together with the help of Georgians all over the state through these meetings and staying in touch since I've been in office.

There is no focus, no message, no "repeat, repeat, repeat"–only mush.

"One of the reasons I have the trouble I have," he admitted afterward, "is because when I talk I say whatever comes into my head and I end up being all over the ballpark. I know the most successful politicians are those who boil everything down to three things and then repeat them over and over again. . . . Elect me and I'll do them—one, two, three. People know what you stand for. I've never been able to do that."

I believe that, because of his extraordinary career-long success, he did not take seriously the idea that he might have to change. This conclusion is buttressed by the defensive—almost passive—posture Fowler adopted toward the campaign during my early visits. In our first meeting, he said, "I'm the incumbent, so the campaign will be attack, attack, attack me. We will figure out how to deal with that when we hear what my opponent says." Later that month, a friend asked him privately, "Have you figured out yet what the big issues will be, the big issues in the campaign?" "No," he answered. "It all depends what the other fella hits me with. Then I'll hit him back and we'll see what happens. It's way too early to be thinking about that."

At the time, he knew that his race would be "a hard hoe," that the contest would be for the votes between 48 percent and 52 percent. And still, he did not seem energized.

The Republicans think I'll be their easiest incumbent to beat— in the South. I'm their prime target. . . . In the polls we've seen, my numbers are low for an incumbent. My pollster is worried that there's a strong anti-incumbent feeling among the voters.

He wants to do five polls a year. I'm not going to do that. I've been through this before. And I know that a lot depends on who the other fella is.

He was waiting for an opponent, and his plan was to counterpunch, not initiate. This defensive posture was consistent with his own failure to adopt a focused, coherent, and positive campaign theme.

His dominant attitude toward his four prospective Republican challengers was, "I want a Republican runoff so they will all run around burning money . . . so our campaign will be only eight weeks long, and we can make the best use of our paid television." Whoever his opponent might be, he said, "what I worry about is the anti-incumbent feeling. I will have to figure out how to handle that because I will be painted as corrupt and one of those long-term incumbents." He had begun to think of Paul Coverdell, former state senator and Peace Corps director, as the most likely primary winner. And he was convinced that a Coverdell campaign "will be desperately negative—attack, attack, attack." He would not be blindsided as Dick Clark had been.

Even so, he remained in an essentially reactive mode. "I'd rather run against Coverdell than the others," he said in April, "because he has a record. We have researched his record and we know its weaknesses. If he attacks me, I can attack him back." If, however, Fowler had a good idea—as he seemed to—of what the general thrust and the intensity of an all-purpose Coverdell attack would be, why wasn't he preparing a positive policy or personal campaign message to counteract it? The danger was, of course, that if he didn't dictate the message of the campaign, someone else might. And that might drag Fowler into a kind of campaign that was not to his liking.

Policy Connections Theme. As I observed Fowler's performance on the campaign trail, it wavered between a policy connection theme and a personal connection theme. His public presentations always drifted toward policy. That was his strong preference. He described himself always as "a public policy person" who examined problems "from a public policy standpoint." He saw himself as someone who was in public service to make good public policy in the Senate. That is what he most enjoyed; that was where he could best exercise his independence; and that was the reputation he most wanted.

The dozen or so campaign speeches I heard focused, Clinton-style, on the need for domestic policy change—in health care, education, and jobs. They were the three things he most wanted to repeat, repeat, repeat. He showed a sophisticated understanding of these issues, as a Senate policy broker might. Even so, he was unable to identify himself closely with any of those policy areas. They were not part of his observable legislative record. And he never put forward any specific, recognizable plan for coping with any of them.

Neither could he derive any electoral leverage from his two major legislative accomplishments in the Senate. Historic preservation and alternative energy research had tiny constituencies. Nor did his personal policy passions—for the environment and foreign affairs—have any visible saliency in Georgia in 1992. Nor could he capitalize on his facilitative work in the Democratic leadership, since it was done on the inside and out of public view.

On the trail, he contented himself with policy generalities. And he often displayed his role as an inside-the-Senate policy broker in the least attractive manner. On the major campaign issue of health care reform, when asked point blank, "What is your position on health policy?" he answered,

Well, I don't know how far I would go into my position. . . . We are going to try to develop a health care policy . . . over the next year and a half. We're gonna have national hearings, one in Georgia in December. We'll have a plan—I say "we"—I guess it will be a Democratic plan. We've been trying to get a plan out of the White House and get their suggestions. . . . And what we will try to do is to get the best suggestions and the best parts of many, many suggestions and then mold them together to try to have a comprehensive reform plan that gets some sort of handle on their costs.... We are going to consider everything.... We'll see what we can put together.

As much, therefore, as Fowler liked to talk about policy, he could not actually claim an identifiable policy record or program for himself.

In one sense, of course, he had a policy record—his votes. They may not have been highly visible, but some of them were well known to identifiable constituencies. The best known were a vote against the Gulf War, a vote to confirm Clarence Thomas's nomination to the U.S. Supreme Court, and strong support of President Bush's 1990 proposed tax increase. None of them was helpful. In each case, he had traded some lukewarm support for some strong opposition. On the war and on taxes, opposition came from among the South Georgians and from the "downscale whites" whom his polls consistently identified as his weakest supporters. On Clarence Thomas, opposition came from among his strongest liberal supporters. Insofar as a policy-oriented campaign was an invitation to voters to consider these three votes, it is hard to see how any one of them would appreciably strengthen his constituency connections.

But Fowler was confident about his policy votes—confident, for example, that his controversial Gulf War and Clarence Thomas votes would not cost him support. "I have a good deal of confidence," he said, "that back-to-back votes like those two will not hurt me, not even two or three votes in a row." And he explained, "People like me because they like my dimensions— not because of any vote. They may not like the way I vote all the time, but I think they trust my judgment. I think I have a bank of confidence that allows me to vote as I think best." That was the degree of independence he wanted. And he believed he had achieved it.

Among the oldest and strongest Atlanta supporters I met, I found agreement that he did indeed have a lot of voting independence. "I'm a banker," said one, "but he has never done anything to help the banks. People may not like the way he votes, but they think he's the best man for the job." Another said, "I'm in the public finance business, mostly the bond business. In all the years that he has been in Congress, he has never cast one single vote in favor of the public finance industry. William Faulkner had a great line, 'People don't love because of, they love in spite of.' That's Wyche Fowler. People support him in spite of some of his views."

A question for 1992, however, was whether those voters who knew little or nothing about his Senate record would feel the same way. Or whether the incumbent senator could hold his old supporters as easily as the incumbent congressman had done.

In the days before he had an opponent, Fowler remained optimistic that any opposition to his controversial votes would subside. In November, he expressed the opinion that "Anita Hill activated a few activists, but I think the general effect will dissipate pretty fast. I think that has already happened with my vote on the Gulf resolution, although the Republicans may want to bring it up." In January, he exclaimed, "I've done twenty-five town meetings in sixteen days, and not one person has asked me about my vote on the war or my vote on Clarence Thomas. Not one." I asked him in October, if he could take back one vote in the last six years, what would it be? He said, "It wouldn't be the war vote or the Clarence Thomas vote or the tax vote—or any major, highly publicized vote."

Later in the campaign, however, he allowed as how those votes may, in the end, have strained voter loyalties. "Politically —just politically—I would have been much better off if I had voted for the war and against Clarence Thomas. I ticked off all those supporters of mine." And, he might have added, he attracted very little support in return. The point is that an intensified attention to policy, which is what his rhetorical campaign was all about, did not seem to make for a strong link to his constituents.

Personal Connections Theme.

While the campaign drifted toward policy connection themes,

it drifted away from personal connection themes—by which I mean themes of identification and attentiveness. "I am a lot like you," "I am working for you," "I have kept in touch with you"—these are the themes of personal representation. Given his difficulties on the policy side, I found this campaign drift increasingly baffling. After all, a personal connection theme had been his recognized strength as a congressman. And the same theme had gotten him elected to the Senate six years before. Besides which, local observers gave him great credit for keeping in touch as a senator. "One thing Republicans can't accuse [him] of is not tending to his flock."[23] "Fowler has done a good job tending to the folks back home, and that is pretty hard for any challenger to overcome."[24]

When I asked his campaign manager how they would cope with a Paul Coverdell "too liberal for Georgia" charge, he emphasized Fowler's underlying personal connections with his constituents.

> Our first defense will be to get him out among the public, let them see him, listen to him, talk with him. He doesn't sound like a pointy-head liberal. He sounds like Georgia. It will be Coverdell who will come across as a silk stocking, country club type. Wyche is more Georgia red clay than Coverdell. His values are Georgia values. He's grounded in the state. That's our most important defense, that he is so good at relating to folks, that he is such a good candidate.

The implication was that the master campaigner running a strenuous personal connections campaign would win. Personal contact and attentiveness is the theme that contributes most to the historic "incumbency advantage" at election time. As such, it was the obvious textbook inoculation against the anti-incumbent attack he believed was coming.

Strangely, too, although Fowler neglected this personal connections theme in the broadest campaign settings—in interviews, commercials, and televised debates—he often leaned on it in selected settings. He certainly had ammunition. He had conducted a record number of two-hundred town meetings—in every one of Georgia's 159 counties. And in small, fund-raising gatherings, he often led off by touting his accessibility. At an Atlanta house party in October, he began typically,

> I have spent my time as a freshman United States senator keeping promises—mainly of accessibility over our state. I've been in 159 counties holding meetings, where I don't make any prefatory remarks, because the only way I know is that you can't represent people unless you come home and find out which policies we're getting right and which ones we're getting wrong.

His travel talk revealed his judgment that his tangible accomplishments—support for the peanut program; disaster relief funds; appropriations for bridges, military installations, educational pilot programs, and rural health care—would count heavily in his reelection.

During a visit in Augusta, he remarked, "I've carried a lot of water for Augusta since I've been in the Senate. I've brought a lot of help to this area." He carried a list of eight local problems he had addressed—with funds, with negotiations, or both—involving historic preservation, railroad crossings, water, buildings, and education.[25] On that basis alone, he privately predicted a 12 percent increase in his Richmond County vote and editorial support from the Augusta paper.[26] In conversation with a South Georgia editor, he said,

> Georgians know me now and know how closely I've worked with the agricultural community and the successes we've had. [They know] how closely I've worked, especially on rural issues such as rural health and saving the money—the Medicare money—for these rural hospitals. And that if I'm to be labeled, I hope it's as a man who gets things done, puts his state and its people first. I've kept my promise to emphasize rural Georgia and our agricultural base … fighting back the efforts of the administration to dismantle the peanut program, leading the two-year effort to make the White House release the disaster relief money [to farmers].

He had serious accomplishments to talk about.

Later, riding through agricultural South Georgia, he talked about his inside work on these matters. "The thing that shifted my support here was getting them the disaster relief," he said.

> They'd been waiting two years to get what was owed to them and they had given up. When Bob Dole put in legislation to help his Kansas wheat farmers, I saw an opportunity ostensibly to "work with him" on that legislation. Actually, I told him that his bill wasn't going anywhere until Georgia's farmers got what was owed them. When that bill went through, everything turned around down there. Everybody was talking about it; and wherever I went, people thanked me for it.

When Fowler, a former soldier, was named honorary grand marshal of a VFW-sponsored Loyalty Day parade in suburban Conyers, some veterans declared a boycott because of his vote against the Gulf War.[27] After marching the parade route without incident, he spoke to the VFW members at their postmarch ceremony. After reminding them that freedom meant "the freedom to say foolish things or even to pass foolish resolutions," he also reminded them of his $1.8 million amendment to preserve veterans' health benefits. He received standing applause and a media judgment that his war vote seemed to be no longer an issue.[28]

This was an insider's accomplishment—one of many potential building blocks for a personal connections theme. Privately, he described what he had done.

> I talked to [Majority Leader] Dole. He was in favor of it— he's a veteran. Then I had to convince [Budget Chairman Pete] Domenici. He was in favor of it [but he was afraid that if he accepted it, things would open up and other amendments would be offered.] But he was afraid of a vote. I convinced him that I didn't care about a vote. So we agreed not to have a vote or a lot of prepared statements either. I had it ready twenty-four hours in advance; I brought it up; and we passed it quickly.[29]

If he didn't push those sorts of accomplishments, no one would do it for him.

On the trail, he carried with him a thick book detailing the benefits he had brought to every section of the state—often because of his strategic positions on the Agriculture and Appropriations committees, not to mention his party leadership connections. "Lyndon Johnson," he noted, "always said the key to success was being able to tell people 'what I did for Culpepper.'" And as we approached a town, he would finger his notebook, musing "Let's see what I did for this Culpepper." Then, when he met privately with the editorial boards of the newspaper, he would routinely bring out his black book of benefits and ask them to publicize those localized successes. "Let's see, what do I have here that I can sell you. What could you write an editorial about."

He did not enjoy doing this, I might add. And he was not a convincing credit claimer. Like fund raising, he saw this solicitation as an activity that compromised his independence—another unwanted encumbrance for someone who wanted to be his own man. Which may help explain his reluctance to embrace home accomplishments as his campaign theme.

Nonetheless, it was the obvious one. When his southern Senate colleagues, Howell Heflin, Bob Graham, Jim Sasser, and Terry Sanford, came to Georgia to campaign for him, they invariably touted his local accomplishments wherever they went.[30] When Sam Nunn spoke for him in public and in television endorsement spots, he listed the many things Fowler had done for Georgia. A less than friendly Georgia commentator recognized as his great strength–"at least a B+"—the fact that he "brought home the bacon."[31] "Senator Fowler had quite a record," said one of Fowler's district office directors, "but it was not highlighted in the media campaign. The closest it came to hitting the target was the Nunn ad."

All his Senate associates made it unmistakably their pro-Fowler theme. But Fowler did not adopt it for himself. He leaned heavily in nearly every campaign speech on the support, the endorsement, and the political cover provided by Nunn. But he did not fully embrace Nunn's arguments on his own behalf.

Thematic Drift

When the election was over, Senator Fowler recognized that he had failed, in his six years, to establish a sufficient connection with a sufficient number of his constituents. "My problem was," he said, "that I could never develop a base. All our polls and interviews showed that people did not know what I had done." His idea was that if people had known of his accomplishments as a senator, he would have withstood the challenger's attacks on him. Enough constituents, that is, would have had their own evidence and would have given him the benefit of the doubt when doubts were raised. Politicians call this trust. And constituent trust is never easy to come by in a single senatorial term. It is harder still in a state like Georgia where historic regional and racial divisions, coupled with contemporary population growth and demographic change, make it difficult for a politician to find a stable base to represent and from which to begin to negotiate for trust. Nonetheless, that is what the transition from challenger to incumbent is all about. As a first-term incumbent, Fowler had to start that blending and building process and had to campaign as if he had an idea of how to represent "Georgia."

When he lamented his lack of a base, I asked him why a campaign theme like "Fighting for Georgia" or "Georgia First" had not been the obvious choice—given his success with that theme in 1986, his available record of accomplishment in the Senate, and his fear of the anti-incumbency mood. "That was our original idea of what the campaign should be," he answered.

> We even picked out the things I had done for each area, beginning with MARTA [Metropolitan Atlanta Rapid Transit Authority]. About a year and a half out, that was our plan. Then our later polls seemed to tell us that it would sound like too much pork, and that was not what people wanted to hear, that they wanted to hear about the major policies. So we switched. We were moved by "the superior intelligence of new information." Maybe it was a mistake.

To my mind, it certainly was a mistake—their biggest. In the end, the Fowler campaigners never "switched" at all. They just drifted.

Indecisively and inconsistently, they shifted emphasis from policy connections, which were his preference, to personal connections, which were his strength. Their initial failure to adopt a sustaining campaign theme or message was the biggest failure of the campaign. It undermined almost every campaign effort that followed.

Moreover, it was a collective failure. In the analysis of Paul Tsongas's campaign, I suggested the importance of quality campaign teams for quality candidates. And I suggested that quality teams, too, can help us to explain election outcomes. The Fowler campaign provides more supporting evidence. The 1992 Fowler campaign team was the same, in name at least, as his 1986 team. But in 1992, they did not serve him so well.

In 1986, they had been young in the business, strongly committed and attentive to their candidate. That campaign had been characterized by collective discipline. By 1992, the two top gurus had become—partly because of their 1986 success— nationally famous. They were fat, happy, and much less focused on and attentive to the Fowler campaign. Pollster Alan Secrest (like Peter Hart in Dick Clark's campaign) was juggling about thirty campaign accounts. At one crucial juncture late in the campaign, he had to farm out his assigned task of directing focus groups. In 1992, media consultant Frank Greer was working in the political stratosphere, handling presidential candidate Bill Clinton's television campaign.[32] And he did not give his personal hands-on concentration to the Fowler campaign until the runoff—when it was too late.

The television campaign Greer devised for Fowler exemplified both inattention and drift. Its "positive" segment began with a warmed-over remake of his 1986 biography featuring the personal connections of "Georgia's man born on Georgia's land." A panel of local political commentators described it as, "don't rock the boat," "safe," "nothing new," "no new ground."

One commentator, Tom Hauck, added, "Greer is not putting a lot into this commercial. He's not giving Fowler enough attention. If I were Fowler, I would fire him."[33]

After playing this "personal connection" ad for ten days, the campaign team shifted to their main set of policy spots in which Fowler, talking to small groups, expressed his concern for health care and education. Members of the team described these policy ads as "insipid" and "disappointing."[34] It was about as sleep-inducing as any so-called positive TV campaign I had ever seen—all the more unfathomable coming from so personally engaging and resourceful an individual as Wyche Fowler.

From my first conversation with a media consultant, in June, I sensed a good deal of indecision between a policy-oriented and a personal-oriented campaign. "I don't want to say it's an experiment we're engaged in, but it is," he said. "Wyche is an incumbent at a time when pork doesn't count like it used to," he continued. "People think it's nice that you got money to restore the courthouse in Augusta. But they want to know about jobs. People are 'big-picturing' it this year."

At the same time, the consultant was staring at a recent poll summary that called for confronting anti-incumbency arguments, not policy arguments. "Institutional arguments against Wyche (junkets, contributions from gas companies, pay raise votes)," it said, "carry more weight than some ideological arguments." This came as no surprise to me. For nearly a year, Fowler's media interviewers had been pressing him hardest on the pay raise issue. And he must have known it would be an issue central to the campaign.

Furthermore, when I asked the consultant about Fowler's campaign assets, he answered, "He's a Georgian. He has roots. He has a family. He's a real guy." It was exactly what his campaign manager had said about "red clay." Fowler's essential strengths, I was being told, were personal strengths, not policy strengths. This fact, I thought, might point them away from "big picture" policy connections toward a 1986-style campaign theme of personal connections. I believed it should have. But it didn't.

I returned when it was all over to talk with the same team member about the personal connections idea. "Why didn't you ever mention his two-hundred town meetings?" I asked. Answer: "We did, on radio. Radio is a very important medium." But it was, of course, television that carried all their hopes and absorbed over half their money. Then, I asked him, "What was your campaign slogan?" Answer: "Working for Georgia." So I said, "I never saw or heard it. Why didn't you ever use it on television?" Answer: "Sam Nunn used it in his TV ad." But that ad was the very one (and the only one) that highlighted Fowler's specific accomplishments for Georgia— the rejected "pork barrel" approach. Apparently, the campaign that wouldn't emphasize pork used its "campaign slogan" only once—on the one and only commercial that advertised pork. In retrospect, the media campaign his consultants gave him was undisciplined and unfocused.

In name, Fowler's team was the same one as in 1986. In that year, this was a quality team matched with a quality candidate. But in 1992, they were not a quality team. And they did not produce a quality effort. By failing to supply Fowler with a consistent and sustaining campaign theme—and particularly by downgrading personal connections—his campaign team contributed mightily to campaign drift and failure.

Coalition Maintenance

But, so, too, did the candidate himself. When he accepted, as he put it, somewhat sassily, "the superior intelligence of new information," Fowler was simply acceding to his own personal preference for policy connections. That is what representation meant to him. Keeping in touch was, I believe, a secondary aspect of representation for him—less enjoyable, less challenging, and more encumbering.

After his victory-without-victory on November 3, he was

quick to dismiss the importance of his town meetings. "All those town meetings don't mean a thing in this time of negative advertising. All that work got us nothing." A staffer echoed, "We didn't get one inch of support from all those meetings." Fowler agreed. After the runoff he commented, "I'll miss my friendships on the Hill. But I won't miss all those town meetings where you say the same things over and over to the same people—most of whom are mad at you anyway. What a waste of time when you could be thinking and reading." These comments hardly reveal enthusiasm.

A campaign aide, who accompanied him to numerous town meetings in rural Democratic areas, said afterward, "He acted very arrogant in those meetings. He lost votes. If he did that in every county, he lost votes there, too. People were turned off. Of the twenty or so [meetings] I saw, that occurred in about every case." The first sin of an elected politician is arrogance. If Fowler had shown some of it in his town meetings, then he had not made optimal use of them as vehicles for keeping in touch.[35]

When I asked his pollster afterward why the campaign team had not emphasized the personal connections theme, he argued that "from his second to his fifth year, Wyche had not sold the idea that he was in touch. The groundwork had not been laid for that theme. The infrastructure was not there. You can't save all your salesmanship for the last year." Poll results, which he called "chilling," for example, showed that between January 1991 and January 1992, the voters had become "substantially less inclined to feel Wyche 'really cares about people like me' despite relative stasis on other personal measures." There were, he believed, candidate-related reasons for rejecting a campaign theme designed to capitalize on personal connections. But that does not mean they couldn't have pushed him harder along those lines.

On the campaign trail, there were hints that Fowler had not, in fact, kept as closely in touch with some constituents as he might have—or as people expected him to. This was easiest to see among his strongest supporters in Atlanta. To some degree, this loosened contact was the inevitable result of his transition from congressman to senator and the necessary adjustment from urban toward rural interests. "I gave up the best district in the United States," he said, "forty square miles, easy to get around in. And I knew everybody. I gave it up for a huge state second only to Texas in the number of counties—159 counties each with its own government. Some of them are without an economic base; and all of them want special attention." The effects of this transition on his efforts to keep in touch cropped up often during my visits.

After a party at Manuels restaurant, a favorite Atlanta hangout throughout his career, he commented on the expectation of his old friends. "I hadn't intended to stay so long, but people kept saying, 'We never see you anymore.' Several people refused to come up and say hello. They just sat there waiting to see if I would come over to say hello to them." A couple of Atlanta women supporters described a general loosening of old bonds. "When he was in Congress," one said, "I used to kiss him whenever we met. Southerners kiss a lot. Now, when I see him, we don't kiss." And another added, "He doesn't represent us anymore. He represents the farmers."

Similarly, the minister of a black church in Atlanta commented from the pulpit one Sunday, "He used to be around here so much that he began to look a little black. Now he's looking pretty white.... We don't see him as much as we used to." Driving away, Fowler reflected, "I didn't appreciate how much of a change it would be going from House to Senate, with seven million people to represent. I can't get around to the churches as often as I used to. And when I go, I can't stay as long. I'm always hurrying to get somewhere else.... I have to get out of Atlanta so I can catch a plane to Waycross."

There was a large and very positive theme to be made out of his transition from House to Senate that might have addressed the uneasiness among his oldest supporters—and his newest ones, too. It was formulated by an Atlanta friend in answer to a question about the senator's most important accomplishment. She said, "He has tried to bring the city of Atlanta and the state of Georgia into a situation of political unity.... Wyche did not accept the idea that an Atlanta person could not hold things together. He has an idea about governing. He really understands what it means to govern."

This idea, that he had brought together a traditionally riven state, was akin to Senator Nunn's theme when he campaigned for Fowler on television and on the stump: "Wyche Fowler promised to represent the whole state, not just Atlanta, and he has done that."[36] Nunn's evidence came from a list of specific accomplishments for specific areas of the state.[37] But with a little imagination, "Working for Georgia" could have been elevated to a broad record of accomplishment that bundled Nunn's recitation of "pork barrel" projects into a more visionary representation of his diverse state as a functioning whole.

Put differently, the signal accomplishment of his 1986 campaign had been the piecing together of a statewide majority coalition that bridged both racial and regional interests. The central task of his 1992 campaign was to hold that coalition together. By any standard, it was a daunting task. He had to reassure his hard-core supporters, who tended to be black and urban, while he retained his weak supporters, who tended to be nonurban and white. And he had to do so in a state with historical sensitivities and a changing demography. He faced an abnormally large gap between his primary constituency and his reelection constituency. The strategy of his opponent was to pick off the weakly supportive elements of the reelection constituency—the white fundamentalists of North Georgia, the white gun owners of South Georgia, the white conservatives of suburban Atlanta.[38]

As a politician, Fowler understood all this. But he may have underestimated how much personal attentiveness would be required to do the reassuring and the retaining. And the suggestion here is that a personal connections theme might have kept him more constantly mindful of the personal requirements of the task and sensitized him even more to the intricacies of maintaining what his friend saw as a remarkably broad statewide governing coalition. Two examples come to mind.

Among his weakly supportive elements was northern Georgia—white, fundamentalist, oriented more toward conservative Chattanooga, Tennessee, than liberal Atlanta, leaning toward Republican for president, but still loyally Democratic in congressional elections.[39] "This area is difficult for me," he offered when we met. "They get all their news from Chattanooga. I've spent an awful lot of time in South Georgia and I've neglected the northern part of the state." He also felt less at home there than in the south, finding it, he said, "very closed ... [with] no initial expansiveness" to someone "from out of town." He needed to retain the support he had there; but he didn't. He did disappointingly on November 3 and worse in the runoff. "On November 24," said his campaign manager, "the worst was our horrendous showing in the Chattanooga media market. It's only 5 percent of the state, but it was critical and we fell through the floor."

During the runoff, Fowler had told a national reporter, "I may be white, but my soul is black." And that comment had been reprinted and widely circulated by his opponents in North Georgia.[40] It was a signature statement that I had heard him use often with black groups with whom he enjoyed exceptional rapport and support. "Black voters are especially loyal," he said. "Over twenty years I have built up a huge amount of goodwill. I believe I have their confidence, their trust, and their respect." His comment was superfluous where black voters were concerned. But it was certainly a strategic mistake to say it statewide in the midst of a delicate campaign to maintain his coalition.

Did he realize what he was doing? Did it make a difference in the outcome? Would a broad personal connections theme have made him more sensitive and constrained the freewheeling candidate from expressing himself? We cannot know. Such a theme might have injected some coalitional discipline into the campaign. As it was, he did not tend to his connections theme. "I suppose voters just felt they didn't know Fowler very well," said a leading North Georgia Democrat. "This area . . . never got used to Fowler."[41]

The single most harmful failure to keep in touch involved his inattentiveness to a core element of his 1986 coalition—the strongly supportive liberal, pro-choice women who had become disaffected in the wake of his vote in support of conservative, anti-abortion Clarence Thomas for the Supreme Court.[42] It was a mistake John Culver would never have made. And it was a more personal mistake than anything brought about by Fowler's House-to-Senate or urban-to-rural transitions.

A full year before the election, one of his oldest and closest associates talked about it. "His vote for Thomas was extremely unpopular with people like me," she said. "I'm comfortable with the idea that he represented the majority of his constituents. But he'll have to do some fence-mending with his friends." When I reported that conversation to the candidate, he agreed that the disaffected women were "some of my strongest supporters." "I'll let the activists cool down," he said, "and then I'll get them together. I will spend time with them, give them my reasons, talk it out, and tell them I need their help, we're on the right side. I'll work to bring them back into the fold." That was November 1991. He did do some of that, in "several small meetings," he said later. "But it was not a priority for me."

His tepid response registered at the level where hard-core support is most needed. In July, his campaign office coordinator said, "We've lost some of our volunteers because of the Thomas vote. Several people had told us, 'I wouldn't work for him again because of the Thomas vote.' Whether that means they won't vote for him, I don't know. But it hurts us with the volunteers." It also may have dampened the endorsement of the *Atlanta Constitution*. After our meeting with the editorial board, with questioning led by a prominent female member, he commented, "They are upset with me that I'm not as pure a liberal as I used to be.... They are particularly mad at me because I won't say I made a mistake in my Thomas vote.... So they will give me a backhanded endorsement." Which they did. "I could have done without their endorsement," he said during the runoff. "It's like you want to call them, and say, 'If that's the way you feel, I'd rather not have your endorsement.'"

The pro-choice activists did not return wholeheartedly to the fold until the runoff, when they organized a furious direct mail campaign and held a well-covered press conference. It was too late. As Fowler noted afterward, "Once they had sent all those messages the first time, there wasn't much they could do to turn everyone around." But the relationship during the runoff highlighted, once again, the degree to which Fowler's personal desire to remain unencumbered could keep him from securing the political support he needed. Joining the broad coalition of women's groups at their press conference, Fowler would not admit to his doubts about the Thomas vote. "The press will emphasize that I told them 'No' when they asked me if I had any doubts," he said as we left. "I shouldn't have said that. I should have said, 'I may have regrets several years from now, but I won't know till then.' I'm my own worst enemy."

His problem was as much the untimely failure to explain his vote and to educate his supporters on his overall record on women's issues as it was the vote itself. Explanation of a vote is especially important when the vote cast is on the winning side, since the consequences of a winning vote remain traceable and visible.[43] Fowler's vote on the Gulf War was on the losing side, and its consequences were blurred. No one I talked to believed that his war vote affected the outcome; and Fowler's own view was, "I don't think that hurt me much."[44]

Fowler's campaign team did estimate that the inaction and the opposition of his female supporters may well have cost him his reelection on November 3. "I don't know how many didn't vote for me," he said during the runoff, "but a lot. I don't know how many 'a lot' is. I know some wanted to punish me. I will admit, privately, that had they gone all out for me, I would have won." With more constant personal enthusiasm for the many-sided process of keeping in touch, he might well have secured the all-out support he needed.

The Fowler campaign — at least to November 3 — was a campaign without a great deal of palpable enthusiasm. Organizationally, the operation was tightly held at the top—as Fowler himself had predicted—by the candidate and his campaign manager. The main body of the campaign staff seemed much more isolated from what was going on than the staffs of the broadly participatory, big-happy-family of the Culver and Tsongas campaigns. Some of this lack of excitement was probably an unintended consequence of a campaign without a positive theme. As one staffer put it, "In 1986, we had a mission. This year, there is no mission."

Among campaigners outside Atlanta, there was a great sense of distance from the top. After November 3, they complained that they got too little attention, too few supplies, and too little say. "The people running the campaign in Atlanta were out of touch," said a top operative in South Georgia. "They did not have their feet on the ground and did not listen to what we were telling them. I could see it coming. We had no signs here, no bumper stickers. Powers were not delegated well. We felt left out of it. The people who tried to coordinate didn't work well with the local people in this area.... It seemed like a very unfocused campaign and it frustrated people here."

The Atlanta people who had some contact with the field operation agreed. "The campaign doesn't reach anyone personally," said one. "It's entirely an electronic campaign. The manager doesn't talk to anyone. That's his biggest problem. What's going on out there? We haven't a clue except for the poll numbers and the media. He thinks everybody out there is busy, but they aren't."

Fowler's personal interactions with his loyal, middle-level campaign staff and volunteer workers seemed to me to lack the sense of attachment, warmth, and appreciation that characterized the Tsongas and Culver campaigns. There were times, I thought, when he could easily have stopped by, talked with them personally, and energized them. But he didn't. Sometimes in private he could be quite critical of their efforts. It seemed as if he felt that a more personal relationship with his staffers would have been another unwanted encumbrance.

A number of signs indicated that Wyche Fowler's campaign team was not of the same quality or as close to him as it had been six years before. In 1986, he resembled Paul Tsongas; in 1992, he resembled Dick Clark.

CHAPTER 6

A CANDIDATE AND A CAMPAIGN II

CAMPAIGN DYNAMICS

ONE OF THE FONDEST HOPES of every candidate and every campaign is to be able to control the events, the dialogue, and the flow of the campaign season. And one of the certainties of every campaign season is that these hopes will be dashed: All campaigns, participants tell us, run out of control to some degree. But the matter of degree and the potential for damage control are crucial. Some environmental conditions are totally beyond the control of the campaigning candidate, and I have paid little attention to them in this study. Where varying degrees of control are possible, however, an outside observer can examine evidence and make judgments.

From my vantage point, it appeared that the Fowler campaigners gradually lost control of the flow of the campaign, particularly as it developed on television. They were put at a huge initial disadvantage by their lack of a positive, defining campaign theme and, relatedly, by the defensive stance adopted by the candidate toward the campaign dialogue. But there were miscalculations by the candidate and mistakes by the team that further hampered their efforts to create a more favorable campaign dynamic or to cope with an unfavorable one.

Candidate Fowler began the campaign with a miscalculation. He underestimated his challenger. In January, he commented, "I think the Republicans are still looking for someone else to run against me.... I think they think Coverdell can't beat me." When Coverdell became his opponent, he told a South Georgia newspaper editor,

> I feel fortunate that I have Coverdell as opposed to, you know, a lot of other people.... I'm proud of my record and I'm certainly not letting the grass grow under my feet in the sense that I've come home and done all my town meetings, tried to stay in touch, that sort of thing—and have. But this anti-incumbent stuff that they're all playing on is tricky business. Coverdell has a record, see. He's claiming he's a big outsider, but he was nineteen years in the state senate; he was Republican party chairman in '86 for Mattingly.... He's not Mr. Newcomer and Mr. Outsider. He's got a public record just like mine. And we can point out the differences in those records and then the public can make their own judgments. I'm comfortable with that.... He's not the kind of candidate who can really stir any enthusiasm. He ran against me for Congress the first time. I know Paul very well.... He will run a very workmanlike campaign, but he's a lot like George Bush in more than manners and mannerisms. He doesn't have any trouble hiring a political hatchet man to hit below the belt when necessary.

Fowler never expressed the slightest respect for his opponent as a person or as a campaigner.

Because Fowler himself was such a talented campaigner, he tended to see a campaign against Coverdell very much as a contest of personal talents. And he derived some of his confidence about the eventual election outcome, I believe, from the expectation that he could control the contest. He was unable to imagine that he could be defeated by Coverdell—so lacking, he believed, in courage, forcefulness, and breadth, let alone spontaneity and wit. He never doubted that when the time came for a head-to-head confrontation, he would take the measure of Paul Coverdell. His disdain drained some of the necessary sense of urgency from the campaign. Difficult decisions that should have been taken could be postponed because, no matter what, the master campaigner of 1986 would surely outshine his opponent.

The candidate was not alone in these assumptions. As the Republican primary shaped up, Coverdell was the preferred opponent of Fowler's campaign team, too, because he, like Fowler, was a political insider. The kind of opponent they most feared—in the year of anti-incumbent sentiment and Ross Perot independence—was a political outsider. "My greatest fear," said one staffer, "is that the recognized candidates will collapse and some wealthy businessman will come along with unlimited funds, will be very successful in the Atlanta suburbs, and make us spend more money than we have to combat him."

Of the four Republicans in the primary, the attractive newcomer Charles Tanksley was the one they most feared. Fowler described him as "a better candidate than Coverdell—more forceful and presentable." "The one that worries me," said another team member, "is Tanksley—forty years old, never been in politics, forceful. He has everything a challenger needs this year, except [big smile] money." And he added, "I pray [fingers crossed] it's Coverdell." It was the conventional wisdom.[1] On August 11 after a Republican primary and a runoff, the challenger became Paul Coverdell.

For a long time, the self-confidence of the candidate and the preferences of the campaign team did not seem to be misplaced. Not, at least, in public. On October 11, an Associated Press story reported that "polls and pundits say Wyche Fowler is a safe bet for reelection."[2] Four days later, the *Atlanta Journal-Constitution*'s campaign story began, "Holding a big lead in the polls, [Fowler] also has seven times more money available than [his] GOP challenger."[3] A seasoned observer called that combination "the recipe for a landslide Fowler victory."[4] And another said, "I don't gather Coverdell's catching fire."[5]

At the time, Fowler was holding a twenty-two point lead in the latest Mason-Dixon poll and a twenty-four-point lead in the *Atlanta Journal-Constitution* poll.[6] Georgia's pundits talked in mid-October as if there were no race, no issues, and no reason to replace the incumbent. Coverdell, they said, had been his party's "weakest candidate."[7] "If he's 14 points down in the middle of October," said columnist Bill Shipp, "he's a dead man."[8] The Dick Clark and John Culver campaigns have shown, however, that while first-term incumbents may get a head start, that may be all they get. Support within their prospective reelection constituency may remain tentative and fragile—even when they are ahead in the middle of October.

While Fowler and his campaigners had felt from the beginning that they would win, they never believed it would be anything but very close. And for some time they had worried that upbeat public polls and published finance reports would produce overconfidence among their supporters. In March, one of them worried that

> there is coming to be an opinion that Wyche is safer than everyone thought last year. People have seen our reports of cash on hand and some [Mason-Dixon] polling data.... which is an improvement over earlier polls. The Republican candidates are held in low regard by the Georgia opinion makers. All this translates into a lack of urgency among our supporters.... They aren't paying attention. Their attitude is: "What? You've got an election?"

In late summer, Fowler admitted, "One of the big problems I have right now is energizing my supporters. They say, 'Oh, you don't have any trouble.'"

There is some evidence that this problem continued all the way to November 3. When I arrived in October, two days after the upbeat mid-October *Atlanta Journal-Constitution* poll, a staffer complained about a continuing lack of energy and organization. "People are calling Atlanta headquarters from places like Macon and Columbus asking for a yard sign," he said. "It's nothing like 1986. In that campaign, people worked; they did anything they were asked. We had a mission. This time, there is no mission. I get around the state and I see it. I guess, everybody seems to think it's over."

At the headquarters later that day, the volunteer coordinator painted a corroborating picture. "We're having a terrible time getting volunteers. When I started, I imagined it would be the easiest thing in the world, but it's been a nightmare." Their comments may have been one more indication of the campaigner's failure to communicate a sense of urgency to his supporters.

When I returned for the runoff in mid-November, the contrast with November 3 was overwhelming. In my notes I wrote, "The change was pretty amazing. An empty, laid-back headquarters had turned into a real campaign." Staffers at the headquarters told me: "The morning after the election, the phones started ringing and they never stopped—four lines lighted up at once." "Everyone wanted to help. People who thought they would give Wyche a scare the first time are now scared to death about Coverdell." "People called to say, 'We didn't know Wyche might lose. We didn't think you needed any help.'" "We have more energy and fire in the belly than in the last six months." "We have a campaign now. We didn't have one before. All we had was 'keep the Atlanta Braves going for seven games and fly in under the radar.'" "Money is no problem; volunteers are no problem; getting out the vote ... that's the problem." Now, they were running scared. But their comments only confirmed the inadequacy of their pre-November 3 campaign—the one they "should have won."

During the runoff, I should interject, the candidate had finally found a theme: "I will support President Clinton and help break the gridlock in Washington." It was, however, a theme that was totally devoid of any emphasis on a representational connection at home—policy or personal. And it totally submerged the free-spirited, freewheeling entrepreneur. He had submerged his independent persona in the hope of winning.

Returning to the situation as of early October, Fowler's own (October 11) poll showed horse race numbers like those reported in the media. He held a twenty-one-point lead, 50 to 29, over Coverdell. Nonetheless, he and his team had found trends to worry about. Fowler expressed concern that "we're having trouble getting above 50 percent." His concern was based on his pollster's "law of politics" that "the challenger will get between 85 percent and 100 percent of the undecideds." The pollster himself worried that "the latest survey shows a relapse of sorts for Wyche, felt most acutely among downscale voters." Campaign manager Johnstone worried because Fowler's positive job approval rating had dropped nine points and his positive favorability rating—the two most closely watched barometers—had dropped five points since the previous week's poll. "It's the trend that bothers me," he said, "because there is no obvious reason for such a significant decline. I'm not saying we're losing or anything like that.... But I do want the race to flatten out pretty soon. And until it does, I'll be nervous. There's a worrisome similarity to 1986. We were twenty points behind against an incumbent and we caught him." As it turned out, his fears were justified.

CAMPAIGN DECISIONS: THE TELEVISION BATTLE

Students of political advertising find that "a common theme" among television consultants is that "media strategy [develops] in stages."[9] The dynamics of the Fowler campaign and the gradual loss of control by the Fowler team can best be traced through the several stages of their decision making about television commercials.

Their first decision was when to begin their television campaign. Their original plan called for eleven weeks of television—three weeks around the time of the Republican primary in late July and eight weeks to wind up the campaign. "I have a big decision to make soon—a $750,000 decision," said Fowler in April.

> The plan is to go on the air with three weeks of TV right around the time of the Republican primary—two weeks before, one week afterward. One idea is to take some of the play away from the Republicans.... We learned this from Mattingly in 1986. Immediately after my victory, he went on TV ... and took all the

momentum out of my victory. But mostly it's to help me establish myself. Nobody knows who I am or what I've done. And my numbers are pretty low.... I need to tell people who I am. But $750,000 will take half my damn money! I'll cut down to two weeks at least.

His campaign manager had already been hesitating because campaign contributions were coming in very slowly. With his goal of "being competitive" with any opponent, he had budgeted $2 million for the eight week endgame.

In June, they decided to cancel the early segment altogether and to spend their money on an uninterrupted eight-week fall campaign beginning in September, even though their opponent might gain traction over the undefined incumbent. They decided, in other words, to run one continuous, high-octane television campaign, as they had done in 1986—albeit with more money and for a longer period. "We will wait until Labor Day," said Fowler. "Coverdell will start negative and we'll see how it goes." In August, a consultant's memo said, "This race has all the makings of a bitter and bruising ten-round slugfest and the candidate who is left standing may well be the candidate with more blood on his gloves than on his chin." But Fowler waited for his opponent to go first.

In retrospect, this may have been a mistake. It was not 1986, and his rope-a-dope strategy was not appropriate for an incumbent. It delayed Fowler's effort to define himself for one month, at a time when each of his prospective opponents had already gained traction. For several months, all four Republican aspirants had been touring Georgia singing the same tune— that Wyche Fowler was too liberal for Georgia. As one report of their primary campaign began, "Three Republican hopefuls for the U.S. Senate attacked incumbent Wyche Fowler as liberal and not representative of the conservative values of most Georgians."[10] In summer, however, when Fowler was leading all four prospective challengers by twenty points in the polls, his campaigners were confident that the decision to wait was not a critical one.[11] In retrospect, it effectively ceded the initiative to the challenger, and it pushed the incumbent far down the path toward a campaign of retaliatory counterattacks.

In the wake of his victory in the Republican runoff primary, challenger Coverdell launched the anti-incumbent campaign Fowler expected. He described the incumbent as "[so] disconnected [that] in no way can [he] claim to represent the views and attitudes of this conservative southern state."[12] His television campaign began with the "too liberal" theme, packaged in a singing jingle by a small-town grandmother, tying Fowler to Ted Kennedy and telling voters to "vote Paul Coverdell in and vote Wyche Fowler out." This first-stage, takeoff commercial did for Coverdell what Paul Tsongas's initial "Tickets" ad had done for him. It pushed a challenger over the crucial recognition threshold.

Coverdell's grassroots campaign continued on this theme to the end. Unexpectedly, however, the challenger's television campaign turned away from the "too liberal" theme and zeroed in on Fowler's personal performance. It surprised the Fowler team. "We thought," said one member, "that Coverdell would go ideological against Fowler. . . . But he stayed away from the ideological and stayed with the personal." That is, he attacked the dimension deemed to be Fowler's point of greatest strength, the dimension left unprotected by Fowler's failure to adopt a positive campaign theme that embraced it.

The challenger's commercials charged that Fowler lied about not bouncing checks at the House bank when he served in that body; that he voted for pay raises and perks for himself and higher taxes for his constituents; that he deceived the voters by leading "a double life," voting one way in Washington and talking another way at home. And all these charges were bundled in a broad lack-of-personal-connections theme with the tag line "Wyche Fowler is taking good care of himself. But you can't trust Wyche Fowler to take care of you." "After sixteen years in Washington, you can't trust Wyche Fowler."

The most devastating out-of-touch, anti-incumbent commercial involved Fowler's alleged check bouncing. In a child custody hearing with his former wife in Texas in 1986, and while he was still a House member, Fowler had said, "Thankfully, we have a bank that doesn't zap me when I bounce a check." That remark, he explained after the election, "was my anarchistic sense of humor. Sue's lawyer was grilling me since I had a 'foreign' bank account, not a Texas bank account. 'What if your check bounced?' he asked. And I shot back sarcastically.... At Sue's request, that court record had been sealed. But the Republicans had gotten it by hook or crook. That is what made me so angry, especially since we had proved that we never bounced a check."

His explanation is certainly consistent with his free-spirited behavior generally—and with its sometime boomeranging effects. In 1986, the Republicans had apparently let it lie harmlessly. In 1992, however, in the context of the highly publicized House bank scandal concerning member overdrafts, it became—despite Fowler's strenuous denials—the stuff of a dynamite negative television ad.

With a picture of a hand on a Bible and the superimposed words "What is the truth, Wyche?" a voice intoned,

> In 1986, Wyche Fowler told a court he had to bounce checks on the House bank to make ends meet. He said, "Thankfully, we have a bank that doesn't zap me when I bounce a check." But now, he's telling Georgia voters, "I never bounced a check." What is the truth, Wyche? Did you lie under oath about bouncing checks, or are you lying now to keep your job? The truth is, after sixteen years in Washington, you can't trust Wyche Fowler.

Since House records did not go back that far, nothing could be proven one way or another. His Houston comment became the great "uncontrollable" of the 1992 campaign. It underpinned all the other Coverdell attacks on Fowler's trustworthiness. And it plagued his campaign to the end.

The Coverdell television campaign was the most completely negative and the most completely personal attack of any, save one, of the thirty-six campaigns I observed. It attacked the character, the attentiveness, and the representativeness of Wyche Fowler. And it was a faceless campaign. The challenger never spoke and never appeared in any of his television ads. And not one of them ever mentioned what he would do if elected. As commentator Bill Shipp said, "It was totally negative. It failed to articulate a single time why Paul Coverdell should be a senator."[13] The challenger was campaigning on television as Mr. X.

From anonymity, Coverdell was able to target Fowler for a lack of personal connectedness—a relationship that Fowler and team had never decided to defend with maximum enthusiasm. At the same time, as Mr. X, Coverdell could simply black out his own persona and record, thus denying Fowler the direct political incumbent versus political incumbent, *mano a mano* comparison he had been counting on. All in all, the Coverdell campaign seemed to be succeeding in doing exactly what the Fowler people believed it could not do: it was successfully portraying Fowler as the untrustworthy insider who had lost touch with his home base. And, by default, it was putting forward a faceless challenger as the outsider alternative. Media observers threw their bouquets at Coverdell's creative, disciplined, and homegrown campaign team.[14]

The Coverdell campaign turned out to be more thematic, more focused, and more successful than Fowler and his team had thought possible. With the election three weeks away, they faced their second strategic television decision—when and how to cope with the Coverdell campaign. Their lead was deteriorating and they were not controlling the campaign dialogue. Said Fowler, "His negative ads knocked us down five points in one week. I'm going to have to make a decision as to how hard we hit back at him."

A memo accompanying Fowler's October 10 tracking poll said, "For Wyche to win, he needs to realize more support among older/downscale, more conservative white Democrats, even if we have to destroy Coverdell in the process." Afterward, one consultant recalled that by the time they faced their second decision, "the window had closed on a pro-Fowler message.... The voters did not want to listen to Fowler's accomplishments.... His issues—health, education—weren't sufficient to hold the line.... [And] Wyche hadn't given us anything to work with.... We knew it had to be a negative campaign against Coverdell." Lacking a strong positive image with which to seek support in his own right, Fowler's only remaining strategy was to drive up the negative image of his opponent.

Early on, the Fowler people had prepared three negative television ads of their own. Each one criticized Coverdell's record as state senator or as director of the Peace Corps. Tutored by focus groups, they considered one of the three to be especially hard-hitting. It attacked Coverdell as soft on crime, for supporting a Willie Horton-type furlough program. It had been prepared to hold in reserve against the ideological, pro-death penalty, anti-pornography attack they thought might come (but never did) as Coverdell's final thrust. All three ads were in the can, to be used only when Fowler was attacked. From the beginning, their bottom line assumption had been that they would be attacked and that they would successfully counterattack. "The wrong lesson," advised media consultant Frank Greer, "is that negative campaigns work. The right lesson is that if you stand up and fight back, you can beat them. If you don't, you'll lose."[15] Pollster Alan Secrest took an even stronger position. "It's accepted now—chop the other guy's legs out before he does it to you."[16]

When Coverdell's attacks came, the Fowler campaigners retaliated in very measured fashion. For a while, nothing; then with one, then two of the three ads—but always holding back the third, most hard-hitting "crime spot." In mid-October, Fowler ruminated about his options. "I don't think I've done anything that would make people turn me out," he said.

The only worry I have is the possibility of a runoff. What would I do if it came to a runoff? Would I nuclear bomb him with everything we've got on him? And we have some awful stuff on him. So far, I won't let it be used. Should I use it now? I think I'm getting some credit for staying positive—at least with the public. Not with the newspapers.... If I go negative, they'll be all over me. I'm going to wait till the end of the week and get one fresh poll. If my lead drops from 16 to 13, I'm going to have to hit back. I won't want to, but I'll have to. So I have postponed making that decision for the time being.

One team member advocated instant and maximum retaliation with all three negative ads the moment Coverdell's first attack appeared. "We waited and waited and waited," he complained later. "We saw the whites of their eyes. We saw their tonsils. And still we did not attack."

When it was all over, Fowler took full responsibility for the decision to make a graduated response.

About three weeks out from the election ... we had to decide whether to go negative and, if we did, how far to go. Well, we decided to go only halfway. We went with our mildest negative ad. As you know, I always felt uncomfortable about going negative. I knew we would have to, but I didn't want to. Some wanted us to go with our toughest ad, to hit him hard right away. I didn't want to and we didn't. They tell me now that if we had done that, we would have won. Maybe they're right.

A plausible explanation is that he did not think he needed to.

Ten days out from the election, with Coverdell's image of Fowler overtaking Fowler's image of Fowler, and with his polls showing that "Wyche remains extremely vulnerable," the team faced their third pivotal television decision. Should they prepare an ad responding specifically to each of the attacks? Should they release their third and hardest-hitting negative ad? Or should they do nothing. On this, they were divided, and they decided to do nothing. Against those who wanted to hit with the toughest negative ad on the grounds that it would appeal to weakly supportive, "down-scale whites," Fowler again said no.

A second consultant explained afterward, "We didn't go with the crime spot. All our research told us it was our most effective ad. But Wyche would not use it.... He did not like it, and if the truth be known, he did not believe he needed it. That was our biggest mistake of the campaign. If we had put it on, we would have won [on November 3]."

A week later, with their polls telling them that if the election were held today, Fowler would likely lose his seat, they revisited their earlier decision. It was their fourth crucial television decision. Again, Fowler vetoed the use of the most negative ad—not, he said, because he thought he did not need it, but because "I had always objected to negative campaigning." Nevertheless, he breached the barrier by permitting the same attack to go forward in a mailing to the Atlanta suburbs.[17] For television, the Fowler campaign decided to prepare a response ad, replying to each one of the various personal attacks in turn, with "supporting editorial comment," and with attribution for each comment flashed across the screen. A third team member believed that it helped—but too late: "There is some suggestion in our postelection polls that without that response ad, things might have been much worse. Wyche got a majority of the late deciders. Had we put the response ad on earlier, it could have made a big difference.... The decision [their third one] not to go with the response ad was the single biggest mistake we made."

Team members could not agree afterward when and how they should have retaliated; but all thought that different decisions might have made a difference. They all agreed that at each of the four points of decision—except the first—they were already caught behind the campaign flow.

When asked for a one-sentence explanation of the outcome, one Georgia pundit said, "I think that Wyche Fowler's failure to answer Coverdell's negative and effective campaign early on cost him the election."[18] He did not define "early on," but most likely he agreed with the assessment of the campaigner who estimated that the immediate use of the soft on crime ad would have gained Fowler thirty thousand votes.

During the endgame, Fowler's genuine ambivalence toward negative campaigning—and his lack of a killer instinct—was surely part of the problem. Since he finally agreed to use his most negative ad in the runoff, one plausible conjecture is that while he may have disliked doing it, he also may have believed that he could win without using the TV ad before November 3. The largest strategic mistake, however, remained his—and his team's—failure to fashion an overarching and protective positive campaign theme. Without it, they lacked the tools to get control of the campaign—either its early positive stage or its later negative stage. That disadvantage manifested itself anew, I believe, as I watched—sometimes at the scene, sometimes from afar—the four televised candidate debates.

CAMPAIGN CONTROL: DEBATES

Given the consensus view among his campaigners that Fowler had won a critical personal victory in his one debate in 1986, his team looked forward in 1992 to debates as a major plus for their candidate. "If Coverdell wins," said one, "I'm going to insist on debates, lots of debates, Lincoln-Douglas debates . . . and we are going to set the rules." There were five debates. But the Fowler camp got no help from them.

When a challenger faces an incumbent in a debate, the challenger needs only to hold his or her own in order to cross the qualification threshold. And that Fowler's challenger clearly did. The incumbent is held to a higher standard: he or she must present six years' worth of accomplishments. And, of course, the incumbent must decide how to package his or her senatorial performance. In this case, I thought the challenger met the test; the incumbent did not.

From the time the two sides negotiated over the debates, Coverdell won media credit for taking the initiative.[19] The format for the debates—ample time for each candidate to ask questions of the other—proved more beneficial to the challenger. He stuck doggedly to his personalized anti-incumbent theme and buttressed it with an attack on Congress as an institution: via term limits, the line item veto, and the balanced budget amendment. His debate themes thus neatly reinforced his media themes in presenting a coordinated and disciplined attack.

And Fowler, without a theme to discipline his presentation, proved ill-equipped to reply in kind.

For one thing, he was thrown off-balance by the thrust of the challenger's campaign. He had wanted and expected debates in which he could demonstrate that he was not an extreme liberal. He had wanted and expected broad policy-oriented debates in which his superior working knowledge of issues such as health, education, and jobs and his superior debating skills would carry the day.

Early on, he was merely baffled when this kind of debate was not shaping up. "All Coverdell said was we've got to get rid of Fowler—no policies, no programs ... no positive thrust. Pretty soon, I would think [he] will start talking policy." "Coverdell's press conference today was just 'Fowler, Kennedy, Metzenbaum.' You would think, wouldn't you, that he could find some way to put on a little more positive face than that for the voters." After a couple of debates, however, he became frustrated and angry.

> I can't for the life of me understand a man who campaigns with-out any program of any sort, who does absolutely nothing except call his opponent a liar and engage in character assassination.... I don't understand why he doesn't talk about his record. There is so much he has done.... He has a lot to be proud of. But he never mentions his public service. He just attacks me.

Fowler had known from the beginning that he would face a negative, anti-incumbent campaign. But he had not prepared a thoroughgoing, pro-incumbent defense.

Why not? Because, I would argue, he did not think he had to. "Do you know what Wyche said when I told him that 51 percent was the best he could expect?" asked a consultant afterward. "He said, 'That's all I need.' Do you know any candidate who would react like that? He thought he could come in under the radar." Fowler may have believed that his opponent would not or could not conduct the kind of single-minded, relentless attack he did conduct. Or he may have been confident that he could handle any person-to-person confrontation when the time came.

Fowler certainly worried about the debates. But it was natural and habitual for him to resist discipline and to rely heavily on his considerable improvisational and entrepreneurial skills. And he treated extensive preparations as another unwanted encumbrance. "I would not presume to brief him," said a top press aide. "And he would not want to be briefed. He would go out of his way to make sure it did not appear that anybody briefed him. If you did make a suggestion, you would worry that he would say just the opposite."

As it turned out, whenever straightforward policy confrontations occurred during the debates, Fowler came across as an active, thoughtful, constructive member of the Senate. And he did carry the debate. The problem was that such clear confrontations occurred only in the interstices of the challenger's all-purpose anti-incumbent attack. On these more numerous occasions, Fowler's performance consisted of personal counterattacks and scattershot sallies that sometimes scored and sometimes didn't and never accumulated into a coherent message. A campaign theme must be carried into the debate; it cannot be created during the debate.

On a purely personal basis, incumbent Fowler could never work up any respect for his challenger. And given, as he was, to free-spirited behavior and humorous storytelling, he often imitated and made fun of his opponent in private. His temptation was to make his private disdain public. And the danger was that in public it would seem condescending and arrogant. Prior to his first debate with Coverdell, one of his campaigners said, "The only thing I said to him was 'Keep your cool.' I wanted to say one other thing, but I didn't dare say it: 'Don't be condescending.'" It would have been good advice. But it would not have mattered.

In the middle of their first television debate, Fowler put this question to Coverdell: "Tell me, what do you think Bobby Cox's [World Series] pitching rotation ought to be?" It was about as unexpected a question as one could imagine, despite World Series fever in Georgia, to an opponent whom he wished to show up, put down, and knock off stride. It was disdainful. It brought a smile from Fowler, laughs from the audience, and protestations from Coverdell—who did not answer either that question (which Fowler asked twice) or the follow-up question: "Name two Braves pitchers." It was an unorthodox and risky move that no handler would have allowed. But it was vintage Fowler, and he entertained himself with it in the car afterward. "That little _____ has been running around pretending he knows something about baseball—like picking the Braves in six in the morning paper. I asked him to name two Braves pitchers, didn't I? He couldn't name them." When I wondered out loud, "How will the voters react," he laughed, "I know how the Braves fans will react."

His baseball ploy and his offstage reaction must be understood in the light of Fowler's love affair with the Atlanta Braves baseball team. The self-described "number one Braves fan," he went often to the stadium. And when he did, he typically helped to broadcast half an inning. During the World Series of 1991, he followed the team to Minnesota. And the most pleasurable event of his campaign season was a foul ball he caught and threw back to the crowd, as captured and replayed—with his running commentary—on Atlanta television.

He used the Braves and even "the catch" to bridge the gap and open communication with varied groups in his reelection constituency. Politically, his connection to the Braves put him in touch with people whom he would not normally reach. And he talked about getting important intensity soundings at the ball park on his Clarence Thomas vote. "The Braves have been good to me," he said one evening at the ball park. "They have brought me support I wouldn't have gotten many other ways—people with high school educations, in the workforce, and white." And later, "When the Indian groups protested the Atlanta Braves chop, Jane Fonda and Ted Turner stopped. But I was sitting right next to them in their box and I kept right on chopping.

I was the only person in the box doing the chop. I get a lot of points with the fans for that." No doubt he was right.[20] And no doubt he did know, in Savannah, how Braves fans would react to his debate ploy.

But there were other aspects of his attachment to the Braves that illuminated the pitfalls of such freewheeling campaign behavior. Media accounts sometimes hinted at the risk of taking his baseball with Ted and Jane.[21] In one focus group, a male participant presented a different perception of the senator at the ball park than Fowler's own. During three rounds of questions, he said nothing. But on the final question, "Any sense for his accomplishments . . . or achievements you associate with him?" he finally spoke up.

> PARTICIPANT #1: I believe a servant like him in his position—One Sunday I was watching the ball game. Mr. Fowler was there. Of course, he was in the Ted Turner [box] next to him. When he got up to go out, I don't know how many people were trying to speak to him. It seemed like what he did best was turning his head, not being face-to-face with anybody. You'd think he was in Russia somewhere. He knew Ted Turner and Jane—knew them real well. But when it was over with, I made a comment to my wife. I said, "Look at him. He thinks he's in Russia. We're strangers."
> PARTICIPANT #2: Of course, you've got to think a public person ought to be able to enjoy a ball game without doing that.
> PARTICIPANT #1: I don't mind a little relaxation. When he went out, in his position, he ought to say hi or something like that.
> PARTICIPANT #3: I don't think he's very friendly.

One person's sense of being in touch can be another person's sense of elitist arrogance. More generally, as the journalist Pete Hamill reminds us, "Politicians come and go, but they all get booed at the ballpark."[22]

In trying to embarrass Coverdell personally on the baseball question, Fowler was on secure ground. In private, he liked to compare their hobbies as reported in the paper. For Fowler: "baseball, fishing, archaeology and poetry." For Coverdell: "yard work and dining out." But in trying to negotiate a reelection constituency of weak supporters, he may have been on less secure ground than he believed. For them, Coverdell's reply may have hit the mark. "Are you serious, Senator? You may think this is a joke, but I don't. This has nothing to do with the Braves. This has to do with the future of our country." Indeed, Fowler's own long-term staffers, watching television, did not find his baseball riposte entertaining or wise. They found it, instead, to be a frivolous bit of condescension ("It demeaned the process") when what was needed was a serious message of accomplishment.

I found his ploy very entertaining. But in light of what he could have done thematically, given the Savannah debate context, I wondered about what he did *not* say during the debate. He had available to him, close at hand, the ingredients of a pro-incumbent, personal connections theme, and he failed utterly to grasp it.

During the drive to the debate, the senator had displayed the morning edition of the *Savannah Morning News*, which endorsed him for reelection because of all he had done for the local economy. Most notably, he had secured funding for the Talmadge Bridge spanning the Savannah River between Georgia and South Carolina. "How's this for timing?" he had exulted. "It's a conservative newspaper, but it is under new ownership and someone there likes me." Then, as we came within view of the majestic bridge itself, he exclaimed, "I got them the money to build that bridge. They had a senator from this very area, Mack Mattingly, and he couldn't get them the money for this bridge. The only promise I made to the people here in 1986 was that I would get that new bridge built. And I did."

Here was the raw material to underpin a sweeping claim of personal representation. And I waited to hear him use it. Yet during the one-hour debate he did not mention either the editorial endorsement or the senatorial accomplishment. The reason, I deduced, was that he had no overarching representational theme into which, almost by reflex, they could be integrated.

In preparation for the final runoff debate, excerpts from the first two debates were shown to both male and female focus groups. "The women," explained one campaigner, "reacted very strongly against Fowler smiling at Coverdell. They said it was arrogant and condescending. To the men, it projected confidence. But the women had a much stronger negative reaction." To wit: "Wyche was a smart aleck." "He looked like a preppie wasp—I'm better than you are." "I didn't like his laughing." "I couldn't stand Wyche."[23] As a result, Fowler's campaigners told him to stop smiling at his opponent.

Before the runoff debate Fowler agreed. "My advisers have told me I must not smile during the debate. For some reason, women don't like that." But after the debate he said, "I know. I smiled at him. But I just couldn't help myself." He might have added, as he had at other times, "I'm my own worst enemy."

Prior to their first debate, Fowler had said, "They're trying to make me blow up." And when it was over, he had asked, "Did my anger show through?" It had not. But under relentless attacks in subsequent debates, with a slipping lead, it became increasingly difficult for him to hold back. In their final debate, he finally blew up—over the use of his Houston check-bouncing comment.

> FOWLER: [I] was fighting to see my daughter in a custody battle.
> COVERDELL: You were fighting to avoid child support payments.
> FOWLER: That's an absolute, bold-faced lie. If you were a parent, you would never stoop to such tactics.[24]

Without a positive theme to set his own course, he had, indeed, been swept into a nasty personal campaign he did not want. "I crave privacy," he said just before the runoff. "When this is over, the first thing I'm going to do is go home and take a long bath to wash all this slime off me."

Accounts of the debates featured charge and countercharge. And when they were over, these exchanges helped listeners characterize the campaign as relentlessly negative.[25] The candidates received equal blame. To this observer, the debates showed that the disciplined campaigner with a consistent theme had carried the campaign to the undisciplined campaigner with an inconsistent theme.

In subject matter, timing, and execution, the Coverdell campaign threw the Fowler campaign off-stride and left them unable to control either the substance of the debate or the momentum of the campaign. When it was over, one team member confessed to their loss of control. "We wanted a campaign of Fowler against Coverdell. The one campaign we did not want was Fowler against Fowler, and that's the campaign we got.... [They] were able to paint their picture of him; and we were not able to paint our picture." The comment is accurate as far as it goes. But the problem with it is this: The campaign team had produced nothing that could reasonably be called "our picture." The team was solidly implicated in the failure.

Campaign Postmortems

Among Fowler's team members, postmortems centered on the November 3 outcome and on the shortcomings of the candidate. One staffer understood the fundamental failure of the team to construct a campaign theme. "We didn't develop an adequate, positive message for the campaign. It was a blur in people's minds. Because he never had a theme or message, he was much more defenseless when the attacks came. He was pretty nearly a blank slate. And we never filled in the slate on Wyche's behalf." But this was a minor chord.

The dominant chord centered on the comparison of the "unsurpassed campaigner" of 1986 and the flawed candidate of 1992. Since the campaign had failed, it had to be Wyche Fowler's fault. He was, after all, the master campaigner. There was passing attention to the contextual change that had occurred in the six-year interelection period, especially the growing whiteness and the growing Republicanism of the Georgia electorate. But it was candidate change that carried most of the explanatory load.

Some aides held strong opinions on this score. "Wyche gave it away. He deserved to lose. There is nothing personal about it," said one. And he explained,

> He was a different candidate in 1992 than he was in 1986. In 1986, he was sincere, attentive, hungry. In 1992, he was aloof, imperial, condescending. In 1986, he listened and worked the state. In 1992, he did not take advice to work the vineyards.... The bottom line is that you've got to want the job and you've got to fight for it. Eighty percent of the blame is at Wyche's feet.

Another expressed similar sentiments.

> I've never been in a campaign before where the candidate did not want to win, did not bust his balls to win, did not have the fire in the belly it takes to win. Wyche Fowler is a great guy, but he was a terrible candidate—undisciplined, arrogant, lazy.... In 1986, he was a great candidate. He won that election because he was such a great candidate. He worked hard and he went everywhere. From the beginning, we thought that he was the one thing we could count on—the one sure arrow in our quiver. But it wasn't there when we needed it. Our slogan should have been: Where is Wyche Fowler?

It is quite likely that the expectations of his team had been set unusually high. And it is quite possible that Fowler's performance was acceptable by ordinary standards. I have no basis for judging. But the tone of these comments demonstrates, at the very least, that Fowler had failed to convince his own team that he was a hardworking and cooperative candidate. Their exasperation with Fowler is surely a testimony to his own independent streak. But it also strongly suggests the absence of another prize-winning campaign effort.

On the trail, I saw a few indications that the campaigner of 1992 might not have been the campaigner of 1986. First, with respect to his own campaign effort, Fowler had asserted in April, "I'm not complacent. I know that the staff will only want me to hit the five media markets. But I think I should go everywhere in the state and shake a thousand hands a day." The instinct was admirable. And it called for the most strenuous of campaigns. In three subsequent visits, however, I never saw him come close to—or try to meet—that goal.[26] Nor did I see a lot of strenuous activity. By mid-October, he was complaining about the schedule and commenting, "If I had to do it over again, I'd change one thing. . . . I wouldn't have any of these breakfasts. I'd start with the 11:00 radio program each day. Then we wouldn't have to get up so early to get where we're going." The next day, when the mayor of Macon had scheduled a press conference and a reception for him in the evening in that crucial city, he decided not to go. He was tired to be sure. But no campaign team or group of eagerly waiting supporters will readily accept that excuse.

Second, I observed at least one notably unskillful campaign performance during the runoff. Vice President-elect Al Gore had come to campaign for Fowler in northern Georgia, where Fowler, badly needed help. Gore, Fowler, two members of Congress, Donna Fowler, whom Fowler had married in the period since his election, and the wife of Congressman Buddy Darden walked through a crowded ballroom and onto the platform. As they walked through the crowd, people around me buzzed: "Is Fowler's wife there?" "Is that Fowler's wife?" "Is Fowler married?"

The local congressman, Ed Jenkins, introduced Gore. Gore spoke, emphasizing Fowler's integrity, as Fowler had asked him to do. Then he introduced Fowler. The two women stood throughout the proceedings; but neither was introduced. Fowler spoke at length; but he did not introduce his wife. When Fowler finished, Congressman Jenkins rushed to the microphone and introduced the two women. Donna Fowler—a warm, attractive, and accomplished woman and a huge campaign asset in every respect—received friendly applause.

Any male campaigner with good working instincts would never have left his recent bride standing alone on the stage without introducing her to the friendly crowd. More than that, any politician in a tough campaign would long since have realized what an enormous help she would be and would have made certain that she was seen and appreciated everywhere they went.

Third, there was his constant preoccupation with the health and comfort of his most valued "friend and mentor" Charles Weltner, who was battling cancer and who died in late August. During the 1992 April recess, when senators facing an election invariably go home to make reelection hay, Fowler took his sick friend, a lifelong student of ancient religions and owner of a world-class library on the subject, on a trip to Turkey and Iraq to pursue their mutual interest in ancient religion and archaeology.

"I am upset and yet sympathetic," said Fowler's campaign manager at the time.

> The trip will have absolutely no benefit for the campaign. It's benefits are in terms of friendship. The campaign manager side of me says this is crazy, horrendous, stupid, and silly. He will come back tired, and we will have lost him for two weeks of valuable campaign time.... The [campaign] schedule is already draining his energy. But he's the only nonrenewable resource we have. We can't raise money without his presence. We can't improve our poll results unless he goes to Georgia.... For Weltner, it is his last trip, almost his deathbed wish. For Wyche, it is his last chance to help his close friend. And for Wyche, it's more important than the campaign. It is his statement that he will not subordinate everything to the reelection chase.... The noncampaign manager side of me has to admire that.

When the campaign was over, he reflected, "Politically, the trip cut the heart out of our campaign plan to have him all over the state. When we had to make scheduling and fund-raising decisions, he was in Turkey." It was also the kind of trip that allowed some in the media to paint Fowler, falsely, as a smug, vacationing front runner, thus diminishing the sense of urgency among his supporters.[27]

Throughout the campaign period, Fowler devoted himself to two urgent projects designed to brighten his friend's last days. He worked to arrange and help fund a special room in the library at Oglethorpe College (Weltner's alma mater) to memorialize Weltner and to house his personal library. He proposed and pushed through the construction of an eternal flame and plaque outside the Georgia Department of Justice building memorializing Chief Justice Weltner. And he rushed it to completion so Weltner could see it on his final trip from the hospital to his home.

During my August visit, Fowler began each day with a visit to the hospital to talk with Weltner and keep him abreast of his various activities. On one of those mornings, I went with him. And we talked about the library and the flame. I have described Fowler, basically, as a person who wanted to be his own man and to operate free of all encumbrances. In this case, the campaign itself had become the unwanted encumbrance. If, at times, Fowler seemed to treat the campaign that way, it may have been because a big piece of his heart was never in it.

Candidate-centered explanations by Fowler's own team found a harsh echo in the postmortems of media observers. Listen, for example, to three members of Atlanta's *Sunday News Conference*, the only regular political round table in the state. After the first, November 3, election, Rick Allen said,

> Fowler has to take responsibility for his own loss in a number of ways, some of which were just personal. His own demeanor was prickly, as we have all noticed, and I think that got across to voters. Fowler charmed his way into the U.S. Senate six years ago by being a gifted storyteller, a warm guy, audiences liked him. This time he was remote and distanced, prickly.... It was his personality that got him in in 1986; and I think it was his personality that kept him out in 1992.[28]

After the runoff, Tom Hauck commented similarly,

> We've seen a different Wyche Fowler in this election than we've ever seen. A lackluster campaign, the irritability of the man.... I don't know what it was, but something personally was bugging him during the campaign. This was not a typical Wyche Fowler campaign; he was not the kind of candidate we've seen in the past.[29]

During the runoff, Dick Williams wrote in his *Atlanta Journal-Constitution* column, "His biggest problem is his personality change. He has gone from a man respected for uphill fights and a sense of humor to whinin' Wyche, a man who thinks his record was on that tablet Moses carried down the hill." [30] "Something happened this year.... Across the state, Democrats have talked about arrogance with a short fuse."[31]

At the same time, columnist Tom Baxter opined that "Fowler is a deep mystery. He has not campaigned with anything like the aplomb and enthusiasm—'the fire in the gut' as one of his closest supporters put it—that he did in 1986."[32]

In a conversation just before the runoff vote, Atlanta television's top political reporter, Bill Nigut, framed the election as a drama of the candidate against himself.

> What interests me is the hubris—the drama of hubris. His obsession with his reelection has affected all the other relationships in his life, with the press and with his old friends. Leave out the press if you like—maybe there's a reason for that. But I don't know how many of his old friends have told me that he no longer pays any attention to them. It has gotten so people think about it in making their vote decision. To me, that's the most fascinating drama of the election. Will it make a difference? Who knows.

After it was all over, the *Atlanta Journal-Constitution* editorial writer, John Head, pulled together several of these candidate-centered themes. "There was something different about Mr. Fowler during his unsuccessful campaign," he wrote.

> He says he was the same person he has always been. I don't believe it and I can't count the number of people—nearly all of them Fowler partisans—who say they don't believe it either. There was a lack of joy in Mr. Fowler's campaign.... [He] seemed out of sorts from the start, even when polls showed his lead exceeded 20 points.... The campaign didn't show me much of the Wyche Fowler who relished politics and could joke easily about himself doing other things with his life. What I saw was a man struggling to hold onto power and not at all pleased at what it apparently took to do it.[33]

The favorite adjective used by the media to describe Fowler's campaign was "lackluster."[34] And their explanation for it centered on a changed candidate.

Wyche Fowler's unbroken career success, his unexpected victory in 1986, the consensus interpretation of his victory as a personal triumph, and his distinctive personal style conspired to produce a candidate-centered explanation of the 1992 campaign and its outcome. If the candidate had won it single-handed in 1986, he must have lost it single-handed in 1992. That was the media view. Political scientists have often described the way in which the media sets expectations and then judges political performance in terms of these expectations. In Fowler's case, they may have set their 1992 expectations of his personal performance too high to begin with. Nonetheless, it is impossible to dismiss the media view.

It is a large part, too, of the view expressed here. Except that our view is disciplined by taking into account the structural difference between the candidate as a challenger and the candidate as an incumbent. As challenger, the candidate can run a positive campaign based on name recognition and qualifications and a negative campaign that calls for a referendum on the incumbent. But the requirements of an incumbent campaign are different and more difficult. To be sure, name recognition and general qualifications must be enhanced, but the beginning of a reputation for some kind of positive on-the-job performance must be added. And that is where the matter of representational theme weighs most heavily on the campaign.

Media people did not push beyond the problems of the incumbent candidate to identify the fundamental problem of the campaign—the lack of an incumbent-related message.[35] Nor did they factor into their highly personalized summaries such related measures as the quality of the advisory team and the control of the confrontational dynamic. A consultant's summary of Fowler's last two focus groups, convened during the runoff, describes the message that Georgia's voters were receiving: "They are more confused than anything else about the Senate race.... They are inclined to like Wyche, but worry that Wyche has been in Washington too long and believe that he may have raised his own pay and bounced checks at the House bank. They clearly are looking for clues and cues."[36]

The incumbent had not given them anything to connect with. And in their "confusion," their doubts about the incumbent's connectedness had taken root.

THE CANDIDATE AND THE MEDIA

Political scientists know that media observers will always have their own interpretation of an election campaign and of its outcome. And we know, too, that media coverage and media perspectives can have an effect on the voters, the candidates, and the outcomes. I cannot assess the impact of the Georgia media on the two sets of votes in November 1992. But I do have some idea, from the candidate's point of view, how the media may have affected the candidate. And since we are looking at a candidate-centered campaign, the candidate's perspective on media effects may be illuminating.

The invitation comes from Fowler himself. For he, in his postmortem comments, took the view that media treatment during the campaign had been instrumental in bringing about his defeat. He explicitly rejected the changed candidate thesis. "I worked just as hard as I ever did. I did not lose for any lack of effort on my part." And he turned the media explanation back on the media. "Our biggest problem," he said early in our conversation, "was with the media." "All things being equal, I should have won. If the media had done their job ... I would have won."

His judgment came as no surprise. For it was not a late-blooming judgment. From our first campaign trip in Georgia to our last, some aspect of his media relationship had achieved special prominence. And the sum total of these several events and contemplations pointed—from the candidate's perspective—to a relationship filled with worry and distrust. Long before he had been defeated, therefore, he had come to believe that his treatment at the hands of the Georgia media had been inadequate, distorted, unfair, and, for all these reasons, damaging to both his current reputation and his future career.

Any discussion of media–candidate relations must begin without illusion. They need each other. The media needs stories; the candidate needs attention. So they are locked in each other's embrace. Sometimes they engage in a mutually satisfactory trade—a good story for some favorable attention. Sometimes, they do not, because as much as they have reason to need each other, they also have reason to be critical of one another. The media's idea of a good story differs from that of the politician; and the politician's idea of favorable attention differs from that of the media.

On the second day of my initial trip to Georgia, for example, Chairman Fowler of the Subcommittee on Conservation and Forestry of the Senate Agricultural Committee, and a critic of the timber sales program, made an on-site inspection tour of logging activity in the Chattahoochee National Forest.[37] He was accompanied by four television crews—two from Atlanta, one from Augusta, and one from nearby Chattanooga. When I asked the senator if this coverage was unusual for him, it triggered a general theme I was to hear often. "It was very unusual," he answered. "I can't get any media coverage. They've all gone local. All they want from me is conflict. If I attacked Newt Gingrich every night, they'd print it. Otherwise, they aren't interested .... They don't care about policy. On the morning that we opened hearings on the reauthorization of the Older Americans Act, I had a meeting in Atlanta with two-hundred senior citizens. It was the kickoff event and discussion. I did it on their timetable. Not one media person showed up." His comment nicely illustrates the difference between candidate and media perspectives.

That is to say, the combination of Fowler's position of special influence, his policy criticism, and his tramp through the woods doubtless made the Chattahoochee visit "a better story" for the media—more consequential, more conflicted, and more visual—than the fairly commonplace kickoff senior citizens hearings. But a picture of two-hundred senior citizens, members of his core coalition joining him in support of a popular policy, made an equally good story from the standpoint of the politician—certainly not deserving of the great disparity in media attention. In any case, his complaint that media people were not interested in public policy was constant and basic to his media relationship.

In April, he complained to a gathering of his strongest supporters, "Two weeks ago, Senator David Pryor and I held a four-hour hearing in Atlanta on a very important problem ... We had five panels of experts. I begged Channels 2, 5, and 11 to come, but they couldn't. Two United States senators and a horrendous problem, and they wouldn't come. They have turned their backs on policy." "They go by the slogan, 'If it bleeds, it leads,'" he exclaimed in the car afterward. "Everything is about fires and accidents and killings now. I used to call them and try to convince them to cover policy.... But I've just about given up."

Because he thought of himself as a public policy person and because he believed he had a favorable public policy record, he held media disinterest in policy hugely culpable for the damaging fact that people did not know what he had done. "The press never told them," he said after his defeat.

> When I passed my historic preservation bill and my alternative energy bill—two bills signed by a Republican president and measurable accomplishments for a freshman senator—the media said nothing about them. There may have been one three-second mention. I tried to go around quietly to the press and the television stations to tell them about my record, but they never wrote about it. If they don't mention it, how would anyone know what I've done?

A veteran Senate aide concurred that "virtually no air time in Atlanta was given to Wyche's historic preservation bill.... It was widely hailed by preservationists ... [but] no one ever knew about it." "We kept a log of media stories on Wyche," he added. "They were all reactive—what did the senator think about this or that foreign event. Nothing *we* tried to get on the air ever got on. And this is irrespective of Wyche's temperament. The problem is that policy is not newsworthy."

Mention of the candidate's "temperament" recalls the judgment of media commentators that he was "prickly," "testy," "irritable," "whinin'" and "a changed person" from the candidate of 1986. Their judgment came mostly from his relationship with *them*. And that relationship was more adversarial than symbiotic, for which Fowler tended to place heavy blame on the media.

In January, he noted, "I still can't get any good media. There are four or five columnists in the state; and they take turns sniping at me." In April, he repeated this sentiment: "There is not one single newspaper columnist in the state of Georgia who has been writing anything good about me." And when it was all over, he said, "There has never been one story about my Senate career printed in the Atlanta press, and there never will be."

However legitimate his complaints may have been, there is evidence that Fowler sometimes treated the media as another of those encumbrances he could do without. One informed Georgia politico explained in July,

> The Georgia press is user-friendly. They are not tabloid journalism. Their attitude is not red meat, screw you. They all want to be like Teddy White—on the inside. So they will write things pretty straight if you talk to them. Wyche's problem ... is that he wants to talk only when he wants to talk. And sometimes when he wants to talk, it's to complain to the press that they didn't get it right when he did talk to them. So he's prickly. And he doesn't hold press conferences. Among Georgia's top politicians ... Wyche gets the least press coverage. But that's because he doesn't give them anything to write about.

There is evidence, too, that Fowler did not establish either a first-class press operation or a stable, helpful one. His chief press aide, when I first arrived, was gone before long; and Fowler did not set up a campaign press operation in Atlanta until October.

The person who headed that operation continued to go home weekends, even during the runoff. Fowler kept his campaigners on what one called "a tight leash," forbidding his consultants to talk to the press and channeling certain press communications exclusively through an overwhelmed campaign manager. It was not a press-friendly operation. And it did little to lubricate his relationships with them.

A January contretemps between Fowler and one of those "sniping" Georgia columnists documents the sensitivity on both sides. In the middle of a political gossip session with several old acquaintances, the senator engaged columnist Bill Shipp in the following exchange.

Shipp: Coverdell was in my office today.
Fowler: Are you going to write a column about him?
Shipp: Probably two or three.
Fowler: How much money has he raised?
Shipp: I can't tell you that. You'll have to read the column.
Fowler: Are you still going to call him the citizen legislator?
Shipp: You'll have to read the column.
Fowler: When are you going to say something good about me? In every one of your columns, you hit on me! "Fowler is too liberal for Georgia. Fowler is vulnerable." You're writing the script for my opponents.
Shipp: You're crazy. I've been saying for weeks that Coverdell is dead in the water, that he's going nowhere. I've been saying that he's looking for a way to get out of the race.
Fowler: Why don't you say something good about me? One week you go after me, the next week Munford goes after me. He's even going after my wife now.
Shipp: You aren't comparing me to Munford, are you?
Fowler: Yes I am. I'm not trying to browbeat you. I'm just telling you the facts.
Shipp: Coverdell has one big advantage. He has no record.
Fowler: How can you say he has no record? Eighteen years in the Georgia Senate, minority leader of the Senate, chairman of the state Republican party, and you say he has no record.
Shipp: He has no national record.

Fowler: He's got a record and we've researched it. And in due time, I'll expose it. He has flip-flopped in the worst way—on abortion, on redistricting, on school prayer. How can you say he's an innocent citizen legislator?

Shipp: He has researched you, too, and has a lot of material he can use.

Fowler: I'm not so sure Coverdell will come in.

Shipp: He's been promised $2 million as soon as he wins the primary.

Fowler: That doesn't bother me one bit. I don't care how much he raises so long as I can match him and respond to any attacks on me. I just want to stay competitive. And I can.

Shipp: [Charles] Tanksley may beat Coverdell in the primary.

Fowler: Well, why don't you write about the Republicans and their primary? Can't you at least give me a break and lay off of me until after the Republican primary? After all, I don't have to run in a primary this time. Doesn't that count for something in my favor? I must have been doing something right the last year.

Shipp: You guys all want 100 percent.

Fowler: Just hold off till after the primary. Then I'm fair game.

Shipp: No. We've got to have a contest.[38]

As we left, Fowler said of Shipp, "All he wants is a contest. He'll write whatever it takes to make sure we have a close contest. What bothers me is that he is such an influential columnist throughout the state."

The incumbent's biggest media worry, however, was not Bill Shipp. It was the *Atlanta Journal-Constitution*. Because 60 percent of Georgia's population lives within twenty miles of Atlanta, because one-third have arrived since the last election, and because, as one politico put it, "75 percent of Atlanta's newsline is set by what the *Atlanta Journal-Constitution* says," that paper catches the lion's share of every politician's attention. Early on, it became evident that Fowler's relations with the state's major paper were troubled.

On my second day in the state, readers of the *Journal-Constitution* were greeted with the headline, "Fowler's Staff Linked to S&L Meeting."[39] Fowler greeted me with an outburst.

I've been accused by some Republican staff reporter of helping to arrange a meeting for a person I do not know and never have met ... with people I don't know and never heard of. It's a typical smear tactic by the Republicans and it has been bought by the newspaper.... I want to kick the _____ out of the [*Atlanta Journal*] *Constitution*. This is the third time they have done this to us, printed a story without checking at all with us to see whether it is true or giving us a chance to answer.

He seemed especially incensed about an earlier editorial criticizing his bill to create a voluntary registry of black landowning farmers as a "quota bill." He had written a lengthy reply to the editor, and they had refused to print it.

A bit later, he found an airport phone and made his call. He said,

About twelve people must have heard me yelling over the phone to the editor of what is supposed to be the great liberal *Atlanta Constitution*, but which has turned into a rag, like *USA Today*. I told him that if he had a shred of responsibility, he would have contacted me before they printed that article.... "You had your own reporter and your own photographer traveling with me half the day yesterday," I said, "and you couldn't find me?" I said if they had any sense of professional ethics, they ought to run an apology, a retraction, and an admission that it was a malicious story. Of course, they won't. It's a terrible paper.

The next day, the paper did publish a convincing denial from several sources, and the story died.[40] But for a day, it discombobulated the candidate. It was my introduction to his particularly unsatisfactory relationship with Georgia's dominant newspaper.

Fowler's most explosive encounter with the *Atlanta Journal-Constitution* occurred during my August visit. The paper's political reporter, Mark Sherman, had gone to Houston to examine the records of Fowler's 1986 postdivorce hearing on child custody and child support, and he had come back with several pages of testimony. They included the sentence about check bouncing that later became the centerpiece of the

Coverdell campaign. When Sherman tracked down Fowler on the campaign trail to present him, in private, with his Houston findings, Fowler burst out of their meeting ballistic with anger.

> Don't you ever, ever come to me again with those kinds of questions about my private life. I've had it with you, Sherman. That is nothing but pure sleaze. What possible public purpose does that sleaze serve? Tell me, what are your sources? Who told you to dig up those court records? Tell me. Tell me. Where did you get that sleazy idea? The bank is the issue. The bank is the issue, not my private life. You stay the hell out of my private life. Go ahead, write your story and get your Pulitzer. Don't you ever come near me again. You're a disgrace to your profession and I'm through with you.

In the car, he continued to fume. "What earthly public purpose, what possible matter of public policy would be served by digging into those court records of a hearing that took place six years ago, six months before I was even elected to the Senate?"

And he went immediately to the newspaper's offices to put that directly to its top brass. "It was like talking to a wall," he reported when he emerged. "That guy wouldn't know journalistic ethics if they hit him. . . . I guess this is the kind of a campaign we're going to have."

In the end, the blowup soured relations all around. The paper printed Fowler's Houston testimony in an op-ed column, accompanied by the Fowler comment, "I will not tolerate this crap."[41] This intemperate reaction helped to give legs to a story that Atlanta's television stations had thus far ignored. In an editorial, the paper described Fowler's "anger," "rabbit ears," "outrage," and "petulance" and wondered about his "reaction to what otherwise would have been perceived as relatively trivial campaign attacks."[42] The paper's pro-Coverdell columnist exulted that "one testy quote . . . has let . . . Paul Coverdell see some daylight."[43] The *Journal-Constitution*'s Mark Sherman, who was assigned to the Senate campaign, was never given a private interview with Fowler, nor was he ever allowed to ride with the candidate during the campaign. He, in turn, wrote a series of less than friendly campaign stories.[44]

In late October, Fowler commented, "The [Atlanta] newspapers are already painting the election as me against myself." During the runoff, a *Journal-Constitution* editorial writer said to me privately, "I think my paper has been very unfair." The paper, of course, survived this subdued warfare. But the incumbent candidate did not.

Fowler's media advisers described his relations with the local media as "terrible" and "disastrous," because they wanted the view of Fowler projected in their paid-for television commercials to be reinforced by the view of Fowler appearing in the papers. And it wasn't. As one adviser explained,

> We had expected the free media to help us rebut the attacks by showing that they were lies.... But Wyche was in a pissing match with the media.... They may not be the greatest; still, they can help you. But you can't treat the media the way Wyche did and expect them to help you. The media was portraying his prickly side and it contrasted with our paid media.... The *Journal-Constitution* devoted two paragraphs of their endorsement calling him a Vidalia onion. It dovetailed perfectly with Coverdell's attacks, not with the picture of Wyche we were trying to present.

And he concluded, "When the free media reinforces the paid media, the positive effect is exponential. When the free media conflicts with the paid media, the negative effect is even more devastating. It's almost a mathematical formula."

During the runoff, Fowler's media relationships were close to the top of his concerns. "We're getting absolutely no free press," was his very first comment to me. "We've had not one positive article [in the *Journal-Constitution*]. But we've had two negative columns by [Jim] Wooten and three by [Dick] Williams." "We're just putting out fires," he said. The principal one was his opponent's recent charge—in debate and in print—that Fowler, who had once helped legislate a decrease in the inheritance tax, now wanted to increase it. He was especially upset with the absence of media help in fighting this charge.

He just lies, and the media will not pick him up on a single one of his lies. We are getting absolutely no free press. They all have some excuse; but not one of them will take him on. His lies just get bigger and bigger. And the biggest one is ... [the inheritance tax]. I'm the author of the bill he accuses me of being opposed to!

His interpretation of media behavior carried over directly into his postmortem. Indeed, media behavior became his leading explanation of the election outcome.

Our biggest problem was the media. We went on TV for four weeks with our positive ads. Then Coverdell came on with his negative attack ad, claiming that I had voted for a pay raise. It was a lie. The media should have stepped in there and said so. But they didn't. When the media takes a stand like that, it usually stops politicians from going further. Instead, they gave a signal to the Coverdell people that they could say anything they wanted to—that there would be no block, nothing to hold them back. Then when they got more negative and we hit back, the media criticized us for going negative. In the end, they [The *Journal-Constitution*] endorsed me in the most backhanded way. That was their revenge for the time I took them to task for their hands-off attitude.... You were there when I went ballistic with Sherman, who had those three pages of testimony of the court hearing and was going to write his story on the basis of those three pages. You remember how mad I was when I went to see the editors after that. That visit was the point when they turned on me. And they just let the negative attacks on my character continue. I did everything I could. I laid out my expenses, all my receipts, gave them all this information there was about the bank business. There has to be a referee; and if the press doesn't do it, who will?

Given his defensive, counterattacking strategy, perhaps he had done all he could. But in terms of fashioning a positive, pro-incumbent strategy, and organizing a media-friendly press operation, Wyche Fowler had clearly not done all he could. It may be that Atlanta's media people, for their part, believed he could not lose on November 3 and therefore felt they could give him a hard time, perhaps teach him a lesson or two, without consequences. If so, they were very wrong. However, any candidate who wants the media to control the dialogue of his campaign has already lost control of that campaign. At which point, complaining about the media will almost surely bring a more focused and less favorable media spotlight on the candidate. Whether or not Fowler's postmortem description of media activity was accurate, his prescription that they referee the contest was unrealistic. More important, it was a measure of the degree to which he had already hostaged his political persona to the interpretation of others.

REFLECTIONS

Wyche Fowler's case suggests how one campaign can be affected by the candidate's interpretation of his or her previous campaign. And it suggests also how the candidate's career experience can affect that interpretation. More generally, politicians make decisions—including campaign decisions—that are based on career experiences. Campaign sequences and career sequences thus intertwine through time. People who wish to explain the success or failure of elective politicians should examine their careers and their campaigns in tandem—as they affect one another.

Wyche Fowler's career and campaign suggest, further, that the interpretation of his previous campaign, combined with the impact of his previous career on that interpretation, led him to a set of miscalculations that may have cost him his seat in the Senate.

In 1986, challenger Fowler did not need a theme; in 1992, incumbent Fowler did. To the degree that he understood the difference, he would prepare himself for a referendum on his six years of activity. The vital importance of a campaign message is, no doubt, the first lesson at every campaign school. As a demonstration of this lesson, the Fowler campaign qualifies as Exhibit A. Without a message, incumbent Fowler constrained his own aggressiveness, dampened the efforts of his supporters, defaulted the campaign initiative to his opponent, and lost control of the campaign dialogue. Since the incumbent did not clearly and consistently define himself, the challenger exploited the ambiguity and did it for him—unfavorably, of course.

By settling for a reactive campaign, Fowler and his team expressed their confidence that Fowler's personal presentational skill would save the day. It didn't. And it didn't because in their confidence, they overestimated Fowler's contribution to his 1986 victory and underestimated the effectiveness of a totally negative anti-incumbent campaign run by a disciplined campaign opponent. In the end, for want of a clear, positive message, Fowler was easily swept into the very kind of personally bitter, nonissue-oriented campaign that he least wanted and that was least favorable to him.

Campaign messages or themes are inevitably about representation. In the case of an incumbent, they are about what he or she has done by way of responding to, and acting in the place of, a constituency. They are about legislator-constituent connections. I have used the term "representational connections" as a summary expression of those connections. The two main ones involve policy connections and personal connections, with candidate effectiveness, of course, relating to either or both. These are not mutually exclusive themes. An even balance between them is possible, but in the campaigns examined so far, there seem to be observable differences in emphasis.

Fowler certainly could have developed either type of connection; but he wavered between them and emphasized neither. The easy and obvious one was the personal connections theme. It combined his interpersonal skills, his concern for local needs, and his historic ability to knit together a governing coalition in a state riven by racial and regional divisions. Inherent in this set of connections was his effectiveness inside the Senate. But his campaign team failed to accentuate this accomplishment; and Fowler, for his own reasons, did not push it.

Political scientists tend to include the discussion of candidates in our election studies only insofar as we can measure their electoral influence indirectly, using candidate experience or candidate expenditures. But Fowler's large impact on his campaign and its outcome had little relation to experience or money. It had much more to do with matters of interpretation, strategy, and theme. These ingredients, and the miscalculations contingent on them, can best be identified by direct observation. So, too, can matters of luck—as in Fowler's bad luck comment in Houston—or matters of style—as in Fowler's entrepreneurial self-confidence.

Central to his victory and his defeat was his freewheeling, free-spirited effort to be his own man and to act free of encumbrances. In important matters of personal behavior he sometimes became, as he often said, his own worst enemy—undisciplined in interviews, condescending to his opponent, and by turns angry and volatile with the media.

Wyche Fowler was a gifted and promising U.S. senator with a career in public service of which he could be justly proud. But he ran a poor reelection campaign. "If I lose," he said during the runoff, "there will be no one to blame but myself."[45] The blame was not entirely his, nor could he remedy all the adverse contextual circumstances. My concern, however, is with the campaign. The campaign was largely his responsibility. So, too, was its failure.

The basic proposition of this chapter is, once again, that campaigns are important to election outcomes and candidates are important to campaigns. In combination, they are important to an understanding of representation. While the Fowler campaign did produce a loser and a winner, it did little to enhance accountability and was therefore not much of an advertisement for representation. Not, at least, on television, where the campaign was conducted. Fowler was inconsistent—between the two campaigns and within one campaign—in presenting himself to the voters. His opponent chose not to present himself to the voters at all. Voters voted, but not in a campaign context that encouraged confidence or trust or predictability of performance. Negative campaigns "work" electorally. However, they contribute almost nothing to accountability and, hence, to representative government.

CHAPTER 7

DURABLE CONNECTIONS I

DURABILITY

REPRESENTATION TAKES TIME. It is a process of continuous negotiation between politicians and citizens. And it is a process that involves both winning *and* fitting. In the short run, every campaigning candidate wants to win. But in the longer run, every candidate wants to negotiate a constituency *fit* that will sustain his or her representational relationship beyond election day. Elective politicians cannot be said to have developed a recognizable constituency fit until they have at least passed the test of one reelection campaign. Challenger campaigns begin the negotiation; incumbent campaigns attempt to continue it. One incumbent success is needed to demonstrate that there is some *durability* to the negotiated constituency relationship.

Dick Clark, John Culver and Wyche Fowler could win, but they could not negotiate a demonstrable fit. Indeed, the three cases, taken together, suggest that six years is never enough time to demonstrate what a durable senatorial fit would look like. The idea of a durable fit calls attention to the importance of repeated interaction between citizens and candidate. As a working assumption, a successful interaction goes something like this: Citizens begin with some vague notion of what an elected representative should look like and should do. On the basis of these vague notions and on the basis of the politician's presentation, citizens render a highly provisional judgment. If the judgment is favorable, the prospective representative becomes a legislator, makes a (six-year) record in office, and returns for a second judgment. This time the citizen has a little more information and a better-developed set of expectations and applies them in making another and, perhaps, more nuanced judgment. Candidate presentation and citizen judgment will repeat itself over as many electoral cycles as the electorate prefers the incumbent representative to the competition.

The more repetitions, the more likely there will be an increase in the information each has about the other, the more mutual adjustment will occur, and the less provisional citizen judgment becomes. With repeated interaction, the two parties get used to each other. The politician becomes content with a recognizable reputation. The citizen becomes predisposed to give the politician the benefit of the doubt. An exchange of openness and trust occurs.[1] The relationship gets reinforced and settles down. The process of negotiation, then, is characterized by a succession of approximations by one party to the preferences, the expectations, and the performance of the other party and the gradual achievement of a durable fit.

This is a subtle and cumulative accommodation. It involves more than winning. And it cannot be fully known through election margins, roll call votes, and expenditure totals. On the assumption, therefore, that durability is the best indicator of a good constituency fit and on the assumption that longevity is the best indicator of durability, I shall explore—in the next two chapters—the constituency connections of a pair of senators with lengthy careers.

CLAIBORNE PELL, RHODE ISLAND, 1978–1990

Among the senators I have followed on the campaign trail, the most durable Senate career is one begun thirty-five years ago and maintained through five reelection campaigns by the Rhode Island Democrat Claiborne Pell—in 1995, the second most senior Democrat in the Senate. When I met him in 1978, he was on his fourth Senate campaign. He had already passed the durability demonstration test twice; and I watched him pass it three more times. When I left him, in 1990, he had achieved a highly successful representational relationship.

Everywhere we went, he was described to me—and he described himself—as a Rhode Island institution. For a number of years, the only question raised among his constituents was not "Do we want him?" or "Can he win?" but "Will he run?" For us, the question is, How does a politician get to be an institution? How do we explain the durability of his constituency connections, of his constituency fit? Because time is such an important variable, my hope is that the narrative approach will bring some answers.

Ambition and Career

Claiborne Pell's political ambition was fueled by his desire to serve the public. Both the ambition and the fuel came from his upbringing in a wealthy, socially prominent, and public service-oriented New York City family. His father served as a congressman, as the chairman of the New York State Democratic party, and later as a diplomat in Europe. "I've always been interested in politics," Pell said when we first met. "My father was in Congress. And so were four other forebears of mine." Pictures of these five ancestors, including one vice president, hang prominently in the senator's Newport, Rhode Island, home and in his hideaway office in the U.S. Capitol. "My father had a great influence on my life," he says. And he echoes his father's idea of "bourgeois oblige": "When you are given things on a silver platter, you ought to do something in return." "I had always been interested in public service," he adds. "In college [Princeton], I had briefly thought about the ministry, then writing, teaching, and the foreign service." He chose the foreign service.

It was the career choice of a young man from a diplomatic family, someone who had lived in Europe as a child, who had traveled in Europe as a young man, who had worked in Europe as an officer in the Coast Guard. But it was hardly a career choice designed to get him to the U.S. Senate. For it did little to strengthen his very tenuous connections with Rhode Island—his family's summer home in Newport, his attendance at boarding school near Newport, and his marriage to a socially and politically prominent Newport heiress.

Pell left the foreign service after seven years in southern Europe and in the United States. He went into investment banking and dabbled in national politics because, he explained, "in Rhode Island, the political chain of command seemed clogged up."[2] He recognized the liability of his weak constituency ties. But, he said, "about 1955, I began thinking about the House, that I could pull it off. The thought came to me then that we are a very mobile society and that my five forebears had all come from different states.... I had thought in terms of the House.... But when Senator [Theodore Francis] Green retired in 1960, I said, 'Why not shoot for that job?'"

Pell was the first person to announce his candidacy.[3] And "his announcement was met with horse laughs among politicians at the State House."[4] Opponents wondered whether he had ever set foot in the State House.[5] In the media, the forty-one year-old was variously described as "a wealthy Newport resident," "a political neophyte," and "a political novice."[6] He presented himself as a "fresh face"—to which an opponent replied, "It's so fresh, nobody has seen it before."[7] In response to his slogan, "Think Well, Think Pell," the opposition taunted "Who the hell is Claiborne Pell?" "My opponent," he remembers, "called me a cream puff."[8] He was a self-starting political amateur.

As a matter of descriptive representation, his candidacy did not seem promising. He was a Yankee in a state populated by immigrants. "When you're a Yankee," he says, "you're in the minority in this state." He was a wealthy patrician in a blue-collar, working-class state. He had no major union backing.[9]

He was a Protestant in a 60 percent Catholic state. He was opposed in the Democratic primary by two former governors one of whom, a four-term governor, was endorsed by the State Democratic Committee. That designation, on the top ballot line, had always been tantamount to nomination. "The primary is a formality" the *Providence Journal* editorialized, "because under present law, they are rigged in favor of the endorsed candidates. The odds are 10 to 1 that candidates picked by the party ... will win."[10] An observer who saw a chance for "a new face" went out of his way to specify "a type ... different from Mr. Pell," someone "who has served an apprenticeship in elective office in the state." [11]

"I was," Pell recalled, "a most unusual candidate. I had no experience in politics. I came from the wrong part of the state. ... I was not in the mold of my predecessors in Rhode Island. ... I was a woodwork candidate. ... I came in through the back door ... from the outside." He had a long way to go to negotiate a fit with his constituents. And he was far from being a Rhode Island institution. He still calls the 1960 primary his most difficult campaign, because of his inexperience. "I started out all alone," he said. "My wife and I were partners, and I owe an awful lot to her. I was so nervous that my arms shook; and they twitched so at night I couldn't sleep. I had to lie on them to keep them still." By all accounts, however, he conducted a vigorous and well-financed antiorganizational campaign in a congenial antiorganizational climate of opinion. He described his support as "negative support from people who didn't like the iron-fisted way the organization ran things." "And," he added, "I think people liked having someone the same age as [John] Kennedy."

He identified himself closely with his party's youthful presidential candidate. "Like Kennedy," he said, "I started early and worked hard. I wasn't afraid to use my family and friends."[12] Media profiles of the early 1960s portray him in the Kennedy image as a decorated wartime officer, a "fit and trim" athlete, a "personable and hardworking candidate," and as someone who "might be mistaken for a screen actor after the pattern of Henry Fonda."[13] "With his personable wife," it was reported, "he campaigned up and down the state, from doorsteps, in boats, on Narragansett Bay and by land and air."[14]

He was not, observers noted, an "effective extemporaneous speaker."[15] But he put his European experience to good use in this multiethnic state by campaigning—on separate radio programs, for example—in French, Italian, and Portuguese.[16] "I'm not as Yankee as I might be," he noted. "Part of my heritage is French. I have lived abroad a great deal. I identify with Europe, especially southern Europe. And I speak their languages—or I used to." In 1960, that presentational skill surely mattered a lot more than it does now.

He argued that he was "well qualified" by virtue of his "four years of military service during World War II, seven years with the Foreign Service and his business experience."[17] And he negotiated the recognition threshold by spending "lavishly" on television and radio, in newspapers and on billboards.[18] Along with "the expenditure of a great deal of shoe leather," he credited the "drip-drip result" of his five-minute weekly radio program that ran for twenty-six weeks.[19] Financially, it was strictly a family affair—no outside money.[20] Pell, his wife, and his father "split all the expenses three ways." His constituents knew, from the beginning, that he came from a wealthy family and was not likely to be obligated to others financially. And they learned that he was a determined, steady, "drip-drip" kind of politician.

Pell won the primary by an unexpectedly large 2 to 1 margin, defying the odds and breaking the mold of party-grown candidates. Media observers called it "smashing," "amazing," and "a startling upset."[21] "I was," he said, "the first unendorsed candidate in Rhode Island history to win a primary." "After I won," he added "the party was very nice to me and endorsed me." It was his last primary. He won the general election easily. And, with one exception, he has won easily ever since.

When it was over, Pell acknowledged, "This is the type of life, the type of work I've had in the back of my mind since I was twenty." He continued, "I think there's a trend toward, well, not necessarily young people, but toward people who look upon politics not as a profession but as a service."[22] He was a prototypical citizen-politician driven by an interest in public service. Like John Glenn, the other public service-oriented citizen-politician in this study, Claiborne Pell came to office brimming with progressive ambition. And, like Glenn, he soon began "thinking up."

Two years into his second term, in 1968, Pell sought the Democratic vice presidential nomination. "I wanted to be vice president in 1968," he said. "[Edmund] Muskie got it ... He was a better speaker than I was; and it was probably a good choice. But I was very keen on it at the time. We spent $800 to $1,000 on it. We had a couple of people going around to the different delegations, and we sent out a letter to all delegates. But it was not to be. I had to erase my copy book on that." It was an amateurish effort. And from then on, his electoral office ambition remained focused on the Senate, and his progressive ambition became fixed on institutional goals.

Pell, like Glenn, never had any desire to return to his prepolitical life. Proponents of term limits—who believe that the amateur citizen-politicians they hope to recruit will happily relinquish progressive ambition, forsake long-term political careers, and return to their prepolitical endeavors—might profitably ponder the contrary evidence from the Glenn and Pell careers.

Pell's 1960 campaign launched him on a career-long effort to negotiate and sustain a satisfactory representational relationship with his constituents. In five subsequent campaigns, he tested, updated, and confirmed the strengths of that relationship. And yet, to the very last, observers professed not to understand those strengths or the patterns of his constituency connections. Twice, the pundits seriously underestimated his support at home—labeling him "the most threatened" eastern senator in 1972 and one of three most vulnerable nationally in 1990.[23] And they were puzzled by his subsequent victories—by six points in a tough campaign test in 1972 and by twenty-four points in an easy campaign test in 1990.

The source of observer puzzlement is that Pell seems so unlike, almost alien to, the people he represents. In 1984, a New England journalist wrote that he was "baffled . . . by the manifest abyss between the patrician office holder and the voters of Rhode Island."[24] In 1990, another regional journalist called Pell an "oddball who is about as remote from the average Rhode Islander as one can imagine."[25] Even his veteran aides and campaigners professed to be mystified. "Politically, he is an anomaly," said one in 1982. "Here is this very blue-collar, very ethnic, very aging population not only electing but carrying on a love affair with their patrician. I don't know what makes it work."

Pell cannot identify with the life experience of his constituents; and they cannot identify with him as "one of us." This disjuncture is thought to be too severe a representational handicap. Yet it is not. We know that descriptive representation, that is, a demographic match, is neither necessary nor sufficient for a lasting constituency connection. Still, the Pell case presents a puzzle and stimulates an analysis. How has he done it?

Policy Connections

Domestic Policy: Accomplishment.

The answer to Pell's success is framed by the distinction between policy connections and personal connections. It begins with the stronger of the two for Pell and the one he solidified earliest in his career—the policy connection. It is not clear how much of a policy record a senator needs before it registers back home. For now, we shall simply say that Claiborne Pell met that need soon enough and Wyche Fowler did not.

The Rhode Island senator is a person with intense preferences about good public policy. He sees himself as a person of strong policy convictions, in a job that gives him the opportunity to implement those views. Over and over, he repeats his seven-word political mantra: "Translate ideas into events and help people." "If you believe in your philosophy of life," he says, "there's no better fulcrum ... than the Senate."

It is of great importance to his career that he got off to an unusually strong policy making start in his early Senate years. His political career, we might say, has been heavily dependent on his *policy career*—by the sequencing of his policy accomplishments. Early on, he played a major leadership role in creating and guiding two pieces of national legislation out of two subcommittees he chaired on the Senate Labor Relations Committee. One established the National Endowment for the Arts and the National Endowment for the Humanities in 1965, and the other created Basic Educational Opportunity Grants for needy college students in 1968. Both subjects were matters of longtime personal and family interest.

Within that same period, Pell was the prime mover in enacting two less visible, but noteworthy, Rhode Island-oriented laws. The High Speed Ground Transportation Act of 1965 reflects both his intellectual interest in this subject—about which he wrote a book—and his constituents' interest in improving rail traffic in the crowded northeastern corridor.[26] Similarly, his Sea Grant College Act of 1967, to establish and aid institutions doing marine research, reflects both his own intellectual interests in the future and the ongoing interests of Rhode Island, the "Ocean State." He was described in the press as "full of ideas and energy" and cited for this "rare achievement by a junior senator."[27] The combination of national legislation plus "seaweed and choo-choo trains" for the state gave him an extraordinarily strong foundation for a career-long policy-related reputation at home.

His two first-term measures were greater policy accomplishments than first-termers Clark, Culver, or Fowler could take credit for.[28] And his second-term policy accomplishments were more formidable still. "In the long run," he says, "the most important thing I've done is the opportunity grants." In 1980, thanks to the initiative of his friend, Senator Tom Eagleton, they were officially designated "Pell Grants." "I owe a great debt of gratitude to Tom Eagleton," says Pell. And indeed he does! For as the father of college scholarships for needy students—now more than 30 million nationally and 160,000 in Rhode Island—he owns a magic bullet in the business of legislative leadership. Those two words—"Pell Grants"—bring him the kind of long-lived, high-profile publicity that few politicians enjoy and most politicians would kill for.

At campaign appearances he is unfailingly introduced with words that were spoken at two Democratic party functions in 1984: "No one person in the United States has done more for education than Claiborne Pell. Hundreds of thousands of young people have been able to go to college because of Claiborne Pell." "Thank God for Claiborne Pell. He's done more for education than any other senator in the history of the United States." At his 1990 campaign kickoff, with spectators waving "I got a Pell Grant" signs, he was introduced as "the Education Senator."[29]

Throughout his career, the Pell Grants program has been the linchpin of his favorable domestic policy reputation at home. More voters mention it spontaneously than any other specific Pell accomplishment. While the number was just 3 percent in 1983, when combined with the other 7 percent who mention "education," it is a major source of his hard-core support.[30] Once its architect, he is now positioned as the protector of its $6 billion budget.[31] To an editor's suggestion, in the 1990 campaign, that he had passed his legislative prime, he answered, "I have a different kind of influence now. I'm not as creative as I once was. But my seniority gives me a greater opportunity to nurture and to expand old programs like the Pell Grants. I can be traffic cop now, pushing programs I like, halting programs I don't like.... It isn't flashy; but the impact on the community is very great." It is the most durable of his programmatic policy connections.

In terms of maintaining Pell's weaker, reelection constituency support, his general policy record is more relevant. In a state that may be the most liberal in the nation,[32] Pell has been a thoroughgoing supporter of the traditional, union-based economic liberalism of the New Deal. He has also—though not without some conflict—been among the most stalwart supporters of the newer social liberalism of the party's northern Democratic wing. Pell's AFL-CIO and his ADA ratings regularly place him close to the top of both scales. *National Journal* rankings in the 1980s placed him anywhere between the second and the eleventh most liberal senator.[33] A *Fortune* magazine voting study in 1989 found Pell to be "the most liberal member of the Senate."[34]

On the campaign trail, his most visible attachment is to the elderly and their social security-related benefits. "The elderly are the most important force in Rhode Island politics," said a top campaigner in 1982. "You must remember, Rhode Island has not changed that much since he was elected. We aren't like New Mexico and Arizona with lots of new voters." Rhode Island ranks second nationally in the percentage of population over the age of sixty-five. During each of my three campaign visits, his schedule reflected that judgment—five senior citizen groups in one day in 1978, seven in two days in 1990. In 1990, their affection for the "senior senator-senior citizen," as he presented himself to them, was palpable and overwhelming. He was invariably introduced with the most outlandish claims for his Senate leadership on behalf of their economic interests, and they accepted those claims with enthusiasm.[35]

In none of the three campaigns I watched did his opponents criticize him on the basis of his domestic policy record. His 1978 poll summary concluded, typically, "there is little evidence that the senator is in any trouble on the list of issues we tested."[36] In his 1984 race, polling on six prominent issues found that "on none of these issues do people's positions have a major impact on [the race]."[37] In short, Pell's policy performance—specifically, generally, and sequentially—has given him a strong base of traditional liberal support in a markedly liberal reelection constituency.

Policy Independence: Vietnam.

To that base, Pell added, or reinforced, strong support from the proponents of a more moralistic liberalism through his early opposition—from 1967—to the Vietnam War. It was a matter of policy. "When you have strong views, as I did with the Vietnam War, you have a chance to put those strong views on the line. If you don't have strong views, there is just the survival thing." "On real questions of morality, like Vietnam, I was willing to go down to defeat," he says. He does recognize that when he first took that position, "he had just been reelected." Still, he took a real risk. He remembers that his anti-war stand split the state Democratic party. During the platform fight at the 1968 Democratic National Convention, he recalls, "I was called a traitor by members of my own state delegation." And he remembers that four years later, his dovish views became a major issue in the hardest-fought, most closely contested campaign of his career.

The 1972 campaign was a heavyweight championship bout against a popular three-term governor and secretary of the navy, Republican John Chafee. In a landslide Republican year nationally and in a state being won by Republican presidential candidate Richard Nixon, Pell was unexpectedly victorious. "The Republicans thought they had me beaten," he says. "I don't know why. Maybe because my opponent ... was a very glamorous fellow. I was dull and gray. I started out 2 to 1 behind in the polls. But I won that one [by 53 percent]."[38] Reports on the campaign make it amply clear that the Vietnam War was an area of major disagreement between the candidates.[39] But it was not deemed to be a factor in explaining the outcome. Local postmortems emphasized Pell's "traditional support in the state's big cities," his personal campaign "in every nook and cranny of the state," and his highly professional campaign team.[40]

For Pell, of course, what was most important about the 1972 campaign was the surprise election result. He still keeps a large, foot-and-a-half-square collage of 1972 victory stories and postmortems on his Senate office desk as a reminder. As political scientists, we, too, are interested in the election result, but as scientists of durability, our larger interest lies in the development of his political career in a representative system. We want to know what Pell's 1972 campaign can tell us about his ongoing negotiations with his constituents.

It tells us two things. First, purely in terms of survival power, the 1972 campaign freed him from any serious electoral challenge until 1990. It gave him eighteen years in which to negotiate the kind of constituency connections that would make him, by 1990, a Rhode Island institution. It was, in this sense, a liberating campaign. Second, in terms of the kinds of connections he would negotiate, the 1972 campaign highlighted a key connective ingredient—his *policy independence*. It was an extension of the organizational independence he displayed in his initial campaign. But it was a more substantive and durable kind of independence. In that sense, 1972 was a reinforcing and solidifying campaign.

Reporters covering the race wrote that "the senator's basic speech everywhere concentrated on his record of independence."[41] As he did this, he had to define for himself the contours and the limits of his representational relationship. And that is what campaigning by "putting [his] strong views on the line" on Vietnam seems to have done for him. In that campaign, he says, "I was an anomaly running against the tide.... I took a chance. I did not represent my state at that time.... Rhode Island was gung-ho for the Vietnam War; and I was called 'New England's Number One Dove.' ... My views on the war were not popular." But, he added, "the party let me have my individuality. They let me be a dove."

Having run a risk, asserted his independence, won party endorsements, and emerged victorious, he could formulate, with greater confidence, the representational rule he often articulated in his travel talk. "If its an economic matter," he says, "I vote my state's interest. On broad issues of war and peace, abortion, prayer in the schools, I vote my conscience ...

even if it's contrary to my constituents." And he believes that his constituents will not hold that rule against him. On every one of our trips through Providence, he called attention to the statue atop the State Capitol of the so-called independent man symbolizing Rhode Island politics. And he would add, "Rhode Island voters are independent voters. They vote for the person." Pell's first and third campaigns were the most influential in shaping his career.

Following the work of Mark Westlye, political scientists have become well attuned to the various characteristics of "hard-fought," as contrasted to "low-key," campaigns.[42] Pell's Vietnam story—in a "hard-fought" campaign—presents developmental characteristics to which we have been less well attuned. Campaigns may have differential effects on careers. A hard-fought campaign is more likely to produce information about constituency negotiations and is more likely to stimulate career-level effects than a low-key campaign.

Pell's assertions of policy independence are basic to his self-image as a politician. As expressed in 1972, they solidified his reputation as a politician who would act independently and take a political risk to stand up for a policy that he believed in. So powerful is independence as a political value in contemporary politics that every politician is constrained to signal his or her independence at some point in a career. Campaigns may provide a congenial strategic setting for such declarations.

Foreign Policy: A Puzzle.

Pell's interest in the Vietnam War is a clue to more than his policy independence. It is a reminder of his lifelong interest in foreign affairs generally (he still carries the United Nations Charter in his pocket) and his reputation in Rhode Island for leadership in that field. His reputation grew apace as he moved steadily up the seniority ladder on the Foreign Relations Committee, from membership in 1965 to the chairmanship in 1986. During his last three campaigns, I heard him routinely introduced as "a man who has given us leadership in foreign affairs," "a man of vision, a man of peace, a world leader," and "someone who has given us great dignity" and "has made the little state of Rhode Island known around the world."

In those years, Pell received some of his highest voter agreement ratings on the statement that he "is a national leader Rhode Island can be proud of." In 1978, voter agreement with that statement (65%) was tied for second out of a battery of twelve positive statements.[43] In 1989, when Pell was chairman of the Foreign Relations Committee, pride in his leadership drew the second-highest level of agreement (83%) in a battery of eight pro-Pell statements.[44] In the 1983 poll, only "foreign policy"—from 14 percent of the respondents—outranked Pell Grant/education in favorable spontaneous mentions.[45] There seems little doubt that a reputation for foreign policy leadership is a strong sustaining element of his Rhode Island connections.

And yet on inspection, that leadership seems to have been largely symbolic. His post-Vietnam passion on the committee was his sponsorship of several international environmental treaties—to protect the seabed floor from nuclear weapons, to protect the environment against wartime modification, and to protect the common global environment against pollution. They were, admittedly, the lowest of low-profile issues. "The things that get me charged up and excited are so esoteric," he said in 1978.

> I've been most interested in the international environment treaties. . . . To see those treaties pass is a great thrill, the greatest thrill of my career. And it will have a lot more bearing on what happens to people in the future than most of what we do. The people of Rhode Island could care less about them. They aren't the least bit interested. . . . But the treaties are what get me really charged up.

The explanation for such enthusiasm lies in Pell's intellectual fascination with the future and with futurology. He has belonged to the futuristic Club of Rome—"The only politician who belongs," he says, "[because] I enjoy that kind of cerebral activity, listening to people lay out their theories." He has also long been interested in paranormal phenomena such as extrasensory perception and its possible uses in foreign affairs. In these enthusiasms, Pell comes across as a person who follows his own muse, a somewhat quirky muse that has led him away from and not toward foreign policy leadership.

Capitol Hill commentaries on his foreign policy activities have not pictured him as a leader in the field. Far from it. Washington scorekeepers have, on occasion, ranked Pell among the "least effective" and "worst" members of the Senate."[46] One article greeted his 1986 promotion with the headline, "Some Doubt New Foreign Relations Chairman Is Dynamic Enough to Preserve Panel's Influence." Congressional staffers refer to the eccentric legislator as "the senator from outer space and Senator Magoo," it said.[47] Another observer, calling Pell a person with "little presence in the Senate," described "a time of doubt about the panel's effectiveness as well as Mr. Pell's leadership."[48] Three years later, Capitol Hill reports carried headlines such as "Senate Foreign Relations Founders: Decline Under Chairman Pell."[49] And reporters were writing that Pell "lacks the drive, sense of purpose, grasp of complicated issues and consensus-building skills"[50] required of a chairman.

It was not a flattering picture. It presented pundits with a reason to doubt the strength of his home connections, and it presented his opponents with a tempting target. Indeed, each of his last three opponents has played off this beltway critique to fashion an anti-incumbent campaign theme. His 1978 challenger charged, for example,

> His name in Washington is "Stillborne Pell," used continually and routinely by ... [the people] with whom he must deal on our behalf. It is a name of derision, ineffectiveness, weakness, denoting a lackluster incapable legislator. It is not a term of affection.... [I]t is a term of ridicule.... The judgment of his colleagues [is] that Senator Pell is totally ineffective, easily manipulated and unable even to push his own legislation. In the last six years, Senator Pell has not sponsored *one*, not *one* piece of major legislation. His record is one big ZERO. (Emphasis in original.)[51]

This opponent got 27 percent of the vote. His 1984 opponent got 27 percent, his 1990 opponent 38 percent. Beltway judgments, in other words, cut no ice in Rhode Island, the only place where it matters to the durability of Pell's career.

And herein lies another Pell puzzle. He was well entrenched at home but not well regarded as a player inside the Senate. This disjunction reminds us—as with John Culver—that a legislator's performance at home and in Washington are two parts of a single representational relationship. At the same time, they take place in vastly different contexts. They require quite different perspectives and priorities. They are not necessarily connected. A senator does not have to do well in both places to do well in one place.

A developmental explanation for this puzzling disjunction lies in the notion of a policy career. In his early years, Pell put together such a strong Senate record of legislative accomplishment—plus a balanced record of partisan policy loyalty and principled independence—that he inoculated himself against the late-blooming, media-generated charge of ineffectiveness. In the field of foreign affairs, it may be enough for his constituents to know that he has achieved a very prestigious and potentially influential position and to be reminded of that fact when, on appropriate formal occasions, his statements and his pictures appear in the media. Pell's highly publicized position as head of the first Senate delegation to the Gulf War region, in the midst of his 1990 campaign, was one particularly beneficial—albeit symbolic—reminder.[52]

A personal explanation of the disjunction is that Pell makes no *claim* to foreign policy leadership. To the contrary, in response to his critics, he is unusually self-deprecating about his legislative talents. "I am not a very good speech maker." "I talk too little in committee." "I have the uncanny facility for making the most exciting matters gray."[53] "I really don't care about glory.... I tend to drop back sometimes."[54] "I'm not one of the great leaders.... I'm not one of the ten leaders or five leaders. I say, 'Let other people have your way.' " An experienced political reporter concluded that Pell "represents a phenomenon not often found in nature: a politician without an ego."[55]

As chairman, he demonstrated a consistent disinclination to wield power or engage in self-advertisement. His chairmanship of the Senate Rules Committee was diagnostic for his later conduct as chairman of the Foreign Relations Committee. Other Rules Committee leaders, Robert Byrd and Wendell Ford, used that chairmanship to accumulate inside power and to achieve formal party leadership positions in the Senate. But Pell's leadership style made it clear that he did not aspire to inside power. He refused to use his control of inside perks such as parking, staff, and office space to build favor-based increments of power within the institution.

Calling the Rules Committee "a headache committee," he said, "I've never been much of a trader or a wheeler-dealer. I try to be fair, to give everyone what they deserve no matter what position they took on other matters. Senator [Howard] Cannon ran the committee more tightly than I have."

He knew all about Chairman Cannon. When Pell first asked for a private Capitol hideaway office, Cannon tried to cut a deal with him. Pell refused to deal and instead waited three years to get the office he was entitled to. "I can't use my chairmanship as a way of wheeling and dealing. You may gain short-term advantage, but in the long run, it won't help." To the later critiques of his Foreign Relations Committee chairmanship, he answered similarly. "I've got no particular strategy to try to outmaneuver my colleagues."[56] "My job is to be fair. The job of the chairman is to be conciliatory, not confrontational, to compromise, get a half loaf ... I'm not going to sit and be a gavel whacker."[57]

Pell is no more aggressive out of committee than in committee. "I don't make a lot of public comments," he says. "I know that's not the way to run for president ... The national press calls me a lot for comments. But if I don't have anything

to say or if I don't have any obligation to speak out, I don't."
He needn't worry. A colleague who travels abroad with him
calls him a "pussycat gentleman" because he invariably gets
trampled underfoot by the rush of other senators whenever a
microphone comes into view. Steven Hess has ranked senators
according to the frequency of their appearances in newspapers
and on television. In the period before he became chairman of
the Foreign Relations Committee, Pell ranked 51st out of 100 in
1965–66, 81st in 1969–70 and 33d in 1983.[58]

Inside the chamber, his relations with his colleagues are
distant and formal. "He comes to the floor to vote and then
goes back to his office," says a longtime aide. "Some of the old
boys will sit in the cloakroom . . . but not the Senator. He doesn't
work the floor. I'm disappointed in him, but he just doesn't
know how." Pell agrees.

> I'm a loner. I have the reputation of wanting to be left alone. If I
> get pressure, my tendency is to go the other way. People know
> that. I have a very low-key style [here he puts his hands in front
> of him, palms down, like an umpire signaling "safe."] I'm not as
> flashy as a lot of people here. But then [here he shrugs], since I've
> been here, I've watched a lot of people flashier than I am come
> and go.

Three of Pell's recent predecessors in the chairmanship—
Senators William Fulbright, Frank Church, and Charles Percy,
all with "flashy" policy profiles—are believed to have undermined their home connections and lost *because of* their committee leadership.[59]

Ironically, then, Pell's durability at home may owe something
to his very lack of leadership aspirations in Washington. In
terms of career durability, the lesson of Pell's experience is
consistent with that of John Culver. An influential institutional
career is no substitute for strong constituency connections. An
institutional reputation can be helpful at the margins, but it is
a luxury. It could not save John Culver; and Claiborne Pell has
survived quite nicely without it.

Institutional Ambition.

Make no mistake, however. Claiborne Pell loves being in the Senate. And he has had plenty of institutional ambition. But he has what he most wants from the institution. And that, I believe, is position, not power. He wants leadership status, not leadership influence. The position, or status, he has always wanted—to fit with his own prepolitical career and to follow the career of his predecessor, his regular house guest, and his "old and revered friend" Theodore Francis Green—is the chairmanship of the Committee on Foreign Relations.[60] In Green's time, that committee was the most prestigious in the entire Congress.

In 1984, Pell's wife, Nuala, who has advised and campaigned hard in every election, told a reporter that her goal was "to see her husband become Chairman of the Senate Foreign Relations Committee."[61] When he reached that goal, the senator called it "a quite thrilling feeling for someone who forty years ago was a young Foreign Service Officer on the lower rungs of American diplomacy."[62] Pell's institutional ambition has been long-standing and strong, but essentially passive. It has not required a lot of highly publicized activity, only a lot of time to let seniority work.

Far more than most of his colleagues, Claiborne Pell operates with a lengthy time horizon. As much as he wanted to be chairman, for example, he said in 1982,

> I dread the thought of the Democrats winning back control of the Senate. I would have to be chairman of Foreign Relations ... and I would have to campaign at the same time. I don't know how I could manage it. When you are chairman, you have to go to all the meetings, and they take so much time.... It would be awful.

Pell has what one longtime staffer calls a "distinctive pace, [which] is basic to the way he does things." "The senator has such a long view of things," says another veteran staffer. "He doesn't care if he gets his name in the paper; if it's not in today, it will get in some other day. He doesn't need a stream of legislative accomplishments. He doesn't worry about defeat. He thinks in terms of generations."

In 1982, Pell got his unorthodox wish—a four-year postponement of his chairmanship. And four years later, he realized his institutional ambition.

Since 1986, his attentive constituents have known that his chairmanship gives him topmost foreign policy status. If he seems content with that achievement, perhaps they are, too. Media coverage at home suggests that this may be the case. When the *Providence Journal*—never a reliable editorial supporter—mentions the unflattering beltway critiques, they usually weigh in with the counterargument that his position holds unmatched potential for Rhode Islanders and that quietly, out of the limelight, he does exploit his position for their benefit.

When Washington pundits were registering serious pessimism about Pell's ability to get the International Nuclear Freeze (INF) treaty ratified,[63] the *Journal* put an optimistic spin on the story. Their headline read, "Now the Treaty's Fate Is Up to Pell." And they called it "Claiborne Pell's baby."

> Washington area experts agreed ... that Pell isn't quarrelsome or flashy, but said he is an effective legislator who works behind the scenes without demanding credit ... [which] may be the best way to get something as complex and politically volatile as an arms reduction treaty ratified.[64]

In 1989, when Washington criticism resurfaced, the *Journal* reported that "critics ... say he has not been as forceful or effective a chairman as his predecessor, while supporters say he adopts the true diplomat's technique of accomplishing his goals." Pell is further described as more patient than his colleagues, as a senator who "gets things done by quiet persistence." While admitting that Pell has little "ability to devise short, snappy sound bites for television," the reporter adds, "while he may not be the most charismatic politician ever, he may be one of the most tenacious."[65] Reassuring assessments like these from the media at home can take the curse off the ineffectiveness critique emanating from within the beltway.

Not surprisingly, the senator takes an unusually benign view of the local media. "I have very good relationships with the [statewide] press," he said in 1990. "They trust me. They've been fair. They begin by assuming you're a liar and you have to prove otherwise. I guess I've done that over the years. I think I'm the only politician in Rhode Island who has not criticized the *Providence Journal* in twenty-two years. That's a record."

Pell's institutional ambition may now fit with constituent and media expectations. He doesn't demand more from his job, and they don't either. For the folks back home, symbolic leadership in foreign policy may be as beneficial as, and a lot less risky than, actual leadership.

Personal Connections

The perceived threats to Pell's durability come mostly from matters of personal style. Incumbent "ineffectiveness" in Washington is a much-used anti-incumbent argument. But it has been tried and found wanting in Pell's case. Another favorite argument used by challengers is that the incumbent is out of touch with the folks back home. And it is the potential of this latter criticism that has been most worrisome for Pell's campaigners.

In 1978, his pollster wrote, "Pell's only major problem going into the campaign is the perception on the part of many Rhode Island voters that he is aloof.... [they] tend to have an image of Pell and his work that is somewhat remote from their day-to-day lives and concerns."[66] Again, in 1989, he wrote, "[our poll] results strongly suggest that Pell has not ... been keeping in touch with the district ... and that he has begun to lose touch with the 'little guy.' "[67]

Doubtless, the blue blood/blue collar demographic disparity fuels this worry. "We have to probe deeply into the personality aspects of Senator Pell," said one staffer, "because we have to keep worrying about his love affair with a blue-collar state." As a contributor to Pell's presumed vulnerability, however, the "out of touch" charge appears to have been no more damaging than the "ineffectiveness" charge. Which leads us to take a direct look at Pell's personal style and his personal connections at home.

Pell's personal style at home is cut from the same cloth as his personal style in the Senate. In neither context is he highly visible or hyperactive. In both places, I found him to be a serious, sober, quiet, even shy, gentleman with old-fashioned preferences for personal privacy, formality, civility, courtesy, honorable behavior, and understatement. He is reluctant to brag or offend and believes in the traditions of obligation and loyalty. His background could easily have produced arrogance, but it has not. Petulance, yes; arrogance, no.

His relations with the people around him tend to be formal, reserved, and distant. He is a lifetime tennis player. But I could not imagine showering and joking with him after a tennis game in a crowded locker room with two high school coaches as I did with John Culver in Iowa. Pell also is a lifetime runner and jogger. But I could not imagine him sitting around—as Dick Clark did in Iowa—in his running shorts and bare feet at a Ramada Inn, having a late afternoon drink with some staffers, reporters, and a political scientist. Sipping sherry in the hush of a private men's club—the Knickerbocker, perhaps—would be more like it. To their staffs, Senators Culver and Clark were always "John" and "Dick." Pell's staff would not dream of addressing him, in or out of his presence, as anything but "Senator Pell" or "the Senator."

Doubtless, these stylistic preferences grew out of a background of old money, social position, boarding schools, private clubs, and family travel abroad. So, too, did some of his personal eccentricities. His clothes—wrinkled suits, ill-fitting coats, scuffed shoes, frayed collars, elbow patches, and short pants—range from downscale preppie to upscale bowery. His figures of speech have the ring of an earlier time and place. "You take an awful lot of guff in this job." "I worry like the dickens about something before I decide." "May I offer you a spot of lunch?"

And there is his absentmindedness about detail. In the van, his wife has to remind him several times which suit pocket his notebook is in. In a grade school classroom, he cannot remember his congressional salary. At headquarters, he watches his opponent's television ads briefly and says, "These are good ads. Whose are they?" These eccentricities are well known in his home state. And every six years, they tempt pundits to proclaim him vulnerable.

On the campaign trail, Pell's stylistic preferences manifest themselves in an ingrained distaste for publicity-seeking and an awkwardness in the modern arts of self-advertisement. The pattern of his home style is identical to the pattern of his institutional style—low-key, self-effacing, and genuine; no bragging, no preening.

On one occasion, as we drove to a personal appearance at a road race—the major media event on the day's campaign schedule—he insisted that we stop and remove all Pell for Senate signs from the sides of the van. "I'm afraid people might be offended," he explained to his mystified young aides. On another occasion, after we had spent the morning and lunch together, I was watching him handshake his way through a hospital. He walked up to me, grabbed my hand, and introduced himself.

He is not notably adept at face-to-face politicking—at shaking hands, remembering names, recalling relationships, making small talk, giving a speech. And he seems uncomfortable when so engaged. After twenty minutes of obligatory table-hopping at a senior citizens dinner-dance, he returned to his wife and said, "Nuala, that took an incredible effort." Speaking of Rhode Island's favorite setting for major political events, Rocky Point, he told a friend, "If there's a hell on earth for me, it's Rocky Point."

Not surprisingly, he delays campaign activity, such as fund-raising, as long as he can. For his 1984 campaign, he raised only 2 percent of his campaign contributions in the first four years of the electoral cycle, compared with the 10 percent average for all twenty nine incumbent senatorial candidates. And for his 1990 campaign, the comparable figures were 6 percent for Pell and 15 percent for all thirty incumbents (see table 2). Pell adheres to the view that "for four years, you are a statesman and for two years you are a politician."

Only once, he said, did he have to bestir himself for more than one year. In 1977, with a possible primary opponent testing the water, he recalled, "We started early. We got the president and vice president down here and made a big deal of it. We scared everyone out of the race." "He gave more attention to the Democratic party in the state, renewed acquaintances and alliances, raised money," said a consultant. "We had it so no Democrat of any significance would run."[68] It brought to the surface the same determination that got him to the Senate in the first place.

Normally, says a veteran campaigner, "he tends to be out of the public eye for fairly long periods of time, so we have to insert him into the state to let people know not just that he is their senator but that he is a candidate for reelection. It is very hard to get him to start campaigning." Claiborne Pell is simply not comfortable anywhere with the hype, the hustle, and the hardball of contemporary political life.

Neither by his personal background nor by his constant personal presence can it be said that he is as closely "in touch with the little guy" as his pollsters would wish. Nor does he claim to be. He knows that he cannot present himself to his constituents as one of them. And it is the essence of his representational relationship that he does not try. "You know the old saying that you can't make a silk purse out of a sow's ear," he once remarked to a friend. "My problem is just the opposite. I'm a silk purse, but sometimes I wish I could be a sow's ear. But I don't know how." "I'm an oddball," he says on the trail. "I'm not in the mold of Rhode Island politicians."

He has made of this presumed handicap a crucial asset. "He knows who he is," says a veteran staffer, "because he was brought up in a tradition. He doesn't wonder 'Who am I?' all the time. He knows who he is because he knows who his family is. It's the family thing.... He came here and does what he does because generations of his family have come here before and done what they did." Pell is unwilling to be anything other than what he is and to adopt any personal style other than that which "the family thing" has bequeathed him. In that spirit, he defends his senatorial performance to his questioners. "I'm not going to change my style. It is me."[69]

Pell's hand-me-down personal style may be inadequate for keeping in touch with his constituency in the short run. But, it is a source of great strength for him in the longer run. It is derived from a long-range generational perspective. It is a stylistic pattern designed to grow in appeal over time and is well suited to the slow but sure negotiation—campaign by campaign—of a constituency fit. Its distinctive characteristics are Pell's steadiness, patience, consistency, stability, honesty, and integrity. These are not the kinds of characteristics that leap immediately to light in a candidate-constituency relationship. They become apparent and encourage constituency connections only with the passage of time. Their appeal is not their excitement but their durability.

Assuming some initial takeoff capacity, as in Pell's first primary campaign, and some early staying power, as in Pell's difficult 1972 campaign, his personal style is ideal for nurturing and achieving a comfortable constituency relationship. To the degree that such a relationship did grow, the difference in personal experience and the shortcomings on the stump—once thought to be Pell's vulnerabilities—receded into the background. They were not what voters came to care about in the long run. Senator Pell was able to get in touch and stay in touch with large numbers of his constituents when they became convinced, by accumulated interactions, that what they saw was what they got. And they came to value and to trust what they saw.

Such was the condition of Claiborne Pell's constituency relationship when I arrived on the scene in 1978. He drew his strongest supporters from among policy liberals and the elderly and from, he said, "little groups that identify with me, the League of Women Voters, the Jewish community, the Portuguese ... little constituencies like university groups, egghead groups, which is what I'd be doing if I wasn't doing what I'm doing." But with his broader and weaker reelection constituency, he said, he had forged a bond based on personal style. "I think people trust me. They know I'm fair and that I do my best. And I have a hardworking office—case work. People know that I have no other ax to grind. I want no other job. I want no more money. They realize that my interests are the state's interest. I have no personal interests." "With the simple people," he concluded, "I have a good bit of trust."

His 1978 poll supported that conclusion. When asked to name, without any coaching, something they liked about Pell, the largest number (15%) mentioned "honest or sincere or straightforward." On a set of fourteen different traits, he scored highest on "honest" and next highest on "knowledgeable." And, on a battery of twenty-one agree/disagree statements, he received his two highest agreement scores on the statement "Pell is a thoughtful person, you can trust his judgment" (68% agreement) and on the statement "Pell is a man of character, he does the right thing" (65% agreement)[70] These are characteristics of style that take time to take hold; but once they do they virtually guarantee durability.

The salience of these personal characteristics probably becomes magnified in the context of a state that has suffered a history of political corruption. With public officials, from mayor to governor to congressman, embroiled in scandal, Rhode Island has been called "Rogue Island," "a scandal-weary state," "a miasma of venality," and "a stronghold of organized crime."[71] Thus a longtime observer of the state's politics says of Pell's constituents, "They look on him favorably because there is no question about his honesty and integrity or having a hand in the cash register."[72] The Senate is often criticized in the press as a body of wealthy millionaires; and Pell has been called the wealthiest of them all.[73] But in Rhode Island, his wealth is not only not condemned, it is well known and, probably, a political asset.

During the three campaigns I observed, Senator Pell's personal favorability ratings were spectacularly high: 74 percent in 1978, 81 percent in 1983, and 75 percent in 1989. (By contrast, Wyche Fowler's favorability scores in 1992 averaged 54 percent.) All three Pell campaigns I saw were triumphant tours among people who felt they knew him, had gotten used to him, liked him, and trusted him.

Negative Campaigning and the 1990 Campaign

It is, we know, a prime characteristic of modern candidate-centered campaigns that they have tended to be increasingly personal. And as they have become personal, they have become increasingly negative and nasty. The rise of negative campaigning, of personal attack campaigning, has been seen by many as a national scourge—lowering the tone of our politics, eroding citizen trust in politicians, and undermining representative government itself. It thrives, we are told, because it works—as, indeed, it did work in the Clark and Fowler campaigns. From a representational standpoint, the curse of negative campaigning is that it distorts the constituency connection of the winning politician by leaving him or her without strongly positive constituency ties. The winning candidate will have earned the legal right to represent a constituency, but the constituents are left without a clue as to how the incumbent would go about doing it.

The definitive expression of Claiborne Pell's personal style is his career-long refusal to employ negative campaigning. And his 1990 campaign became the classic demonstration of the strength of that stance. In that campaign, his team used Pell's rejection of negative campaigning to control the issues, the dialogue, and the dynamics of the contest. They kept his opponent on the defensive; they made the media his ally; and they turned a putatively close race into a runaway victory. In so doing, they preserved a vestige of idealism in politics.

Pell had stated his view of negative campaigning on the trail in 1984.

> My opponent has conducted the most unpleasant campaign of any I have had. She has begun lately to use strong adjectives like "gutless," "arrogant," "aloof," words like that. I have not replied to any of her accusations and I do not intend to. That's in keeping with my policy of twenty-four years of running a positive campaign. I have never attacked any opponent or responded to attacks by my opponent. I have a reputation for always conducting a positive campaign, no matter how tough the campaign may be. And I've had two very tough campaigns … I know that many of my colleagues feel you must become negative. I don't. To me, positive campaigning is good politics.

These views are consistent with Pell's unaggressive, gentlemanly approach to politics. His steadfast adherence to them is seen as a sincere expression of Pell's values and not as a strategic ploy.

For Pell and his aides, the validation of these propositions came in the defining campaign of his career—against John Chafee in 1972. As Pell explains,

> I was supposed to be gobbled up by John Chafee, but I wasn't. I would have been gobbled up if he hadn't made one mistake. He went negative. He was ahead by 2 to 1 about six weeks before election day, when suddenly he went negative. He didn't have to; and I never understood why he did. Little old ladies in tennis shoes started coming up to me and saying, "I'm a Republican, but you are being such a gentleman by not hitting back, that I'm going to vote for you." The big laborers came up to me and said, "Pell, where's your guts?" I didn't respond, because I knew they would vote Democratic anyway, whereas the little old ladies would not have. I have always believed that negative campaigning will not work. And I'm proof that it doesn't.[74]

That was the historical lesson, the interpretation that Pell carried away from his 1972 campaign. It was the guiding interpretation he brought with him to his 1990 campaign.

In 1990, Pell faced, for the first time since 1972, a quality challenger. Claudine Schneider had represented half of Rhode

Island in Congress for ten years. She was young, energetic, media-oriented, and liberal. For most of her tenure, she had been the best known and the most popular Republican vote-getter ever. Since 1984, she had posed the major political worry for the Pell campaigners. According to Pell's 1989 poll, her overall job performance and favorability ratings were just as high as Pell's. On some job performance measures—"understands and cares about people like you," "stands up for the little guy," "keeping in touch back home"—she scored substantially higher than Pell. And in the horse race, she led him 49 to 42 percent.[75] "I started out as the underdog," said Pell. "It was just like 1972."

The early spring line in 1990 placed Pell among the five most vulnerable Senate Democrats and calculated his chances at "no better than a toss-up."[76] The Republicans targeted the seat as one of their two or three most likely takeovers.[77] A local expert explained Pell's plight. "She fits the profile of a challenger who wins, and he fits the profile of an incumbent who loses." [78] The nation's pundits expected it to be "one of this year's closest," "one of the year's tightest Senate campaigns.[79]

It wasn't. In fact, it wasn't at all like 1972. In 1990, Pell gave a convincing demonstration of an airtight constituency fit. He won 62 to 38 percent. For the third time, the assorted pundits had underestimated his political prowess.

Pell won by capitalizing on his established personal style and by using that strength to take control of the campaign. In a strategic sense, the burden was on the challenger to give voters a reason to turn out of office a popular long-term incumbent. However well Schneider might score in the polls, Pell also scored high. On a battery of eight standard performance questions, Pell received by far his highest agreement ratings on the "personal character, integrity, and ethics" question. He received his next strongest agreement rating on the statement, "He is a national leader Rhode Island can be proud of." "Keep in mind," wrote his pollster, "that these are truly excellent ratings which show a lot of support for Pell."[80]

By 1990, both Pell's policy and his personal connections were contributing to his overall ratings. In addition, the polls showed that Pell supporters registered more intense preferences than did Schneider's. Schneider could not win without criticizing Pell. And since they differed little on policy, her criticisms had to focus on his personal style—too old, too tired, too out of touch, too ineffective. Schneider had to decide, therefore, how strong a personal critique to level against an experienced and respected incumbent—one who began the campaign by saying of his challenger, "She's a very fine woman. We share many ideas, many interests and I like her very much."[81] When, if ever, and how strongly should she "go negative"? That was the central question of Schneider's campaign. From beginning to end, the question absorbed the challenger and everyone who followed her campaign. As early as May, Rhode Island observers were assuming that she would have to go negative to have a chance. But they differed on her ultimate prospects. One said that it "would backfire against a beloved institution like Pell." Another said, "The question is whether he will reciprocate or pull a Dukakis and get massacred as a result."[82]

The strategy of the Pell campaigners was to prevent Schneider from running a hard-hitting, strongly negative campaign against him. To that end, they tried to keep her dilemma and her decisions as much in the public eye as possible, thus subjecting her to Pell's example and to public disapproval of negative campaigning. By emphasizing Pell's well-known commitment to positive campaigning, they encouraged Schneider to make similar public commitments early in the campaign.

Which she did. February: "[It] is going to be one of the most unusual races in the country. We both believe in a kinder, gentler campaign." July: "We have a very congenial race going and we both honestly believe that it is possible to run a civilized race as opposed to one that is plagued by attacks and counterattacks." August: "Claiborne Pell and I are going to try to keep this a very above-board campaign."[83] Pell's team took the position that the two candidates had an agreement, "a sacred contract you might say," not to campaign negatively—an agreement that placed constraints on Schneider, not on Pell. Media people expected to witness a Marquis of Queensbury campaign. And they primed themselves to monitor any deviation therefrom.

In late August, polls showed that Pell had a widening lead and that he was reaping favorable publicity for traveling in the Gulf War zone. A Schneider consultant talked to a reporter about the need "to get tough" and to "draw some contrasts" and hinted menacingly at a predisposition to "go negative."[84] Pell's camp reacted swiftly and preemptively—in a blistering public letter from campaign manager to campaign manager— to reiterate Pell's traditional position, to remind Schneider of her vow to stay positive, to accuse the Schneider camp of reneging on her promises of a positive campaign, and to demand a repudiation of the consultant's comments.[85]

The letter had two effects. In the short run, it threw the Schneider camp on the defensive; and they quickly replied that the consultant's comments had been misconstrued.[86] In the long run, it kept Schneider on the defensive by focusing media attention on the negative content of Schneider's commercials. The subsequent media watch kept her campaign under the gun by calibrating every nuance in her commercials for their degree of negativity.

Would she or wouldn't she? became the central question for the media. Newspaper headlines followed the flow: "Senate Campaign Becoming Negative," (Sept. 17) "Schneider Unveils Contrast Ads," (Sept. 20) "Schneider's Ads Walk Tight Rope" (Sept.13).[87] They were, in effect, pro-Pell headlines. And as mild as her contrast ads were, Pell's aides decried them as "negative" while their own innocuous ads continued to detail his record. At week's end, Schneider opened their debate by saying, "We all love Claiborne Pell." And the event—their one major confrontation—drew the headline, "Civility Not Hostility Marks Face Off."[88]

A week later, Pell's team applied their preemptive coup de grâce. They ran a pro-Pell anti-negative campaign ad in which seven average, sidewalk citizens suggest that Schneider is conducting a negative campaign against a man who wouldn't think of doing such a thing. The script:

> "Don't just put everybody down."
> "I don't approve of negative campaigning."
> "Pell has outstanding achievements."
> "His word is his bond; he will never go back on his word."
> "A negative campaign is going to backfire."
> "Negative campaigning doesn't work and especially someone going negative on someone like Senator Pell."
> "It's just trying to undercut a good guy, that's all."[89]

The ad ran for two weeks.[90]

Pell's top aides call it "the turning point" of the campaign. "The ad didn't mention her," said one. "But the message was: both candidates have promised not to do any negative campaigning; the people of Rhode Island do not want negative campaigning. Senator Pell has never done any negative campaigning. No one else should do any negative campaigning. It was brilliant. We inoculated the environment to the degree that she was boxed in and could not go negative." The ad only heightened interest in the will she or won't she question.

Schneider's answer seemed to be that she couldn't decide. In talking to reporters, she escalated her attack on Pell and invited the media to corroborate her view. But she hired a new consultant to produce a gentler set of television commercials with the theme that "they are two of a kind, one with a proud past, one moving to the future." In the space of a few days, the calibrating headline on the campaign changed from "Schneider's Campaign on a New Tack"[91] to "Pell Is Silent as Schneider Continues Personal Attacks" to "Schneider Ad Hails Pell While Calling for Change."[92] Observers spoke of the "confusion," "indecision," and "hesitation" of her campaign.[93] "It's not clear where they're headed," said one. "She's been tiptoeing toward a more aggressive stance, but she hasn't really come out swinging. I don't think she's sure if she wants to go for broke."[94]

Pundits agreed that the challenger would have to go negative to win. "Either she wants to be nice or she wants to be a United States senator."[95] "You have to go negative as well as positive if you are going to beat an icon."[96] But they expressed the opinion that it might be too late, that it might have worked earlier but wouldn't now. "If she goes negative," said one reporter, "I think it will backfire on her. For some reason, there seems to be this attitude, 'Hey, you don't badmouth Claiborne. You can badmouth anybody else you want, but not Claiborne.'"[97] That was exactly the attitude the Pell camp had intended to reinforce.

When I arrived about one week before election, Pell expressed pleasure with her conduct. "We agreed that neither one of us would engage in negative campaigning, and it's been free from that so far. I've been a good senator; she's been a good congresswoman. I like her ... I guess this has been the most positive campaign in the United States this year." At that point, he had an unbeatable twenty-three-point lead. He should have been pleased. He had established the rules of engagement, rules that gave him the advantage of the status quo. He had controlled the dialogue of the campaign, the central issue of the campaign, and the outcome.

Schneider's reluctance to go negative remained topic number one among Pell's campaigners. "We were surprised," said one top strategist, "that she didn't go after him any harder than she did. She could have run a very different campaign. She could have roughed him up. That would have given us a lot of trouble. There are a lot of ways in which we could have been roughed up. . . . Why she didn't do it, I don't know; but it made it much easier for us."

Schneider said only that "it was her decision to stay positive." But the answer—apart from her personal preferences—has to lie in the formidable, perhaps impregnable, barrier presented by the favorable personal reputation of the incumbent.

The Institution

As we drove along the campaign trail 1984, Pell patted his chest and asked me, "Why should I, among all politicians, be so successful without ever doing any negative campaigning?" I answered, "Because you have a good reputation and you are behaving consistently with that reputation." Then he asked, "But how did I get that reputation to begin with?" I laughed and dodged, "I wasn't following you then." I still cannot answer his question.

As a general matter, since positive reputation building and the demonstration of consistency take time to develop, I expect that negative campaigning would be most effective against short-term incumbencies—as in the Dick Clark and Wyche Fowler cases—and less so as incumbency lengthens and as the strength of a favorable personal reputation grows. From this viewpoint, Schneider's problem was not that she didn't go negative early enough in the campaign but that she didn't go negative early enough in Pell's career.

By 1990, Claiborne Pell had a reputation among his constituents as a man of integrity—financial integrity in the sense of being personally honest and, equally important, political integrity in the sense of being honest with his constituents, by being himself. In his 1989 poll, on a battery of agree/disagree questions, his highest score was 70 percent constituency agreement that "Pell's integrity and honesty are above reproach." And in another battery of eight standard job performance questions, his highest ratings—83 percent positive, 55 percent extremely positive—came on the statement that Pell is "a person of great personal character, ethics, and integrity."[98] The strongest citizen approval items were the same as they had been in 1978.

It is very hard to launch a negative attack against someone who has come to be perceived as a virtuous person and in a campaign that has been framed in terms of that virtuous reputation. Perhaps the best summary of Pell's reputation is that he does not come across as a "politician," at least a politician of the sort so many citizens have come to view with cynicism and distrust.

His 1990 campaign contained some suggestive indicators of constituent trust. To begin with, there was the strange poll result showing voter belief that Pell, one of the most liberal of senators, was more conservative than his Republican opponent. Moreover, the poll indicated that voters were predisposed to vote for the perceived liberal candidate. But they didn't.[99]

Early in the campaign, in the first joint appearance of the two candidates, Pell was asked to identify a recent piece of legislation he had pushed through that had helped the people of Rhode Island. He answered, "I couldn't give you a specific answer. My memory's not as good as it should be."[100] In many contexts, this would be devastating ammunition for a too-old, time-for-a-change argument. In Rhode Island, it had no effect.

Later in the campaign, a Pell staffer studying paranormal phenomena wrote the secretary of defense that he had discovered a secret code by reading foreign policy speeches backward. Here was more ammunition for a charge of aging eccentricity; but when the news came, Pell gently supported the offender's odd adventure and nothing came of it.[101]

These stories illustrate what it means to enjoy constituency trust. From the voters' standpoint, the body of pro-Pell information they had built up over a long period was so strongly held that they were disinclined to take into account any new information coming in via the campaign. There was no predisposition to change their established opinion of Pell. In Georgia, in 1992, with very little knowledge of incumbent Fowler, the voters were strongly predisposed to take in new information from the campaign. Voters gave incumbent Pell every benefit of the doubt, but not incumbent Fowler. With Pell, there were no loose threads and no single thread that could be pulled to unravel his incumbency. The voters had tuned out.

Much was made in the national press of the timing of the Gulf War crisis and the publicity boost Pell received from it during the campaign.[102] When it was all over, Pell said, "My opponent was dogged by bad luck."[103] But bad luck had nothing to do with Schneider's defeat. Bad luck is a short-term factor; Pell's strength is a long-term factor. Pell's comment—gracious, conciliatory, charitable—says a lot, however, about his long-term appeal. The *Journal's*'s political analyst got it right in his postelection analysis when he called Pell "the best loved Rhode Island politician of his era" and summed up, "At the personal level that sometimes prevails in the privacy of [the] polling booths, the quirky, courtly Pell drew from a seemingly bottomless well of good will."[104] That is a good working description of constituent trust.

By 1990, Pell had become a Rhode Island institution, the ultimate stage in constituent trust. I believe that was precisely the representational fit he had spent thirty years negotiating for. Often, in his travel talk, he would measure his career against that of his predecessor, Theodore Francis Green, who served for five terms and retired at the age of ninety-three. Pell spoke of their longevity, their continuous occupancy of the same office space in the Providence Federal Building, their status at home. In 1978, he said, "I've tried to act in the tradition of Theodore Green. If I have, that means Rhode Island has had the same kind of senator since 1938. We both have had our independence."

Six years later, he commented,

> Seniority can be a big advantage; but it allows your opponent to pick out a few votes and concentrate on them. [Pulling a piece of paper out of his wallet.] I have cast 8,809 roll call votes during my career. There is plenty of opportunity to find fault with some of those votes. But perhaps I have become an institution in Rhode Island. That happened to Theodore Green.... I may be in the same position that he was.

Earlier in 1984, he had even proposed to test this proposition. "I wanted," he said, "to run a campaign like [Senator] Bill Proxmire [Wisconsin] or [Senator] George Aiken [Vermont]. I did not want to spend any money on the campaign—no money for TV or anything else. My advisers argued very strongly against it, and I eventually gave in." One of those advisers said, "He wanted to validate the idea that he had become an institution in the state. Whether he had or not—and I think perhaps he had—this was not the basis on which to run a campaign."

In 1990, when it was clear he would win handily, I asked the senator if, now, he saw himself as an institution. "I think it has happened," he said. "I know I have wished it would happen sometime. It didn't happen twelve years ago; and it didn't happen six years ago. But it has happened this year. I have been victorious after having run, warts and all, with all my imperfections on display—my interest in the paranormal, for example. It's a good feeling to have run just the way you are without pretending to be something you aren't." The last comment captures the essence of Pell's durable appeal: he is what he is; Rhode Islanders have a reasonably good idea of what he is, and they have decided to keep him.

By 1990, the burden of proof had been placed heavily on any challenger. "People may disagree with him," one editor told me, "but they all say, 'I like Claiborne Pell.' Nobody has anything against him." The preservative in his representational relationship—both milewide and mile-deep—is the simple matter of good character. For Claiborne Pell, good character has been good politics. And good politics, in this case, brings a durable representational fit.

CONCLUSION

By the mid-1990s, the only question left to ask about Claiborne Pell was not Can he win? but Will he run? A 1995 speculation began, "at 76, Sen. Claiborne Pell is a political *institution* in Rhode Island.[105] How did he get to be a Rhode Island institution? How, despite the descriptive difference between himself and his constituents, despite the disjunction between his Washington reputation and his home reputation, despite the marked absence of an aptitude for modern campaigning, did he get elected to represent his state six times? How, despite these and other short-run handicaps, did he win the degree of constituent support and trust that made possible his overwhelming 1990 election victory, against a distinctively high-quality challenger? The explanation, as I have argued throughout, is partly developmental and partly personal.

On the developmental side, the matter of timing is crucial. An amateur, driven by a desire for public service, he got started by running a hard, grassroots campaign at a time when organizational control over nominations was weakening. And he followed quickly with an unusually productive record of legislative accomplishments—both national and local—in his earliest Senate years. His legislative accomplishments, moreover, fit the policy preferences of a dominantly liberal, Democratic constituency.

When after two terms he faced his toughest campaign test, the timing and the content of his policy career had left him well positioned to defend himself with a combination of Washington success and home support. To which he added a crucial display of independence on the Vietnam issue, the one and only policy issue that ever posed a threat to his support base. The 1972 campaign proved to be the linchpin campaign of his long political career. He emerged with solidified domestic and foreign policy connections and with eighteen years of immunity from serious electoral challenge. From that time on, his constituents supported him, as "a leader Rhode Island can be proud of" even when his leadership was more symbolic than substantive.

When, in 1990, a serious electoral challenge did appear, he had added to his strong policy connections an equally strong set of personal connections. That achievement had taken more time; and the fact that he was able to develop policy support before personal support became important to his longevity. From the moment of his emergence on the local political scene, the greatest threat to the development of any durable constituency connection had come from his difficulties in personal style. By family background and life experience, a seemingly unbridgeable gulf separated patrician Claiborne Pell from his working-class constituency. And this gulf left him vulnerable, in theory, to the charge that he was too disconnected from the people he represented.

The evidence from his career indicates, however, that descriptive representation, that is, "he is one of us," is not necessary for a successful representational fit—provided only that some alternative personal connection takes its place. In Pell's case, it was his integrity—about money and about himself as a politician—that forged the personal link. In the last half of his career, his constituents gave him their very highest poll scores on personal characteristics such as integrity, character, ethics, and honesty.

The final element in Pell's durability was his consistency. Throughout this study, I have emphasized the need to look at politicians over time. Careers are built over time. Personal reputations are acquired over time. Campaign learning takes place over time. Constituency connections are negotiated over time. And a politician's consistency over time can be the key to the successful negotiation of careers, reputations, campaigns, and connections.

Lack of consistency—as in the Fowler case—confuses constituents, feeds the media's appetite for inconsistency, generates dissonance between free media and paid media, and in general opens possibilities for political attack or self-destruction. Pell fell short of consistency between his Washington performance and his home performance. He achieved consistency in his style but not in his reputation. And his lack of representational consistency did provide some opportunity for exploitation by his opponents. But, in the end, his career demonstrates that a senator does not need to become an institution in Washington to become an institution at home.

Representation is, at bottom, a home relationship. At home, some consistency of presentational style is the essential underpinning of a positive reputation. That reputation, in turn, is essential to winning the benefit of the doubt from constituents; and that constituent trust is, in turn, essential to a durable representational fit. Claiborne Pell took the long view of his public service and, in his own words, "steered a steady course" throughout his career. He stayed in character and kept himself remarkably free of political and personal trouble. His career-long refusal to conduct negative campaigning—whether he needed it or not—exemplifies both this consistency and the blend of personal and political integrity that his constituents came to respect and value.

Table 2. Pell Campaigns and the Electoral Cycle, Money Raising

	Money Raised (in 100,000s)					
	1st 2 yrs.	%	2d 2 yrs.	%	3d 2 yrs.	%
4th term						
1979–84	6.2	1	5.8	1	45.3	98
Total	757.3					
Senate avg.	134.2	4	172.2	6	2,579.0	90
Total	83,704.2					
(N=29)						
5th term						
1985–90	56.4	3	66.8	3	2,138.2	94
Total	2,261.4					
Senate avg.	401.4	6	516.4	9	3,763.0	85
Total	140,440.0					
(N=30)						
Source: Federal Elections Commission.						

CHAPTER 8

DURABLE CONNECTIONS II

DAVID PRYOR, ARKANSAS, 1978–1994

DAVID PRYOR OF ARKANSAS came to the Senate in 1978, eighteen years after Claiborne Pell. By 1995, he had now been a senator longer than three-quarters of his colleagues. And his representational relationships are as durable as those of Pell or any other senior senator. He has spent nearly thirty-four years representing an Arkansas constituency—twelve years representing smaller than statewide constituencies and almost twenty-two years representing statewide constituencies.[1] He had been elected to public office eleven times, by means of either a successful primary campaign or a successful general election campaign. During that time, he faced more reelection campaign tests than Pell. In 1990, he was one of five senators who ran unopposed for reelection. This chapter explores the underpinnings of his long-lasting representational connections.

Pryor's elective office ambition at home and his institutional ambition in the Senate have been driven by the sheer love of involvement in politics. Like Pell, Pryor inherited his interest in politics and his Democratic party allegiance from his family. But otherwise, it is hard to imagine a greater contrast in background and experience. Pryor is the son of a south Arkansas

Chevrolet dealer and sheriff. He grew up in the small town of Camden where he gained early local recognition playing high school football. He was educated at Henderson State University, the University of Arkansas, and the University of Arkansas law school. On graduation, he returned to Camden, started a weekly newspaper, and entered politics at the bottom of the elective office ladder. With Pryor, there is no Pell-like puzzle of descriptive representation. He has deep roots in the constituency he represents. His zest for politics is inseparable from his familiarity with its Arkansas context. And it is easy for large numbers of Arkansans to identify with him and to think of him as "one of us."

"My father," says Pryor "had a great influence on me. He taught me to stay close to ordinary people. He was a common people's man. He had only an eighth-grade education, but he understood human nature." From our earliest acquaintance, it became clear how thoroughly Pryor lived his father's lesson. My first day in Arkansas, in 1978, I listened to the two-term governor assure his audiences, "I'm going out of town for a spell, but I won't forget where I came from." A month later—under the approving gaze of local observers—he rented a U-Haul, packed up his furniture, and drove to Washington.[2] During our first Capitol Hill conversation, in January, he expressed his continuing concern for keeping in touch.

When I asked him what actions of his would most likely alienate his constituents, he answered in terms of his personal identification with them, not in terms of his policy decisions. "If you talk down to them or presuppose that this town has all the answers, or if you go back home and talk as if you were smarter than they are. They would say, he's gone up there and gotten uppity. He's got Potomac Fever—that sort of stuff. People are very sensitive to change in a person." A couple of minutes later, he worried about a weakening of identification as a result of his transition from governor to senator. "A governor is a special person in the South," he said.

There's a special relationship between a governor and the people in the South that doesn't exist elsewhere. No matter how long I'm in the Senate, I don't think I can create that relationship with the citizens. They don't look upon congressmen and senators with the same warmth.... In the South, a senator is a step sideways, a step to a role that is not so well defined for them. They can tell you how the governor relates to their lives. But if you ask them how a senator relates to their lives, they aren't sure.

The idea was that he would now have to work extra hard to stay in touch.

From my first 1978 visit, I believed that success in "staying close to ordinary people" would not be a problem for him. And I periodically returned to Arkansas to check that belief— in 1979, 1982, 1984, and 1994. I was right. For all of his seventeen years in the Senate—and not excepting the man who is now president of the United States—David Pryor has been known, by common consent of Arkansas's political observers, as the state's "most popular politician."[3] This chapter is an effort to understand—personally and developmentally—that remarkable constituency fit.

Personal Connections

To travel with Pryor in his home territory is to learn that what he most enjoys about politics is his contact with ordinary people and that what interests him most about politics are the lives and the problems of ordinary people. In describing Claiborne Pell's home connections, I took his partisan policy performance as the starting point, because it provided us with a more reliable foundation than his quirky personal style. In David Pryor's case, it is his personal style that is the foundation for his durable representational fit. And it must be seen to be believed.

Travel talk with Pryor consists of endless stories about the people he has connected with in each town and county. Humorous, nuanced, and touching, they are a way of savoring the relationship of politics to people. "Arkansas," he says, "is like a family. It's a state of wonderful characters." "Aren't the people of Arkansas great," he exclaims. "Isn't this a great state." From the outside, Arkansas may seem markedly homogeneous. But not to Pryor. "Every little town has its own character," he says, driving through the state. "You go thirty miles away and that town will be different from the one you are in." "I don't think there is any town or any county in Arkansas about which I can't tell a story. And I can tell a story about almost any person I've met in Arkansas."

Storytelling is much more than Pryor's way of savoring the everyday life of his state. It is the best clue to his intensely personal view of politics and to the network of personal connections that forms the hard core of his political support. To be sure, there are numerous demanding interests in the state's political life—farming, lumber, poultry, oil and gas, blacks, the elderly, teachers, organized labor, government employees—and the senator has fairly consistent attachments to some of them. But he must be known, first of all, not by any career-long interest group attachments but by his career-long personal appeal, one-on-one, to the ordinary citizens of the state. "His real strength," says a former staffer, "is an organizational network linking general store to general store."[4] A veteran local observer agrees. "While friends-and-neighbors political strength is usually a regional phenomenon," he writes, "it is not for Pryor."[5] His career-long negotiation with the citizens of Arkansas has been a dominantly retail performance.

To come off the road and sit with him for an hour in a Little Rock hotel lobby and eat an evening meal with him and some friends in a Little Rock steakhouse is to experience a steady flow of exchanges with people (six in the lobby, nine during the meal) who stop by to say hello, introduce themselves, discuss a mutual friend, share a reminiscence, ask for an autograph, leave a problem, give advice, or tell a story. These personal encounters put flesh on his travel talk. It would not be correct to call them interruptions or intrusions, for the senator is as eager to make contact as they are. He would hate to miss someone with whom he might find a common bond. With each person, he is warm, animated, and responsive. And he listens. It is altogether a remarkable display of senatorial accessibility.

After his encounters in the hotel lobby, he said, "If I had to self-critique myself, I'd say that I'm not senatorial enough. I don't act—you know—like senators are supposed to act. But you can't teach an old dog new tricks." Perhaps not senatorial in the Claiborne Pell sense—dignified and distant—but senatorial in the sense of taking a genuine interest in whatever is on the minds of his constituents. Shortly after his "self-critique," he returns to form. "That's what makes Arkansas so great," he says. "Everybody you meet knows somebody you know." At dinner, someone quoted a local manicurist as saying, "The only politician I really like is David Pryor. He is one of us." Pryor turns to me, pokes me in the arm to make sure I heard it, and says, "You see, one of us, one of us." It is the essence of his reputation at home.

Political scientists believe this high degree of personal contact is partly a function of state size.[6] Arkansas is a small state of four congressional districts. But Rhode Island—with two congressional districts—is even smaller. And Claiborne Pell's durability has almost nothing to do with close personal contact with his constituents. So something more than sheer size is involved.

With the arrival of Bill Clinton on the national scene, all of us have learned a great deal about Arkansas politics.[7] And we now know that extensive personal contact with citizens is a hallmark of *all* Arkansas politicians. It is expected of them, as it is not expected of politicians in Rhode Island. We must, therefore, think of Pryor's political style also as function of a statewide political culture.

In Pryor's case, however, there is yet another highly individual ingredient involved. He is simply better at Arkansas-style politics than anyone else. He is, in the words of Diane Blair, the leading academic student of the state's politics, "the acknowledged master of the personal touch in contemporary Arkansas politics."[8] Or, as the veteran newsman Ernest Dumas puts it,

"Friends-and-neighbors politics, not ideology, wins here, and David Pryor is the all-time embodiment of it."[9]

Arkansas reporters and columnists make the same generalization. They call him "without question the most popular politician in Arkansas," "the state's most beloved politician," "the people's senator," and "the most popular office holder in Arkansas."[10] They report poll results showing that "[alone] among the state's top politicians, negative opinion about Pryor has remained in single digits."[11] Dumas states,

> [Senator Dale] Bumpers and Pryor have about the same favorability level. But Bumpers' negatives are higher. Pryor's negatives have always been extremely low. If you talk to political people, they will say, I can devise a campaign that will beat Bumpers. But no one can devise a plan that would beat Pryor. Clinton's favorables go up and down. Sometimes his favorables are very high. But he has high negatives.[12]

Journalists focus, too, on Pryor's accessibility. "He relishes spending time with everyone." "Nobody loves shaking hands more." "No one enjoys meeting people and trading stories.... as much." "His enthusiasm for talking to fellow Arkansans is evident." "A key to his popularity is his intense and apparently genuine sense of personal care and concern for others." They call him "personable," "folksy," "unassuming," "a real nice guy," and an "unabashed aw-shucks politician," who is "known and loved across the state."[13] "He is better with constituents than any other politician in Arkansas," says veteran reporter Brenda Blagg.[14]

On the trail, it is easy to see why local observers say that he "has fun in politics" and "relishes politics on the Arkansas level."[15] He travels in a cocoon of good feeling; and it envelops others. As one small-town daily editorialized, "He makes everyone—the common folk as well as the movers and shakers—feel welcome around him."[16] Claiborne Pell always seemed uncomfortable in grass-roots politicking and slightly distressed by my presence. Pryor was totally relaxed in both respects. Handshaking his way through a crowd of teachers, for example, he looks over at me, winks, smiles, and says, "Isn't this a funny way to make a living." Or he introduces me to a large group of lawyers, saying, "He has studied the Senate carefully and out of one hundred senators, he has chosen four who are *destined* [long pause and laughter] for jail!"

His self-image is resolutely unpretentious. In a couple of conversations about his regular radio broadcasts, for example, he casts himself as "ol' David Pryor."

> Press Secretary: Yesterday, one lady told me, "I heard David Pryor on the radio the other day and I sure like him." So I asked her, "What did he say?" She said, "I don't know."
>
> Pryor: (laughing) She probably thought, "There's ol' David Pryor up there doing something. He sounds pretty good."
>
> Pryor: (during a broadcast) We've got an energy problem. And it's time to shell down the corn.
>
> Fenno: (afterward) Is that a favorite expression of yours?
>
> Pryor: (laughing) I don't know why I said it. But I can see some ol' guy driving a pickup down the road. He'll say, "That's ol' David Pryor saying we've got to shell down the corn. That's tellin' 'em."

When he fills out his own name tag at functions, he simply prints "David." "He has an extraordinary ability to relate to people," says Blair. "Everybody calls him David and they think of him as their next-door neighbor."[17]

When Pryor is introduced to his audiences, the accent is on his personal qualities, not, as with Pell, in terms of his policy accomplishments or his senatorial status. To the Arkansas Education Association: "David Pryor, he is just about the most perfect person I know." To the Russellville Rotary: "David Pryor has something most politicians do not have—humility." To the Arkansas NAACP: "David Pryor is a decent, caring individual. He will still talk to you no matter what your problem is today, just as quick as he would have years ago before he got into statewide politics." Pryor's response to such introductions is invariably self-deprecatory. He says that his humility comes from having "a lot to be humble about" or that being described as "warm" really means that he is "not so hot."

For several months between 1991 and 1993, he was felled by a heart attack and then by a heart bypass operation. In January 1994, I went to Arkansas as he resumed his travels at home. At a gathering of trustees, administrators, and doctors of the Children's Hospital in Little Rock, I found that neither he nor his home relationships had been affected by his absence.

> Pryor: It's been several years since I've been here. And I've been wanting to come by for a long time to get myself reinvigorated.
> Welcoming trustee: I know you've said it's been some time since you've been here and a lot has happened here—the research and the building and all. But one thing is the same. You are still our most respected and most popular politician. And when I say that, I mean that you have the love and the trust of the people of this state.
> Pryor: You're as out of touch as I am.

After the meeting, our hospital tour guide edged over to me. "What Herschel said is the truth. David is the most loved politician in Arkansas," she said. "Why?" I asked. "Because he speaks for us and we trust him." It is a simple relationship to articulate. But it is not, as we have already seen, a simple relationship to negotiate.

Pryor's conception of politics-as-people applies equally to his relations with fellow politicians in Arkansas. During a 1994 gathering of the state's politicians at the obligatory Annual Coon Supper in Gillett, numerous movers and shakers volunteered to me the same description as the journalists. "Everybody loves David Pryor." "He knows half the people of Arkansas by their first names." "He's the most popular politician in Arkansas." "He doesn't put on airs." "His secret is that he likes people." He was accompanied that day by several people who had helped manage and finance the two campaigns against him in the defining three-way primary face-off in 1978. And these comments flowed as freely from former opponents as they did from lifelong supporters.

Here again, he recalls lessons he absorbed as a teenager.

One thing my father taught me was to neutralize your opposition. Do not go into combat with your opposition, neutralize
them. His first race was against an incumbent, Sheriff Tom Ellis.
Tom and his friends ran the courthouse ... and my father joined
the reform group.... He went to all of Tom Ellis's friends and
said, "I know you have to vote for Tom Ellis. I'm not going to
hold it against you. I want you to be for me when you find you
can't go with Tom." He neutralized them, and before long they
became his supporters.

"The moral of the story," he adds, is "don't burn your bridges.
The person who opposes you today may be with you down
the line." In 1984, a top member of Pryor's reelection campaign
team was a man who had been a top adviser in 1972 to Pryor's
bitter opponent, Senator John McClellan. Said the adviser, "This
campaign is filled with people from the campaigns of those
who ran against him. David makes bridges with people who
opposed him. He doesn't make them into enemies."

McClellan was the only person ever to defeat David Pryor in
an election. And it was only on McClellan's death that Pryor
was able to get to the Senate. Even so, early in his first term, he
and his wife drove down to North Carolina and back in one day
to visit with McClellan's widow and to help her with a personal
problem. The individual who told of that trip also reported that
"Mrs. McClellan said David Pryor was nicer to her than anyone
else in the state of Arkansas in the years after her husband's
death."

The same characteristic decency is revealed, too, in a visit
involving another political enemy, Orval Faubus. When Pryor
was a "young Turk" state legislator, Faubus had been his main
target; and in 1974, Pryor had become governor by defeating
Faubus for the Democratic nomination. Still, Pryor reported, in
1982,

I was scheduled to dedicate a Confederate cemetery two weeks
ago and I saw that Governor Faubus was going to be there, too.
So I called him up. "This is David Pryor." "Hello, senator, how are
you?" "How are you going to get to the dedication ceremonies

on Thursday?" "I was planning to drive up." "Why don't I come around and pick you up. We can drive up together and swap war stories." We had the most delightful trip. You would have loved to have been in the back seat listening to the conversation. I had a wonderful time. He's a real historian. He remembers names and dates and places. We were mortal enemies. I was philosophically opposed to almost everything he did. But sometimes you can learn from your enemies.

That kind of personal attentiveness to others is good politics in Arkansas. But its origins precede politics, and its consequences transcend politics.

Not surprisingly, the man I saw in Washington was the very same informal, outgoing man I saw in Arkansas. He comes to the office each morning just as he hits the campaign trail, with an untied necktie slung over his shoulder—to be put on only as necessary. During the year (1981–82) I spent at the Capitol, I occasionally found him sitting at the receptionist's desk answering the day's first telephone calls. And it was not at all unusual to find him later in the day in the receptionist area visiting with tourists from home. After watching the newly elected senator for nearly a year, one influential Arkansas political reporter concluded,

> Spending some time with Pryor in his office makes it clear why many political observers believe he will become the most unbeatable politician in Arkansas in a few years. Like every politician here, Pryor receives a string of visitors in his office every day. Unlike other politicians, Pryor loves it. The task of greeting constituents, often a burden to other legislators, appears to be Pryor's greatest joy.[18]

Two years later, a senior staff aide emphasized the senator's concern for the treatment of constituents who come to the office.

> He wants to know, "Are they being treated right? Do they feel at home?" If he meets them in the hall, he'll ask them if they got their passes [for the White House or the House and Senate galleries]. If they say no, he'll come back into the office and want to know why. "Are we telling people who get their White House

passes that they can also go to the FBI?" For the first year and a half, these are the sorts of problems we would talk about, almost exclusively. He gets very upset if every individual doesn't get the best possible treatment.

During that same conversation, the senior aide reported, not unrelatedly, "Our polls show he's got 95 percent name recognition and an 85 percent approval rate. In fact, right now, he's the most popular politician in Arkansas."

So far as I can tell, that generalization never changed. Everything I have seen and read confirms it. As Pryor expresses it, "As a congressman, governor, and senator, I feel like I've developed a special relationship with all the people of Arkansas, that we understand each other."[19] "If you level with them, they'll level with you," he says. "As long as they think you are shooting square with them, they give you the flexibility to do what is right."[20] When asked why he is so popular, Pryor uses the word that best captures the essence of a durable, long-term constituency connection—trust. "Well, I think—I hope—that the people of Arkansas feel there's a relationship between us. I hope they feel they can trust me. They may not be happy with every vote I cast, but I think they know I represent their interests."[21]

In an era so widely characterized by assertions of a "disconnectedness" between politicians and citizens, Pryor's strong personal connectedness to the citizens of Arkansas is a remarkable accomplishment.

Policy Connections: Constituency Perceptions and Agriculture

Constituent trust, of course, cannot survive on personal connections alone. Policy counts, too. On his support base of personal connections, Pryor has negotiated over time a set of policy connections. Conceptually, if not actually, the relationship between the two sorts of connections has been mediated by his perception of his constituency. In taking positions on matters of public policy, a representative must take constituency preferences into account. And this cannot be done by adding up all his one-on-one relationships, however vast and informative they might be. There must be a perceptual framework within which the politician builds constituency connections.

When asked to describe the makeup of his constituency in its broadest terms, he says, "Arkansas is a proud state, ferociously independent in politics." And he quickly links citizen independence to the dominantly rural character of the state. "Even the most urbanized sections or neighborhoods have a rural philosophy of independence, because most of them grew up on a farm in the south or east or northwest part of the state.... People are proud of the rural communities they came from. I call Camden my home—15,000 people."

In his mind's eye, Arkansas is very much a state of small farms, small business, and small towns. "Small business people and farmers are the cement that has held this country together," he says. These perceptions of an independent, rural electorate fit nicely with his attentiveness to "ordinary people" and his down-to-earth, person-to-person style for relating to them.

He is, not surprisingly, most comfortably at home in unbuttoned, small-scale, rural settings. "[He] loves to press the flesh in rural Arkansas," writes a seasoned political observer. "His idea of a good time is getting out of the city and talking to people who appreciate the importance of a good sheriff."[22] In 1979, he dispatched seven Washington staffers to the "real Arkansas" to spend a summer week learning the state by working ordinary jobs alongside ordinary people. "They won't stay in Little Rock," he said. "They will travel to small cities and towns ... and listen to folks at the cattle barns and the café's. "[23]

On the way to a 1978 campaign rally in Stuttgart, Pryor commented,"They wanted to have the dinner at the Stuttgart Country Club. I said no. I don't campaign at country clubs. It smacks too much of the rich and the highbrow. People say, 'You say you're just one of the ordinary people and then you come to town and go off to the country club.' " His discomfort in country club settings was apparent a year later when he went to a Little Rock country club to deliver a speech on energy policy to a large group of yuppie professionals. Afterward, the district aide who accompanied us discussed Pryor's performance.

> He doesn't make good speeches in Little Rock. In Springdale the other night, he was tired, he had a cold, but he gave a great speech. Technically, he gave the same speech last night in Little Rock. But in one case he had the crowd and in one case he didn't. He doesn't like the country club atmosphere. You heard him say how he picked at his food. He didn't enjoy it. He likes dirt roads and streams and the countryside. And that's where he gets his votes.

"It was like driving with a flat tire," agreed the senator. "They weren't my crowd."

Pryor's perception of his home constituency begins with its regional components. Arkansas, unlike Rhode Island, is a state where political lessons begin with geography lessons.[24] "When I go back home," he says, "I'd rather pay more attention to geographical areas of the state, to two or three towns there, than to groups." During my first day in Arkansas, a veteran staffer instructed me,"You have three very different mentalities in one state. In the northwestern part of the state, you have a midwestern mentality; in the eastern part of the state, you have a southern mentality; in this part of the state (Little Rock), you have a southwestern mentality."

Pryor describes Arkansas similarly as "a composite of diverse entities." Riding through the rolling Ozarks in the northern part of the state, he explained that "the Delta is a different world from the one we are in now. Fayetteville is a different world. The southern part of the state, where I come from, is a different world." And, riding in the flat southeastern "grand prairie," he comments that the state's wealth used to be "in this region—rice, timber, oil," but it has moved "to the north with industry, poultry." "The northwest part of the state," he says, "is busting at the seams."

His political calculations begin by emphasizing these regional differences. The southern and eastern (or Delta) regions are traditionally the most Democratic. And they are pillars of his reelection constituency. In regional terms, his solid, reliable support comes from the south. "I do best," he says, "in the southern part of the state. That's where my congressional district was. The eastern area always thought I was a little too liberal." Over time, however, Pryor has built his statewide reelection constituency by gradually adding the eastern region to his primary constituency in the south.

The figures at the end of this chapter present a rough picture of the senator's changing regional support patterns—from his unsuccessful runoff primary in 1972 (fig. 8.1) through his successful runoff primary in 1978 (fig. 8.2) to his general election victory in 1984 (fig. 8.3). In every case, his hard-core support in the south is evident. Along the eastern side of the state, between 1972 and 1978, he increased his support among Democrats in nearly every county. And in the 1984 partisan contest, he carried the eastern region as strongly as the southern one.

The political importance of rural Arkansas has been highlighted by Diane Blair in her descriptions of twenty-six pivotal "rural-swing districts," which are most indicative of changing vote patterns.[25] They are scattered throughout the state (designated with an X on figs. 8.1, 8.2, and 8.3). Of these twenty-six, Pryor captured thirteen in 1972, fourteen in 1978, and twenty-four in 1984. While it is fair to assume that this rurally oriented politician does well throughout this rural state, it is also true that he has done increasingly well in the most politically sensitive rural areas.

In career terms, the three regional support charts display a two-step development—the first from 1972 to 1978, and the second from 1978 to 1984. To explain these changes, it is useful—as it was in the case of Claiborne Pell—to think in terms of David Pryor's policy career.

The change in his support pattern between 1972 and 1978 can be explained largely by a marked change in his policy orientation. As a labor union-supported, reform-oriented congressman running against a veteran conservative incumbent, Pryor was the more liberal of the two candidates in the 1972 runoff primary. And, said an aide, "John McClellan successfully wrapped him in the liberal-labor flag." In 1978, candidate contrasts were reversed. "Against Jim Guy Tucker," says Pryor, "I didn't look so liberal. I was a governor who had to say no, who had to hold down spending, who balanced the budget, who ran the biggest business in the state and ended up with a surplus. That sold the people in the east, and I did well there." These changes in his policy orientation, and to a new reputation as a fiscal conservative, best explain the regional shift in his support patterns between 1972 and 1978.[26]

An explanation of the second and more dramatic increase in his Delta region support, between 1978 and 1984, needs to take into account his six-year policy performance as a senator. That performance begins with his attentiveness to agriculture. If there is a dominant economic interest in the eastern region of Arkansas, it is farming. And if there is a dominant economic component to Senator Pryor's successful negotiation with the eastern Delta region, it is the agricultural one.

Campaigning in 1978 in Stuttgart, "The rice-growing Capital of the World," he promised a dinner audience at the high school, "I hope I become a member of the Senate Agriculture Committee. I want to become a member of that committee. If I get to the Senate, I'm going to make the point loud and clear that in all the Department of Agriculture, there's not one advocate of the rice industry, not one salesman for the rice industry."

In Washington, Agriculture was the first committee assignment he requested; an agriculture assistant was the first specialist he hired; and a comprehensive agriculture bill was the first bill he introduced. Within six months, his top staffer in the state surveyed the results of this early negotiation with the state's agricultural constituency: "In Arkansas, parties don't count; regions count," he said. "Pryor's stand on agriculture has gotten him solid support among the farmers in the eastern, Delta area."

In 1980, a top staffer in Pryor's Washington office provided a glimpse of the kind of service to Arkansas's farmer-constituents that added the glue of personal relationships to policy performance.

> The farmers' groups were here for a week and made this office their headquarters. This office was their headquarters last year, too.... We gave them the full run of the office.... One newspaper wrote an article saying that while the farmers felt at home here in the office, they did not feel that way in Bumpers's office. They felt they were intruding there. As you know, that's Pryor's stock in trade—people. Another paper wrote that when the farmers had Bumpers in a room, wringing him out on the issues, Pryor was taking the farmers' wives on a tour of the Capitol.... We also set up a little agenda for them so we wouldn't have any "idle hands, idle minds." Some of the rice farmers have beaver problems—the beavers come in and eat the rice. So we set up a meeting with the Interior Department on beaver control. Other farmers have problems with the herbicides they spray on crops. So we set up a meeting with EPA on that. We brought the bureaucrats over here and set aside a room for the meeting.

In a 1980 discussion of recent Arkansas politicians, two Farm Bureau leaders emphasized that Pryor has "understood rural people," and they commended him, especially, for being "accessible to everybody."[27]

At the Weiner Rice Festival in 1984, I listened to a reprise of Pryor's Stuttgart appearance six years earlier. "It has been one of the joys of my service in the Senate," he told a large crowd, "to serve on the Agriculture Committee and to stand up for the Arkansas rice farmers." And he regaled his audience with the story of his much-publicized mini-filibuster to keep loans and target prices for rice in the agriculture bill.

> I stood up, talked about the importance of rice, and started to read rice recipes. Howard Baker walked over to me and asked whether or not I intended to filibuster. I said I had no such intention but that I did have several hundred rice recipes that I might read! He walked away, and I kept reading recipes. Pretty soon, Bob Dole

came over and said, "OK, what do you want?" We called for a quorum and worked it out.[28]

As we drove away, he commented, "I've worked very hard with the farmers of the state. I should do well in all the farming areas."

Agriculture Committee service may or may not be one of his great joys; but in his 1984 reelection campaign, his defense of the Rural Electrification Administration became a major issue in his favor when his opponent proposed its abolition. At the time, his poll results showed his popularity rating ("high and very high opinion of") at 64 percent among "farm households" and his opponent's at 39 percent.[29] When I asked Pryor to name the most important long-run career accomplishment of his first term, he answered, "Getting on the Agriculture Committee." In 1984, a veteran columnist wrote that "Pryor is known in Arkansas as the farmer's best friend."[30] In 1989, he became the committee's second-ranking Democrat. He chaired its most powerful Subcommittee on Agricultural Production and Price Stabilization, with jurisdiction over 75 percent of the farm program. This policy-oriented representational connection is depicted by the darker regions of figure 8.3.

Policy Connections: Populist Constituency and Reform

When pressed to place a covering ideological label on his entire geographic constituency, he used the term "populist." "I think all Arkansans are populists," he said. "We are a populist people." [31] "We are independent thinkers and proud of our pioneering spirit, which is more populist than it is liberal or conservative." Accordingly, he describes himself as "more populist than liberal or conservative," or alternately, "somewhere between a moderate and a maverick." It is a self-definition that avoids ideological labeling and allows for the kind of pragmatic responses to contextual change that his policy career reveals.

In conventional policy terms, Pryor's House and Senate

voting record is that of a southern moderate—one of the racially liberal "New South" politicians who emerged on the national scene in the 1960s and 1970s. During his three terms in the House, his conservative coalition score began close to the average of southern Democrats and then grew steadily away from them—moving from 61 percent support in his first term to 43 percent and then 20 percent—while his southern colleagues remained in the 62 to 66 percent range throughout. In the Senate, his conservative coalition score averaged 62 percent in his first term and 51 percent in his second. Nonetheless, his opposition scores have usually landed him on *Congressional Quarterly*'s list of the least supportive of southern Democratic senators.

When, in 1981, he joined "a group of about ten moderate-to-conservative" Democratic senators,[32] he explained it by saying, "Between [Jesse] Helms and [Ted] Kennedy there has to be a middle position. On food stamps, for example, Helms has his knife out to gut the program, and the McGovernites, the nutrition people, want to give it to everyone. There has to be a middle position there. Our idea is that we can make a difference by developing that position." Ideologically, Pryor occupies the middle position. As such, he is well placed to adopt a shifting array of nonagricultural policy enthusiasms.

In policy matters, he also calls himself "a generalist." And in the Senate, his policy enthusiasms have tended to follow an earlier antiestablishment reformist bent. "I was a bit of a reformer in college," he recalls, "writing for the newspaper. But I think it was my experience as a [student] driver for Governor Francis Cherry in his 1954 campaign against Orval Faubus that made me angry at the system. Faubus beat Cherry . . . and from that day on everything Faubus was for, I was against."

After college, he started the crusading weekly *Ouachita Citizen*, "an independent newspaper devoted to the best interests of the people of Ouachita County and South Arkansas." It was a direct challenge to the established hometown *Camden News*; and it brought him the lifelong opposition of both the *News* and the influential Hussman chain of South Arkansas newspapers of which the *News* was a part. "It was crazy," he says. "If I had had $50, I would have declared bankruptcy. But I didn't have the money." In what one local friend called "a feisty move by a feisty guy," Pryor hired a black woman as his first assistant. He editorialized against the "old guard leadership of the [Arkansas] House" in favor of a city manager for Camden and inveighed against the Washington handling of taxpayers' money.[33] The paper folded on his election to the state legislature.

"I made my first reputation in politics as a reformer," he says. "In the state legislature, I was known as a Young Turk. I tried to get rid of the poll tax and clean up nursing homes, things like that." He was, recalls the journalist Ernest Dumas, "a hell raiser" and "an anti-Faubus liberal." So out of favor was he with the established leadership, Pryor recalls, that "I had a resolution praising Winston Churchill after he died and I couldn't even get recognized by the Speaker." "The first bill I introduced required competitive bidding for all state and local highway contracts. The first year I got four votes. After six years, it passed by six votes." "I noticed recently," he noted with satisfaction, that "several of those fellows went to jail." As governor, despite his conservative turn, he offered several antiestablishment initiatives.[34]

Pryor's populist predilections have led him—gadfly style— to a variety of crusading, reformist investigations in the Senate. At his request, the General Accounting Office has conducted well over one hundred investigative studies.[35] But the objects of his predilections and his crusades have a commonality: they stem from the primacy of people in his thinking about policy. Comparing two *Gazette* reporters, he gives his kudos to the one "who captures the human side, the personal side, of politics— who sees the person who thanks me for the social security check or talks to me about someone we know." He does not see the world in terms of abstractions or philosophies. He sees it in its human dimensions, and he identifies problems most readily when he sees them on a human scale. He moves from thinking about people to thinking about policy.

The difference from Claiborne Pell's habit of mind is striking. Recall Pell's intellectual interests and his operating code: "Translate ideas into events and help people." In fact, the early version of Pell's credo lacked any reference to people. Those words were added later.[36] Pell is something of a policy wonk; and many of the ideas that interest him are quite esoteric. For Pryor, it is the other way around. He got into politics because he likes people. Once in office, he found that addressing the problems of ordinary people made politics worthwhile. For Pryor, people's problems come first, then ideas about policy. That is the lesson of his storytelling, his personal encounters, and his accessibility.

Pryor is moved to policy action more by instinct than by analysis, by the feeling "in my gut" that something is just plain wrong. "I need something to make my blood boil," he says. And a top adviser agrees: "He's usually outraged about something." He needs a cause to stir his interest; and once interested, he sees himself as engaged in a crusade to right some wrong. If you want to get his attention to a problem, therefore, present him with an example of a wrong being done to some identifiable individuals and let him work his way, inductively, toward the larger public policy issue involved.

The prototypical case of Pryor's instinctive people-to-policy approach is his career-long interest in the care of the elderly. It was the mistreatment of an individual that triggered its congressional phase. "My efforts in this area began," he told a reporter, "when my mother wrote me a letter about her great-aunt who she thought was receiving poor treatment in an Arkansas nursing home. My mother kept telling me how bad the nursing home was and I said conditions could not be that bad; and, not only was it as bad as she said it was, it was worse."[37]

When Pryor's efforts to persuade the leaders of the House of Representatives to investigate the nursing home industry failed, he took matters into his own hands. He investigated nursing homes as an undercover weekend employee; he set up, in a rented trailer, his own committee of Capitol Hill volunteers to research the industry; and he pushed for a separate House Committee on Aging.[38] He has been especially protective of the elderly ever since.

Arkansas ranks among the top half-dozen states in its percentage of people over the age of sixty-five. Journalists at home write that "he is known nationwide as a friend of the elderly," and they describe him as "the champion of the elderly" and "the principal heir of [Rep. Claude] Pepper's legacy."[39] In July 1984, his popularity rating ("high and very high opinion of") stood at 77 percent among citizens ages 60 and older.[40] It is, perhaps, a form of justice that by 1989 he had enough seniority to become chairman of the Senate's Special Committee on Aging. In 1994, the legislative director of the American Association of Retired Persons (AARP) described Pryor as "the most visible and the most effective spokesperson for older Americans in Congress."[41]

In chapter 2, I discussed Pryor's crusade against the excessive use of outside consultants by the government. Again it was a specific instance that moved him to action. He happened to share a taxi in Washington with two men who were, he said, "debating the amount they should charge a federal agency for their services." After debating between $12,000 and $25,000, they decided on the higher figure. As Chairman of the Governmental Affairs Subcommittee on Post Office and Civil Service, he launched an investigation into the government hiring of consultants or "the invisible bureaucracy." And he concluded that "the American taxpayer is being ripped off by a $2 billion industry."[42] He passed amendments cutting the money available for consultants to various agencies ($100 million from Defense) and introduced the Consultants Reform Act of 1980.[43] His efforts landed him on CBS's *60 Minutes* and brought him notice back home. "Senator Pryor is showing an instinct for can't miss issues in his first term," editorialized the *Gazette*.[44]

In later years, he took on at least two more nationally publicized reformist causes. I did not investigate the triggering circumstances. But the impulse and the effect were the same as before. As chairman of the Finance Committee's Subcommittee on the Internal Revenue Service, he held hearings on the intimidation of individual taxpayers by the Internal Revenue Service, and he wrote the Taxpayer's Bill of Rights.[45] "The president of IBM did not write me to tell me how the IRS had put him into bankruptcy," he said. "However, hundreds of small businessmen did write to relate sad stories. The little people of the world are easy marks for the IRS, and I suspect that is why they are frequent targets. These people do not have batteries of accountants and tax attorneys waiting to do battle with the IRS."[46] The Taxpayer Bill of Rights became law in 1988. And the state's leading paper called it "the best thing he has ever done as a senator."[47]

This anti-bureaucracy crusade was reminiscent of an earlier one. In connection with the debate on the expulsion of Senator Harrison Williams, he attacked the untouchable FBI for what he saw as its menacing entrapment procedures. "It is a matter," he said, "that should strike fear into the hearts of not just senators. Generally, as has been said, we can take care of ourselves. But I am worried about John Smith. I am worried about Mary Doe. They are defenseless. If the Federal Bureau of Investigation ever wants you, it is going to get you."[48] It was another defense of the ordinary citizen caught in the maw of a powerful bureaucracy.

In the 1990s, Pryor took on the pharmaceutical industry for what he called its price gouging on prescription drugs for the elderly. "I enjoy an uphill battle when the odds are against me," he said of this cause. "It gets my adrenaline pumping. This is the kind of issue I like because I feel I'm right. I feel I'm on the right side."[49] He told another reporter, "We're going to go after those dudes. They're going to wish they had never heard of me."[50] And he explained it to me as "the white hats against the black hats."

In all these cases, what makes Pryor's blood boil is a perceived abuse of power whereby some "big guys" are taking unfair advantage of some "little guys." Thus defined, his causes are populist causes. "He enjoys bucking the establishment," says a top Senate aide. The senator himself admits that "ol' Pryor, once a year he likes to get in a big brawl."[51]

His stands against powerful institutions of one sort or another—a media chain, the state legislature, federal bureaucracies, private industries—have been a consistent thread in his policy career. To be sure, his stance is a calculated one; but it is also instinctive. And his instincts are a product of his close "one of us" association with the lives of ordinary Arkansans. Talking to reporters in 1990, he reflected on his career-long populist predisposition. "If I had it to do all over again, I'd double my efforts for the little guy. Big guys look after themselves and big guys stick together."[52]

In general, Pryor does not gravitate naturally to involvement in the more ideological, controversial, and publicity-generating policy problems of the day. He gravitates, instead, toward what he calls "living room issues." They are issues of right and wrong that have arisen because some establishment practice adversely affects the everyday life of ordinary citizens. They are issues that are understandable to average citizens and are meaningful subjects of their everyday conversations.

In choosing such manageable issues, Pryor exhibits a quality rarer in a politician than good speech-making. He is a listener. And listening—as in a living room—is an activity he emphasizes over and over. In describing his job, he says, "It's a relationship of sitting on the porches with the people and listening to them. I've tried to listen to the people and translate their hopes into reality."[53] In our travels, whenever we came upon a group engaged in some activity, he would refuse center stage, saying, "I'll just sit here and listen." If anyone cares what Arkansans have on their minds, David Pryor is probably the best person in Arkansas to ask.

Early in my visits to Arkansas, I came to understand that Pryor's desire to keep in touch, and to listen, rested on another rare quality—his ingrained respect for citizen reactions to government performance. For him, keeping in touch and listening are matters of good public policy as well as matters of political support. The burning issue of 1979, for example, was energy. And Pryor was critical of the energy policy makers (of his own party) for their inability to communicate at ground level with the general public. It was not the substantive policy that concerned him as much as it was the point of contact between policy maker and citizen.

Of one influential senator, Pryor said,

> He knows everything there is to know about energy. He has all the facts and figures, the numbers of barrels of oil needed per day per state and the amount of oil needed to make gasoline. But he can't talk to the common man. He can't make it understandable. He talks over their heads.

Of an influential energy administrator, he remarked similarly,

> He's a smart man, but he's a theoretician. He is aloof and is not in touch with ordinary people at the gas pump. He should step aside in favor of someone with common sense and courage. . . . I have called for his resignation.

Pryor was arguing that policy expertise was not enough, that there must also be a healthy representational component in the making of public policy.[54]

In his book about President Clinton, the Arkansas political writer John Brummett repeatedly describes Pryor as the president's "common sense adviser."[55] Pryor's ability to discern and to communicate citizen concerns is a deliberate choice—a choice that depends on the importance he attaches to his close grass-roots contact with the citizenry and on the respect he accords their assessments. It is, then, as a representative "one of us" that he chooses his policy issues and pursues his policy career. His policy connections are heavily informed by his personal connections, and these two bases of his constituency connections are compatible and reinforcing.

Media Interpretations

David Pryor's investigative enthusiasms have kept him relatively free from ideological controversies that break along liberal-conservative lines. His self-definitions — "populist," "moderate," "maverick"—eschew these rubrics. Nonetheless, there are times when he must make choices on matters with unavoidable liberal-conservative dimensions. They are the most difficult for him personally, and they are the ones that are made most visible by the media at home.

For most of his Senate life, Pryor has been under the watchful eye of the liberal *Arkansas Gazette* (now the *Democrat-Gazette*), until 1991, the dominant statewide newspaper. Its relations with Pryor reflected the stages of his policy career. In his Young Turk days in the Arkansas legislature, he said,"I was the darling of the *Gazette*. I could do no wrong." As primary challenger in 1972 and as candidate for governor in 1974, "they supported me [because] I was more liberal than my opponent." But when, as governor, Pryor proposed turning some of the state's taxing power over to local governments, he said in 1981, "They turned against me. We came to a parting of the ways; and they have been after me ever since."[56]

They went after him for what they deemed his conservative-leaning votes—on food stamps, the balanced budget amendment, flag desecration, and the windfall profits tax, for example.[57] And it is probably the case that anybody who measures his pragmatic voting record on high-profile liberal-conservative issues will find something to criticize.

Criticism of individual votes sometimes escalates into a more general criticism. When Arkansas's political reporters combine an assessment of his votes with an assessment of his investigative activity, their judgments are two parts appreciation, one part skepticism. They praise the constituency connectedness of everything he does. But they also convey the reservation that he could or should have acted more boldly on controversial issues. The suggestion is that "his decisions on issues are made to catch the political winds."[58]

Their reservations are sometimes couched in faint praise. "As a senator, Pryor has developed a knack for finding issues that appeal to American taxpayers."[59] "[He has] an uncanny ability to read the public pulse—and to use it. He knows what will sell."[60] "[He has] a tendency to approach issues in a general symbolic way, but often not in substance."[61] Others suggest that his "low negatives" result from his avoidance of controversial matters: "The issues he has seized upon have been carefully selected, but uncanny in their popular appeal.... Pryor has not sought to unravel the energy conundrum or wrestle with SALT II or inflation on any kind of comprehensive scale.... [He has] a penchant for popular issues and facile solutions."[62] Others are quite blunt: "When it comes to avoiding ideas, Pryor's career has provided the model. His success has taught a whole generation of Arkansas politicians how to win elections in an intellectual vacuum."[63] All agree that the policy work he has done, he has done well. But they want him to do more.

Media reservations express, of course, their own expectations about senatorial activity, their penchant for senatorial involvement in the comprehensive and intellectual treatment of large policy problems. Just how much their unmet expectations influence Pryor's reputation at home, I cannot say. Probably very little, if at all. For one thing, they are balanced, inasmuch as they show appreciation as well as skepticism. And in the final analysis, Pryor's policy choices are ones his constituents believe represent their interests or at least are ones his constituents seem not to find problematic. As one prospective Republican opponent in 1990 put it in declining the honor, "How can you run against a guy who beats up on the IRS?"[64]

Media expectations and reservations do, however, have a basis in reality. They are indicators of Pryor's choices about where to commit his personal resources. Pryor tends to avoid large policy pronouncements or noteworthy media appearances. Compared with Pell, for example, he is not a policy intellectual. His watchdog investigations have given him a gadfly reputation as someone clearly lacking the patient, long-term perspective of the bookish Foreign Relations chairman. Pryor cannot claim to be the legislative architect of any sweeping and readily recognizable policy accomplishment like the Pell Grants program or the National Endowments for the Arts and the Humanities. Nor do his polls reveal much spontaneous citizen recognition of any special area of legislative activity. His agricultural and elderly policy concerns are only barely visible in unguided voter comments.

A skeptical media may, quite legitimately, want more from him. They may, however, undervalue the legitimacy that ordinary citizens give to policy work designed to protect them against big institutions. In any case, it would be hard to argue that "the most popular" and "the most beloved" politician in Arkansas has made inappropriate policy choices, not, at least, in a representative system of government.

Policy Independence: Nerve Gas

In marked contrast to these media reservations, my own earliest observations in Arkansas produced quite a different view of David Pryor's public policy involvements. His crusade against the manufacture of nerve gas for military use demonstrates his willingness to tackle an issue of broad scope and limited popularity. In this case, the prospective benefits of nerve gas manufacture would accrue to his own constituents while the prospective costs of the manufacturing would be borne globally. But he leaned hard against the prevailing local interest and toward the global interest.

The issue dominated my initial trip to Arkansas in 1978. Through a leak from the Pentagon, Governor Pryor had learned of Defense Department plans to manufacture nerve gas at the National Center for Toxicological Research (NCTR) in Pine Bluff, Arkansas—in a county (Jefferson) within his old congressional district and one that he carried in every statewide election. As he began to think about it, his opposition to the Arkansas site and to the manufacture of nerve gas in general crystallized. Since an estimated two hundred jobs and $200 million were at stake, he knew his position would be unpopular in Pine Bluff, the state's fourth-largest city.[65] The question I found him debating when I arrived was whether to hold a press conference the next day to announce his opposition.

At lunch, an aide advised him to wait until the day after the election: "Hold it [the press conference] on November 9," he recommended. "These people are worried about their jobs." To which Pryor replied, "But there's more to it than jobs. We can already kill each other a thousand times over. I think if we are going to fight a war, we should fight with clubs and sticks." He made no decision but kept worrying about the problem. "I'm the only person in the state who cares," he said that afternoon. "It's a one-man issue. I called [Arkansas Senator] Dale Bumpers this morning and talked to him about it. He doesn't care. Nobody cares but me. But every gut instinct tells me I should go ahead." And on that familiar basis—moral outrage and gut instinct—he did.

On the plane to Jonesboro the next morning, he said, "I decided to let it rip and go ahead with the press conference. The trouble is, nobody cares but me." His conversation with Jonesboro's congressman was no help. On the flight back, he continued to worry. "This press conference makes me feel less easy than any one I have ever held," he said. "The devil of it is I don't know why I'm doing it. I just feel compelled to, that's all. When I told [Congressman] Bill Alexander, he told me in his own way that I ought to wait.... He asked me why I was doing it. And I told him I didn't know why, but I had to. He kinda shook his head."

Back in Little Rock, Pryor worked on a letter to President Carter expressing his views. And later, as we walked to his press conference, he said, "I may be walking into a trap. I may be making a big mistake this close to election." At the news conference, he said (among other things),

This has worried me a great deal. There's a tremendous apathy about this issue that worries me even more.... Morally, I find it repugnant—the production of nerve gas.... I'm here to say that the production of nerve gas in Pine Bluff is a tragic mistake.... Economic reasons are the important reasons for producing nerve gas in Pine Bluff, Arkansas. I know the people of Pine Bluff; they are proud of their community and would not want to profiteer from this suspect adventure. I think the people of Pine Bluff would want to see the NCTR expand and play a more positive role.... I could have waited very easily till after the election. But I think a decision like this has no relation to a political race.... A decision of this magnitude and this moral climate is one you can't wait on. I wrestled with it all week, hoping someone else would come forward. When no one did, I felt I had to get it off my chest.

Afterward, he told an aide to call the person in charge at Pine Bluff. "Tell him I did it out of moral compunction and that I did it before election so people will not think I have my feet planted firmly in sawdust." Then he added, "We probably just went down nineteen points in the polls." Moments later, he found some Pryor-style perspective. "One thing I know," he said, "and that is that one hundred years from now, what I just did will not make any difference and no one will remember. We'll all be dead [long pause] of nerve gas!"

He carried that large issue with him into the Senate. And his opposition to nerve gas production brought him into alliances with other senators in the Military Reform Caucus, which advocated substantial changes in Pentagon policy. "Chemical warfare is not the important part of the [antimilitary] movement," he said in 1982. "People don't parade with signs saying Stop Chemical Warfare. But it's part of the same movement; it's part of the war, war, war movement." For that part of the reform movement, at least, Pryor became a recognized leader. "It came up two or three or four times every year," he said in 1984. "I'd get my six thick briefing books and go over to the floor one more time to do battle on it."[66]

In that fight, he found a target he had not identified when he first took up the issue in 1978: it was the Pentagon, the biggest of all big institutions against which to mount a populist attack. As he put it in 1984,

I hate ... the nerve gas people. They just want something for

> themselves, without regard for security. They're a bunch of hypocrites.... It's just a matter of constituencies.... they all want something. That's the way the Pentagon works. The nuclear people have their missiles and they are happy. The tank people have their M-1 tanks and they are happy. But here's this one group that doesn't have anything, so they decide they ought to make up some new nerve gas. They are ripping people off for their own benefit.... And that makes me mad.

It was one more ripoff to make his blood boil.

His lengthy association with policy on nerve gas helped him in achieving his elective office ambitions at home. "It was important," he said, "because it showed a commitment on my part. It showed I would stand up and fight for something, that I would be tenacious when I thought I was right." Along with his investigation into government consultants, he said the nerve gas issue brought him the most visibility in his first term. "Reporters, as you know, operate with boxes or pigeonholes— Tower, MX missile; Domenici, budget; Pryor, nerve gas. For them, I was identified with it.... The fact that I was opposed to it when it was manufactured in my state and would cost jobs and that I was opposed by people in the state made it more interesting." In 1994, a leading state politician still framed the issue just that way: "David took on the state's business establishment on that one."[67]

In the 1984 reelection campaign, Pryor's opponent took the same position he did. So it was not an issue. But the publicity certainly helped to confirm Pryor's reputation at home as a crusader against bigness. In that sense, the nerve gas crusade was vintage Pryor—with the same gut instinct serving as trigger and with the same establishment target as all his other causes. At the time he took his stand, however, it was not the popular cause—in Arkansas or in the nation. And he fought as the leader of a Senate minority throughout the 1980s. It was not a demonstration of some "uncanny knack." It was not, as the media might have it, taken because "it would sell." It was not "symbolism." And it carried political risk. To media skeptics, if they cared, it presented unmistakable evidence of his willingness to finesse political popularity to work in large, controversial policy areas. David Pryor's nerve gas battles were a close equivalent to Claiborne Pell's stand on Vietnam—a strategic declaration of his policy independence.

In 1982, I found him, as always, wary of becoming a single issue senator.

> I don't go around knocking people over the head on the subject. For one thing, I'm sick of the issue. For another thing, I don't want people to think that every time they see me coming, I'm going to talk to them about nerve gas. [He flinches and ducks his head.] "Here comes Mr. Nerve." [He opens his eyes wide and laughs.] When John Warner and I meet, all we ever talk about is nerve gas.

Nonetheless, in response to my question in 1984 about what helped him most in his first six years to advance his *institutional* goals, he answered,

> Probably [my work on] nerve gas. It showed that I could learn about a subject and become, if not an authority, at least more knowledgeable than most. There weren't three people inside the beltway who knew as much about nerve gas as I did. I didn't know all that much about it. But everyone thought I did. It showed I could take the lead on an issue. The nerve gas fight has helped me the most with my colleagues, with my peers.

For students of the modern Senate, it is a nice example of the ability of today's senators to gain knowledge and influence far beyond the confines of their committee assignments.[68] It is also an example of the ability of senators to use extracommittee activity to forward their institutional goals. Pryor, we know, brought special institutional ambitions with him to the Senate— to fit into the community life of the Senate and to achieve influence within it. Unlike Pell, he had a strong desire for political involvement inside the institution. While he hardly could have predicted it when he took up the issue, his nerve gas activities undoubtedly helped him to achieve this goal.

Having explored David Pryor's highly personal political style in Arkansas, it becomes clearer how perfectly suited he is to the life of the Senate. To begin with, he brings to the institution a strong sense of community. In this most individualistic of political institutions, where a good deal of information processing and decision making takes place in face-to-face encounters, a politician who relishes person-to-person politicking, who nurtures and thrives on personal relationships, is in his element.

One time-honored path to influence inside the institution depends on the knowledge one senator has about the goals, preferences, styles, and interests of other senators. That is the kind of knowledge that a gregarious, civil and decent person like Pryor acquires without trying. And from all that I observed, he moves around the Senate, as in Arkansas, in an atmosphere of friendly equality, never full of himself, always respectful of others. Early in 1995, a veteran Washington columnist called him "everybody's favorite senator."[69] His conception of politics as personal relationships is as much his guide in one community setting as it is in the other. And his career—as we learned in chapter 2—has prospered in both places because of the dual applicability of that conception.

Campaign Tests

Pryor has conducted nineteen election campaigns: six primaries, three runoffs, and ten general elections. Except for one general election contest (1984), all of his serious campaign tests involved a nominating contest among his fellow Democrats. My information as gleaned from travel talk and occasional press commentary is totally inadequate for an account of any of Pryor's campaigns, much less their results. Nonetheless, a few glimpses can buttress our picture of his representational strengths and help to explain the durability of his career.

In general, his campaign reminiscences have a distinctively large personal component. He sees them primarily as tests of his personal performance and his personal connections. Policy

connections are a secondary consideration.
1966: House Primary.

Pryor's 1966 runoff campaign for election to the Congress was his first national-level campaign. His recollections of that campaign are candidate centered. He described his opponent: "Richard Arnold was a child prodigy. When he was in first grade, they used to take him around to schools where he would recite roman numerals from one to one thousand—backwards. He was one of the smartest people in the state—first in his class at Yale University, Phi Beta Kappa, first in his class at Harvard Law School. But he was a poor campaigner." Of Arnold's personal style, Pryor recalled that "his coat sleeves were so long that when he went to shake hands, you couldn't tell whether or not his hand was going to come out of his sleeve."

The defining moment of the campaign, says Pryor, was a television speech he gave in the face of some negative assaults by the Arnold campaign team. As Pryor tells it, the theme of his speech was a personal one.

> He was trying to paint me as a tool of organized labor. He circulated a story late in the campaign that I had received a $50,000 contribution from the Teamsters Union and that an agent of Jimmy Hoffa had flown the money into some remote airstrip in Arkansas.... Then a little later, a bunch of us were sitting around in Wayne's Drug Store [in Warren] one day when someone came in with a flyer that had been placed in every rural mailbox. It was a big picture of Stokely Carmichael, who was all the rage then, saying that he supported David Pryor for Congress. There he was with his beads and his shark-tooth necklace. Pretty soon, other people started coming into the store with the same flyer. We decided right then and there that I had to go on TV. I could feel myself slipping fast ...
>
> I gave what I call my "Poor Richard" speech. It was very corny. I started by saying, "I hope no one will mind if I speak directly to an old friend of mine, Richard Arnold. Richard, I have known you for years. I know that you have placed this Stokely Carmichael flyer in every mailbox. I know you have circulated this Jimmy Hoffa story. I know you didn't mean to do that. It isn't like you. Why did you do it?"

It was the greatest speech of my career. Arnold told me later that the speech broke his back. He said that before the speech, he thought he was going to win. He said those two charges were the greatest mistake of his life, that he took bad advice and was ashamed of it.

Like so many of his political relationships, he sees this as a one-on-one personal encounter with his opponent. There was, of course, a policy context, involving organized labor and civil rights. And there was a hit-back strategy. But the essence of the campaign, as he saw it, was a one-on-one contest that turned on personal skill and personal integrity.[70]

1972: Senate Primary.

When Pryor reminisces about his unsuccessful 1972 challenger's campaign for the Senate, its personal aspects again take center stage. His reflections concern the campaign's effect on him and on his career. He speaks of his impatience and frustration with the "claustrophobic" effect of "the seniority system in the House" because "it would be fifteen years before I ever had any degree of influence." He believed there was an opportunity to make an upward career jump. "With many of the older senators falling by the wayside and with eighteen-year-olds now having the vote," he said, "I thought the time was right."[71] It wasn't—not quite. He almost pulled it off. He received 41.4 percent of the vote to McClellan's 44.7 percent in the primary and 48 percent in the runoff. If his vaunted political instincts failed him in this case—and there is plenty of doubt about that—it is the only time. Some even say the closeness of the race kept his career alive.[72]

The conventional story of the campaign is that among Pryor's earliest financial supporters were the state's McClellan-hating labor unions and that McClellan successfully tagged Pryor as a liberal tool of the labor bosses. The centerpiece of this story is McClellan's aggressiveness in winning their debate—a performance that overwhelmed Pryor despite his down-home disclaimer that his campaign funds "came from the overalls pockets and the cookie jars of the people of Arkansas." There is little doubt that Pryor remembered that debate and the aggressiveness of his opponent. His own tactics in 1978 and 1984 strongly indicate as much.

But on the trail Pryor rehearsed different lessons—lessons of personal relationships and personal growth. He wonders out loud, for example, what if he had approached the seventy-six-year-old, thirty-year veteran incumbent differently. "Senators love this place," he says of the Senate,

> especially when they are challenged. Then, they'll really fight to keep the job. They never want it as badly as when someone wants to take it away from them. I've always wondered whether I should have behaved differently in 1972. If I had gone directly to John McClellan and said, "I want to run for the Senate, but I don't want to run against you," would he have dropped out? I don't say he would have, and I don't know that he would have, but I'll always wonder what would have happened if I had behaved differently than I did.

Pryor's travel talk focuses, too, on other career-related lessons he took away from the 1972 campaign—lessons that assume a long-term negotiation with the people of his state. "People watch a person very closely in a campaign, especially, I believe, in defeat. They want to know how a guy takes defeat. In 1972, what kept me in public life was that I was considered a good loser. People told me the best talk I ever gave was my concession speech." "I never had any regrets about my first race for the Senate," he said. "It was a hard, clean race. I got beat. I came back and I had the chance to be governor, which was a great opportunity for me. Perhaps I wasn't ready to be a senator then." From a career-length perspective, the suggestion is that two elections to the governorship vastly strengthened his negotiating position statewide.

1978: Senate Primary.

Pryor's first successful Senate campaign took place in 1978. In a primary described to me as "a clash of the titans of their time," he was opposed by two members of Congress, Jim Guy Tucker and Ray Thornton. In a campaign Pryor described as dull and his campaign manager called boring, each candidate parlayed his congressional district strength to divide the vote 35 percent, 33 percent, and 32 percent, respectively. Because he had twice run successfully statewide, "I was expected to get 40 percent," Pryor said in 1978. "But I fell 5 percent short. That had a great effect on my supporters [in the runoff against Tucker]. They really got out and worked every county, every town, every precinct, every box. They worked day and night; they did cartwheels and turned the election around. In some places, I went from 35 percent to 60 percent; and I beat him in his own home county of Pulaski [Little Rock]."

He added, "In this election, the teachers, the unions, and the special interest groups—not one of them endorsed me. They supported Jim Guy Tucker." Their opposition allowed Pryor, the budget-balancing governor, to brand Tucker in the manner that John McClellan had branded him. "I tell you that this was not the year to run with the support of special interest groups. We turned those endorsements right around on Tucker and made him wish he had never gotten them. I told people, 'It's you and me against them.' And it worked." Press observers remarked that McClellan would have been proud of the lessons he taught Pryor, but the senator himself never offered the connection.
1982: Interlude.

In the year of Pryor's triumph over two of Arkansas's political giants, the other giant, Attorney General Bill Clinton, was elected to the governorship. When, in 1979, we bumped into Hilary Rodham, the governor's wife, I asked the senator whether—as rumor had it—Clinton was likely to run against him in 1984. He said, "I don't know the answer to that question." It was all he would ever say on that subject. But three years later, the relationship between the two ambitious politicians emerged as a major thread of my October 1982 visit.

Pryor had just returned from a trip to China, to find himself faced with a decision concerning his endorsement of a gubernatorial candidate. Clinton was running to retake his job as governor from the man who had taken it from him in

1980, the Republican incumbent, Frank White. White, a former Democrat, was a longtime Pryor friend, who had worked for him when Pryor was governor. Clinton was, of course, the Democratic party standard bearer. There was a belief, fanned by a White campaign ad and accepted by most of Pryor's staff, that if Clinton won, he would run against Pryor in 1984. Pryor dearly preferred to finesse his endorsement dilemma. "It's a real downer for me," he said. "I wish I'd stayed in China."

His friends within the Clinton camp were pressuring Pryor to endorse Clinton by spending the next day with him on the campaign trail. As he put it to a friend, "The Clinton people want to suck some of my blood." "I don't think," Pryor protested, "that a politician can transfer his allegiances to another politician. The Clinton people are paranoid. They think I talk to Frank White every night before I go to bed. They want me to cancel my schedule tomorrow."

Clinton eased the problem by declaring privately and publicly that he would not run against Pryor in 1984.[73] Pryor said he could not change his speaking schedule; but he agreed to visit the Clinton headquarters to shake hands with the candidate there, as the cameras rolled. When asked what he said to Clinton, he replied, with typical self-deprecation, "I told him it would probably cost him four points in the polls." On the way back to his office, he commented, "I made a few Clinton people happy, and I made a lot of White people unhappy. I hope they forget in two years. Frank White will understand, but the people who support both him and me will not." That evening, he closed the book. "I have done my duty today."

Bill Clinton needed David Pryor in this case. And Pryor gave Clinton just enough to help him. The end result for Pryor was that he maintained his partisan loyalty and his independence from Arkansas's most dominating politician. "If he wins," Pryor mused, "his mind will not be on Arkansas. On Wednesday morning, he'll be accepting congratulations from Yell County and Harrison and Mountain Home, but his mind will be on the vice presidency."

In later years, the wary and dutiful relationship of 1982 developed into genuine friendship. And Pryor was unreservedly and crucially helpful to Clinton in later periods of need.[74] As this is written, it is noteworthy and diagnostic, however, that despite the reams of investigative journalism devoted to Clinton's Whitewater affair and to the vast web of interconnections that characterize the dealings of the political-business elite of Arkansas, David Pryor's name has been markedly absent. That is to say, he has remained very much his own man.

His independence is very important to him. In 1994, he still recalled a nasty 1978 *Arkansas Gazette* cartoon that greeted his election to the Senate by portraying him as a little boy in a sailor suit entering a clubhouse and saluting the Senate's most conservative members. "If I had ever behaved that way," he said, "people would have pointed at me and said, 'He's a whore.' If there is one thing people can recognize and can't stand, it's a whore." By 1994, his sixteen-year tenure seemed to him a sufficient warrant of his senatorial independence.

1984: Senate Reelection.

In 1984, he faced his first—and most critical—reelection test. It was the only serious partisan challenge of his career. His opponent was the strongest Republican votegetter in the state, three-term Congressman Ed Bethune. In Pryor's 1994 retrospective on that campaign, it was strictly a personal encounter. He said later,

> In 1984, I didn't have any vision or any sense of history. I wasn't thinking about the future or the past. I saw it as a matter of personalities. Our families were friends; our wives played bridge together; we raised our kids together. We were friends, and he was running against me. When I would meet him in the campaign, I would ask him, "Ed, why are you running against me?" He would say, "You went to Washington and became too liberal."

Bethune was, indeed, a down-the-line Ronald Reagan conservative, one of Congressman Newt Gingrich's closest sidekicks in starting the Conservative Opportunity Society in the

House.[75] He framed the 1984 campaign as an ideological contest, conservative versus liberal. His theme was the need for expanded individual freedom and a smaller, less intrusive government. President Reagan, holding a commanding thirty-point lead over Walter Mondale, came to Arkansas to campaign for the man they said would help to keep Republican control of the Senate.

Pryor, in contrast, framed the campaign as a contest between two individuals—one guided by close attention to ordinary people's problems and the other guided by abstract doctrines at a far distance from everyday life. On the campaign trail, Pryor would tell reporters, "[Ed] talks about all these global things. I think it's time to talk about issues that affect Arkansas and Arkansas people."[76] "Ed is concerned with national issues. He is not looking at state issues. He is not involved with the protection of farmers, and he shows disregard for the elderly."[77] "I have tried during my entire political career not to tell people what you need," he stressed, "but basically to listen to you ... [to try to put] myself in the shoes of the people of our state."[78] And a veteran observer concurred that "the heart of Pryor's down home campaign [is that] rigid ideology overrides compassion and gets in the way of representing real people with problems."[79]

Pryor's construction of the campaign contest played, of course, to his great strengths in personal connectedness. In four polls taken from July 1983 to July 1984, his "immense popularity" (in the words of his pollster) averaged 74 percent.[80] And the average level of agreement with the statement "Pryor is a quietly effective, common sense kind of guy" stood at 73 percent. With respect to the pollster's favorite indicator of underlying incumbent strength, "Do you think David Pryor has performed well enough as a U.S. Senator to deserve reelection or do you think it is time to give someone else a chance to do better?" Pryor's support had hardly changed for a year and, in July, held strong at 65 percent. His lead in the horse race question was 61 percent to 28 percent.

His campaign message was encapsulated in the slogan "Arkansas Comes First." And in July, 71 percent of the likely voters agreed with the statement "Pryor puts Arkansas first—he votes to make sure Arkansas is taken care of before anything else."

In their August debate, Pryor hammered home his campaign theme and used it to frame the contrast between himself and his opponent.

> Ed has had an awful good time poking fun at the idea that Arkansas comes first. Ed has a different philosophy of what a senator should be. Ed is so concerned with graphs and charts and national policy that he's truly forgotten the real everyday problems we face here at home. The election is not about which political party controls the Senate, but about who is the best senator. It's not about those percentages and charts and graphs and tables you carry around. It's about you and it's about me, Ed. It's about me and the people of Arkansas and their seat in the Senate.

Moments later, he hit on a personal note reminiscent of the 1968 "Poor Richard" speech.

> He can't make a speech without calling me an ultra liberal. I have a 60 percent congressional caucus [sic] voting record. It's credibility, Ed, and it's hypocrisy, Ed, in this campaign, that you have injected, it's distortion.... Really, when you get down to it, all we have left is our credibility and our integrity. Ed, I'm going to be honest with you. I'm ashamed, because I think you're about to lose both.

And he closed by restating "the real issue": "Which individual can best represent Arkansas? Who has been the most effective member of Congress? Ask him what he's done to put his state first."

Privately, he used equally strong language to link his battle at home to his battle in Washington. Both, he said, made his blood boil. "There's a fairly close connection between my attitude toward Ed Bethune and my attitude toward the people who want nerve gas. I get mad at both of them because I hate self-righteousness and hypocrisy. There's nothing I hate more than people who think they are completely right and you are completely wrong. That's Ed Bethune. I just can't get along with such people." In the electoral and legislative contexts alike, he displayed his deep pure distrust of ideology.

When I arrived in mid-October, Pryor was still holding a twenty-four-point lead in the polls; and he was running a classic front runner's campaign. "Our situation now is damage control. Stay out of intersections and don't run any red lights. If we don't make any mistakes, we'll be all right." He reported on the progress of the campaign.

> I spent hours in the summer in the back of cafes with twenty or so people getting together our county committees and a county coordinator.... The fruits of that hard work are being felt today.... I've never had as good an organization as I have for this race.... I haven't had one bit of trouble raising money for this campaign.... In July and August we went through the stage of confrontation, firing charges back and forth. That became very unproductive and I withdrew from that.... As part of that stage, we ran a series of seminegative ads [because] we wanted people who were hearing about him for the first time to hear negative things about his record. In September, we moved into the stage we're in now, just hard politicking.

Four of his television ads praised his "Arkansas First" record. Two of them attacked Bethune for voting against the lowering of electric rates by the Rural Electrification Administration and for voting against a social security protection measure. His pollster reported in midsummer, however, that "there is little to indicate that either your or Bethune's media has affected your image very much. One exception may be in the area of your theme 'Pryor Puts Arkansas First'—where your media seems to have been effective."[81]

Confronted with Ronald Reagan's equally large lead in the state and with his opponent's charge (from *Congressional Quarterly*) that he voted against the president more often than any other senator, Pryor spoke often of the "ferocious independence" of Arkansas voters. It was demonstrated in 1968, he said, by their support for an independent (George Wallace) as president, a Republican (Winthrop Rockefeller) as governor, and a Democrat (William Fulbright) as senator. To which he would add, "I'm hoping and praying they do the same thing in 1984."

For his part, Ed Bethune seemed to have no doubt that if he could get through to people, he could convince them that Pryor was a typical tax-and-spend liberal, that they were conservative Reaganites at heart, and that they should vote Republican for senator as well as president.[82] But press accounts highlighted Bethune's frustrating inability to make the sale. Said one, "Bethune found it impossible to burn the solid little personal bridges Pryor had built in a lifetime of Arkansas politics."[83] Columnist Paul Greenberg characterized the reaction Bethune's challenge was provoking among Arkansas's rural voters.

> Hey, does ol' David *look* like a liberal to you? Does he *talk* like one? ... David is a Democrat. But mostly he's just David ... [who] went over to his momma's house in Camden ... and set down on the front porch in his overhauls and allowed as how he was fixin' to run again. That can't be no liberal; it ain't even hardly a politician.... Our idea of politics down here is to vote for who you like, who you trust and who's gonna look after folks.[84]

And that trust, it appeared, was being tendered to "ol' David," by a sizable constituency.

A top Pryor campaigner summarized their reading of the polls. "All the image polls [show that] people like the senator, but they don't know why. There is that flat, shallow level of support all across the board. Bethune's theory is that if he can puncture the crust at some point, he can break it up and drill deep. The problem is, he can't puncture it. It's amazing."

A brief look inside one such poll provides some added nuances. In early October, a random sample of 200 eligible voters were asked their vote preference. Fifty-seven percent of the respondents (113) declared their preference for Pryor. The Pryor voters were then asked, "What, if anything, good or bad comes to mind when I mention the name David Pryor."[85] Of this group of prospective supporters, 19 had no response to the open-ended question. Considering only those remaining 94 respondents who preferred Pryor and who did answer the "good or bad" question, fully two-thirds, 63 (66%) mentioned some personal quality of Pryor's—from "good man" and "good job" to specifics such as honest, friendly, courteous, intelligent, courageous, fair, reasonable, considerate. With some overlap, one-fourth of Pryor's supporters (25%) said (perhaps in response to his "Arkansas Comes First" theme) that he had helped "Arkansas," "the state" or "the people." And, again, with some overlap, 16 (17%) mentioned Pryor's work in a general policy area. Half of these—less than 10 percent of the Pryor supporters—mentioned help for the farmers or the elderly. There was no mention of nerve gas or consultants. It was not a large policy yield. But it was a large and—albeit vague— dominant personal yield.

Campaigns can strengthen or weaken careers. When asked to think in advance about the effects of his campaign, Pryor articulated the vital link between his constituency support at home and his governing activity in Washington. My question was, "What would be the effect on your career of a victory of 52 percent, as opposed, say, to a victory of 62 percent?" His answer was,

> A lot. If I win by 62 percent, I can be more freewheeling in the Senate. If I win by that much, I can become more active in the arms control debate. I can have more leeway in everything I do. And if I have a 62 percent margin, people back home will say, "You can run against David Pryor next time if you want to, but you'll be wasting your time." If I were to win by 52 percent, I'd be a cripple; and I'd be on everyone's hit list six years from now.... If I get 60 percent, I'll be strong in the Senate and in the state. If I get 58 or 57, I'll probably be strong. But if I get 55 or 54, I don't know. I would not feel confident. It would have a big effect on me psychologically.

Winning the election by any margin possible is the proximate goal of every politician. But negotiating a constituency fit that produces leeway, or trust, is a different matter. And it may be the next most important goal of every elective politician. Pryor's comment suggests that some sort of outsized winning margin, after repeated exposure to the electorate, may be interpreted by politicians as an indicator of constituent trust.

In the theory and the practice of representative government, constituent trust is always a contingent relationship, subject to interelection testing and testing at the next election. The best we can ever say of any representational relationship is that a renewal seems very likely. That was David Pryor's situation. But it was prudent to worry about it. As he said, "It's a trust of the people, and you are a custodian of that. You don't own it."[86] The race tightened up a little toward the end. Nonetheless, the 57 percent margin he got proved every bit as diagnostic for his future as the 60 percent he would have preferred. That certainly was the all-important media interpretation at home. As two experienced *Arkansas Democrat* observers saw it, "Pryor crushed Bethune in a walk."[87] "The whipping he gave Bethune makes it highly unlikely that he would ever draw major league opposition again."[88]

As his 1990 reelection drew near, the prophecy became true. "He is a dynamite politician," said Ed Bethune. "His skills just improve with age.... David Pryor is tough to run against. I can testify to that!"[89] And he also said, "David Pryor can hold that seat as long as he wishes to hold it."[90] No Republican candidate could be found to run against him in 1990. His "most likely challenger" declined with the comment, "[He] is an institution in Arkansas. [I] wouldn't want to participate in a suicide mission."[91] Pryor was reelected for a third term with 100 percent of the vote. Over his political lifetime, he had negotiated a representational relationship as solid and secure as that of Claiborne Pell.

In sum, David Pryor's negotiated fit with his constituents is based primarily on his personal style and secondarily on his pragmatic populism in matters of policy. What is more, they have reinforced one another. The main thrust of his political activity is to keep both himself and the government in touch with the ordinary citizen. He campaigns and he legislates as a representational "one of us."

Moreover, his highly personal view of politics is well suited to the Senate, in both its individualistic and its communitarian aspects. And he has been able to achieve his institutional goals— as a confident player and as an institution builder—without altering his behavior. "He never behaves different from what he is," says political reporter Brenda Blagg. "He is the same in D.C. as he is in Arkansas." For him, the idea of "the beltway" as the infamous dividing line between the politicians and the rest of the country has no meaning.

With so much consistency and reinforcement between his preferences and his activities, he avoided the problems of John Culver, who believed that accomplishments in Washington could compensate for a lack of connectedness at home. He has avoided the inconsistencies of Wyche Fowler, whose failure to push an aggressive "Georgia Comes First" campaign opened him up to charges of a disconnected "double life," saying one thing at home and doing another thing in Washington. And he has avoided all the representational puzzles presented by Claiborne Pell—the personal distance from his constituents, the disparities in representation between home and Washington. In the 1990s, after three senatorial elections, David Pryor was a politician at the top of his game.

TWO INSTITUTIONS: PRYOR AND PELL

David Pryor and Claiborne Pell share a remarkable durability. And yet, by no strength of anyone's imagination could the folksy populist have been successful in urban, ethnic Rhode Island, or could the liberal patrician have been successful in poor, rural Arkansas. Constituent preferences and expectations— regarding policy and style—make a difference.

The two men have relied on a very different balance of activities in connecting with their constituencies. Pell relies heavily on his policy record and on his strength as a patient legislator. Pryor relies heavily on his outgoing presentational style and his skill as a campaigner. Pryor is a gregarious, instinctive, emotional politician. Pell is an awkward, bookish, cerebral one. They took different career paths to get to the Senate; and they pursued different institutional goals after they arrived. Pell was a political amateur who found institutional fulfillment in seniority and status; Pryor was a political professional who found institutional fulfillment in association and involvement. There is, I conclude, no recipe for senatorial longevity.

While there is no recipe, there are a few basic ingredients. A Pryor–Pell comparison suggests some intriguing commonalities. Which returns us to an earlier question: What does it take for a senator to become an institution? The short answer is time. The long answer is when a solid majority of your constituents feel they know you, know enough about you to trust you, and are not much interested in learning more.

For the long answer, it is personal performance that matters most. At least that is the view from the campaign trail, where personal style dominates policy. On the trail, policies count, but mostly as vehicles through which each candidate displays and communicates a political persona. It matters that Senator Pell opposes the Vietnam War, but it matters more that he uses it to display his political independence. It matters that Pryor investigates government consultants, but it matters more that he uses it to portray himself as a watchdog against bureaucratic waste. Within constraints set by the strongest policy preferences of the constituency, therefore, the individual politician presents a persona and acquires a reputation that underpins his or her durability. Within policy limits prescribed by liberal expectations in Rhode Island and by moderate-populist expectations in Arkansas, Pell and Pryor each fashioned a favorable and distinctive political persona.

In one basic quality, however, their personae were remarkably similar. And that quality was their *authenticity*. However different the content of each senator's policy vehicle might be, each set of constituents finds its own senator's persona eminently believable. And that is the crucial commonality. Both men are distinctively open and honest—almost naive— in letting their constituents know who they are as individuals. Both senators have recognizable roots; they know who they are; they are comfortable with who they are; and they come across to their constituents as authentic individuals. "With David Pryor," says a veteran observer, "what you see is what you get, and he doesn't get many complaints."[92] With Claiborne Pell, too, what you see is what you get. Both are among the least image conscious and the most self-effacing politicians I have met. The Arkansas journalist Ernest Dumas says, "Unlike most politicians, David Pryor does not seem to have an ego." Associated Press reporter James Drinkard writes similarly of Pell: "He represents a phenomenon not often found in nature: a politician without an ego."[93] Each has become, over time, a real, knowable human being: the one of neighborly decency, the other of grandfatherly rectitude.

Both senators' authenticity is buttressed by their *consistency*. They are the same people at home as they are in Washington. They are the same people in their media advertising as they are in the flesh. Their representational relationships are relatively free of fabrication or distortion. Their presentation to their constituents has been consistent over time—Pell especially in terms of policy, Pryor especially in terms of personal style. Both have steadfastly pursued career-long policy interests—Pell with foreign policy, Pryor with policy on issues concerning the elderly. Neither man has tried to reinvent himself for public consumption.

Taken together, authenticity and consistency go a long way toward explaining durability. But there is a third ingredient in the Pryor-Pell recipe: *good character*. To begin with, the cardinal sin of a representative is arrogance; and no one has accused either senator of that. What you see and what you get from each of them is a high degree of personal and political integrity.

On the personal side, there is unselfishness and honesty. Neither senator is thought to be "in it for himself." On the political side, there is the willingness to take an unpopular stand on moral grounds: in Vietnam, on nerve gas. Each senator is thought to be "his own man." Besides which, each is the soul of civility. If we suspend cynicism for a moment, we might add that Pryor's belief in the wisdom of ordinary citizens and Pell's belief in the value of positive campaigning have even brought a touch of idealism into their politics.

In both cases, constituent judgments have moved beyond personal character to encompass political character as well—by which I mean aspects of their public life as opposed to aspects of their private life. Samuel Popkin argues that citizens can and do make both sorts of judgments and that in doing so, they use information they take in from campaigns. He also suggests that judgments about personal character are the easiest to make and, therefore, that they tend to drive out more complex judgments about political character.[94] To extend his argument, it seems likely that repeated campaign interaction between politicians and constituents increases the likelihood that judgments about political character will gain in importance. That is to say, repeated negotiation increases the amount and the reliability of information available to constituents.

The two cases also suggest that the better equipped constituents are to make judgments about political character and public performance, the more satisfied they are likely to be with the overall accountability connection between themselves and the politician. Campaigns establish a framework for accountability. And repeated campaign success—durability—enhances accountability.

Some such pattern seems to have emerged, over time, for Pryor and Pell. After repeated interaction, a substantial majority of citizens in both states have arrived at a similarly settled and summary judgment about the political character of their senator. And that judgment is that neither one is an ordinary "politician"—not, at least, of the sort the public now so heartily dislikes and deplores. Both senators have managed to transcend the all-purpose category of "politician" and the condemnation that goes with it. And they have become institutions.

Even if this description is accurate and even if authenticity, consistency, and good character have produced durability and accountability, no further generalization is possible. Two senators from small states are hardly representative, much less a sample.[95] In Rhode Island and Arkansas, citizen knowledge, acquaintance with politicians, retail-scale campaigns, and notions about political character—however undeveloped—are at least possible. Long before we begin to generalize, we would want to know how such possibilities hold up in the television campaigns of the megastates[96] where judgments about political character can be swamped by politicians who invent and reinvent themselves in campaigns that seem inevitably to be personal and negative.

Furthermore, Pell and Pryor have engaged in numerous statewide campaigns—six for Pell, five for Pryor. [97]And none of the other studies in this book looks beyond the first reelection campaign. If we are to watch the repetitious development of candidate-citizen interaction over time, we would want to look at the middle stages of negotiation, at some second or third reelection campaigns. We cannot, therefore, know how relevant the Pryor–Pell commonalities might be for politicians campaigning and connecting in other states and at other stages in their careers. For anyone interested in representational durability, the ideas expressed here are only a beginning.

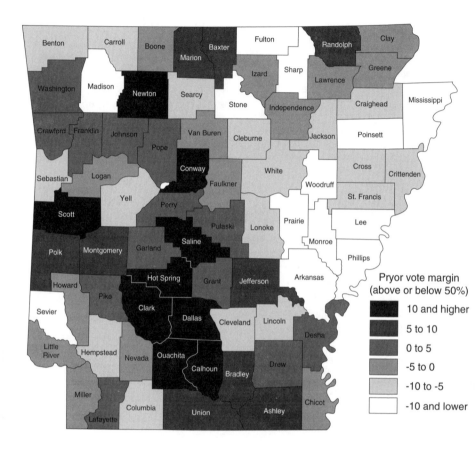

Figure 8.1. Regional Support, 1972 Senate Runoff Primary, Pryor–McClellan.

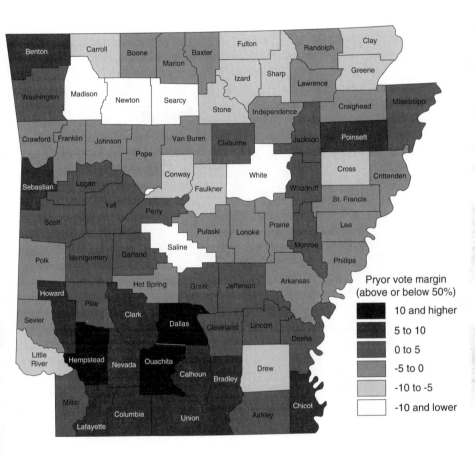

Figure 8.2.   Regional Support, 1978 Senate Runoff Primary, Pryor–Tucker.

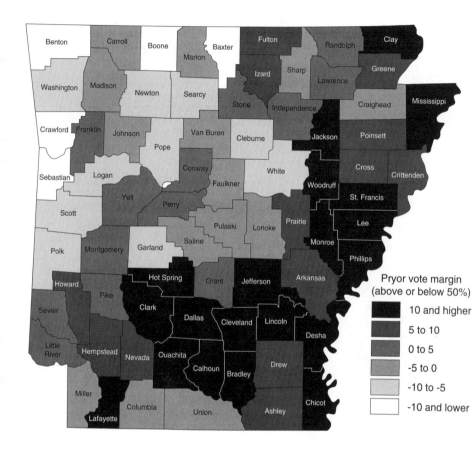

Figure 8.3. Regional Support, 1984 General Election, Pryor–Bethune.

CONCLUSION

REPRESENTATIVE DEMOCRACY IS A GRAND EXPERIMENT. The idea that ordinary citizens freely elect other ordinary citizens to make certain decisions on their behalf and then hold them electorally accountable is not foreordained. It cannot be taken for granted; it is not simple to maintain; and it is not readily appreciated. For political scientists, it requires an understanding of the two sets of citizens who make it work—the politicians who want to be elected and the voters who do the electing. Since the voters have the last word, it is appropriate that political scientists have devoted the lion's share of our research to them. But at the same time, we need to keep a research eye on the politicians. And this book takes a look at a few. It is, admittedly, a biased, episodic, and astigmatic look. But it takes politicians seriously, by adopting their perspectives and by listening to them as they go about the business of making representative democracy work.

The main activity of politicians in a representative government is to take collective action on certain matters of public concern. For that purpose, they have created lawmaking institutions such as Congress. But their decision making inside such an institution and the acceptance of their decisions by citizens outside that institution depend, in turn, on quite a different cluster of political activities. Every legislative politician pursues a career, campaigns for office, and builds constituency connections. And those three interconnected activities account for the essential representational component in every legislative decision. Taken together, they create the underlying infrastructure of a representative democracy. Our shorthand summary for the complex of activities involving careers, campaigns, and constituency connections is "the politics of representation."

Representational politics begins with the interest and the desire of individual citizens to get involved, run for office, and become politicians. Our exploration is based on the idea that it is worthwhile for political scientists and citizens to take a close-up, in-depth look at a few such individuals. Because the primary observational vantage point has been the campaign trail, the analytical spotlight has focused on the campaigning politician. And it has focused, perforce, on the home constituency. I have looked, occasionally, at a politician's activity inside the legislature. I have done so, however, not to explain legislative decision making, but to find clues to the legislator's representational relationships at home.

The study of representation begins with ambition and ends with accountability. And the book has been organized to move from a focus on careers to a focus on campaigns and then to a focus on constituency connections. The career-campaign-connections sequence poses a succession of related questions: Why do I want to be a representative? How do I get to be a representative? How do I manage to remain a representative? Two chapters of the book centered on the seeking of representation; four chapters centered on the testing of representation; and two chapters centered on the achievement of representation.

A persistent theme has been the desirability of studying the various activities of our politicians developmentally, over some period of time. I have conceptualized the representational relationship as a continuous negotiation between politician and constituents. And I have conceptualized campaigns as critical events and sequences in that negotiating process. Aspiring politicians campaign for citizen support; if enough citizens like what they see better than the alternative, they give the politician their provisional support contingent on performance and representation, to be followed by another citizen accounting, and so on. As the negotiation repeats itself over time, however, citizen information accumulates, citizen trust increases, the constituency fit grows more comfortable on both sides, and the bonds of accountability become easier to identify. At some point, after repeated interaction, the representational relationship may become noteworthy for its durability.

The first concept employed to harness the element of time is the career—the sequential accumulation of ambition, experience, and accomplishment by which we identify and follow each individual politician. Primary attention has been given to the elective office career and the institutional career; occasional attention has been paid to the prepolitical career, the policy career, and the constituency career.

Chapter 1 emphasized the potential importance of understanding the prepolitical career—as it helps to direct and to constrain a politician's subsequent behavior and as it contributes to a politician's reputation. Chapter 2 emphasized the importance of digging beneath the idea of ambition to its motivational sources to explain both electoral and institutional behavior. Taken together, the two chapters conveyed the notion that knowing the prepolitical career and/or the motivational sources of ambition will help us to discern distinctive, consistent, career-long patterns of choice and behavior for individual politicians. Because random events and luck—good and bad—often help to shape career opportunities, however, prediction seems to be impossible.

The study of careers has been linked to the study of campaigns because campaigns are among the most prominent milestones in every career. Chapters 4 through 6 discussed six campaigns—but with no concerted effort to explain outcomes. In every case, however, candidate interpretations and behavior clearly helped to shape the campaign; and the campaign, in turn, contributed to the outcome. In every case, the story focused more on the things candidates can control than on the things he or she cannot control. We have concentrated more, for example, on candidate conduct within certain identifiable constraints than on the macrolevel campaign context.

In chapter 3, a pair of primary challenger campaigns were used to identify the early stages of a campaign and to identify some of the nonpartisan ingredients of successful and unsuccessful challenger campaigns. Each ingredient is well known separately. But the introduction of a campaign dynamic invites the inspection of interactions among competing candidates and within campaigns as they involve challenger quality, campaign teamwork, the timeliness of campaign decisions, and the money–media relationship. The differentiation of primary and reelection constituencies was introduced, too, for use in the later descriptions of incumbent–constituency negotiations.

Negotiation involves learning. And chapter 4 examined campaign learning—as it takes place across a sequence of three same-party, same-state campaigns. At each stage in the sequence, the interpretation—by each candidate of the preceding campaign(s)—provided the linkage. Two incumbent campaigns suggested the performance criteria that differentiate primary challenger campaigns from incumbent campaigns. And those two losing campaigns, when compared with the third successful campaign suggested what can be learned (candidate strategy) and what cannot be learned (candidate experience and predispositions) from previous campaigns. Policy connections and personal style connections—and the balance between them—were introduced and used to discuss incumbent strengths and weaknesses in their negotiations with constituents. The campaign consequences of an incumbent's behavior inside the Senate were also explored.

Chapters 5 and 6 examined a single campaign over a longer period of time and in greater depth than any of the others. In so doing, it incorporated much of what had been discussed before. The campaign was that of a progressively ambitious, public service-oriented politician with a fairly long political career, who won election to the Senate as a challenger and was negotiating his incumbency relationship for the first time. Contrary to elite expectations, it turned out to be a losing campaign. The candidate's own contribution to the loss was central to the analysis, as were the developmental and interpretive sequences from his first to his second campaigns and within the second campaign itself. Among the campaign decisions subject to the control of the candidate and the campaign team, decisions about message content and media timing were given special scrutiny.

Taken together, the chapters on careers and campaigns suggested that when we political scientists study careers, we might profitably study campaigns, and when we study campaigns, we might profitably study careers.

Chapters 7 and 8 explored the successful negotiation of a representational relationship by two senators with lengthy careers and multiple campaigns. Their career motivations, their campaigning abilities, their senatorial performance, and the strengths of their constituency connections could hardly be more different. Neither one could get an ounce of political traction in the other's state. Yet their constituency connections display similar attributes—of reputation, information, and trust. And each is now described, accordingly, as "an institution" in his own constituency.

Taken together, the final chapters suggested that while the mix of ingredients will vary widely from person to person and context to context, some ingredients are common to all successful candidate–constituency negotiations. As common denominators, several candidate-centered attributes of success such as authenticity, consistency, and good character were given special emphasis. These commonalities emerged only after repeated interaction and repeated testing involving the behavior of the candidate and the response of the constituency over a considerable period. By emphasizing, therefore, the importance of careers and campaigns for the building of constituency connections, the final chapters concluded our three-sided exploration of the politics of representation.

For many political scientists, steeped in sampling as a basis for generalization, these case studies will no doubt generate questions about generalizability. While they do contain variety, they are in no sense a sample. If "generalization now" is the goal, this book cannot be of much help. If, however, the exploration of representational relationships has stimulated an appetite for "generalization later," then maybe the book can help.

Quite apart from the particular suggestions of the various cases and chapters, the sum total of these candidate-centered cases suggests some general research directions. By focusing on the politicians, by looking at the interconnections among their several political activities, and by aiming to understand representation, we have made suggestions that may encourage the broadening of current research perspectives. To the degree that these suggested changes in focus are already under way, the cases discussed here will help strengthen both incentive and argument.

Three such broadening suggestions have emerged from the case studies. First, in our studies of careers, we might move beyond our dominating focus on the decision to run or not to run for some given office and focus more broadly on the relationship of career decisions to the campaigns and to the constituency connections that come before or afterward.

Second, the study of campaigns might be moved beyond the dominating focus on voters and beyond the dominant notion that campaigns are worth studying only to explain electoral outcomes. A focus on the campaigning candidate may encourage us to think of campaigns in the context of the candidate's career and constituency connections. And it may lead us to broaden our focus beyond the study of election outcomes toward the study of representation.

Finally, the study of constituency connections might encourage us to supplement our dominantly cross-sectional studies of representation with a sturdier emphasis on longitudinal analyses. And these analyses might probe, in some depth, changes in the cultivation, the makeup, and the strength of constituency connections over time. It we think of representation as a matter of negotiation between politician and constituency and if we think of negotiation as a matter of repetitious candidate presentations and citizen reactions, then we shall have to adopt a more process-oriented, developmental perspective. And the study of representational durability suggests that the end product of successful negotiation over time may be a better sense of accountability on both sides of the citizen–politician relationship.

The literature of political science does not lack for studies of representation. But the idea remains large and elusive, embracing many manifestations and interpretations—of its significance, its scope, its applications, and its impact. The complexity of the subject seems to have dictated an incremental literature. This book, for its part, explores only individual—rather than collective or systemwide—representation and accountability. Despite the wealth of research, we are regularly reminded of the unsettled state of the subject by the inability to assess with sufficient confidence and authority the persistent criticisms aimed directly at the Congress and indirectly at our system of representative government. So this is no time to close down the piecemeal research enterprise.

Early in the book, I expressed the hope that if citizens were to study the politics of representation, they might temper the blanket condemnation they so commonly and so vigorously visit on our politicians. And I expressed the further hope that some discriminating assessments might emerge. Admittedly, some politicians may do very little to encourage the citizenry to make such distinctions and must, therefore, shoulder some of the blame for their fate. That is particularly the case where the nature of the campaign makes accountability difficult. For the most part, however, the politicians I traveled with did present sufficiently variegated profiles and performances to encourage differentiation and critical judgment by the citizenry. Indeed, the cases discussed here make it clear that there is no one model politician or one best politician. Victorious candidates included a nonpolitical hero, an upbeat conservative, a downbeat liberal, a competitive loner, a folksy crusader, and an oddball patrician. Politicians noteworthy for exemplary intelligence, leadership, commitment, and resourcefulness were among the losers.

It is their diversity, not their uniformity, that characterizes campaigning politicians. Indeed, representation is predicated on assumptions about diversity and about ways of turning that diversity into patterns of governing. To the degree that we ignore the diversity of our legislators, we may fail to understand our representative institution.

The eleven politicians in this book did connect, or tried to connect, with their constituents in diverse ways. Even more, they worked to connect with their primary and reelection constituencies in different ways. Their constituency connections cannot be dismissed with the simple judgment that all of them are out of touch. Indeed, it takes very little discrimination to demonstrate that disconnectedness is *not* the chronic and fatal systemwide malady it is thought to be. There are, however, nearly as many formulas for success in connecting as there are senators. Getting connected is not simply a matter of getting elected. Negotiating a constituency fit is a different process and requires a separate scrutiny.

Occasionally, observers from the media will lift a legislator out of the Washington crowd and examine his or her connective patterns at home. When they do, they produce a foothold of information, however tiny and temporary, that positions us to make discriminating judgments. Where congressional critics are concerned, the aim of this book has been to encourage any and all such footholds of additional knowledge about individual politicians. Our representative democracy rests on the quality of our politicians as well as the quality of our institutions. The more we know about the representational activities of our politicians, the better we can judge the health of the system of government that we value so highly and on which our future surely depends.

NOTES

INTRODUCTION

1. In this respect, this book takes up where a previous campaign-oriented monograph leaves off. See Richard Fenno, *The United States Senate: A Bicameral Perspective* (Washington, D.C.: AEI, 1983).

2. Richard Fenno, *Home Style: House Members in Their Districts* (Boston: Little, Brown, 1978), introduction

3. The article is by Richard Morin, *Washington Post Weekly Edition*, 29 May–4 June 1989. The best scholarly study of the subject is John Hibbing and Elizabeth Theiss-Morse, *Congress as Public Enemy* (New York: Cambridge University Press, 1995).

4. Barbara Sinclair, *The Transformation of the U.S. Senate* (Baltimore: Johns Hopkins University Press, 1989); Ross Baker, *House and Senate* (New York: W. W. Norton, 1989); Steven Smith, *Call to Order* (Washington, D.C.: Brookings Institution, 1989); Roger Davidson, "The Senate: If Everybody Leads, Who Follows ...," in *Congress Reconsidered*, 4th ed. , ed. Lawrence Dodd and Bruce Oppenheimer (Washington, D.C.: CQ Press, 1989); C. Lawrence Evans, *Leadership in Committee* (Ann Arbor: University of Michigan Press, 1991)

5. Donald Matthews, *U. S. Senators and Their World* (Chapel Hill: University of North Carolina Press, 1960), 68

6. These books were *The Making of a Senator, Dan Quayle,* 1989; *The Emergence of A Senate Leader: Pete Domenici and the Reagan Budget,* 1991; *Learning to Legislate: The Senate Education of Arlen Specter,* 1991; and *When Incumbency Fails: The Senate Career of Mark Andrews,* 1992. All published by CQ Press, Washington, D.C.

1. PREPOLITICAL CAREERS

1. David Mayhew, *The Electoral Connection* (New Haven: Yale University Press, 1974), 5.

2. Joseph Schlesinger, *Ambition and Politics* (Chicago: Rand McNally, 1966); David Rohde, "Risk-bearing and Progressive Ambition: The Case of Members of the United States House of Representatives," *American Journal of Political*

Science 23, no. 1 (1979): 1–26; Linda Fowler, *Candidates, Congress and the American Democracy* (Ann Arbor: University of Michigan Press, 1993).

3. Gary Jacobson and Samuel Kernell, (*Strategies and Choice in Congressional Elections* (New Haven: Yale University Press, 1981).

4. John Hibbing, *Congressional Careers* (Chapel Hill: University of North Carolina Press, 1991).

5. The argument is fleshed out and more fully applied in Richard Fenno, *The Presidential Odyssey of John Glenn* (Washington, D.C.: CQ Press, 1990).

6. Myra MacPherson, "The Hero as Politician: John Glenn's Hard Road," *Washington Post*, 12 January 1975.

7. Richard Fenno, *Home Style: House Members in Their Districts* (Boston: Little, Brown, 1978), chap. 1.

8. Joe Klein, "The Right Stuff," *Rolling Stone*, 24 November 1983.

9. Edward Whelan, "Look Out Folks, John Glenn Has Landed," *Cleveland Magazine* (Summer 1974).

10. David Canon, *Actors, Athletes and Astronauts* (Chicago: University of Chicago Press, 1990).

11. Bernard Weinraub, "Glenn Maintains Upbeat Mood in the Wake of Disappointment," *New York Times*, 26 February 1984.

12. The argument of this section is elaborated and extended in Richard Fenno, *The Making of a Senator, Dan Quayle* (Washington, D.C.: CQ Press, 1988).

13. Rohde, "Risk-Bearing and Progressive Ambition."

14. Fenno, *The Making of a Senator, Dan Quayle*.

15. Dan Quayle, "Turning the Senate Away from Trivial Pursuits," *New York Times*, 21 September 1984. *Congressional Record*, Daily Edition, 28 June 1984, S8533–36; 12 September 1984, S10957–60; 3 October 1984, S12801–2; 28 September 1984, S12271–77; 13 January 1987, S689–90. Nadine Cahodas, "Panel Proposes Senate Committee Changes," *Congressional Quarterly*, 1 December 1984.

16. Michael Barone and Grant Ujifusa, *Almanac of American Politics* (Washington, D.C.: National Journal, 1988), 393; Richard Cohen, "Dan Quayle," *National Journal*, 12 April 1986; Rob Gurwitt, "*GOP Arms to Elude GOP Senate* Takeover in '86," *Congressional Quarterly*, 20 July 1985; "Politics," *Washington Post*, 13 April 1986.

17. Elizabeth Bumiller, "The Charmed Life of Indiana's Golden Boy," *Washington Post*, 11 January 1981.

18. See Richard Fenno, *The Emergence of a Senate Leader: Pete Domenici and the Reagan Budget* (Washington, D.C.: CQ Press, 1991), introduction.

19. Phil Duncan, ed., *Politics in America, 1990* (Washington, D.C.: CQ Press, 1989), 1143.

20. Fenno, *The Presidential Odyssey of John Glenn*, epilogue.

21. Mary Sharkey, "Glenn Sits up Straight," *Plain Dealer*, 14 October 1992.

22. Mike Curtin, "Glenn's Outrage Disguises His Inattention to '84 Debt," *Columbus Dispatch Forum*, 10 November 1992. In 1994, Glenn was still calling Dewine's 1992 campaign the "dirtiest" in Ohio history and complaining that Dewine challenged his patriotism. Tom Diemer, "With Glenn on His Wing, Hyatt Flits Around Ohio," *Plain Dealer*, 1 November 1994.

23. David Broder and Bob Woodward, *The Man Who Would Be President* (New York: Simon and Schuster, 1992,) 56, 12.

24. Richard Fenno, *Watching Politicians: Essays in Participant Observation* (Berkeley: Institute for Governmental Studies, 1990), chap. 2.

2. POLITICAL CAREERS

1. People interested in the careers of America's contemporary politicians can begin with Alan Ehrenhalt, *The United States of Ambition: Politicians, Power and the Pursuit of Office* (New York: Random House, 1991), and Shirley Williams and Edward Lascher, eds. , *Ambition and Beyond: Career Paths of American Politicians* (Berkeley and Los Angeles: University of California Press, 1993).

2. Lewis Anthony Dexter, *The Sociology of Politics* (Chicago: Rand McNally, 1969).

3. Wendy Schiller, "Bill Sponsorship in the United States Senate: Opportunity and Constraint" (Ph.D. dissertation, University of Rochester, 1993), chap. 4; Wendy Schiller, "Senators as Political Entrepreneurs: Using Bill Sponsorship to Shape Legislative Agendas," *American Journal of Political Science* 39 (1995): 186–203; Barbara Sinclair, *The Transformation of the U. S. Senate* (Baltimore: Johns Hopkins Press, 1989), chap. 8.

4. Rachelle Patterson, "How One Senator Decides," *Boston Globe*, 24 June 1979.

5. David Rogers, "Tsongas—Keeping His Own Agenda," *Boston Globe*, 20 April 1980.

6. On Chrysler, see Peter Sleeper, "Tsongas 'Swing Vote' on Loan for Chrysler," *Lowell Sun*, 23 November 1979; Peter Sleeper, "Tsongas Faces Pressure from Unionists on His Proposal for Chrysler," *Lowell Sun*, 7 December 1979; Miranda Spivack, "It's Tsongas on Chrysler," *Springfield Daily News*, 11 December 1979; *Congressional Record*, Daily Edition, 30 November, 1979, S17543–44. On Alaska lands, see Peter Sleeper, "Tsongas, Alaska and Lowell," *Lowell Sun*, 7 November 1979; David Rogers, "Tsongas' Key Role on Alaska Bill," *Boston Globe*, 3 August 1980; Robert Furlow (AP), "Alaska Lands Bill Advances in Senate," *Boston Globe*, 19 August 1980; *Congressional Record*, Daily Edition, 19 August 1980, pp. S11188–89.

7. The speech can be found in *Congressional Record*, Daily Edition, 16 June 1980, S7086–87.

8. The book of poetry is William Cohen, *Of Sons and Seasons* (New York: Simon and Schuster, 1978); the diary is William Cohen, *Roll Call* (New York: Simon and Schuster, 1981); see also, Scott Thompson, "Sen. Cohen, A Renaissance Man and Poet," *Christian Science Monitor*, 11 October 1985.

9. Sandra McElwaine, "Bill Cohen—The Poet-Politician from Maine," *Washington Star*, 12 January 1979. The Maine version is Ann Pincus, "Wonder Boy of Capitol Hill," *Maine Magazine* (January/February 1977).

10. Tim Ahern, "Iran Arms Probe Puts Cohen Back in Spotlight," *Portland Evening Express*, 31 March 1989.

11. See Stephen Wermiel, "Portrait of a Man Alone," *Boston Globe*, 28 July 1974; John S. Day, "Senatorial Candidates Size Each Other Up," 15 October 1990.

12. Michael B. Antonio, "Cohen Builds Reputation in Defense Area," *Portland Press Herald*, 2 January 1982.

13. Lou Cannon and George Wilson, "President Backs Build Down," 13 May 1983; Pat Towell, "New Reagan Arms Initiatives Get Cautious Capitol Hill OK," *Congressional Quarterly*, 11 June 1983; William Cohen, "Impact of Build Down," *Congressional Record*, Daily Edition, 22 June 1983; Lou Cannon, "Reagan Sends Team Back to Arms Talk with New Proposals," *Washington Post*, 5 October 1983; Steven Strasser, "A New Push for 'Build Down,'" *Newsweek*, 17 October 1983.

14. *Congressional Record*, Daily Edition, 21 October 1988, S17113.

15. Pryor's career is treated at length in chapter 8.

16. Morris Cunningham, "Use of Consultants Attacked by Pryor," *Commercial Appeal*, 13 October 1979.

17. *Congressional Record*, Daily Edition, 5 December 1985, S16915–16; *Congressional Record*, Daily Edition, 7 August 1987, pp. S11601–06.

18. Fred Barnes, "Bests, Worsts, Misfits and Others," *Roll Call*, March 1989; Alan Ehrenhalt, *Politics in America* (Washington D.C.,: CQ Press, 1991), 630.

19. Christopher Madison, "Cohen: It's No Replay," *National Journal*, 7 March 1987.

20. Steve Campbell, "Cohen Wields His Defense Power," *Maine Sunday Telegram*, 13 May 1990.

21. Marsha Ginsburg, "Maine's Regular Guys Play Hard Ball in D.C. ," *San Francisco Examiner*, 27 July 1987; Jack Germond and Jules Witcover, "As Sen. Cohen Observes, President Should Have Known About Politics," *Portland Press Herald*, 15 January 1987; David Nyan, "Remember Our Maine in Washington," *Bangor Daily News*, 3 February 1987.

22. For the atmosphere of my visit, see John Day, "Cohen's Duties in Washington Detract from Reelection Plans," *Bangor Daily News*, 30 October 1990.

23. Martin Tolchin, "Questioner of the President's Men," *New York Times*, 15 December 1986.

24. Mara Henson, "Pryor Wins No. 3 Position in Senate Leadership," *Arkansas Gazette*, 30 November 1988.

25. Janet Hook, "Senate Plans to Meet Nov. 13 to Select Its Leaders," *Congressional Quarterly*, 10 November 1990; David Rogers, "Ford Is Elected Democratic Whip in the Senate," *Wall Street Journal*, 14 November 1990.

26. Jeffrey Stinson, "Popularity for Pryor Still Rising," *Arkansas Gazette*, 7 May 1990.

27. Anthony Moser, "Folksy, Caring Image Major Forces Behind Pryor's Success," *Arkansas Democrat*, 18 February 1990.

28. John Harwood, "Sen. Pryor Gains New Prominence as Clinton's Closest Ally in Congress," *Wall Street Journal*, 22 February 1993.

29. Janet Hook, "Race to Fill Mitchell's Shoes Highlights Party Divisions," *Congressional Quarterly*, 12 March 1994. Once he decided not to seek the top job, it seemed only prudent to step off the leadership ladder to give someone else a chance. Janet Hook, "Senate Race Narrows to Two: No. 3 Job Suddenly Opens," *Congressional Quarterly*, 23 April 1994.

3. PRIMARY CHALLENGER CAMPAIGNS

1. Prepared by the Harwood Group for the Kettering Foundation, *Citizens and Politics: A View from Main Street* (Dayton: Kettering Foundation, 1991); Center for the Press, Politics, and Public Policy, *Campaign Lessons for 1992* (Cambridge: Harvard University Press, 1991); Dan Balz and Richard Morin, "An Electorate Ready to Revolt," *Washington Post Weekly Edition*, 11–17 November 1991; *Los Angeles Times*, "Political Reporters Find Politics Today Disenchanting," *Rochester Democrat and Chronicle*, 6 January 1991.

2. Edward Carmines and Richard Champagne, "Voting in Senate Elections: A Review and Future Research Agenda," *Congress and the Presidency* 17 (1991): 139–57.

3. Warren Miller, Donald Kinder, and Steven Rosenstone, "The Systematic Study of Senate Elections, 1990–1993," Proposal to the National Science Foundation, National Election Studies, University of Michigan, January 1990.

4. Steven Finkel, "Reexamining the 'Minimal Effects' Model in Recent Presidental Campaigns," *Journal of Politics* 55 (1993): 1–21; see also, John Hibbing and John Alford, "Economic Conditions and the Forgotten Side of Congress: A Foray into Senate Elections," *British Journal of Political Science* 12 (1982): 505–16.

5. Mark Westlye, *Senate Elections and Campaign Intensity* (Baltimore: Johns Hopkins University Press, 1991); Gary Jacobson and Raymond Wolfinger, "Informational Voting in California Senate Elections," *Legislative Studies Quarterly* 14 (1989): 509–29; Charles Franklin, "Candidate Strategy and Voter Response in the 1990 Senate Elections," Paper prepared for the annual meeting of the American Political Science Association, Washington, D.C., 1991; Edie Goldenberg and Michael Traugott, "Evaluating Models of Voting Behavior and U.S. Senate Elections," Paper prepared for the annual meeting of the Midwest Political Science Association, Chicago, 1985; Samuel Patterson and Thomas Kephart, "The Case of the Wayfaring Challenger: The 1988 Senate Election in Ohio," *Congress and the Presidency* 18: 105–119.

6. Barbara Salmore and Stephen Salmore, *Candidates, Parties and Campaigns*, 2d ed. (Washington, D.C.: CQ Press, 1989).

7. Ibid. , 7.

8. Samuel Popkin, *The Reasoning Voter* (Chicago: University of Chicago Press, 1991),116.

9. Salmore and Salmore, *Candidates, Parties and Campaigns*, chap. 3.

10. Linda Fowler, *Candidates, Congress and the American Democracy* (Ann Arbor: University of Michigan Press, 1993).

11. Alan Abramowitz and Jeffrey Segal, *Senate Elections* (Ann Arbor: University of Michigan Press, 1992), 120.

12. Janet Box Steffensmeier and Charles Franklin, "The Long Campaign: Senate Elections in 1992," in *Democracy's Feast*, ed. Herbert Weisberg (Chatham, N.J.: Chatham House Press, 1994).

13. Salmore and Salmore, *Candidates, Parties and Campaigns*, chap. 1.

14. Fowler, *Candidates, Congress and the American Democracy*, chap. 4; Gary Jacobson, *The Politics of Congressional Elections*, 2d ed. (Boston: Little Brown, 1987).

15. Alan Abramowitz, "Explaining Senate Election Outcomes," *American Political Science Review* 82 (1988): 385–403; Pevrill Squire, "Challengers in U. S. Senate Elections," *Legislative Studies Quarterly* 14 (1989): 531–37; Charles Stewart, "A Sequential Model of U.S. Senate Elections," *Legislative Studies Quarterly*, 14 (1989): 567–601; L. Sandy Maisel, "Quality Candidates in House and Senate Elections, from 1982–1990," in *The Atomistic Congress*, ed. Alan Hertzke and Ronald Peters (Armonk, N.Y.: M. E. Sharpe, 1992). A recent effort to include the "skill" factor is Pevrill Squire, "Challenger Quality and Voting Behavior in U. S. Senate Elections," *Legislative Studies Quarterly* 17 (1992): 247–63

16. Editorial, *New York Times*, 1 June 1978.

17. David Canon, *Actors, Athletes and Astronauts* (Chicago: University of Chicago Press, 1990).

18. David Wald, "Dick Leone," *Newark Star-Ledger*, 31 May 1978.

19. T. R. Reid, "A Scholar-Athlete Pivots into Politics," *Washington Post*, 22 May 1978.

20. Press release, "The Senate Primary: Candidates Not Well Known," Eagleton Institute of Politics, 19 May 1978.

21. Charles Hucker, "Sen. Case's Reelection Battle is the Center of Attention in New Jersey," *Congressional Quarterly*, 27 May 1978.

22. Ramona Smith, "Leone Has Defense for Party Line," *Trenton Times*, 6 April 1978.

23. Robert Sam Anson, "The World According to Garth," *New York Times*, 30 October 1978; John Goldman, "For Super Campaigner, Politics Is All," *Los Angeles Times*, 21 February 1978.

24. David Wald and Stuart Marques, "Maguire Quits Race for Senate," *Newark Star-Ledger*, 7 February 1978.

25. David Wald and Dan Weissman, "Byrne Backs Leone for Senate," *Newark Star-Ledger*, 11 February 1978.

26. Editorial, *New York Times*, 4 June 1978.

27. David Wald, "Leone Campaigns in Hudson," *Newark Star-Ledger*, 2 June 1978.

28. Ramona Smith, "Hudson, Essex Hard on Leone," *Trenton Times*, 19 March 1978; Wald, "Dick Leone"; Reid, "A Scholar-Athlete Pivots into Politics."

29. David Wald, "U. S. Eyes Senate Race in New Jersey," *Newark Star-Ledger*, 21 May 1978.

30. David Wald, "Bradley Wins; Case and Bell Close," *Newark Star-Ledger*, 7 June 1978. See also Lee Lescaze, "New Jersey Trying to Overcome a History of Corruption," *Washington Post*, 2 March 1980.

31. Reid, "A Scholar-Athlete Pivots into Politics."

32. Wald, "Dick Leone."

33. Charles Hucker, "Bradley and Kaye vs. Leone and Garth," *Congressional Quarterly*, 22 July 1978; Wald, "U. S. Eyes Senate Race in New Jersey."

34. Quoted in Lawrence Longley and Walter Oleszek, *Bicameral Politics* (New York: Yale University Press, 1989).

35. Robert Turner and Norman Lockman, "Tightening Massachusetts Race for U. S. Senate," *Boston Globe*, 30 August 1978.

36. Robert Healy, "The Democratic Name Game," *Boston Globe*, 31 July 1978.

37. *Springfield Daily News*, 12 September 1978.

38. Internal Memo: To Dennis Kanin from Rich Arenberg, "Poll Data," 30 June 1978.

39. B. Drummond Ayres, "Tsongas Played Underdog Role to Oust Brooke in Senate Race," *New York Times*, 11 September 1978; Norman Lockman, "The Demise of Brooke: Six Months of Trouble," *Boston Globe*, 11 November 1978.

40. Gilbert Scharfenberger, "Massachusetts Elects a Governor and a United States Senator: A Comparative Analysis of the 1978 Elections" (Ph.D. dissertation, Massachusetts Institute of Technology, 1982), 171, 213.

41. Press release, "Post Election Poll Released by Tsongas," 5 December 1978.

42. Associated Press, "Tsongas Out Thanking Voters Who Elected Him," *Portland, Maine Press Herald*, 9 November 1978.

43. Mark Westlye, *Senate Elections and Campaign Intensity*, pp. 12–13.

44. Peter Lucas, "A Pro Explains How to Bankroll a Campaign," *Boston Globe*, 5 December 1979.

45. Robert Healy, *Boston Globe*, 15 September 1978.

46. Jeff Barnard, "Tsongas Settling into Senate Seat," *Cape Cod Times*, January 1980.

4. A SEQUENCE OF CAMPAIGNS

1. Charles Franklin, "Senate Incumbent Visibility Over the Election Cycle," *Legislative Studies Quarterly* 18 (1993): 271–90. See also Robert Erikson, "Incumbency and U.S. Senators," paper prepared for Stanford Conference on Senate Elections, November 1991.

2. Marjorie Randon Hershey, *Running for Office: The Political Education of Campaigners* (Chatham, N.J.: Chatham House, 1984).

3. In her book, Hershey studied the pro-life movement in Iowa; she and Darrell West compared the Clark and Culver campaigns from that angle. See chaps. 7 and 8. See also note 10 below. Their work was doubly helpful to me.

4. Frank Nye, "Senatorial Slot Open; List Names," *Cedar Rapids Gazette*, 10 February 1972; James Larew, "A Party Reborn," honors thesis, Harvard University, 1976.

5. *Ibid.* Staff writer, " 'Interested,' Says Former Culver Aide," *Cedar Rapids Gazette*, 10 February 1972; Barbara Salmore and Steven Salmore, *Candidates, Parties and Campaigns* (Washington, D.C.: CQ Press, 1989), 120.

6. Larry Wilson, " 'Walker' Dick Clark Trails in Iowa Race," *Omaha World Herald*, 13 September 1972.

7. *Congressional Quarterly*'s informants never wavered in predicting Clark's defeat. See the following issues: 24 June 1972, 1509; 7 October 1972, 2522; 14 October 1972, 2832–33; 28 October 1972, 2781; 4 November 1972, 2905. The last citation showed Clark twenty points behind in the *Des Moines Register*'s "Iowa Poll," as of 12–15 October.

8. Frank Nye, "Democrat Challengers Predict Wins Tuesday," *Cedar Rapids Gazette*, 2 November 1972.

9. Wilson, " 'Walker' Dick Clark Trails in Iowa Race."

10. Marjorie Randon Hershey and Darrell West, "Single Issue Groups and Political Campaigns," paper delivered at the annual meeting of the Midwest

Political Science Association, Cincinnati, 1981.

11. Election survey, Peter D. Hart Research Associates, 4–6 October 1978.

12. Election survey, Peter D. Hart Research Associates, 4–9 March 1977.

13. Reprint of article on Dick Clark, by John Hyde, from *Des Moines Sunday Register*, 10 September 1978.

14. Dennis Farney, "A New Great Schism, This Time a Political One, Divides Catholics in Iowa Races and Nationally," *Wall Street Journal*, 21 January 1988; "Iowa," *Congressional Quarterly*, 25 February 1984.

15. Hershey, *Running for Office*, 190 passim.

16. Ibid. , 190–91; Bill Peterson, "Foes of Abortion Aim at Hill Deadly Dozen," *Washington Post*, 11 February 1979.

17. Robert Klaus, "Iowa Democrats Put Stress on Organization," *Des Moines Register*, 14 September 1979; Daniel Pedersen and David Yepsen, "Carter Aides Fight 'Overconfidence'," *Des Moines Register*, 13 January 1980.

18. Laura Weiss, "Tough Election Fights Forced Some Members to Moderate Their Stands," *Congressional Quarterly*, 2 June 1979, 1064.

19. Postelection survey, Peter D. Hart Research Associates, 9 March 1979.

20. Daniel Pedersen, "Fitzgerald Gains on Ray, Poll Shows," *Des Moines Register*, October 15 1978. The figures were Clark 50%, Jepsen 39%, 11% undecided. These were virtually unchanged from July and September.

21. Albert R. Hunt, "Political Pollster Examines Causes of Losing Effort," *Wall Street Journal*, 8 February 1979.

22. Postelection survey, 9 March 1979. All quotes in this and the next two paragraphs are from this survey.

23. David Alpern, "1978's Wobbly Polls," *Newsweek*, 27 November 1978.

24. Election survey, 4–6 October 1978. These quotes and those in the next paragraph are from this survey.

25. Election Survey, 4–9 March, 1977. These quotes and those in the next paragraph are from this survey.

26. Klaus, "Iowa Democrats Put Stress on Organization"; David Nyan, "Second Thoughts in Iowa," *Boston Globe*, 17 August 1979; Hershey and West, "Single Issue Groups and Political Campaigns"; James Flansburg, "Iowa Parties Take Care Not to Awaken 'Wrong Voters,'" *Des Moines Register*, 7 September 1980.

27. According to Westlye's classification, the Clark-Jepsen contest was a "hard-fought" campaign. In terms of our more measurable variables—closeness of outcome and campaign spending—it was. But in terms of the preferences and the strategy of the incumbent, it was a "low-key" campaign. The October *Congressional Quarterly* summary, on which Westlye based his classification, missed both of these candidate and campaign factors. Westlye's classification is a valuable one. Still, as he says, it is only a first cut into a complex subject. See *Congressional Quarterly*, 14 October 1978, pp. 2832–33; Westlye, "Senate Elections and Campaign Intensity," 207, chap. 2.

28. "Clark, Loser to Jepsen, Figures That's Enough," *Quad City Times*, 17 June 1981.

29. Culver's work on the endangered species act was the substantive focus of Elizabeth Drew, *Senator* (New York: Simon and Schuster, 1979).

30. Jack Anderson and Tony Capaccio, "Jack Anderson Rates the Congress," *Washingtonian*, October 1980; a *New York Times* editorial had even endorsed him as "an outstanding member of Congress" when he was in the House, 26 October 1992.

31. Drew, *Senator*.

32. Election Survey, 4–9 March 1977.

33. Daniel Pedersen, "Culver Sprints Ahead in Poll on Senate Race," *Des Moines Register*, 9 September 1979. The April figures were Culver 35%, Grassley 31%, undecided 34%.

34. Mark Shields, "Losing Principles," *Washington Post*, 9 January 1981; Rowland Evans and Robert Novak, "Iowa's Defiant Liberal," *Washington Post*, 31 August 1979.

35. The finest work on the importance of policy connections to Senate election outcomes is by Gerald Wright. Cf. Gerald Wright and Michael Berkman, "Candidates and Policy in United States Senate Elections," *American Political Science Review* 80 (June 1986): 568–88; Gerald Wright, "Coalitions in Elections for the United States Senate," paper prepared for presentation at the Annual Meeting of the Southern Political Science Association, Savannah, Georgia, November 1993; Gerald Wright, "Policy Voting in the U.S. Senate: Who Is Represented?" in *The Changing World of the U.S. Senate*, ed. John Hibbing (Berkeley: Institute of Governmental Studies, 1990).

36. On Culver and NCPAC's campaign against him, see "Endangered Liberals," *Newsweek*, 30 June 1980; Bernard Weinraub, "Million Dollar Drive Aims to Oust 5 Liberal Senators," *New York Times*, 24 March 1980; Brad Bannon, "NCPAC in the 80's: Action and Reaction," *Campaigns and Elections* (Winter 1983); Richard Cohen, "Are the Senate's Liberal Democrats Becoming an Endangered Species?" *National Journal*, 14 July 1979. On Culver and *Christian Voice*, see David Yepsen, "The Message From Pulpit: Political Clout," *Des Moines Register*, 7 September 1980.

37. Arnold Garson, "Culver Catches Up with Grassley," *Des Moines Register*, 31 August 1980. The figures were Culver 47%, Grassley 46%, undecided 7%. In July they had been 36%, 53%, 11%.

38. Stanley Kelly, Jr. , "Campaign Propaganda in Perspective," in *The President*, ed. Joseph Ray (El Paso: Texas Western Press, 1969).

39. The Grassley and Culver campaign ads were obtained from the Political Commercial Archives at the University of Oklahoma, Norman. Personal thanks to Julian Kanter for his help.

40. The observers were curators at the University of Oklahoma's Political Commercial Archives.

41. Daniel Pedersen and Arnold Garson, "Slight Gains for Carter, Culver in Poll," *Des Moines Register*, 12 October 1980. The figures were Culver 47%, Grassley 46%, undecided 9%.

42. In April 1979, his approval rating was 40%, disapproval 18%, and no opinion 42%. Daniel Pederson, "Culver Sprints Ahead in Poll on Senate Race."

43. Arnold Garson, "Grassley Overtakes Culver," *Des Moines Register*, 2 November 1980.

44. Democratic State Committee of Iowa, "1980 Election Statistics," Pt. IV,

Selected Group Vote Analysis.

45. Garson, "Grassley Overtakes Culver."

46. Thomas G. Ryan, "Did Shift in Iowa Catholic Votes Lean to Clark's and Culver's Defeat?" *Des Moines Register*, 23 November 1980.

47. Ibid. Democratic State Committee 1980 election statistics.

48. Ryan, "Did Shift in Iowa Catholic Votes Lead to Clark's and Culver's Defeat?"

49. James Dickenson, "Don't Be Fooled by Charles Grassley's Yokel Image," *Washington Post Weekly Edition*, 8 April 1985.

50. Ibid.

51. Dennis Farney, "Senate Race in Iowa Is a Seesaw," *Wall Street Journal*, 17 October 1984; Jack Germond and Jules Witcover, "Negative Campaigning in Clean-Politics Iowa," *National Journal*, 27 October 1984; See also Dennis Farney, "In Wake of Scandal, Sen. Jepsen Relies on 'Damage Control,'" *Wall Street Journal*, 18 June 1984.

52. George Anthan, "Jepsen-Harkin Race Pivots on Iowa's Farm Economy," *Des Moines Register*, 14 May 1984.

53. As in Gerald Wright, "Representation and the Electoral Cycle in the U. S. Senate," Paper prepared for the annual meeting of the Midwest Political Science Association, Chicago, April 1993.

5. A CANDIDATE AND A CAMPAIGN I

1. "14 Democratic States Look Solid," *Congressional Quarterly*, 24 October 1992, 3343. "Democrat Favored" was their designation. The rationale: "War vote flap subsides. Strong ads, country charm lift Fowler."

2. *Congressional Quarterly*, 11 October 1986, 2416–17.

3. Phil Gailey, "Jordan of Georgia Looks to Battle for Senate Seat," *New York Times*, 18 December 1985; Jay Beck, "The Triumphant Defeat of Hamilton Jordan," *Campaigns and Elections* (November/December 1986); Barbara Salmore and Stephen Salmore, *Candidates, Parties and Campaigns*, 196–202.

4. "Georgia," *Congressional Quarterly*.

5. Salmore and Salmore, *Candidates, Parties and Campaigns*.

6. The senators involved were John Glenn, Arlen Specter, Mark Andrews, and Pete Domenici, respectively.

7. Hershey, *Running for Office*, chap. 4; Marjorie Randon Hershey, "Explaining Election Results," paper prepared for the annual meeting of the American Political Science Association, Atlanta, 1989.

8. See note 3 above.

9. Carin Dessauer, "Georgia Senate: Mattingly's Third Strike," *Political Report*, 20 February 1987.

10. Salmore and Salmore, *Candidates, Parties and Campaigns*, 201.

11. Alan Ehrenhalt, ed. , *Politics in America: The 100th Congress* (Washington, D.C.: CQ Press, 1987), 354–55.

12. Michael Barone and Grant Ujifusa, *The Almanac of American Politics, 1990* (Washington, D.C.: National Journal, 1991), 298.

13. Michael Hinkelman, "The Duke's Short List Includes One Wyche Fowler," *Atlanta Business Chronicle*, 13 June 1988.

14. Alan Secrest, "Learning the Lessons of 1986," *Election Politics* (Winter 1986–87): 7.

15. Dessauer, "Georgia Senate."

16. For example, Carrie Teegardin, "Newcomers to Suburbia Bolster Republican Party," *Atlanta Journal-Constitution*, 12 November 1992.

17. Salmore and Salmore, *Candidates, Parties and Campaigns*, 199.

18. A good account of his early career can be found in "An Interview with U.S. Senator Wyche Fowler," *Journal of the Medical Association of Georgia* (January 1988).

19. Jackie Calmes, "Fowler Plucks Plum Assignment," *Atlanta Journal-Constitution*, 2 December 1980.

20. Speech at Fowler fund raiser, Atlanta, 2 November 1992.

21. Stan Darden, "Republican Wins Apparent Narrow Victory in Georgia," UP On-Line, 25 November 1992.

22. John Kingdon, *Candidates for Office: Beliefs and Strategies* (New York: Random House, 1968).

23. Mark Sherman, "Fowler Enjoys Easy Campaign as Republican Foes Struggle," *Atlanta Journal-Constitution*, 21 June 1992.

24. Frank LaMonte, "Folksy Ads by Fowler Popular," *Augusta Chronicle*, 20 October 1992. See also, Helen Dewar, "Georgia Voters Seem to Have Fowler on Their Minds," *Washington Post*, 9 May 1992.

25. "Local Accomplishments of Senator Wyche Fowler, Jr., 1987–1992, Augusta Area." Mimeograph.

26. He did not receive the paper's endorsement; and his vote in Richmond County went up 1.3%—from 48.3% in 1986 to 49.6% (on November 3). It dropped to 45.2% in the runoff.

27. Bill Osinski, "Political Sniping Mars Rockdale Parade Plan," *Atlanta Journal-Constitution*, 23 March 1992.

28. Mark Sherman, *Atlanta Journal-Constitution*, 27 April 1992.

29. *Congressional Record*, Daily Edition, 9 April 1992, pp. S5197-S5199.

30. Gregg Bass, "Fowler Colleagues Stop in Moultrie to Get Out the Vote," *Moultrie Observer*, 24 November 1992; Terry Toole, "Fowler Wins in Miller County," *Miller County Liberal*, 25 November 1992; Dean Poling, "Carter Makes Exception for Fowler," *Valdosta Daily Times*, 21 November 1992; Mark Kelly, "Demo, GOP Stump Here," *Cordele Dispatch*, 24 November 1992.

31. Bill Shipp, "Why Race Went Bad for Fowler," *Marietta Daily Journal*, 15 November 1992.

32. Jerry Hagstram, "Greer's Year," *National Journal*, 7 November 1992.

33. "Sunday News Conference," Channel 36, Atlanta, 4 October 1992.

34. They can be found—picture and text—in *Atlanta Journal-Constitution*, 27 September and 17 October 1992.

35. Other observers picked up the same problem. "His flip, sometimes arrogant style, wears thin with many whose support he needs at home." David Rogers, "Political Eyes, Funds Turn South to Bloody Duel of Fowler, Rival in Georgia Runoff for Senate," *Wall Street Journal*, 20 November, 1992; "He believed his own press clippings. He seemed to have all the answers. Staff criticism

was discouraged. Sycophancy worked better." Shipp, "Why Race Went Bad for Fowler."

36. Richard Fogaley, "Nunn Calls Fowler 'Effective,' Urges Colleague's Reelection," *Savannah Morning News*, 27 October 1992.

37. In his TV ad saying Fowler "has worked effectively to promote economic development for our state," he mentioned: Moody Air Force Base, the Talmadge Bridge, Metropolitan Atlanta Rapid Transportation Authority, Atlanta University Complex, small business centers.

38. Grover Norquist, "Coverdell's Winning Strategy," *American Spectator* (March 1993).

39. Barone and Ujifusa, *Almanac of American Politics, 1990*, 311–12, 315–16.

40. Helen Dewar, "Democrats Seek to Pull Georgia's Fowler Back From Political Precipice," *Washington Post*, 18 November 1992.

41. John Meacham, "Surprise Strength on Nov. 3 Boosts Coverdell's Hopes," *Chattanooga Times*, 12 November 1992. See also Rogers's "Eyes, Funds Turn South. . ." In 1995, the Democratic congressman from North Georgia switched parties and became a Republican, *Roll Call* (April 1995).

42. Julie Hairston, "Wyche and the Women Scorned," *Business Atlanta*, (September 1992); AP, "Fowler's Votes Cost Him Support of Former Allies," *Athens Banner-Herald*, 4 October 1992; Thomas Edsall and E. J. Dionne, Jr. , "The Vote That Split Liberal Core," *Washington Post Weekly Edition*, 21–27 October 1991.

43. Douglas Arnold, *The Logic of Congressional Action* (New Haven: Yale University Press, 1990).

44. CBS exit polls on 3 November were not conclusive. Among the people who disapproved of his vote, 29% voted for Fowler anyway. And among Fowler's voters, 35% disapproved of his vote.

6. A CANDIDATE AND A CAMPAIGN II

1. For example, pollster Claiborne Darden, in AP, "Fowler Battles Republicans," *Albany Sunday Herald*, 12 April 1992.

2. AP, "Fowler is a Shoo-in, Polls, Pundits Predict," *Augusta Chronicle*, 11 October 1992.

3. Mark Sherman, "Fowler Also Has Big Fund-Raising Lead," *Atlanta Journal-Constitution*, 15 October 1992.

4. Merle Black quoted in Mark Sherman, "Fowler Has Huge Lead Over Coverdell in Poll," *Atlanta Journal-Constitution*, 10 October, 1992.

5. Charles Bullock quoted in Frank LaMonte, "Folksy Ads by Fowler Popular," *Augusta Chronicle*, 20 October 1992.

6. John Meacham, "Fowler's Lead Big in Georgia," *Chattanooga Times*, 9 September 1992; Sherman, "Fowler Has Huge Lead."

7. "Sunday News Conference," Channel 36, Atlanta, 18 October 1992.

8. Ibid.

9. Lynda Lee Kaid and Dorothy K. Davidson, "Elements of Video Style: Candidate Presentation through Television Advertising," *New Perspectives on Political Advertising* ed. Lynda Lee Kaid, Dan Nimmo, and Keith R. Sanders (Carbondale: Southern Illinois University Press, 1986).

10. Ben Wright, "GOP Hopefuls Outline Views," *Columbus Ledger-Enterprise*, 20 May 1992; Mark Sherman, "GOP Uses Old Strategy, Labeling Senator Liberal," *Atlanta Journal-Constitution*, 22 June 1992.

11. *Atlanta Daily News*, 14 June 1992.

12. Frank LaMonte, "Coverdell Shifts Primary Gears to Face Dem Incumbent Fowler," *Augusta Chronicle*, 13 August 1992.

13. "Sunday News Conference," Channel 36, Atlanta, 8 November 1992.

14. Ibid. "Sunday News Conference," 29 November 1992; Dick Williams, "The Former Democrat Behind Paul Coverdell," *Atlanta Journal-Constitution*, 28 November 1992.

15. Quoted in Paul Taylor, "The Trick Is to Get Vicious Carefully," *Washington Post Weekly Edition*, 16–22 July 1990.

16. Quoted in Paul Taylor, "Consultants: Winning on the Attack," *Washington Post*, 17 January 1989.

17. Mark Sherman, "Fowler Ad Plays on Suburban Crime Fears," *Atlanta Journal-Constitution*, 30 October 1992.

18. Bill Shipp, "Sunday News Conference," Channel 36, Atlanta, 29 November 1992.

19. Frank LaMonte, *Savannah Morning News*, 17 September 1992; "Sunday News Conference," Channel 36, Atlanta, 8 November 1992; Dick Williams, "A Runoff Too Tough to Predict," *Atlanta Journal-Constitution*, 7 November 1992.

20. Rod Hudspeth, "Politician Who Loves Baseball Can Be Trusted," *Marietta Daily Journal*, 1988; Colin Campbell, "Nine Innings with Wyche Fowler," *Atlanta Journal-Constitution*, 2 October 1991; John Meachman, "Fowler Is Calm, Collected," *Chattanooga Times*, 15 October 1992.

21. Mark Sherman, "Fowler Enjoys Easy Campaign as Republican Foes Struggle," *Atlanta Journal-Constitution*, 21 June 1992; Dillard Munford, "A Close Look at Wyche," *Marietta Daily Journal*, 13 October 1992; Mark Sherman, "Incumbent Fowler Finds Himself in Good Shape Heading into Stretch," *Atlanta Journal-Constitution*, 25 October 1992.

22. Pete Hamill, "Winding Up for Spring," *Washington Post*, 9 March 1981.

23. Cooper and Secrest, "A Qualitative Investigation Conducted for Wyche Fowler for Senate."

24. Mark Sherman, "Attacks Get Personal in Senate Race," *Atlanta Journal-Constitution*, 20 November 1992.

25. Tom Baxter, "Senate Race an Omen of Worse to Come?" *Atlanta Journal-Constitution*, 23 November 1992; Mark Sherman, "Senate Race Never Got Beyond Nasty," *Atlanta Journal-Constitution*, 11 November 1992; Mark Sherman, "Coverdell Victor in Squeaker," *Atlanta Journal-Constitution*, 25 November 1992.

26. Other observers said the same thing. Sherman, "Senate Race Never Got Beyond Nasty"; David Von Drehle, "Sen. Fowler Defeated in Runoff," *Washington Post*, 25 November 1992; Frank LaMonte, "Incumbency Blamed in Fowler Loss," *Augusta Chronicle*, 29 November 1992.

27. Bill Shipp, "Somewhere Fowler Is Smiling," *Rockdale Citizen*, 20 April 1992.

28. "Sunday News Conference," Channel 36, Atlanta, 8 November 1992.

29. "Sunday News Conference," 29 November 1992.

30. Dick Williams, "Is Fowler Back to Old Self?," *Atlanta Journal-Constitution*, 21 November 1992.

31. Williams, "A Runoff Too Tough to Predict."

32. Tom Baxter, "Senate Race Turnaround Resembles '82 Contest," *Atlanta Journal-Constitution*, 19 November 1992.

33. John Head, "Did System Wear Down Fowler?" *Atlanta Journal-Constitution*, 7 December 1992.

34. AP, "Senate Foes Battle Tight," *Valdosta Daily Times*, 25 November 1992; David Von Drehle, "Coverdell Takes Slim Runoff Lead," *Washington Post*, 11 November 1994.

35. One exception: Editorial, "Coverdell Ran a Better Race," *Atlanta Journal-Constitution*, 26 November 1992.

36. Cooper and Secrest, "A Qualitative Investigation Conducted for Wyche Fowler for Senate."

37. Picture and story: John Harmon, "Fowler, Feds Tour Forest, Debate Timber Subsidies," *Atlanta Journal-Constitution*, 7 August 1991.

38. For some of Bill Shipp's sniping, see "Coverdell Takes on 'Wafflin Wyche' in Race," *Athens Banner-Herald*, 24 November 1991; "Non-Truth Telling an Epidemic," *Rockdale Citizen*, 15 April 1992; "Polls Shaped Sen. Fowler's Thomas Vote," *Athens Banner-Herald*, 20 October, 1991.

39. Mike Christensen, "Fowler's Staff Linked to S&L Meeting," *Atlanta Journal-Constitution*, 7 August 1991.

40. AP, "Lawyer: Fowler Staff Had No S&L Role," *Atlanta Journal-Constitution*, 8 August 1991.

41. The controversy can be followed in Ron Taylor, "Metrospective," *Atlanta Journal-Constitution*, 30 August 1992; Steve Harvey, "Fowler Foe Hints at False House Bank Statements," *Atlanta Journal-Constitution*, 1 September 1992; Bill Shipp, "Don't Look for a Gentlemanly Campaign for Senate Seat," *Columbus Ledger-Enquirer*, 3 September 1992; Michael Hinkleman and Emory Thomas, Jr. , "Handling of Fowler Story Criticized," *Atlanta Business Chronicle*, 4–10 September 1992; staff and wire reports, "Coverdell Seeks Review of Fowler's Account," *Brunswick News*, 24 September 1992.

42. Editorial, "Sen. Fowler, Please Lighten Up," *Atlanta Journal-Constitution*, 21 September 1992.

43. Dick Williams, "A Quiet U.S. Senate Campaign Gets a Hot Foot," *Atlanta Journal-Constitution*, 1 September 1992.

44. Compare, for example, his lead paragraph on the first debate with that of Frank LaMonte, who was allowed to ride with Fowler. Mark Sherman, "Fowler, Coverdell Have First Debate," *Atlanta Journal-Constitution*, 10 October 1992; Frank LaMonte, "Fowler Raps Coverdell in Radio Debate," *Athens Banner-Herald*, 10 October 1992. See also Mark Sherman, "In Debate, Coverdell Says Fowler Lied," *Atlanta Journal-Constitution*, 19 October 1992; Mark Sherman, "Fowler, Coverdell Keep a Tightening Race Bitter to the End," *Atlanta Journal-Constitution*, 31 October 1992.

45. LaMonte, "Incumbency Blamed in Fowler Loss."

7. DURABLE CONNECTIONS I

1. As used by politicians on the campaign trail and in this book, trust is a general long-term phenomenon—one factor among others that helps to explain voting decisions in the legislature, constituency receptivity at home, and voter predispositions at election time. It is a word rarely heard in the travel talk of first-term senators and sometimes heard in the travel talk of long-term senators. It is a cumulative notion. No doubt, it is partly the cumulative result of many individual voting decisions that have been calculated, defended, and explained, one at a time, over the length of a legislative career. But more than that—cumulative presentations of self, for example—is involved, too. An excellent discussion of the conditions under which legislators perceive or do not perceive constituent trust when they vote and a stimulating argument for conceptualizing trust on an issue by issue, vote by vote, contextual basis is William Bianco, *Trust* (Ann Arbor: University of Michigan Press, 1994). See also, Suzanne Parker and Glenn Parker, "Why Do We Trust Our Congressmen" *Journal of Politics* 55 (1993): 442–53; and Stephanie Greco Larson, *Creating Consent of the Governed* (Carbondale and Edwardsville: Southern Illinois University Press, 1992).

2. Special report, "New Face in Politics," *New York Times*, 30 September 1960.

3. Joseph Shanley, "Senate Race Wide Open," *Providence Journal*, 10 April 1960.

4. "New Face in Politics."

5. *Providence Journal*, 29 August 1960.

6. AP, "Newcomer Wins Senate Primary," *New York Times*, 29 September 1960; John Fenton, "Pell Plans Drive in Rhode Island," *New York Times*, 30 September 1960; Special report, "3 in Rhode Island Seek Green's Seat," *New York Times*, 18 September 1960; "New Face in Politics."

7. "McGrath Aims Fire at Rivals in Party," *Providence Journal*, 20 July 1960. For an underground attack, see "Pell Invites Check on His Expenses," *Providence Journal-Bulletin*, 2 August 1960.

8. Bernard Weinraub, "New Foreign Relations Chief is Not a Cream Puff," *New York Times*, 2 February 1987.

9. "Roberts Gets State Backing of AFL-CIO," *Providence Journal*, 21 May 1960. When an opponent called him a "cream puff," however he said, "I rushed out and got the bakers union to endorse me." Weinraub, "New Foreign Relations Chief Is Not a Cream Puff."

10. Editorial, "The Primary Law Should be Revised," *Providence Journal*, 17 March 1960.

11. Edward Milne, "R. I. Democrats Consider Ticket," *Providence Journal*, 3 April 1960.

12. "Rhode Island," *Congressional Quarterly*, 11 November 1960.

13. Francis Stevenson and Jerry Lisker, "A Senate Nor'easter: Pell of Rhode Island," in *Congressional Record*, Daily Edition, 19 January 1966, 568–69; "New Face in Politics."

14. "3 in Rhode Island Seek Green's Seat."

15. "New Face in Politics."

16. See advertisement, *Providence Journal*, 25 June 1960.

17. "Pell Attacks 3 'Myths' about His Campaign," *Providence Journal*, 16 August 1960. See also Shanley, "Senate Race Wide Open"; "Newcomer Wins Senate Primary."

18. For example, newspaper advertisements appeared in the *Providence Journal* on 16, 17, 22, 23, 25, 26, and 27 September. (Primary day was the 28th.)

19. "Pell Attacks 3 'Myths' About His Campaign."

20. "Rhode Island," *Congressional Quarterly*; Fenton, "Pell Plans Drive in Rhode Island."

21. "Pell Victorious by 38,000 Votes," *Providence Journal*, 29 September 1960.

22. "Rhode Island," *Congressional Quarterly*.

23. "The East," *Congressional Quarterly*, 7 October 1972; "Democrats Striving to Break Even," *Congressional Quarterly*, 17 February 1990.

24. George Higgins, "Mother Jones' Own McCarthyism," *Boston Globe*, 9 June 1984.

25. John Fitzgerald, "Hot Rhode Island Race Turning Out to be Tepid," 17 October 1990.

26. Claiborne Pell, *Megalopolis Unbound* (New York: Praeger, 1966).

27. Stevenson and Lisker, "A Senate Nor'easter."

28. His NEH accomplishment is described in Ernest Cuneo, "Rhode Island Senator Won Place in History for Aid to Art, Education," *Newport Daily News*, reprinted in *Congressional Quarterly*, Daily Edition, 25 August 1978.

29. M. Charles Bakst, "At Kickoff, Pell Stresses Past—And Future," *Providence Journal*, July 1 1990.

30. "Rhode Island Senatorial Poll #1, 1983," 25 November 1983.

31. Rochelle Stanfield, "School Aid Granted Pell-Mell? Maybe Not," *National Journal*, 13 November 1993; "The Pell Record," Reelect Sen. Pell Committee, 1992, 16.

32. John Wilkerson and Larry Bartels, "Measuring State Party Ideology," Working Paper 8911, University of Rochester, June 1989.

33. "Democrats, Republicans Move Further Apart on Most Issues in 1983 Session," *National Journal*, 12 May 1984; "A Year of Continuity," *National Journal*, 17 May 1986; "Shift to the Left," *National Journal*, 2 April 1988; "Partisan Patterns," *National Journal*, 19 January 1991. Pell ranked fifth, eleventh, second, and tenth in those years.

34. Daniel Seligman, "Keeping Up," *Fortune*, 24 February 1992.

35. Polls showed him consistently with leads of over 60% with voters over age 64 or 65. Darrell West, ed., *The Public Opinion Report*, vol. 3, no. 4 (September 1990) (Providence: Taubman Center, Brown University, 1990); Kevin Sullivan, "Poll Shows Pell's Lead Has Widened," *Providence Journal*, 9 September 1990.

36. Cambridge Survey Research, "An Analysis of Political Attitudes in the State of Rhode Island," January 1978, 122.

37. Cambridge Survey Research, Tubby Harrison, "Rhode Island Poll #1, 1983," 25 November 1983.

38. John P. Hackett, "Chafee Lead Over Pell Approaching 2–1 Margin," *Providence Journal*, 5 March 1972.

39. "Rhode Island," *Congressional Quarterly*, 7 October 1972, 2562; 28 October 1972, 2781; 4 November 1972, 2902; M. Charles Bakst, "Pell, McGovern Link Argued," *Providence Journal*, 12 October 1972.

40. John P. Hackett, "Pell, Tiernan, St. Germain Easy Victories," *Providence Journal*, 8 November 1972.

41. John P. Hackett, "Pell Advocates Stronger Navy," *Providence Journal*, 27 June 1972.

42. Mark Westlye, *Senate Elections and Campaign Intensity* (Baltimore: Johns Hopkins University Press, 1991), chap. 2.

43. Cambridge Survey Research, "An Analysis of Political Attitudes in the State of Rhode Island, 1978." The wording was, "He's a statesman and I'm proud to have him as my senator."

44. Harrison and Goldberg, "1990 Rhode Island Senatorial Poll #1," 27 September 1989. In 1983, he had an equally high agreement score (75%) on a somewhat different wording of the same idea. "Pell has a great deal of seniority and influence in Washington and this gives Rhode Island a bigger voice than most other small states." Harrison and Goldberg, "Rhode Island Senatorial Poll #1, 1983," 25 November 1983.

45. Ibid.

46. Jack Anderson, "Distinctions Made Between Doers and Non-Doers," *Washington Post*, 10 September 1981; Eleanor Randolph, "The Best and the Worst of the U.S. Senate," *The Washington Monthly* (January 1982).

47. Frederick Kempe, "Some Doubt New Foreign Relations Chairman Is Dynamic Enough to Preserve Panel's Influence," *Wall Street Journal*, 15 January 1987.

48. Jonathan Fuerbringer, "Some Political Chasms that Await the Arms Treaty," *New York Times*, 7 December 1987.

49. Helen Dewar, "Senate Foreign Relations Panel Founders: Decline Under Chairman Pell Is Exacerbated by Helm's Tactics," *Washington Post*, 10 October 1989.

50. Ibid.

51. Reynolds for U. S. Senator Committee, "News Release," 23 October 1978.

52. "Pell to Head Lawmakers Group to Meet with Mideast Leaders," *Providence Journal*, 29 August 1990; C. Eugene Emery, Jr. , "Pell's Mission Includes Mail Call to Middle East," *Providence Journal*, 31 August 1990; John Mulligan, "Mideast Crisis Through Media Spotlight on Pell," *Providence Journal*, 13 September 1990.

53. Kempe, "Some Doubt New Foreign Relations Chairman is Dynamic Enough to Preserve Panel's Influence."

54. AP James Drinkard, "Rhode Island Senator Shrugs Off the Glory," *Rochester Democrat and Chronicle*, 13 October 1991.

55. Ibid.

56. Fuerbringer, "Some Political Chasms that Await the Arms Treaty."

57. Brian Fuller, "Claiborne Pell," *Providence Business News*, 1 January 1990.

58. Stephen Hess, *The Ultimate Insiders: U. S. Senators in the National Media* (Washington, D.C.: Brookings Institute, 1986).

59. Albert Hunt, "Prowess Restored to Senate Committee Is Likely to Lapse as Lugar Steps Down," *Wall Street Journal*, 5 January 1987; Dewar, "Senate Foreign Relations Panel Founders"; Fuerbringer, "Some Political Chasms that Await the Arms Treaty."

60. "Speculation Grows on Green Vacancy," *Providence Journal*, 13 January 1960; "New Face in Politics."

61. Elliot Krieger, "Nuala Pell," *Providence Sunday Journal Magazine*, 12 August 1984.

62. John Goshko, "For Pell, Tests Await on Resurgent Panel," 11 November 1986.

63. Fuerbringer, "Some Political Chasms that Await the Arms Treaty."

64. Jody McPhillips, "New Treaty's Fate Is Up to Pell," *Providence Journal*, 9 December 1987.

65. Jody McPhillips, "The Elder Statesman Stays in Stride as He Puts 30-Year Record on Line," *Providence Journal*, 15 November 1989. See also Jody McPhillips, "Senator Pell, Marathon Man," *Providence Journal*, 8 October 1989. For a similar post-1990 contrast, compare in Washington, Carroll J. Doherty, "Subcommittee Plan Created to Revive Senate Panel," *Congressional Quarterly*, 2 February 1991; Christopher Madison, "A New Look for Sen. Pell's Committee," *National Journal*, 2 February 1991; and, in Rhode Island, John Mulligan, "Pell Relishes Role in Shaping History from Sidelines," *Providence Journal*, August 11, 1991.

66. Cambridge Survey Research, "An Analysis of Political Attitudes in the State of Rhode Island," 1978.

67. Memorandum from Tubby Harrison, "1990 Rhode Island Senatorial Poll #1," 27 September 1989, 6, 19.

68. William Lanouette, "The Selling of the Candidates, 1978," *National Journal*, 4 November 1978.

69. Weinraub, "New Foreign Relations Chief Is Not a Cream Puff."

70. The last statement was tied (at 65%) with the "Statesman ... proud" statement. Cambridge Survey Research, "An Analysis of Political Attitudes in the State of Rhode Island," 1978.

71. Katherine Whittmore, "Rogue Island," *Lears* (March 1991); Christopher Daly, "Scandal-Weary State Gears for Next Drama," *Washington Post*, 5 September 1993; John Yang, "House Democrats Weigh Ouster of Chairman of Banking Panel, but Dislike Potential Successors," *Wall Street Journal*, 31 December 1986.

72. Elmer Cornwell, in Kempe, "Some Doubt New Foreign Relations Chairman Is Dynamic Enough to Preserve Panel's Influence."

73. Steven Pressman, "Detailed Listing of Senator's 1982 Finances," *Congressional Quarterly*, 3 December 1983.

74. Thomas O'Toole, "Sen Claiborne Pell Defeats Ex-Gov. John Chafee in Rhode Island," *Washington Post*, 8 November 1972; Hackett, "Chafee Lead Over Pell Approaching 2–1 Margin."

75. Harrison and Goldberg, "1990 Rhode Island Senatorial Poll," 27 September 1989.

76. Ken Bode, "Senate Control: Who Cares?" *New York Times*, 17 May 1990;

Michael Oreskes, "Outlook for GOP: Senate Gains in '90, a Showdown in '92," *New York Times*, 3 May 1990.

77. R. W. Apple, Jr. , "Senator Staging Startling Comeback in Bid for Reelection in Rhode Island," *New York Times*, 6 October 1990.

78. Darrell West, in Adam Pertman, "In R. I. , Pell Faces a Big Battle to Retain His Senate Seat," *Boston Globe*, 20 May 1990.

79. Helen Dewar, "Over Here, Sending Aid Over There Isn't Too Popular," *Washington Post Weekly Edition*, 23–29 April 1990; Leslie Philips, "A Leader Takes on a Legend: Sen. Pell in Tough Campaign," *USA Today*, 24 August 1990.

80. Harrison, "1990 Rhode Island Senatorial Poll #1," 27 September 1989.

81. Fuller, "Claiborne Pell."

82. Guy Dufault and Darrell West, in Pertman, "In R.I., Pell Faces a Big Battle to Retain His Senate Seat."

83. As quoted in letter from Mary Beth Cahill to Robert Rendine, Jr. , 10 September 1990.

84. Adam Pertman, "Negative Campaigns Getting Cautious," *Boston Globe*, 9 September 1990.

85. Letter, Mary Beth Cahill to Robert Rendine, Jr.

86. Robert Trott, "Claudine Camp Denies Negative Ads Planned," *Newport Daily News*, 13 September 1990; Robert Trott, "Schneider Camp Disavows Article on Negative Ads; Candidates to Debate," AP Wire Service, 12 September 1990.

87. The first and third headlines were in the *Providence Journal*. The second was an AP wire story by Ross Sneyd.

88. Scott MacKay, "Civility, Not Hostility, Marks Faceoff," *Providence Journal*, 24 September 1990.

89. Jody McPhillips, "Anti-Negative Ad Irks Schneider Camp," *Providence Journal*, 4 October 1990.

90. Jody McPhillips, "Schneider's Campaign on a New Tack," *Providence Journal*, 11 October 1990.

91. Jody McPhillips, "Pell Is Silent as Schneider Continues Personal Attacks," *Providence Journal*, 12 October 1990.

92. Jody McPhillips, "Schneider Hails Pell While Calling for Change," 17 October 1990.

93. Ross Sneyd (AP), "Pell–Schneider Campaign Is a Classic," *Baltimore Sun*, 21 October 1990; McPhillips, "Schneider's Campaign on a New Tack"; Fitzgerald, "Hot Rhode Island Race Turning Out to be Tepid."

94. Darrell West, in McPhillips, "Schneider's Campaign on a New Tack."

95. Ibid.

96. Patrick Devlin, in Adam Pertman, "Senate Campaign Has Been Gentle So Far," *Boston Globe*, 7 October 1990.

97. Fitzgerald, "Hot Rhode Island Race Turning Out to be Tepid."

98. Harrison and Goldberg, "1990 Rhode Island Senatorial Poll #1," 27 September 1989. In his March poll, "Poll #2," the results on the "character, ethics, and integrity" question were very close—83% positive and 49% extremely positive.

99. Harrison and Goldberg, "1990 Rhode Island Senatorial Poll #1," 14–15.

100. John Mulligan, "A Forgetful Pell Trips in 1st Debate with Schneider," *Providence Journal*, 2 August 1990.

101. John Mulligan, "Pell Aide Chastised for Alert," *Providence Journal*, 19 October 1990; John Mulligan, "Pell vs. Schneider Senate Race Takes on an Added Dimension," *Providence Journal*, 20 October 1990.

102. See note 50 above.

103. Mulligan, "Pell Easy Victor over Schneider."

104. Ibid.

105. *Roll Call*, 20 February 1995.

8. DURABLE CONNECTIONS II

1. See chapter 2.

2. Editorial (and picture), *Mena Evening Star*, 15 December 1978. "This may be a good man.... We think he has the right idea in demonstrating that his new riches have not inflated his ego to such an extent that he is too proud to drive his own furniture to Washington."

3. Rex Nelson, "On the Road with David Pryor: He Loves Visiting Arkansas," *Arkansas Magazine*, 26 April 1987; John Brummett, "Inimitably Casual Pryor Travels Among Constituents to Get Rejuvenated," *Arkansas Gazette*, 6 September 1987; Paul Greenberg, "Pryor's Stand Shows Why Bork's in Trouble," *Paragould Daily Press*, 14 October 1987; John Robert Starr, "Pryor as Vice President? Not a Bad Idea," *Arkansas Democrat*, 20 May 1988; Anthony Moser, "Folksy, Caring Image Major Forces Behind Pryor's Success," *Arkansas Democrat*, 18 February 1990; Rex Nelson, "In the Cattle Barn, Whitewater's a Ways Off," *Arkansas Democrat-Gazette*, 10 April 1994.

4. Skip Rutherford, "Politics Is Personal in Arkansas," *Arkansas Gazette*, 4 April 1984.

5. Ernest Dumas, "Pryor's Down Home Campaign," *Arkansas Gazette*, 30 August 1984.

6. John Hibbing and Sara Brandes, "State Population and the Electoral Success of U.S. Senators," *American Journal of Political Science* 27 (1983):808–19; Mark Westlye, *Senate Elections and Campaign Intensity* (Baltimore: Johns Hopkins University Press, 1991), chap. 7; Bruce Oppenheimer, "The Representational Experience: The Effect of State Population on Senator-Constituency Linkages," paper prepared for annual meeting of American Political Science Association, September 1994.

7. Diane Blair, *Arkansas Politics and Government* (Lincoln: University of Nebraska Press, 1988), chap. 14; John Brummett, *Highwire: The Education of Bill Clinton* (New York: Hyperion, 1994); Thomas Friedman, "Of 3 Arkansas Pals and a Raccoon Roast," *New York Times*, 27 March 1993.

8. Blair, *Arkansas Politics and Government*, 59.

9. Dumas, "Pryor's Down Home Campaign."

10. See note 3 above, articles by Brummett, Nelson, and Moser. See also Jeffrey Stinson, "Popularity for Pryor Still Rising," *Arkansas Gazette*, 7 May 1990.

11. Moser, "Folksy, Caring Image Major Forces Behind Pryor's Success"; Stinson, "Popularity for Pryor Still Rising."

12. Interview with Ernest Dumas, Little Rock, Arkansas, 6 January 1994. Unless otherwise specified, comments by Dumas are from this interview.

13. See notes 3 and 5 above.

14. Conversation with Brenda Blagg, Fayetteville, Arkansas, 4 January 1994. See also Brenda Blagg, "Sen. Pryor's Advice: Never Lose Your Sense of Humor," *Warren Eagle Democrat*, ca. January 1988.

15. Nelson, "On the Road with David Pryor."

16. Editorial, *Paragould Daily Press*, 10 January 1990.

17. Quoted in Pamela Strickland, "Some Governors Never Die, They Become Senators," *Arkansas Democrat*, 6 August 1989.

18. Tom Hamburger, "Pryor in the Senate," *Arkansas Gazette*, 21 October 1979.

19. Moser, "Folksy, Caring Image Major Forces Behind Pryor's Success."

20. Nelson, "On the Road with David Pryor."

21. Moser, "Folksy Caring Image Major Force Behind Pryor's Success."

22. Nelson, "In the Cattle Barn, Whitewater's a Ways Off."

23. "Back Roads Trip Called Important, Uplifting by Pryor," *Arkansas Gazette*, 17 June 1979. See also Bob Ferguson, "Pryor Aides Hear the 'Folks,' " *Benton Courier*, 23 August 1979; Tom Hamburger, "Arkansas Tired of 'Dating Carter,' 6 Pryor Aides Say," *Arkansas Gazette*, 6 August 1979.

24. Boyd Gibbons, "Easy Going, Hardworking Arkansas," *National Geographic*, March 1978.

25. Blair, *Arkansas Politics and Government*, 84–87.

26. The best account of Pryor's governorship is Diane Blair, "David Hampton Pryor, 1975–1979," in *The Governor of Arkansas*, ed. T. P. Donovan and W. B. Gatewood, Jr. (Fayetteville: University of Arkansas Press, 1981).

27. JoAnn Pryor, "Farm Leaders Assess Governors' Success," *Arkansas Democrat*, 28 December 1980.

28. *Congressional Record*, 88th Congress, 2d sess., 22 March 1984, 6387, 6402–3, 6406–7.

29. Harrison and Goldberg, "Arkansas U.S. Senate Race Poll #4," April 1984.

30. Starr, "Pryor as Vice President? Not a Bad Idea."

31. Paul Barton, "Pryor Keeps Battling Bloated Bureaucracy, Buffing Populist Halo," *Arkansas Democrat*, 1 April 1990. An excellent discussion of Arkansas populism is Roy Reed, "Clinton Country," *New York Times Magazine*, 6 September 1992. An intriguing historical treatment is David Pryor, "Eight Days in Arkansas: How Huey Long and Hattie Caraway Planted Populism in State Politics," speech transcript, Little Rock, Arkansas.

32. Helen Dewar and Richard Lyons, "10 Senators Team Up to Nudge Democrats to Right," *Washington Post*, 31 January 1981. See also Paul Barton, "Pryor Holds Middle Ground... Political Balance Makes Senator Invincible," *Arkansas Democrat*, 20 November 1989.

33. Editorials, *Ouachita Citizen*, 5 February 1959, 8 October 1959, March 1959, passim.

34. Diane (Kincaid) Blair, "The Arkansas Plan: Coon Dogs or Community Service," *Publius* (Winter 1978). See also Blair, "David Hampton Pryor."

35. Barton, "Pryor Keeps Battling Bloated Bureaucracy, Buffing Populist Halo."

36. The original version was "to translate ideas into production." Francis Stevenson and Jerry Lisker, "A Senate Nor'easter: Pell of Rhode Island," reprinted in *Congressional Quarterly*, Daily Edition, 19 January 1966, 568.

37. Rex Nelson, "Pryor Recalls Early Efforts to Help Elderly," *Arkansas Democrat*, 8 December 1988.

38. Norman Miller, "In Search of Fame: A Congressman Finds It's Possible to Emerge from Faceless Crowd," *Wall Street Journal*, 2 August 1971.

39. Editorial, "Senator Pryor Rides Out," *Arkansas Gazette*, 2 October 1989; Brenda Blagg, "Pryor Champion of Elderly Again," *Springdale News*, 13 December 1988; Terry Lemons, "Pryor Grows into Role as Leading Legislator on Issues of Aging," *Arkansas Democrat Gazette*, 5 July 1994.

40. "Arkansas U. S. Senate Race Poll #4," April 1984.

41. Lemons, "Pryor Grows into Role."

42. Gale Arnold, "Pryor's Ride to Result in Senate Probe," *Arkansas Democrat*, 7 October 1979; Morris Cunningham, "Use of Consultants Attacked by Pryor," *Memphis Commercial Appeal*, 13 October 1979; "Consultants a 'Ripoff' Pryor Charges," *Arkansas Democrat*, 16 November 1979.

43. Gale Arnold, "Pryor Has $100 Million Consultant Item Removed," *Texarkana Gazette*, 11 November 1979; *Congressional Record*, Daily Edition, 26 June 1980, pp. S8482–501, and 10 September 1980, S12389–90.

44. Editorial, "Buying Private Advice," 18 October 1979.

45. *Congressional Record*, 6 August 1987, S11397–400; Susan Dantzer, "Reining in the Tax Man," *Newsweek*, 13 July 1987.

46. Rex Nelson, "Smiling Coon Dog," *Arkansas Business*, 2 December, 1991.

47. Editorial, "Pryor and IRS," *Arkansas Gazette*, 1 June 1987. See also George Arnold, "Pryor Stands Up to IRS," *El Dorado News Times*, 24 June 1987.

48. *Congressional Record*, 10 March 1982, S1899.

49. Jeffrey Stinson, "Pryor: Loves Senate, Loves Going to Work," *Arkansas Gazette*, 7 May 1990.

50. Blagg, "Pryor Champion of Elderly Again."

51. Stinson, "Pryor Loves Senate, Loves Going to Work."

52. Ibid.

53. Scott Charton, "Arkansas Senators Agree: Hard Work Put Them in Their Positions of Power," *Arkansas Democrat*, 5 September 1984.

54. An exquisite case of his struggle to break through the brilliance of an intellect in order to find and assess the essential human being beneath is the senator's public wrestling with the Supreme Court nomination of Robert Bork. *Congressional Record*, Daily Edition, 1 October 1987, S13268–69.

55. Brummett, *Highwire*, 143, 179, 206, 223.

56. A later appraisal of this performance, one closer to mine, is Rex Nelson, "Pryor Sinks Stereotypes of Accusers," *Arkansas Democrat*, 4 October 1987.

57. Paul Greenberg, "David Pryor Echoes Big Oil," (from *Arkansas Gazette*) printed in *North Little Rock Times*, 6 December 1979; Tom Hamburger, "Pryor's Voting Scores," *Arkansas Gazette*, 3 February 1980; John Brummett, "Leadership Grades Range from A to E," *Arkansas Gazette*, 7 August 1989.

58. Hamburger, "Pryor's Voting Scores."

59. Nelson, "Smiling Coon Dog."

60. Hamburger, "Pryor's Voting Scores."

61. Hamburger, "Pryor in the Senate."

62. Robert L. Brown, "An Inside Look at our Men in Washington," *Arkansas Times* (June 1980).

63. Paul Greenberg, "Sen. Pryor Says Something Provocative," *El Dorado News*, 3 January 1989. See also Greenberg, "David Pryor Echoes Big Oil."

64. Michael Arbanas, "There's No Talk of Competition Against Pryor: High Popularity Discouraging," *Arkansas Gazette*, 9 October 1989.

65. The Pine Bluff reaction to their "Pryor problem" can be found in UPI, "Nerve Gas Supported by [Mayor] Moore," *Arkansas Gazette*, 9 September 1979; George Wilson, "Nerve Gas Production Opposed," *Washington Post*, 23 March 1982. The $200 million figure comes from Mary McGrory, "John Tower Knows that Even Doves Spare the Pork Back Home," *Washington Post*, 8 February 1983.

66. He played a leading role in anti-nerve gas debates on 16–17 September 1980, 21 May 1981, 13 May 1982, 13 July 1983, 8 November 1983, 22 May 1985, 3 February 1986, 6–7 August 1986, 12 May 1988. His "crusade" can be followed in the *Congressional Record* on those dates.

67. Former speaker of the Arkansas House of Representatives, John Lipton. Early local approval of Pryor's stand as moral and independent can be found in editorial, "A Vote of Conscience," *Arkansas Gazette*, 26 May 1981.

68. See Barbara Sinclair, *The Transformation of the U.S. Senate* (Baltimore: Johns Hopkins University Press, 1989).

69. Mary McGrory, "A Balanced Budget Number Show," *Rochester Democrat and Chronicle*, 3 March 1995.

70. Pryor concluded this 1984 recollection of Arnold: "He's a federal judge now. Some day he may be on the U.S. Supreme Court. That's where he belongs." Twice, he was on President Clinton's short, short list for that very appointment.

71. Rex Nelson, "On the Road with David Pryor."

72. Diane Blair, "The Big Three of Late Twentieth-Century Arkansas Politics: Dale Bumpers, Bill Clinton and David Pryor," *Arkansas Historical Quarterly* (Spring 1995).

73. David Terrell, "Looking Ahead to the '80 Races," *Arkansas Gazette*, 29 July 1979; Jeffrey Katz, "The Roar of the Crowd," *Arkansas Democrat*, 17 August 1980; Wes Zeigler, "White Ads Speculate on Political Ambition of Gubernatorial Foe," *Arkansas Democrat*, 27 October 1982; "Clinton Calls Senate 'Bull' a White Ploy," *Memphis Commercial Appeal*, 27 October 1982; "Pryor Disregards Ad Hinting Challenge by Clinton in '84," *Arkansas Democrat*, 29 October 1982.

74. For Pryor's campaign help, see Howard Fineman, "The Inner Circle," *Newsweek*, 26 October 1992; John Harwood, "Sen. Pryor Gains New Prominence as Clinton's Closest Ally in Congress," *Wall Street Journal*, 22 February 1993. A recent public example is the letter from Senators Bumpers and Pryor to the *New York Times*, 26 August 1994.

75. Anthony Moser, "Bethune Differs Sharply with Pryor," *Midweek Magazine*, 12 September 1984.

76. Randy Fears, "In This Corner, David Pryor," *Hope Star*, 22 August 1984.

77. Derwood Brett, "Pryor Stresses Love of State," *Mena Star*, 22 August 1984.

78. Brenda Blagg, "Pryor Asks Help in Campaign, Criticizes Bethune's Record," *Springdale News*, 19 August 1984.

79. Dumas, "Pryor's Down Home Campaign."

80. All the poll data that follows comes from this source: Tubby Harrison, Memorandum to Senator David Pryor, Arkansas U. S. Senate Poll #4, April 1984.

81. Harrison, Memorandum to Senator David Pryor.

82. John Brummett, "Two Nice Guys Plan to Finish First in the U.S. Senate Race," *Arkansas Gazette*, 19 August 1984.

83. Brenda Blagg, "Sen. Pryor's Advice: Never Lose Your Sense of Humor," *Warren Eagle Democrat*, 2 December 1987.

84. Paul Greenberg, "Bethunery and Strange Pryorities in South Arkansas," *Arkansas Times* (May 1984).

85. Harrison and Goldberg, "Arkansas U. S. Senate Poll," 11 October 1984. The total sample was 400, but the other 200 were separated and then asked their vote preference. The Bethune voters from the group were asked the same open-ended question about Bethune.

86. Charton, "Arkansas Senators Agree."

87. Moser, "Folksy, Caring Image Major Force Behind Pryor's Success."

88. Starr, "Pryor as Vice President? Not a Bad Idea."

89. Harwood, "Sen. Pryor Gains New Prominence as Clinton's Closest Ally in Congress."

90. Scott Charton, "GOP Has Not Lined Up Target for Sen. Pryor," *Jonesboro Sun*, 12 March 1989.

91. "Pryor Running with $800,000: Campaign Funds May Scare Off Potential Challengers," *Arkansas Democrat*, 8 August 1989.

92.

93. James Drinkard (AP), "Rhode Island Senator Shrugs Off the Glory," *Rochester Democrat and Chronicle*, 13 October 1991.

94. Samuel Popkin, *The Reasoning Voter* (Chicago: University of Chicago Press, 1991).

95. The work of Bruce Oppenheimer makes it very clear that the representational relationship is affected by state size. See Bruce Oppenheimer, "The Representative Experience: The Effect of State Population on Senator-Constituency Linkages," paper prepared for the annual meeting of the American Political Science Association, New York, 1–4 September 1994.

96. See the discussion of "large arena campaigns" in California by Bruce Cain, "Lessons from the Inside," in *The 1990 Governor's Race*, ed. Gerald Lubenow (Berkeley: Institute of

97. In April 1995, David Pryor announced his retirement from the Senate. Five months later, Claiborne Pell announced his retirement from the Senate. There was no doubt expressed by anyone, anywhere that both would have been easily reelected. For the stories, see Rex Nelson, "Among Friends, Pryor Lets Go of 'Temporary Lease' on Seat, *"Arkansas Democrat Gazette*, April 22 1995; Jody McPhillips and John Mulligan, "Pell Bows Out Gracefully," *Providence Journal*, September 6, 1995. For editorial comment, see "David Steps Down," *Arkansas Democrat Gazette*, April 22, 1995; David Nylan, "U.S. Politics Will Be the Poorer for Claiborne Pell's Retirement," *Boston Globe*, September 6, 1995.

INDEX